SO-AUV-672

Beginning Facebook Game Apps Development

Wayne Graham

Apress®

Beginning Facebook Game Apps Development

Copyright © 2012 by Wayne Graham

This work is subject to copyright. All rights are reserved by the Publisher, whether the whole or part of the material is concerned, specifically the rights of translation, reprinting, reuse of illustrations, recitation, broadcasting, reproduction on microfilms or in any other physical way, and transmission or information storage and retrieval, electronic adaptation, computer software, or by similar or dissimilar methodology now known or hereafter developed. Exempted from this legal reservation are brief excerpts in connection with reviews or scholarly analysis or material supplied specifically for the purpose of being entered and executed on a computer system, for exclusive use by the purchaser of the work. Duplication of this publication or parts thereof is permitted only under the provisions of the Copyright Law of the Publisher's location, in its current version, and permission for use must always be obtained from Springer. Permissions for use may be obtained through RightsLink at the Copyright Clearance Center. Violations are liable to prosecution under the respective Copyright Law.

ISBN-13 (pbk): 978-1-4302-4170-6

ISBN-13 (electronic): 978-1-4302-4171-3

Trademarked names, logos, and images may appear in this book. Rather than use a trademark symbol with every occurrence of a trademarked name, logo, or image we use the names, logos, and images only in an editorial fashion and to the benefit of the trademark owner, with no intention of infringement of the trademark.

The use in this publication of trade names, trademarks, service marks, and similar terms, even if they are not identified as such, is not to be taken as an expression of opinion as to whether or not they are subject to proprietary rights.

While the advice and information in this book are believed to be true and accurate at the date of publication, neither the authors nor the editors nor the publisher can accept any legal responsibility for any errors or omissions that may be made. The publisher makes no warranty, express or implied, with respect to the material contained herein.

President and Publisher: Paul Manning
Lead Editor: Steve Anglin
Developmental Editor: Ben Renow-Clarke
Technical Reviewer: Eric Rochester
Editorial Board: Steve Anglin, Ewan Buckingham, Gary Cornell, Louise Corrigan, Morgan Ertel, Jonathan Gennick, Jonathan Hassell, Robert Hutchinson, Michelle Lowman, James Markham, Matthew Moodie, Jeff Olson, Jeffrey Pepper, Douglas Pundick, Ben Renow-Clarke, Dominic Shakeshaft, Gwenan Spearing, Matt Wade, Tom Welsh
Coordinating Editor: Brent Dubi
Copy Editor: Valerie Greco, Heather Graham
Compositor: MacPS, LLC
Indexer: SPi Global
Artist: SPi Global
Cover Designer: Anna Ishchenko

Distributed to the book trade worldwide by Springer Science+Business Media New York, 233 Spring Street, 6th Floor, New York, NY 10013. Phone 1-800-SPRINGER, fax (201) 348-4505, e-mail orders-ny@springer-sbm.com, or visit www.springeronline.com.

For information on translations, please e-mail rights@apress.com, or visit www.apress.com.

Apress and friends of ED books may be purchased in bulk for academic, corporate, or promotional use. eBook versions and licenses are also available for most titles. For more information, reference our Special Bulk Sales–eBook Licensing web page at www.apress.com/bulk-sales.

Any source code or other supplementary materials referenced by the author in this text is available to readers at www.apress.com. For detailed information about how to locate your book's source code, go to http://www.apress.com/source-code/.

For Anna, Stella, and Caroline.

Contents at a Glance

Contents... v

About the Author.. x

About the Technical Reviewer xi

Acknowledgments xii

Introduction xiii

■Chapter 1: First Steps.. 1

■Chapter 2: JavaScript Boot Camp 15

■Chapter 3: It's All About Context: Canvas Basics 49

■Chapter 4: The Plan: Idea to Design 69

■Chapter 5: Essential Game Components.. 81

■Chapter 6: Your First Game: Alien Turtle Invasion 109

■Chapter 7: Social Components and HTML5 Games................................. 145

■Chapter 8: Introducing the Facebook Platform 171

■Chapter 9: Facebook Developer Tools 201

■Chapter 10: Creating Your First Facebook Game.................................... 231

■Chapter 11: Adding Facebook Components... 265

■Chapter 12: Launching Your Game 301

■Chapter 13: HTML5 Game Engines.. 333

■Chapter 14: Facebook Fuzed 355

Index.. 405

Contents

Contents at a Glance iv

About the Author x

About the Technical Reviewer xi

Acknowledgments xii

Introduction xiii

▓Chapter 1: First Steps 1

Gaming in the Browser 1

HTML5 and the Canvas Element 2

Game Terminology 3

    Game Views 3

    General Terms..8

Game Genres 12

Summary 14

▓Chapter 2: JavaScript Boot Camp 15

What Is JavaScript? 15

Testing Out JavaScript..18

    Firebug..18

    Chrome 19

    Debugging...20

Comments...21

Data Types 22

Variables 23

Operators 25

    Assignment 25

    Comparison 26

    Arithmetic Operators...26

    Logical Operators..27

    String Operators..28

    Special Operators 30

Data Structures 32

    Array 32

Flow Control..34

if..else 34

Switch 35

Loops 36

Functions 38

Variable Scope 39

Special Variables 41

Document Object Model...42

Guess the Number Game 43

Getting Good with JavaScript 46

Summary 47

Chapter 3: It's All About Context: Canvas Basics 49

Canvas: The 2D Context 50

First Shape..51

Triangles and Lines...55

Translation and Rotation...58

Simple Motion 60

Debugging Tools 66

What About Mobile?..67

Summary 68

Chapter 4: The Plan: Idea to Design 69

The Design Process 69

Brainstorming 70

Identify Your Audience 71

Identify Your Competition 72

Artistic Direction 73

Project Review 74

Feature Cull..75

Planning Milestones..76

Code 77

Deployment...77

User Testing 78

Launch 78

Summary 79

Chapter 5: Essential Game Components.. 81

Types of Graphics 81

Graphics Tools 83

Graphics Design Process 85

Sketch...85

Refine..86

Produce..86

Techniques 90

Lighting..90

Depth...94

Color..95

Focus and Blur...96

Movement...96

Drop Shadow 97

Audio 97

Creating Sounds 98

   Software 98

   Hardware 100

   Recording 101

   Royalty-Free Sounds 102

   Preparing Your Audio 103

Understanding Copyright 104

   Creative Commons—BY(CC-BY) 105

   Creative Commons—BY—Share Alike (CC-BY-SA) 105

   Creative Commons 0 (CC0) 105

   Gnu General Public License (GPL) 105

   Apache 2.0 106

   MIT 106

   Dual/Multi License 106

Summary 107

■ Chapter 6: Your First Game: Alien Turtle Invasion 109

Defining the Game 109

   Define the Audience 110

   Identify the Competition 110

Boilerplate 111

Coding the Engine 114

Adding Textures 136

Adding Sound 140

Summary 143

■ Chapter 7: Social Components and HTML5 Games 145

Social Mechanics in Games 146

Tic-Tac-Toe 146

   The Rules 150

   The Board 150

   Keeping Track 152

   Adding Some Intelligence 156

   Going Further 161

   Next Steps 170

Summary 170

■ Chapter 8: Introducing the Facebook Platform 171

The Facebook Development Platform 171

Creating Applications with the Facebook Platform 173

   Basic Info 176

   Cloud Services 176

   Facebook Integration 177

Software Development Kits 178

Your First Facebook Application 178

   Prerequisites 178

   Facebook Setup 183

Using the Graph API 187

   Searching 193

Facebook Query Language 196
Facebook SDKs 198
    Setting up a Development Environment 198
Summary 200

Chapter 9: Facebook Developer Tools 201
Developer App 201
Open Graph Protocol 201
    Open Graph Types 203
    Open Graph Stories 206
    Aggregations 209
    Achievements 210
Credits 216
    Credit Callback 223
    Troubleshooting 223
Roles 224
Insights 226
Summary 229

Chapter 10: Creating Your First Facebook Game 231
Project Planning 231
    Define the Rules 231
    Identify Your Audience 232
    Competition 232
Developing the HTML Game 234
    Project Setup 234
    Game Code 235
Facebook Integration 249
2.0 Ideas 262
Summary 263

Chapter 11: Adding Facebook Components 265
Adding Levels 265
Adding a Timer 271
Working with Databases on Heroku 273
Recording Puzzle Information 278
Tracking Achievements 283
    Assigning Achievements 287
Customizing the Authorization Dialog 288
    Creating Your Privacy Policy 290
    Defining Your Terms of Service 291
    Adding Your Terms of Service Policy 292
Deployment Concerns 293
Summary 298

Chapter 12: Launching Your Game 301
Website 301
    WordPress 302
    WordPress Plugins 306
    Social Plugins 308
Facebook Pages 308

Customizing Your Page 314
Promoting Your Page 320
Advertising 320
Content 321
Plug 321
Targeting Ads 321
Interaction 322
Cycle II 322
Cycle III 323
Driving Likes 323
Create a WordPress Category 323
Facebook Tabs 324
Launch Checklist 329
Content and Style 329
Functional Testing 330
Finishing Touches 330
Ongoing 330
Summary 330

■**Chapter 13: HTML5 Game Engines**... **333**
Development 333
Open Source 334
Canvas Advanced Animation Toolkit 334
Cocos2d.js 340
Crafty 343
LimeJS 346
melonJS 350
Play My Code 350
PixieEngine 351
Paid Game Engines 352
ImpactJS 353
Isogenic 353
Summary 354

■**Chapter 14: Facebook Fuzed**.. **355**
Game 355
Tiled Map Editor 356
melonJS Framework 362
Creating the Game files 362
Background 373
Facebook Score API 373
Summary 390

Index.. **405**

About the Author

Wayne Graham heads the Research and Development division of the University of Virginia's Scholars' Lab, a digital humanities research center. He holds a Master's Degree from the College of William and Mary in History, and has over a decade of experience as a developer and systems administrator, with work in a variety of fields including computer graphics, high performance computing, geographic information systems, augmented reality, and architectural history.

Wayne can be found online on Twitter @wayne_graham and on github (waynegraham).

About the Technical Reviewer

Eric Rochester is Senior R&D Developer at the Scholars' Lab at the University of Virginia. He started programming games in BASIC on a TRS-80. He's written a program or two since then, and he still has fun writing a game every so often.

Acknowledgments

I would like to thank all of the hard working editors who helped on this book. I am indebted to the editorial team who offered advice and their encouragement throughout the writing phase. I am grateful for the work Steve Anglin did bringing the initial idea to fruition, Ben Renow-Clarke for his comments and advice, Brent Dubi for answering all of my many questions along the way and his work in ensuring the process went smoothly. Additionally I would like to thank the copy-editors Valerie Greco and Heather Graham for the invaluable feedback they provided.

I would like to thank my colleagues at the Scholars' Lab for their support during the writing of this book. In particular, I would like to thank Bethany Nowviskie for not only encouraging me to undertake this project, but ensuring that all of us have research time to pursue our own endeavors.

Lastly, I want to thank to my wife Anna, and daughters for putting up with me through this project. Anna's support and encouragement (as well as her smiles and polite nods as I ramble about code) helped me work through many coding issues. Her support, understanding and encouragement helped me immensely in this project.

Introduction

When I wrote the first book on Facebook's APIs in 2008, the platform suffered from a lot of the growing pains many nascent technologies do. There was a distinct lack of documentation, the APIs were changing on an almost weekly basis, and many of the APIs seemed to grow organically, and independently of one another. Facebook had been growing astronomically for several years, and with the launch of their API platform, were positioning themselves to expand their user base even further with over 845 million monthly visitors today.

With this kind of user growth, Facebook engineers had some really interesting technical problems to tackle. How do you scale a system to handle this many users? How do you enable users to interact with their information in meaningful ways? How do allow developers access to your platform in a meaningful way that does not impinge upon the privacy of Facebook users? How do you create an API that is logical for developers to use?

Facebook engineers took on all of these problems, and in the case of the API Platform, rethought and re-implemented the older REST APIs in favor for the Graph API. Having worked with the older APIs, I was impressed with how well thought out the service ended up being, and the implementation of a JavaScript API really opened up a lot of possibilities for developing applications on the Facebook Platform.

While Facebook was working on their platform, the first of what has become known as the HTML 5 standards was published. This standards body introduced specifications for a set of technologies that web developers had either complained that were absent from the HTML specification, and would work on the emerging mobile market. These specifications included definitions for how to work with animation (canvas), how local storage for off-line web applications would work, and included native support for audio and video components, among many other elements that web developers had been requesting for years.

While these specifications were being developed, web browsers were making some real strides in not only their ability to handle the new HTML 5 specifications, but their underlying JavaScript engines took major steps to increase the performance of web-based applications. With the major performance enhancements to the various JavaScript engines in different browsers, browser-based games that did not require the installation of Adobe's Flash plugin began to be a real possibility.

The emergence of a standards-based approach to browser animation and the browser's ability to handle more complex JavaScript efficiently has seen a move by developers to various HTML 5 technologies for components of their games. However, there is not currently a dominant platform to deliver these games. The success of companies like Zynga in the realm of social gaming show great promise for game developers in the realm of social gaming applications, and the Facebook platform provides game developers with an easy-to-use set of APIs to integrate in to their game.

When I was approached about writing an update to the *Facebook Developer's Guide*, and we began the conversation about what an update to that book would look like, we quickly realized that there is a great opportunity for game apps on the Facebook platform. Much of the first book was focused at addressing showing how to use a new technology that has since been superseded by documentation and posts by Facebook engineers, and many great blog posts, I thought it would be interesting to write a beginner's book on building browser-based games using HTML 5 technologies for the Facebook platform.

This book is aimed at individuals who have some JavaScript, CSS, and PHP experience. I try to lay out not only coding techniques that can help you develop your game, but also where to find resources for your games (e.g. images and audio), as well as tips for successfully developing a project. I walk through several different types of game development techniques, from building your own space shooter to a platformer built with a game engine. There are tips and tricks for deploying your game, advertising on Facebook, and building the social aspects of games on the Facebook platform. If you have developed HTML games, you may find a lot of this book too basic for your needs. However, if you are somewhat new to JavaScript development, and want to learn more about developing browser-based games and their integration with the Facebook platform, this is the book for you!

Chapter 1

First Steps

Facebook has emerged over the last several years as the dominant social space. Their astronomical growth has made it *the* platform for social interaction on the web. Although there have been some hiccups along the way with privacy concerns, Facebook continues to grow and provide a space for users worldwide to interact with one another. Facebook has also introduced a new breed of casual social gaming to the world. Individuals who would never consider themselves gamers are suddenly spending real money to play games such as Farmville, Mafia Wars, War Commander, and SpaLife. The success of companies like Zynga and CrowdStar have made companies including Electronic Arts take notice and start rethinking some of their games for social play.

If you are reading this book, you are undoubtedly interested in building social games. Building games can be very rewarding, but getting started can be daunting. If you haven't had any experience with game design, the whole idea can seem quite overwhelming. Even if you have a great idea for a game that you would like to share with people on Facebook, you may find turning that idea into code and deploying it for people to use can be a whole different story. How you design the interface, add motion, build graphics, and interact with users can get confusing very quickly. The biggest piece of advice I have is: don't worry, we have all been there. And this book is, after all, a place to break down and explore the process.

Building games is a complex endeavor no matter how you slice it. Don't worry though, I break it down into manageable steps. Before we start building games together, I introduce you to some general game concepts and terminology, particularly as they relate to building games to play in web browsers. In this first chapter, to help orient you for your first foray into game design, I discuss some of the general concepts of game design, common online gaming genres, their terminology, and the role the browser now plays in the online game-development environment.

Gaming in the Browser

Until quite recently, most games developed for the browser have used Flash. In fact, many of the popular games on Facebook still use Flash as their runtime environment. However, as mobile devices began growing their market share, Flash became a less attractive option for delivering interactive applications. Perhaps the biggest single reasons revolve around the power and memory requirements required for the Flash runtime. On a desktop machine, this goes somewhat unnoticed (although you may notice some slowdown in other applications, or your fans spinning up), but on a mobile device this is far more noticeable as it drains the battery and noticeably slows the performance of your application to make it appear sluggish. A bit of a religious battle over the use of Flash came to a head in 2010 when the late Steve Jobs, Apple's CEO at the time, commented that the iPad would not support Flash, citing security holes and its CPU load. In late 2011, this war seems to have ended as Adobe announced it would discontinue development of the Mobile Flash runtime beyond version 11.1 to focus its efforts on delivering content via HTML 5 for mobile devices. The company will continue to develop the Flash player for desktop environments, however, it does appear that the future of mobile rich Internet applications is with the browser-based HTML 5 technologies.

To be fair, when Flash was introduced in the 1990s, web browsers were not capable of much more than displaying text and images, and Flash allowed developers to add multimedia and sophisticated animations to web pages. However, browsers have come a long way and are now capable of rendering multimedia natively, animations at a high enough frame rate to ensure smooth movements, and even storing data locally. Coupled with some clever software engineering that optimizes the execution of JavaScript, developers are beginning to leverage the capabilities of the browsers to deliver games and applications that work no matter if you're on Windows or OS X, but also an iPad or Android device.

HTML5 and the Canvas Element

The HTML5 Specification, although still in draft, defines many new properties that describe how a browser should implement a bevy of new features. The specification defines new elements for encoding content (HTML) and presentation styles (CSS), as well as APIs for local and "web" storage, background processes, bidirectional communication, geolocation, and device orientation (through JavaScript APIs). The specification also combines HTML elements and JavaScript to define native, browser-based support for audio and video, as well as how browsers should render two-dimensional content. The specifications are still in draft format, but browser developers are racing to build these features into their current generation of browsers.

I focus a lot of attention in this book on the native support for rendering 2D content. The specific HTML element that allows developers access to this rendering API is named "`<canvas>`" and serves as a container element for rendering "graphs, game graphics, or other visual images on the fly" (http://www.whatwg.org/specs/web-apps/current-work/multipage/the-canvas-element.html). By itself, the `<canvas>` is just a container element, but when coupled with a JavaScript API, it provides developers with a powerful runtime platform without the need to install third-party plugins.

NOTE: The HTML5 specification started in 2004 as the Web Applications 1.0 specification with the Web Hypertext Application Technology (WHAT) Working Group. It moved to become the starting point of the HTML working group of the World Wide Consortium (W3C) in 2007, and as of the writing of this book in 2011, is still under development. The specification is expected to move to the Candidate Recommendation stage in 2012. In order to become a full W3C recommendation, the bar is set at "two 100% complete and fully interoperable implementations." However, most modern browsers already implement many of the main features of the specification.

One of the great things `<canvas>` gives you that other elements do not (e.g., `<div>`) is pixel-level access to graphics, as well as a large number of methods for drawing and manipulating images, pixels, and text.

It is worth noting that `<canvas>` is not the only game in town for dealing with graphical assets. Another tool developers have access to is inline SVG (Scalable Vector Graphics). Where elements drawn to the `<canvas>` are bitmap (pixel-based), SVG elements are vector shapes. These shapes can be as simple as drawing a circle or square, or exceptionally complex polygons. SVG has been around for a while, however, the HTML5 specification allows developers to use SVG tags directly in their HTML, and no longer requires a third-party plugin. I do not cover SVG in the context of gaming in this book, as it is not often used for games because rendering of the shapes can be slow inasmuch as these shapes attach the HTML Document Object Model (DOM).directly. I am covering game development, therefore performance is more important than being able to manipulate elements via the DOM. Hence, the `<canvas>` element, which handles everything as a pixel, is a better choice for gaming applications.

Game Terminology

Are you familiar with terms such as isometric, sprite, and avatar? As you begin developing games, you will quickly find a high degree of specialization, with specific jargon used when talking about the games. However, it is important to have a basic understanding of these terms, and what they mean as you come across them in the book. Most of these terms are further described in later chapters, but I want to give you a preview of the main terms here.

Game Views

Games use different perspectives as part of the game mechanics. Can the player see everything through the characters' eyes? From above, or the side? Each of these are classified by their *point-of-view*.

- **Isometric:** This is one of the most popular views, as it allows developers and artists to use some tricks to create a 3D environment without creating an entire 3D world. Sometimes called 2.5D, this game view looks down at the game space from a slight angle, giving the game more dimension than a flat 2D space. This is used in popular Facebook games like Farmville as it gives the illusion of 3D.

Figure 1–1. *This is an example of an isometric game view. Courtesy of LostGarden via Creative Commons BY license.* http://www.lostgarden.com/2009/03/dancs-miraculously-flexible-game.html

- **Top Down:** The top-down perspective shows a "god's-eye" view of the playing area. Classics including Civilization, Super Sprint, Minesweeper, Solitaire, and the original Zelda, as well as more modern cult classics such as Dwarf Fortress are examples of this top-down perspective. This perspective is useful in providing the player with the visual world around them so they can make decisions on where to move, or make a play.

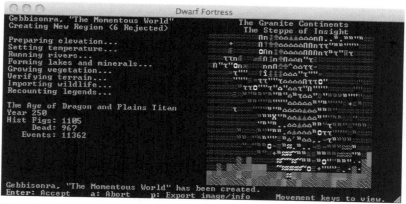

Figure 1–2. *Dwarf Fortress World Creation*

- **Side Scroller**: This view allows players to see what is happening from the side. This view will be familiar to you if you've played Super Mario Brothers.

Figure 1–3. *This is an example of a side-scrolling game view. Courtesy of Open Game Art.*
http://opengameart.org/sites/default/files/preview_19.png

- **Chase**: This is a popular perspective with many sports games where the camera follows a character or action in a 3D game. Most hockey, golf, and football games leverage this perspective to change the angle to optimize the player's view of the game.

Figure 1–4. *Screenshot from Extreme Tux Racer courtesy of Extreme Tux Racer website;*
`http://extremetuxracer.com/screenshots/035/tux_sshot_10.jpg`

- **First Person**: With this perspective, the user views the game from the character's point of view. This is a popular view for "shooter" style 3D games (e.g., first-person shooters) where the player views the world through the eyes of his or her game avatar.

Figure 1–5. *Screenshot from Urban Terror courtesy of Urban Terror website;*
`http://www.urbanterror.info/files/static/images/pics/presentation/shot0016.jpg.`

- **Third-Person View**: A player view where the players can view the characters they are playing and the world around them. This 3D view is very close to the first-person view, but allows the player to view the body of the character (or vehicle containing the character) to allow the player to have more information about what is going on around him.

Figure 1–6. *Screenshot from Armagetron Advanced courtesy of the Armagetron Advanced website;*
http://armagetronad.net/screenshots/ss_ctf_3.png

General Terms

- **AAA Game:** This refers to games that are developed with big budgets and large staff to produce a high-quality game. Because of the size of the code base, there is exhaustive testing of the gameplay and codebase, high-quality graphics, polished audio–visuals, and generally a large marketing campaign to drive sales. If you have seen a commercial for a game in a magazine or on television, most likely you are looking at what the developers believe is a AAA game. On Facebook, there are quite a few AAA-level games (Zynga, EA, and others have developed quite a few), but it is important to remember that your first games will not be on the same level as these games. However, write a few games very well, and you may find yourself working with a group that turns your idea into a AAA-level game!

- **Algorithm:** An algorithm is a set of logical steps that describe how to solve a problem. These steps can then be implemented in a programming language, such as JavaScript or PHP, to provide your program with a set of operations to solve a procedure.

- **Application Programming Interface (API)**: A code library that allows different application systems to interact with one another. For this book, we use APIs that allow your code to interact with the user's browser, as well as APIs for interacting with data from Facebook's systems.

- **Assets**: These are the noncode elements of your game, especially sound and image files that interact with your codebase.

- **Artificial Intelligence**: Depending on the style of game you are developing, the player may need to interact with (or combat) the game. Artificial intelligence is code you write that allows pieces of the game to act in a logical way. For instance, you may have a board game such as chess that can be solved automatically, or any "enemy" character in a game that needs to interact with your player (e.g., attack or run away). Although these algorithms can get quite complex, at their base level they are designed to fake how humans might interact with their environment in logical ways.

- **Avatar**: From the Hindu concept of an incarnation of a deity on earth, an avatar in the gaming sense refers to in-game characters that represent the player. Avatars "stand in" for players in the game, and serve as proxies for experiencing the "game" world.

- **Collision Detection**: Detecting a collision between two (or more) objects is a major component of many games. For instance, in the game Super Mario Brothers, detecting when a Goomba strikes the Mario *sprite* is a major component of the gameplay.

- **Framework**: In programming, this is a set of libraries (or code) that provides generic functionality that can be selectively integrated, modified, or ignored by a software developer.

- **Map**: A map, in the game sense, defines the universe (or a subset) of the game.

- **Multiplayer**: A game that allows more than one player.

- **Raster Graphics**: Sometimes referred to as bitmaps, raster graphics refers to data structures that represent points of color (as opposed to *Vector Graphics*). These points of color are two-dimensional representations of resolution-dependent information. JPEG and PNG files are examples of raster graphics.

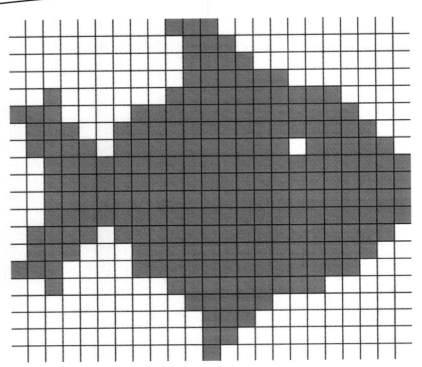

Figure 1–7. *Raster-based fish at 20 x 23 pixels. Courtesy of Andres -horn- Hornig via Creative Commons Attribution Share-Alike license:* http://upload.wikimedia.org/wikipedia/commons/5/54/ Raster_graphic_fish_20x23squares_sdtv-example.jpg.

- **Realtime**: A game in which there are no restrictions on when the player can make a play (e.g., there are no turns).

- **Render**: In the computer science world, this refers to taking data and converting it into a visual form. For our games, we render different assets on the screen for our players.

- **Single-player**: A game for a single player. The game play revolves around a single player's interactions with the world or stage for the duration of the game. Any additional players to help move the gameplay along are controlled by the game designer.

- **Sprite**: Generally this is a two-dimensional manifestation integrated into a larger scene. This used to refer to assets that moved in a game scene that would not need to have the entire screen redrawn, but has shifted its definition to refer to any sort of graphic overlay integrated in a scene.

Figure 1–8. *Sprite Sheet of Tux, the mascot of Linux by Mj Mendoza IV, via Creative Commons Attribution Share-Alike License (http://opengameart.org/content/tux-the-linux-mascot).*

- **Turn-based**: A game in which there are restrictions on when players can make a play. Games such as Sid Meier's Civilization series and Blizzard's StarCraft series integrate a turn-based system as the central game-play mechanism.

- **Vector Graphics**: A set of geometric points, lines, curves, and multiline shapes (polygons) that are based on mathematical formulas. Vector graphics are used heavily in Flash-based games, and have the advantage of being able to scale easily to any resolution. With the advent of the HTML5 specifications, you have access to vector graphics in the DOM through the `<svg>` element set.

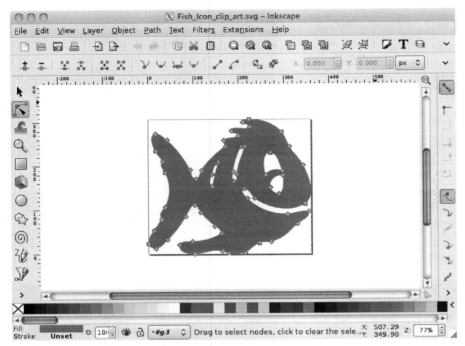

Figure 1–9. *A fish drawn as a vector graphic in Inkscape*

Game Genres

Games are categorized by conventions that describe a central component of gameplay. Games can fit into several categories, or define their own. Although not an exhaustive list, here is a list of many of the more popular game genres. For Facebook gaming, games that you can play for short durations and still make progress (and keep the attention span of the player) do best. Simulation games are quite popular (Farmville), as well as puzzle games (e.g., Bejeweled) and casino games (e.g., Texas HoldEm) hold quite a bit of the gaming market share. Games that require a lot of time investment tend not to be very popular as most people play these games in very small time increments.

■ **Action**: Action games focus on timing, reflexes, hand–eye coordination, and quick thinking to maximize player scores. This genre typically showcases a series of levels with different themes, with a level boss to defeat before moving on to the next level. Games in this genre include classics such as Super Mario Brothers, Pac-Man, and Donkey Kong.

- **Adventure**: These are games showcasing interactive storytelling and puzzle-solving. This is one of the oldest game genres, based on the 1970 computer game, Adventure. Some examples of this genre include Myst and King's Quest. These were popular in the 1980s and early 1990s, but this genre has seen a decrease in popularity.

- **Casino**: These are games that emulate games available in casinos. These games range from card games including Blackjack and Poker, to slot machine emulators to Keno. Many of these games are played for fun, but where legal, these games can be played with real money.

- **First-Person Shooter (FPS)**: Arguably a subgenre of Action games, the FPS genre leverages weapon-based combat as its major gameplay component, typically in a 3D or isometric first-, or third-person view. Examples of this genre include Doom, Halo, and Call of Duty.

- **Puzzle**: A very popular genre for "casual" gamers. Also referred to as a logic game, these games challenge your cognitive skills, usually in a timed setting, rather than your reflexes. Games such as Tetris, Mahjong, and maze games are examples of puzzle games.

- **Horror**: Sometimes referred to as survival horror, these games emphasize puzzle-solving and evasion rather than heads-on engagement. The horror-survival genre utilizes sound and lighting design, as well as scarce resources, to help the player feel vulnerable in the gameplay. Examples of this genre include Silent Hill, Resident Evil, and Left 4 Dead.

- **Sports**: These games emulate sporting games including football, baseball, and hockey.

- **Simulation**: Simulation games mimic some real-world experience. Although there are realistic simulators such as flight and driving simulators, there are a growing number of games like Farmville (and its clones) that simulate other real-world social interactions.

- **Role-Playing Games (RPGs)**: Role-playing games allow you to control a character (or party of characters) and make decisions that affect the game play. Engaging players in the story line is important in this genre as they need to take on the persona of their character, and buy into the storyline for it to be engaging. These scale from single-player games, to the larger MMORPG (massively multiplayer online role-playing games). Dragon Age, Star Wars: Knights of the Old Republic, and World of Warcraft are examples of this genre.

- **Strategy**: The strategy genre is typified by emphasizing strategic, tactical, and logistical challenges. Examples of this genre include Civilization, Starcraft, and Red Alert.

Summary

Getting started with game design and interacting with the Facebook API can be a daunting task, and in this chapter I introduced some of the major topics covered in the book, as well as some more general information about terms related to game design. In the next several chapters, we get more in-depth with some of these topics, including working with JavaScript, the Facebook APIs, and the canvas element.

Chapter 2

JavaScript Boot Camp

JavaScript is one of the most predominant languages in use today. There is virtually no website that you can visit these days that does not leverage JavaScript to do anything from improve your experience with the site's content to recording robust analytics about how you are using the site. JavaScript's flexibility in allowing developers to choose a style of programming that best fits their style is one of its greatest assets (or, if you are a pessimist, one of its greatest faults), and engineers have put in a lot of work to squeeze every bit of optimization into their JavaScript engines to ensure this code executes as quickly as possible. This chapter introduces you to some of the important JavaScript concepts that we use throughout the rest of the book.

What Is JavaScript?

If you talk to a stuffy academic type, you might hear him describe JavaScript as a dynamically typed, prototype-based language with first-class functions. If you are scratching your head about what that means, don't worry, you're not the only one. A more pedestrian explanation of what JavaScript is would be that it is a language designed to allow developers of web applications to add dynamic, and interactive, elements to web pages. Although this does gloss over quite a large swath of the capabilities of JavaScript, it does describe the role the language plays.

One of the really nice features of JavaScript is that it allows developers to choose a style of programming that makes sense to them. Because of the way JavaScript is organized, every function is an object (a Function object). If you are unfamiliar with JavaScript object orientation as a programming concept, think of JavaScript functions as a special kind of collection of properties (variables) and methods. JavaScript is what is referred to as a prototype-based programming language, which was intended to encourage developers to focus their efforts on working with behaviors. However, if you are more comfortable with a *class*-based approach to your code, JavaScript is flexible enough to allow you to code in that style. Another nice feature in JavaScript is that the language is dynamically typed. This means that you do not need to declare data types explicitly, saving you some potential headaches when you are getting up and running with the language. We cover data types in more detail in just a second.

NOTE: Dynamically typed languages are sometimes referred to as "duck-typed." There is an old adage that goes, "If it talks like a duck and walks like a duck, it's probably a duck." In the world of computer programming, dynamically typed languages allow you to create variables without explicitly declaring their data type. Thus, I can set var x = 1;, then proceed to use that variable to perform mathematical operations because the JavaScript engine will automatically determine that x is a *numeric* data type. This is different in a static (or strongly) typed language such as Java where you would need to make decisions about the precision of the x variable (e.g., int x = 1;), which affects the memory allocation for your program. The main technical difference in the approaches comes down to when the data are evaluated. JavaScript engines evaluate the data when they are executed, then manage resources appropriately. Static languages will evaluate the data when the software is compiled. However, from a developer perspective, letting the JavaScript engine take care of some of these concerns allows you more time to focus your efforts on the system you are developing.

JavaScript is implemented in browsers by highly specialized JavaScript engines that do the heavy lifting of converting the JavaScript code into the results on a web page. As you have probably experienced, every browser vendor has a slightly different take on the World Wide Web Consortium (W3C) standards for HTML. This is no different for the implementation of JavaScript. Some of these choices come down to decisions on how to best optimize the execution of code for performance, however, most modern browsers support at least a good interpretation of the ECMAScript 5 specification. If you are unfamiliar with this, ECMA is an international standards organization that promotes standards. In the case of JavaScript, the standard from which the language is derived is ECMAScript. There are actually several languages that derive from this standard, including ActionScript (for Flash) and ECMAScript for XML (E4X).

To deal with the variations in not only the HTML standards, but how JavaScript engines interact with the browsers, there has been a lot of effort put into JavaScript frameworks that endeavors to build consistency across browser platforms, saving developers much time and effort when targeting multiple browsers for their applications. Libraries such as jQuery standardize the selection of DOM selectors across multiple browsers, and mask the complexities of weird edge cases in how the browsers behave. Table 2–1 displays the most popular browsers, their engines, and the ECMA standard they support. It is worth noting that the Mozilla Foundation maintains the official JavaScript specification, so most JavaScript engines target the ECMA standard and list themselves as "compatible" with JavaScript. This can be a bit confusing if you are building all of your code from scratch, which is another reason libraries such as jQuery have become so popular.

Table 2–1. *Browser JavaScript Engines*

Browser	Engine	ECMA Standard
Chrome	V8	ECMA 5.1 (ECMA-262), edition 5
FireFox	Spider Monkey	ECMA 5.1 (ECMA-262), edition 5
Internet Explorer	Trident	ECMA 5.1 (ECMA-262), edition 5
Safari	Nitro	ECMA 5.1 (ECMA-262), edition 5

As you can see, the JavaScript engines that ship with the latest editions of all the major browsers ship with an engine with similar capabilities.

NOTE: One approach that leverages the power of JavaScript that has been getting a lot of press recently is Node.js. Node.js is a set of libraries built on top of Google's V8 JavaScript engine, which powers their Chrome browser, that allows developers to run their JavaScript code outside the browser. The promise of this technology is that developers will write JavaScript for both the client (the browser) and server (the back end). Sharing the same language on both the client and server, with special attention to the scalability of the software across servers, holds a lot of promise for the future of high-scalability applications.

Node.js takes JavaScript, which has traditionally run in the browser, and allows you to run it outside the server. The clever part is that by using the same V8 engine that Chrome uses, you no longer need to learn multiple languages to do front-end and back-end development. Having to jump among Ruby, Python, or PHP and HTML and JavaScript on a project can cause all kinds of errors to crop up when you write JavaScript in your Ruby code, or PHP in your JavaScript. The promise of a single, high-performance system that uses the same language style is a big draw for a lot of developers. Node.js is definitely something to keep on your radar.

In this book, we use JavaScript extensively to build up our Facebook application. Not only are our games written in JavaScript using the HTML5 canvas API, but we use a combination of Facebook-supplied JavaScript to interact with our users, as well as custom JavaScript to improve the overall user experience of our application. JavaScript in user interface design goes a long way in masking the complexity of applications when done well, and the design of modern interfaces on sites such as Facebook has trained users to expect web pages to work in specific ways that we cover in later chapters. All of this is to say that JavaScript is perhaps one of the most important languages on the web today, and will continue to grow in importance as browsers continue to improve their performance, and will shift its role from browser-only applications to a lingua franca for application development.

Testing Out JavaScript

Depending on your browser of choice, there are a few different options you have to follow along with the code snippets I use in the rest of the chapter. Although I typically use Firefox for my development, I have been switching more and more between the tools in Firefox and those in the Chrome Developer Tools. Each has a slightly different approach to organizing its feedback to help you detangle what is going on in your code.

Firebug

I have been a long-time Firefox user, and a big reason has been the Firebug tool (http://getfirebug.com/). This Firefox extension adds a console so you can not only debug and trace what is going on in your JavaScript code, but also inspect and edit HTML elements (including CSS in realtime), analyze network usage for assets, profile and log your JavaScript, and quickly find errors. Beyond these tools, the console also has the ability to execute JavaScript on the fly. This last feature is what you can use to test out the JavaScript in this chapter without needing to write an HTML file that calls a JavaScript file.

Firebug is listed in Firefox's Addons Directory, however, I usually point my browser at the version that is hosted on the Firebug site. If you point your browser at http://getfirebug.com/ and click on the "Install Firebug" button at the top, you will be directed to a page with the current versions of Firebug that you can install. Depending on what version of Firefox is available when you install the plugin (Firefox has adopted a much faster revision release schedule, going from Firefox 5 to Firefox 8 in 2011 alone) that is appropriate for your version of Firefox, just be sure to read which versions are compatible with your browser version.

After the plugin has been installed and Firefox has restarted, you should have a new button with a bug on it.

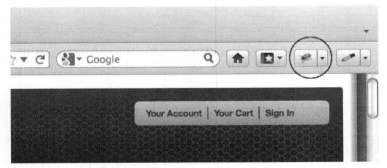

Figure 2–1. *Firebug button in Firefox*

Clicking on the button will toggle the tool on and off. You can also launch the tool through the menu system at **Tools ➤ Web Developer ➤ Firebug ➤ Open Firebug**.

The Firebug console defaults to launching in the bottom of the browser window, but can be separated into another window. For the examples in this chapter, when the Console tab is selected, you can type JavaScript code on the right-hand side, and when you click "Run" the code will execute on the left.

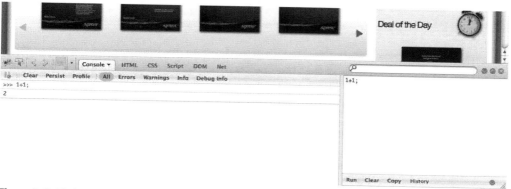

Figure 2–2. *Firebug console evaluating the expression 1+1*

Firebug is a great tool, one that I use almost every day. These tools are so useful in fact, that they are starting to be evaluated in future versions of Firefox. You can download the Aurora Firefox browser which has a feature called Scratchpad that gives you a text editor to evaluate your code.

```
Scratchpad
1  /*
2   * This is a JavaScript Scratchpad.
3   *
4   * Enter some JavaScript, then Right Click or choose from the Execute Menu:
5   * 1. Run to evaluate the selected text,
6   * 2. Inspect to bring up an Object Inspector on the result, or,
7   * 3. Display to insert the result in a comment after the selection.
8   */
9
10 1 + 1;
```

Figure 2–3. *Aurora Scratchpad*

I believe Scratchpad is quite nice for looking at different pieces of code, but it lacks some of the feedback that a tool like Firebug provides when evaluating your code. It does, however, provide a nicer (e.g., larger) space to work with some of your JavaScript, and if you are already using Aurora, it does not require installing a plugin.

Chrome

As I mentioned earlier, I have found myself switching back and forth between the developer tools in Chrome and Firebug for Firefox. There is a special Developer Channel for Chrome through the Chromium project (http://www.chromium.org/getting-involved/dev-channel). This will allow you to receive updates to Chrome, as well as unlocked tools especially for developers. There are a lot of channels on that page, just be sure to get the "Dev" channel for your operating system.

Once you have the proper Dev channel installed, you can access the tools by clicking on **View ▸ Developer ▸ Developer Tools**. You can also use the keyboard shortcut of ⌘+ ⌥+ I (OS X), or shift + ctrl + I (Windows). This will open the tools at the bottom of the screen, as Firebug does. You can get to the Console tools for JavaScript by clicking on the Console tab.

Figure 2–4. *Chrome Developer Tools JavaScript console*

One of the differences between Chrome's implementation of the JavaScript console and Firebug's is that there is no separate editor for the JavaScript. You simply type it in directly to the console, and when you hit the "Enter" key, the line is evaluated.

Debugging

Both Chrome Developer Tools and Firebug support several features to make debugging much easier. I find myself using one feature in particular to help detangle what is going on in my code a lot: logging. Both tools support logging tools that will dump as much information as you need through the console.log function. You simply call the function in your code, with whatever message or bit of code you want to check in the following format,

```
console.log('Shall we play a game?');
```

Firebug and Chrome Developer tools will then evaluate the log statement and print it out to the console.

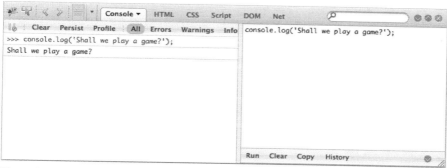

Figure 2–5. *Firebug output of console.log() function*

The `console.log` is an invaluable tool for getting information about what is actually happening in your code (and not what you are expecting). Because it provides immediate feedback regarding what is going on in your code, I use this function in the code snippets I present throughout the rest of the chapter.

Comments

When you are writing code, you will find it useful to write notes that explain some piece of code, but are not actually executed. There are two styles of commenting that JavaScript provides: inline (on a single line) and multiline. The syntax for these are slightly different, with inline comments starting with two characters "//" followed by the comment. These are meant to be on the same line as the comment, and are used either to explain what is happening on a line of code, or to quickly keep a line from executing during debugging. Multiline comments begin with the "/**" characters and end with the "*/" characters. Multiline comments allow you to put more detail into an explanation, or remove a larger block of code from execution during debugging.

Listing 2–1. *JavaScript Comment Examples*

```
// single line comment

var x = 1; // x is equal to one

/**
 * Multi-line comment spans more than one line.
 *
 * Like this one.
 */

alert('Hello World'); // executes

// the code below does not execute
```

```
/**
for(var i = 0; i < 10; i++) {
  alert("Hi, I have said this " + i + " times.");
}
*/
```

Comments are a very useful piece of your development, but if you do use comments to keep your code from executing, remember to clean up before you go live with your project.

Data Types

As I mentioned earlier, JavaScript is a language that is dynamically typed. By this I mean that the language infers a lot of what you can do with certain data by the type of data you use. If you passed 2 + 2 to a JavaScript engine, most likely you want to perform a mathematical operation and get the result of the operation (4) and not print out "2 + 2." However, if you had "JavaScript" + "Rocks," adding these together to get a numeric value doesn't make much sense.

In programming languages, these are called data types, and in JavaScript, the JavaScript engine dynamically interprets this information. That's not to say that you don't need to know about data types and sometimes assign them yourself. Why is this important? Didn't I say that JavaScript is dynamically typed? Shouldn't it just work? One hopes it will, but you can get into some issues pretty quickly if you are not a little careful, so it's a good idea to know what is going on under the covers to help debug your code. For me, the biggest issue I have encountered reading code is when someone accidentally places quotes around a numeric data type, or getting Boolean and numeric types mixed. Here is a quick rundown of some of the basic data types that JavaScript interprets from your code that you will use on a very regular basis.

- **Strings**: Contain character data, usually to be read by a human and are denoted by single or double quotes (but not mixed). For example, if you have a status that you want to output to a user, you could create a variable with the message:

  ```
  message = "Hello World";
  ```

- **Numbers**: Contain numeric data (data that can be added, subtracted, multiplied, divided, etc.). Numbers do not require quotes when they are declared.

  ```
  answer = 43;
  ```

- **Boolean**: True or false values; useful in evaluating the "truthfulness" of a result. Boolean values can either be the words "true" or "false" (without the quotes) or the numeric values 0 or 1. However, to be very clear when coding, it is a good idea to use the word version.

  ```
  fun = true;
  ```

- **NaN:** This data type stands for *not a number*. This is a special data type that is generally thrown as an error because you are mixing a numeric data type with some other data type and the JavaScript engine does not know what to do.

```
2 * "JavaScript" // When evaluated, will be NaN since you cannot multiply a ↵
string by 2
```

- **null:** A special keyword denoting an unknown piece of data. This is sometimes used to create a value that will be evaluated later and does not use quotes around the word "null."

```
container = null;
```

- **undefined:** A property (e.g., a variable) that has no value associated with it.

```
facebook; // when evaluated, will be undefined
```

Depending on the data type, you will have access to different operators to manipulate the data (we cover operators a bit further on), but logically it makes sense that if you are dealing with numbers, you most likely want to perform a mathematical operation. If you have two strings, most likely you want to do some other type of operation, such as concatenation (joining together), or finding if a string contains certain characters.

Variables

Variables in JavaScript, as in most languages, can be thought of as named "buckets" that associate names with data that can be used in a program. Information for different variables is stored in memory, which allows you to access that information with a name that points to those data in memory. For example, if you were writing a program that would convert degrees in Fahrenheit to degrees in Celsius, you might store the degrees in a variable in order to do multiple calculations on it.

Listing 2–2. *Simple JavaScript Variables*

```
var degrees = 51;

var celsius = (degrees - 32) * 5 / 9;

console.log(degrees);
console.log(degrees * 2);
console.log(celsius);
```

Figure 2–6. *Firebug variables*

JavaScript variables must begin with a letter, an underscore ("_"), or dollar sign ("$"). Variables that have a numeric value in the first character are illegal (no numeric characters). If you find yourself needing to use a variable name that has a number that would best describe the data being stored, you can just spell out the number. Remember, these names are just to give you, as the developer, a convenient way of referencing some value(s) somewhere else in your code.

Listing 2–3. *Proper and Improper JavaScript Variable Names*

```
// correctly named variables
var _legalVariable;
var $legalVariable;
var legalVariable;
var fourDozen;

// incorrectly named variables
var 4dozen;
var ♥nyancat;
```

> **NOTE:** Starting with JavaScript 1.5, which most modern browsers support, Unicode letter characters are also valid in variable names. Before JavaScript 1.5, variable names such as 今日 の (Japanese for "today") were not valid, forcing developers to use (from their perspective) foreign characters in their code. Although intended for foreign languages, the specification states that the first character in a variable name needs to be a character (not a number). A variable name such as ſcholar (the first character is a long-s) is a valid variable name because the long-s is a character and not a symbol. As an example, the variable name i♥javascript, although true, is not valid as it contains a Unicode *symbol* (♥), whereas the "ſ" character is a unicode character (an "s").

Notice that I prefixed all of the variables in Listing 2–3 with the word "var." When writing JavaScript, you should always prefix your variables with var to ensure your variables are appropriately *scoped*. I cover scope in more depth later in this chapter, but as a rule, always use var when declaring variable names.

NOTE: A good rule to use when naming variables is to use meaningful names within the context of your code, and shy away from variables with underscores and dollar signs. These variable names imply some special meaning to developers, especially those who have worked in other languages. For example, a variable named with an underscore (e.g., `var _privateVar;`) implies a private variable, but does not actually provide any security. Avoiding $ in your variable names is also important as several JavaScript frameworks map certain components to this symbol.

Operators

Now that we have covered some of the types of data JavaScript has available, and how you can store that information, we need to go over how to do something with these data. There are several categories of *operations* you can perform in the JavaScript language. You can assign and compare data, perform calculations with data, evaluate logic, and manipulate string data. JavaScript also has a set of special operators that amount to programming shortcuts for making some common programming structures with fewer keystrokes.

Assignment

This set of operators allows you to assign variables to data. There are some shorthand ways whereby JavaScript allows you to interact with data assignment to save some of the repetitiveness of programming.

Table 2–2. *JavaScript Assignment Operators*

Shorthand	Expanded	Example
x += y;	x = x + y;	var a = 2; a += 3 // evaluates to 5
x −= y;	x = x − y;	a −= 1 evaluates to 1
x *= y;	x = x * y;	a * = 3 evaluates to 6
x /= y;	x = x / y;	var b = 6; b / = 2 evaluates to 3
x %= y;	x = x % y;	b % = 2 evaluates to 0

Comparison

Comparing data is extremely important in any programming language. If you have done any programming in the past, you will find these operators very familiar.

Table 2–3. *JavaScript Comparison Operators*

Operator	Description	Usage
==	Equal operator returns true if the operands are equal.	true == true; "truth" == "truth";
!=	Not equal operator returns true if the operands are not equal.	true != false; "7" != 7;
===	Strict equals returns true if the operands are equal and the same type.	7 === 7;
!==	Strict not equals returns true if the operands are not equal and/or not of the same data type.	"7" !== 7;
>	Greater than returns true if the left operand is greater than the right operand.	7 > 3;
<	Less than returns true if the left operand is less than the right operand.	3 < 7;
>=	Greater than or equal returns true if the left operator is greater than or equal to the right operator.	7 >= 7; 10 >= 7;
<=	Less than or equal to returns true if the left operand is less than or equal to the right operand.	3 <= 3; 3 <= 7;

Arithmetic Operators

Arithmetic operators allow you to perform calculations on numeric data. You do not need to tell JavaScript explicitly which data type you are using, however, these operations logically only work for numbers. Beyond the add, divide, subtract, and multiply operators you are probably familiar with, JavaScript includes a set of arithmetic operators that help with common needs in your programming.

Table 2–4. *Arithmetic JavaScript Operators*

Operator	Description
++	Increment operator adds one (1) to the operand. This works for prefix (++x) to add one and then return the value of x, and postfix (x++) to return the value before incrementing its value.
--	Decrement operator subtracts one (1) from the operand. Like the increment operator, it works on operators in both the prefix (return the value after decrements) and postfix (return the value before decrement).
-	This operator holds a different meaning if it is a prefix of a numeric operator. Although 3 – 1 returns 2, if you prefix a variable with the negative operator, it multiplies the number by –1, giving you the operand's (the variable) negation (the number multiplied by –1).
%	The modulus operator returns the remainder of the division of two operands. For example, 7 % 2 returns 1 (e.g., 7/3 = 2 with a remainder of 1).

Listing 2–4. *Javascript Arithmetic Operators*

```
var x = 1;
++x; // increment x before evaluating x
x++; // increment x after evaluating x
--x; // decrement x before evaluating x
x--; // decrement x after evaluating x
-x;  // multiply x by -1

1 % 2; // 1
4 % 2; // 0
```

Logical Operators

In the flow of your program, you will inevitably need to evaluate some logic to handle different conditions in your program. Logical operators use *Boolean* values (true or false) to evaluate a specific condition. These operators are typically used to help make decisions in your code. For example, in a Facebook game, you may need to create a check in your code that the user is logged in to Facebook AND clicked on your application. If these two conditions do not exist, you can make decisions in your code on what to do next.

Table 2–5. *JavaScript Logical Operators*

Operator	Usage	Description
&&	var1&& var2	The logical AND operator returns var1 if it can be converted to false; otherwise it returns var2. This operator essentially checks that both var1 AND var2 evaluate to true.
||	var1 || var2	The logical OR operator returns true if var1 or var2 can be converted to true. This check essentially evaluates if either of the conditions is true.
!	!var1;	The logical NOT operator returns false if the operand can be converted to true. This operator is commonly used to ensure that a variable does not evaluate to a specific value in the flow of your code.

String Operators

String data have an operator that allows you to concatenate (link) different string data together. This is done with the "+" operator, and unlike numeric data types, the string concatenation operator is interpreted differently by the JavaScript engine. Instead of returning the result of the arithmetic operation, the concatenation operator returns the result of putting the two string operands together.

```
"Java" + "Script";
```

This example just returns the string "JavaScript," but you can take this much further by combining special formatting characters such as the "newline" character (which is \n). Take the following opening of Thomas Hardy's poem "I Look Into My Glass," with each line broken into its own variable then put together on a single line.

Listing 2–5. *JavaScript String Concatenation*

```
var line1 = "I look into my glass,";
var line2 = "And view my wasting skin,";
var line3 = "And say, 'Would God it came to pass";
var line4 = "My heart had shrunk as thin!'";
line1 + "\n" + line2 + "\n" + line3 + "\n" + line4; // each line is split using the
'newline' (\n) character
```

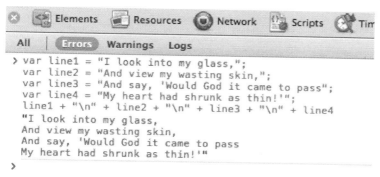

Figure 2–7. *Poem evaluated in Chrome Developer Tools*

The string concatenation operator also has special shorthand for concatenating strings:

Listing 2–6. *More JavaScript String Concatenation*

```
var line5 = "For then, I, undistrest";
var line6 = "By hearts grown cold to me";
var line7 = "Could lonely wait my endless rest";
var line8 = "With equanimity.";
var stanza = line5 + "\n";
stanza += line6 + "\n";
stanza += line7 + "\n" + line8;
stanza;
```

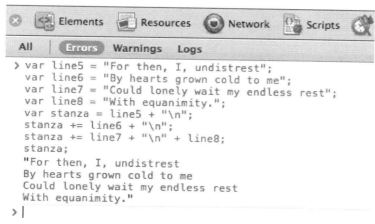

Figure 2–8. *Poem using string shorthand operator*

This example shows how you can utilize a variable to build up strings for your program, and use them to output information to the user.

Special Operators

JavaScript also provides a set of operators that do not fit cleanly into the above categories, but nonetheless are important. Some of these provide programming constructs that are shorthand for operations, whereas others provide facilities for interacting with data.

Ternary

This is a shorthand operator for evaluating simple if/else statements. The syntax that follows is quite compact, but contains a true/false evaluation, followed by a "?" and what to do if the statement is true, followed by a ":", then what to do if the statement is false.

```
statement ? true : false;
```

This operator is meant to save typing by the developer. Take the following example with an expanded if/else statement, and a shorthand to evaluate the doctor character on two different shows.

Listing 2–7. *JavaScript if/else Operator*

```
// without the operator
var show;
var doctor = "Hugh Laurie";

if ( doctor == "David Tennant") {
  show = "Doctor Who";
} else {
  show = "House";
}
```

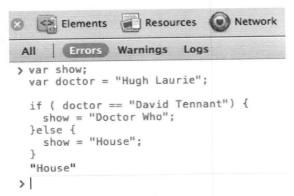

Figure 2–9. *Example if/else code*

Now we can do the same thing with the ternary operator.

Listing 2–8. *JavaScript Ternary Operator*

```
var show;
doctor = "Hugh Laurie";
show = (doctor == "David Tennant") ? "Doctor Who" : "House";
show;
```

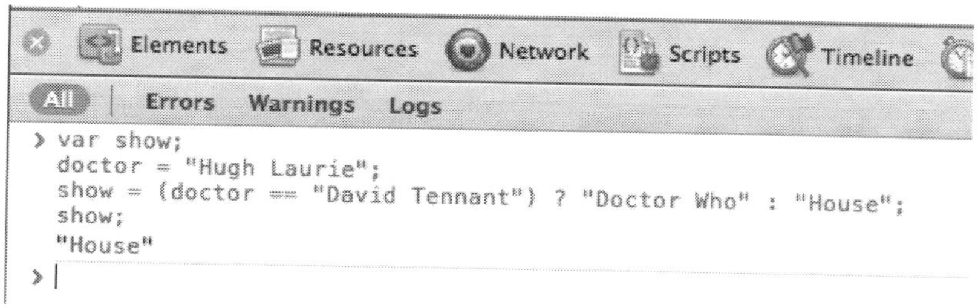

Figure 2–10. *Example ternary code*

The ternary operator is important inasmuch as it provides a shortcut that makes the footprint of your program smaller. One of the many performance factors in JavaScript is how fast you can get the file containing your program from your server to the client. When you have the chance to condense your code logic, it is always a good idea to do so.

New

The new operator creates a new instance of a predefined object such as Array, Date, or String, or one a programmer defines for use in the execution of a program.

Listing 2–9. *JavaScript New Operator*

```
var today = new Date();
var game = new Game();
```

This

In JavaScript, "this" is a reserved word that refers to the current object. Although a bit abstract at this point, "this" refers to the calling object in a method. We get more into the use of "this" later, but for now, think of it as a special variable. Using the this operator, you have access to the class properties using either array, or dot, notation, from within a function.

Listing 2–10. *JavaScript this Keyword*

```
this["property"];
this.property;
```

typeof

In JavaScript this returns the datatype of the operand. As this is an operator (and not a function), parentheses are optional.

Listing 2–11. *JavaScript typeof Operator*

```
var car = "Corvette";
var number = 3.1415;
var now = new Date();

typeof car;
typeof number;
typeof now;
typeof metaphysical;
```

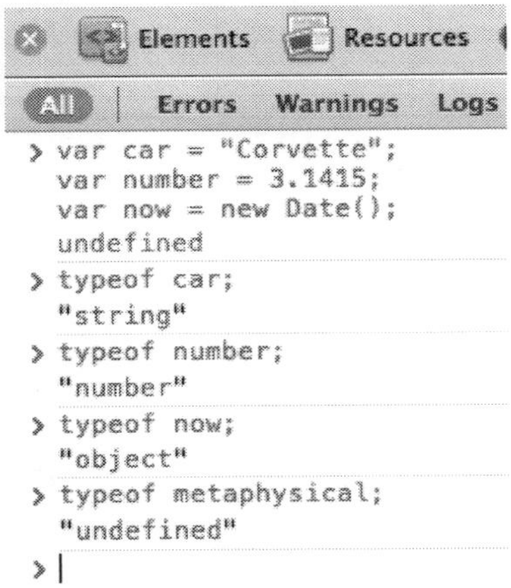

Figure 2–11. *Typeof operator*

This is not an exhaustive list of all the operators in JavaScript, but it does provide you with many of the most commonly used operators and their functions.

Data Structures

You will find in your programs that you routinely need to store information in certain areas of your program. Data structures are designed to store information efficiently and provide convenient mechanisms for passing data around in your code. Different data structures have different ways of accessing and addressing the information contained within, and having a general idea of how the built-in data types work will help you choose the one that is right for your program.

Array

An array is one of the most common data structures used in JavaScript. An array is one of the predefined objects in JavaScript and provides a convenient structure to store an ordered set of values that you can access by name or by their position within the array.

Arrays can contain any type of data, and can be instantiated with no parameters (an empty array), or with data to store in the Array:

Listing 2–12. *JavaScript Array Literal*

```
var myArray = new Array();
var anotherArray = new Array("Cool Array", myArray, 1, 3.1415);
console.log(anotherArray);
```

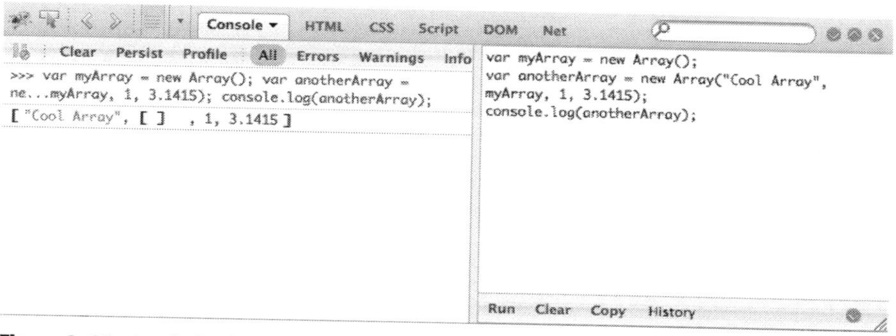

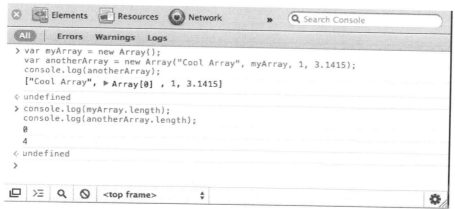

Figure 2–12. *JavaScript Array literals*

You also have access to the number of elements contained within an Array with the length method:

Listing 2–13. *JavaScript Array Length*

```
console.log(myArray.length);
console.log(anotherArray.length);
```

Figure 2–13. *JavaScript Array length*

You can use a for loop to then iterate over each element in an Array and use them:

Listing 2–14. *JavaScript Array Iteration*

```
for( var i = 0; i < anotherArray.length; i++ ) {
    console.log(anotherArray[i]);
}
```

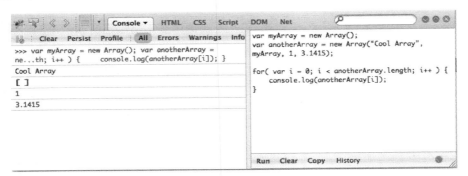

Figure 2–14. *JavaScript Array iteration*

This is only a very preliminary introduction to the JavaScript Array just to introduce the basics of what an Array does, and how to work with it. We use this structure a lot in subsequent chapters.

Flow Control

Flow control refers to the logic you use in a program to make decisions. One of the functions of a program is to contain logic to make decisions, and these statements provide a logical way of expressing that logic. Expressions in flow control are contained within blocks, delimited by curly braces ("{", "}"). Although there are certain conditions in which the braces are optional (e.g., a one-line check), I have always found it best to include them for readability, if not your own, then for the next person who sits down with your code.

if..else

This is a simple construct for checking conditions within a block of code. With this syntax, you check for explicit conditions to be met. Using this construct, every condition will be evaluated.

Listing 2–15. *JavaScript if..else*

```
var x = 5;

if(x < 5) {
  //do something
} else if (x == 5) {
  // do something else
} else {
  // in case none of the conditions are met
}
```

Switch

There are cases when the if/else syntax is inefficient, as it needs to evaluate each condition before evaluating the next line of code. There is another construct in JavaScript that allows your code to evaluate conditions more efficiently and break out of the evaluation, named `switch`. A switch statement evaluates an expression, and then matches a label to execute some code. To stop the evaluation, simply pass `break` to the code, otherwise the evaluation will continue to the next symbol. If none of the case evaluations is met, a `default` case (if defined) will return its values.

Listing 2–16. *JavaScript Switch*

```
var description;
var coffee = "Kona";
switch(coffee) {
  case "Blue Mountain":
    description = "Sweet, good body";
  break;
  case "Kona":
    description = "Robust, earthy, balanced";
  case "Sumatran":
    description = "Deep, dark";
  break;
  case "Starbucks":
    case "Dunkin Donuts":
    description = "With enough cream and sugar, almost anything is good.";
  break;
  default:
    description = "I don't know about that coffee…";
}
```

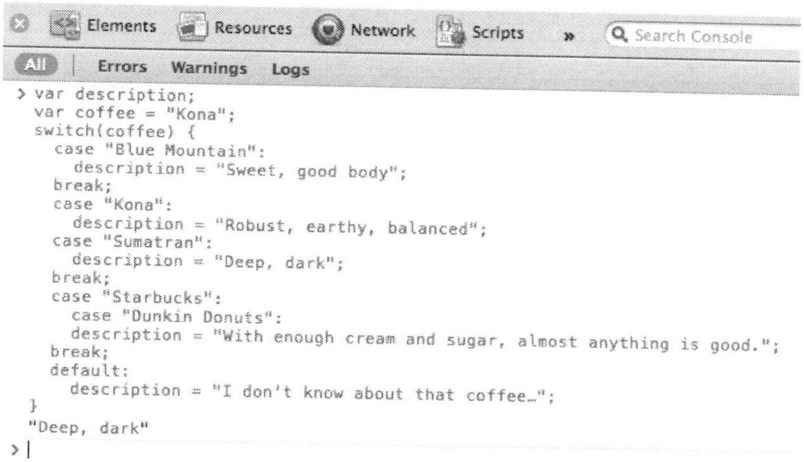

Figure 2–15. *Typeof operator*

When you run this, you may be expecting to see "Robust, earthy, balanced" and be surprised that the return value is "Deep, dark." This is due to a condition in the code called *fall through.* With the switch statement, if you do not explicitly add the break *keyword*, the code will "fall through" to the next statement until there is a break. You can use this behavior with a cleverly ordered set of case statements to execute several operations, or logically group collections together to execute functions, however, it is a best practice to always add the break keyword in the case statement.

Loops

Loops allow you to repeat steps until a specified condition is met. JavaScript has several different syntax for expressing the conditions of the loop, as well as explicit statements to jump out of the loop.

For Loop

A for loop repeats until a specified condition evaluates to false:

Listing 2–17. *JavaScript for Loop*

```
for(var i = 0; i < 10; i++) {
  // do something 10 times
}
```

While Loops

A while loop repeats until a specified condition evaluates to true:

Listing 2–18. *JavaScript while Loop*

```
i = 0;
while( i < 5) {
    i++; // do something 5 times
}
```

Do/while

Similar to the while loop, this syntax places the logic to perform before the exit condition. You use this method to execute a loop before evaluating the condition, ensuring that the loop executes at least one time before exiting.

Listing 2–19. *JavaScript do/while Loop*

```
i = 0;
do {
  i += 1;
} while ( i < 5 ); // also do something 5 times
```

Loop Statements

There are two JavaScript statements that expressly allow you to exit, or continue, a loop operation. Commonly used with logic, these help you code logic to handle edge cases in your loops.

- ▪ **break**: In its most basic form, break terminates the loop that is being currently executed. There is additional functionality for the break statement to take a label, which will terminate the specified statement.

- ▪ **continue**: As with break, continue will terminate a loop, but will continue the next iteration of the loop. Unlike break, continue does not entirely terminate the execution of a loop.

Listing 2–20. *JavaScript do/while Loop*

```
for(var i = 0; i < 10; i++) {

  if(i === 3) {
    break;
  }

  console.log(i);
}
```

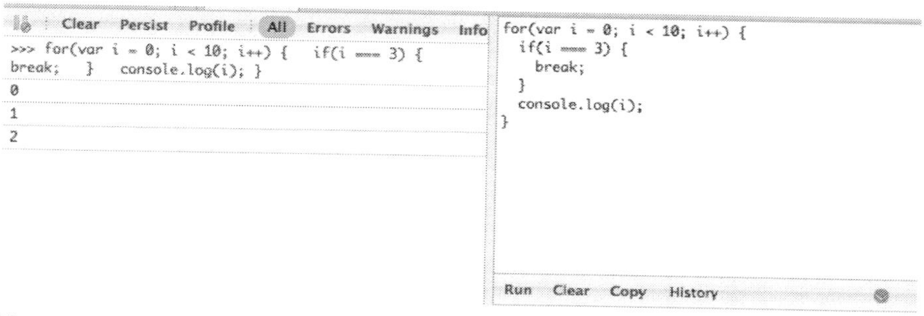

Figure 2–16. *Loop example with break*

Notice that this snippet produces the result 0, 1, 2. When the iterator value (i) evaluates to 3, the break statement is called and the loop stops evaluating the code. This is useful if there are conditions in which you want to break out of a loop to continue your code logic elsewhere. The continue statement is slightly different. Take the following example.

Listing 2–21. *JavaScript do/while loop*

```
for(var i = 0; i < 5; i++) {

  if(i === 3) {
    continue;
  }

  console.log(i);
}
```

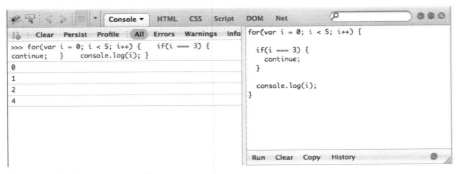

Figure 2–17. *Loop example with continue*

Notice that this prints 0, 1, 2, and 4, skipping 3. The `continue` statement in a loop is useful when you want to have a special case to "skip" in your loop.

Functions

Functions are pieces of code within your program that perform a specific task. By using functions, you are able to write reusable code, not only within the context of the program you are writing, but also with other programs that you may write. In JavaScript, a function consists of the keyword `function`, followed by the name of the function, a list of arguments, and the JavaScript statements.

The contents of a `function` (the function body) include some coding logic, and even calls to other functions. This is a way in which you can share bits of code throughout your program. However, on its own, a function is never executed. It needs to be called in the execution of your code. This is done by *calling* the function by its name. Take the following example which defines a function `sayWhat()` to log the word "what" to the console. It is called by executing the function in the code.

Listing 2–22. *JavaScript Function*

```
function sayWhat() {
  console.log("What");
}

sayWhat();
```

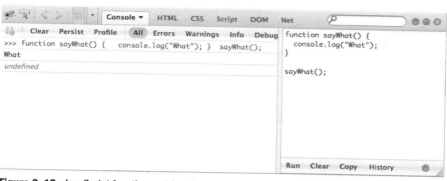

Figure 2–18. *JavaScript function and function call*

Variable Scope

When you declare a variable, you not only want access to the information, but you want to protect it from being changed. JavaScript has a construct called a `function` that allows you to define a block of code that you can call later. This approach makes it easier to write less code throughout your program by breaking your program into component parts. When you declare a variable within a `function`, you should intend to access that from within that `function`. You could imagine a scenario where you created a variable named `count` in one function that was used as a counter (a numeric data type), and in another function you intended to have a separate variable named `count`, which creates an array to store some data regarding the numbers of different items. When you execute a block of code, which `count` variable are you talking about now? The JavaScript engine has to deal with this, and if it gets it wrong, it will cause your program to act in unexpected ways.

To deal with this scenario, programming languages introduce a concept called *scope*. For functions within your program, you want the scope of each variable you declare to be *local*, that is, the information stored in that variable to be explicitly for that function, and to exist only for the duration of that code execution.

But what if you need to keep a piece of information so other functions can share those data? You can do this with a global variable. This allows a variable to be used from anywhere in your program. You declare this the same way as a local variable, just outside a function. If you do not add the `var` keyword to a variable declaration, the JavaScript engine will infer that it is a global variable. Because there is not an explicit "global" keyword in JavaScript, and anything not prefixed with the keyword "var" is considered a global variable, it is a best practice to always use the `var` keyword to declare your scope explicitly, even if you intend for it to be a global variable.

The previous examples in this chapter have all assigned variable names to different data types. The example in Listing 2–22 can be considered a "dangerous" example as it infers a global scope. You could run into a situation very quickly with the code where you reset the value of `myVariable`, which may not be your intention when writing the code. Let us take a look at another example of how not explicitly declaring scope can get your program into trouble:

Listing 2–23. *JavaScript Global Scope Confusion*

```javascript
otherVariable = new Array("javascript", "rocks", 1);

function setVariable() {
  otherVariable = "Hello ";
}

function setAnotherVariable() {
  otherVariable = 1;
}

console.log("display otherVariable " + otherVariable);
setVariable();

console.log("after calling setVariable():" + otherVariable);

setAnotherVariable();
console.log("after calling setAnotherVariable():" + otherVariable);
```

Figure 2–19. *JavaScript scope confusion*

Both of the functions in Listing 2–23 assign otherVariable in the *global scope,* which can lead to confusion in the logic in your code, and make it more difficult to debug issues that will arise because of the confused global scope. As stated before, it is a really good habit expressly to ensure all variables are explicitly scoped to ensure your code does not accidentally overwrite information that you will need in the execution of your program. Let's go ahead and rewrite these functions to make sure we do not overwrite the global scope:

Listing 2–24. *JavaScript Global Scope Clarity*

```javascript
var otherVariable = new Array("javascript", "rocks", 1); // otherVariable array is ↵
available for the entire script

function setVariable() {
  var otherVariable = "Hello "; // otherVariable is not available from outside this ↵
function
}
```

```
function setAnotherVariable() {
  var otherVariable = 1; //otherVariable is not available from outside this function
}

console.log("display otherVariable " + otherVariable);

setVariable();
console.log("after calling setVariable():" + otherVariable);

setAnotherVariable();
console.log("after calling setAnotherVariable():" + otherVariable);
```

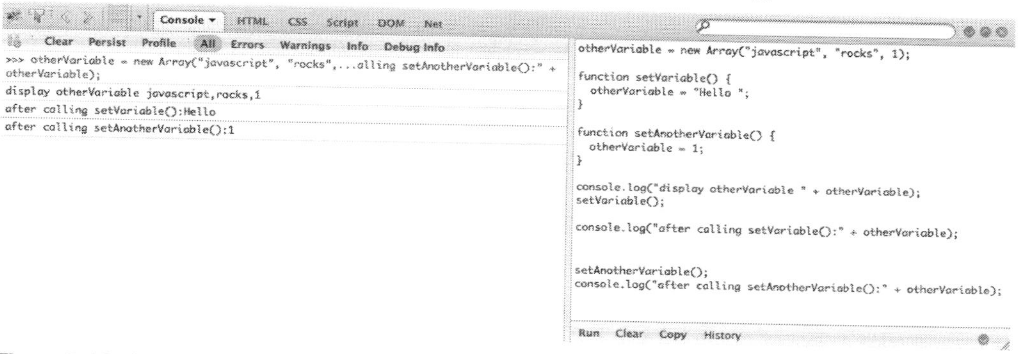

Figure 2–20. *JavaScript scope example*

Notice that now there are no side effects from setting the otherVariable variable in different functions. The global variable otherVariable remains the array with the values "javascript", "rocks", and "1", and the functions do not reset its value.

Special Variables

There are a couple of special variable classifications in JavaScript that you should be aware of when writing your programs.

- **Constant**: A read-only variable that uses the const prefix and the variable names are often capitalized by convention. Once set, a constant's value cannot be changed during the execution of the script. One caveat with a constant, setting one within a function definition will raise an error; constants can only be set outside a function.

  ```
  const PI = 3.14159265; // sets a global constant of PI
  ```

- **Global Variables**: These are declared in the same manner as a local variable, just outside a function definition. You use these within a script to handle passing information between functions. Unlike a constant, a global variable can be reset by functions in a script:

Listing 2–25. *JavaScript Global Variables*

```
var count = 5;

function incrementCount() {
  count = count + 1;
}

incrementCount();
console.log(count); // count evaluates to 6
```

As you begin to write your programs, you will find that using some standard coding conventions when naming and using variables will save you a lot of debugging time. Remember, capitalize your constants, use the var prefix for all of your variables, and use meaningful names for your variables. As your code gets more complex, you will find that using a standard approach will give you more time to work on innovating new features for your applications rather than debugging old ones!

Document Object Model

Everything I have discussed in this chapter up to this point has been part of the JavaScript language. However, one of the most important parts of working with JavaScript is in interacting with web pages. This occurs through an application programming interface (API) that browsers provide which allows you programmatic access to the content on a web page. At its heart, the document object model (DOM) provides a structural representation of the web page, which allows you, as a programmer, to write scripts to modify the content and visual representation of the information in a programmatic way.

It is worth pointing out that the DOM specification is implemented in slightly different ways by the different browser vendors with slightly different interpretations of the W3C specification. A lot of work has gone into different frameworks to make working with the DOM far less painful than it was, and currently jQuery seems to be winning the hearts and minds of developers. If you find yourself needing to work with the DOM, do yourself a favor and take a look at a framework such as jQuery, MooTools, or YUI.

Part of the DOM specification provides an event model that allows you to react when a user interacts with your application in a specific way. For instance, to start a game, you may create an element on an HTML page that has a "click" event that starts the game when clicked. There is a dizzying array of events, and we cover many of them in future chapters as we build our games together.

It is worth pointing out that most of this book is devoted to using canvas to develop games for Facebook which does not actually use the DOM. However, the DOM is an important piece of the overall development of your Facebook application as it provides mechanisms for interacting with the user on the page.

Guess the Number Game

Because this is a book on writing games in HTML5 for Facebook, let's walk through an example that implements a simple game, reinforcing the techniques in this chapter. For this example, we build a High–Low game, where the computer chooses a random number and you try to guess what it is.

The first thing we need to do is to define the rules of the game, and the expectations. As this is just meant to show off some of the code I have discussed in this chapter, the first iteration of this game is pretty bare bones. However, there is a second iteration of the code base with a few more bells and whistles (e.g., interface enhancements) that make the game look a bit nicer in the source code for this book.

For this game of High–Low, the program needs to generate a random number for the user to guess. This could be any number, but for the time being we just keep the numbers between 1 and 10. The user needs to be able to enter a guess, and get feedback from the program, either a hint to lower or raise her guess, or that she has successfully guessed the correct number, as well as to track the number of guesses to provide a "score" for how quickly the player was able to guess the number.

Let's start breaking this down into code. We need to store at least two numbers for the life of this program: the answer and the number of guesses. We know we want the number of guesses to start at 0, therefore we can set that number, while leaving the answer variable undefined.

Listing 2–26. *High-Low Global Variables*

```
var answer;
var guesses = 0;
var hint = '';
```

Now, let us look at creating a function that will set a random number within a given parameter. We want this to be a bit flexible, and allow the function to take a parameter, but not require this maximum number to seed the function. We also create a function that evaluates if a given guess is correct, returning a string of "Higher . . ." for low guesses, "Lower . . ." for high guesses, and "You Win!" if the answer is correct.

Listing 2–27. *High–Low Game Components*

```
function randomNumber(seed) {
      seed = seed || 10;
      return Math.floor(Math.random() * seed + 1);
}

function checkGuess(guess) {
      var hint = '';
      var parsedGuess = parseInt(guess, 10); // make sure the guess is a number

      guesses++;

      if(parsedGuess == answer) {
        hint = 'You Win!';
      } else if (parsedGuess < answer) {
        hint = 'Higher...';
```

```
    } else {
      hint = 'Lower...';
    }

    return hint;
}
```

Believe it or not, all of the components needed for this game are now done, but let me talk a little about some of the gotchas here. In the checkGuess function, notice that I used the parseInt function to ensure that the input I receive is a numeric data type. The second parameter (radix) represents the numeric system I am using. Although a base10 system is the default, it is always better to declare explicitly this value in the function so there is no question about the number system you are using.

Also, I used a couple of tricks in the randomNumber function. First, I want to allow the function to be executed without a seed parameter (randomNumber()). To do this, I evaluate the seed parameter, and set it to 10 if it is undefined.

Now, all that is left to do is integrate this code into a web form, and interact with the user input. We use some HTML boilerplate code to write the form.

Listing 2–28. *High–Low HTML Wrapper*

```html
<!doctype html>
<html>
<head>
<meta charset="utf-8">
</head>
<body>
<div class="hint">Guess a number</div>
<div class="guesscount">0</div>
<form id="game_form" name="game_form">
<label for="guess">Guess</label>
<input type="text" name="guess" />
<a href="#" value="Guess!" id="guess" class="button">Guess</a>
</form>
</body>
</html>
```

With this rudimentary HTML in place, we can focus on the interactions between the guesses and the HTML. To accomplish this, I use the JQuery framework to handle letting my code know when the DOM has been loaded, and when the anchor tag "Guess" has been clicked to submit an answer to the code.

Listing 2–29. *High–Low jQuery Loader*

```javascript
$(document).ready(function() {
        answer = randomNumber(10); // generate a new random number when the DOM is ready

        $("form a#guess").click(function() {
          var guess = $("input:first").val(); // read the first guess
          var guessHint = checkGuess(guess);  // check the guess

          $('.hint').html(guessHint)
          $('.guesscount').html(guesses)
        });
});
```

Now, for the entire HTML and JavaScript in a single file that can be played on your browser:

Listing 2–30. *Complete High–Low Game*

```
<!doctype html>
<html>
<head>
<meta charset="utf-8">
<script src="https://ajax.googleapis.com/ajax/libs/jquery/1.7/jquery.min.js"></script>
<script type="text/javascript" charset="utf-8">
    var answer;
    var guesses = 0;
    var hint = '';

    function randomNumber(seed) {
      seed = seed || 10;
      return Math.floor(Math.random() * seed + 1);
    }

    function checkGuess(guess) {
      var hint = '';
      var parsedGuess = parseInt(guess, 10); // make sure the guess is a number

      guesses++;

      if(parsedGuess == answer) {
        hint = 'You Win!';
      } else if (parsedGuess < answer) {
        hint = 'Higher...';
      } else {
        hint = 'Lower...';
      }

      return hint;
    }

    $(document).ready(function() {
        answer = randomNumber(10); // generate a new random number when the DOM is ready

      $("form a#guess").click(function() {
        var guess = $("input:first").val(); // read the first guess
        var guessHint = checkGuess(guess);  // check the guess

        $('.hint').html(guessHint)
        $('.guesscount').html(guesses)
      });
    });
</script>
</head>
<body>
<div class="hint">Guess a number</div>
<div class="guesscount">0</div>
<form id="game_form" name="game_form">
<label for="guess">Guess</label>
<input type="text" name="guess" />
<a href="#" value="Guess!" id="guess" class="button">Guess</a>
</form>
```

```
</body>
</html>
```

Figure 2–21. *High–Low game*

Really the only thing to note here is that I am loading the jQuery library from the Google CDN (content delivery network) before I call jQuery code. As long as you load jQuery before any of your code, you can place your DOM interactions anywhere on the page. If you adhere to the wisdom of Paul Irish and his wonderful HTML5 boilerplate, JavaScript should be loaded at the bottom of the page to make page parsing even faster. However, for our purposes here, I just kept everything in the header.

> **TIP:** You can not only target specific versions of the JavaScript hosted on the Google CDN, but also keep up with incremental releases by manipulating your calling URLs. To target the 1.6.3 version of jQuery, your URL would be `https://ajax.googleapis.com/ajax/libs/jquery/1.6.3/jquery.min.js`, to target any 1.6 release, simply drop the .3, and to stay up with all of the releases (e.g., 1.7, 1.8, etc.), simply drop the .6.3 from the URL `https://ajax.googleapis.com/ajax/libs/jquery/1/jquery`.

Getting Good with JavaScript

There is a lot I have not covered in this chapter on JavaScript. Every few years there are entirely new books that come out on the subject matter, and in order to get really good with JavaScript, you need to practice, and keep up with current trends.

I thought I would list a few good books that get much further into the details of JavaScript and its implementations on different browser platforms.

- Earle Castledine, and Craig Sharkie. *jQuery: Novice to Ninja*. Collingwood: SitePoint Pty, Limited, 2010.

- Douglas Crockford. *JavaScript: The Good Parts*. Cambridge: O'Reilly, 2008.

■ Marijn Haverbeke. *Eloquent JavaScript: A Modern Introduction to Programming.* San Francisco: No Starch Press, 2011. `http://eloquentjavascript.net/`.

■ Christian Heilmann. *Beginning JavaScript with DOM Scripting and Ajax.* New York: Apress, 2006.

■ John Resig. *Pro JavaScript Techniques.* New York: Apress, 2006.

■ Stoyan Stefanov. *JavaScript Patterns.* Cambridge: O'Reilly Media, 2010.

■ Nicholas Zaka. *Professional JavaScript for Web Developers.* 2nd ed. Indianapolis, IN: Wiley Pub., 2009.

Summary

This chapter just scratched the surface of the JavaScript language, but it does give you many of the tools you need to begin getting good at JavaScript. Knowing when to leverage a framework such as JQuery or MooTools, how to debug what is going on in your code, and how the language interacts with the browser are all things you need to know to start building games.

In the next chapter I go into much more detail on the canvas element. The HTML5 canvas element allows developers to create graphics directly in the browser without the need for third-party browser extensions. The JavaScript I have covered to this point is just the basics, but gives you context for what comes later as we begin to develop games for Facebook.

Chapter 3

It's All About Context: Canvas Basics

The emerging HTML5 specification includes facilities for developers to leverage the power of the browser to start to build applications that feel more like native applications. In the past, where you may have written a game in Flash using Adobe's tools, you now have the ability to do many of the same things inside the browser without needing to download a third-party extension. Because the browser manages the implementation of the specification, developers can also take advantage of the power and memory management the browser provides.

Specifically for this book, we look at the canvas element introduced in the HTML 5 specification and implement games on the Facebook platform. The canvas element provides developers with an API for drawing pixels on web pages. Although there are methods for drawing simple shapes on a canvas (rectangles and arcs), it is worth noting that the canvas element is not designed to render shapes. Shapes are actually part of another API (the SVG API) that is specifically designed to optimize the rendering of complex shape patterns on the screen. In contrast, the canvas API is meant to render pixels. This is a bit of an abstract between drawing shapes and pixels inasmuch as these most likely look the same in the end, but the big difference comes in the SVG elements becoming part of the document object model, meaning that they can be manipulated with tools such as jQuery. By contrast, canvas elements can only be manipulated within the context of the program rendering the current pixels in the canvas.

In the previous chapter I covered some of the basics of JavaScript syntax. These syntax basics allow you to write the logic you will need to integrate different APIs into your application. This chapter gets into the basics of how the canvas API works, with examples for its usage. Making the jump from knowing the syntax structures to API calls can be tricky if you have not worked with different APIs before.

Canvas: The 2D Context

The canvas element in HTML is a complex beast. The specification was originally meant to cover both two- and three-dimensional contexts. However, as of the writing of this book, the 3D context was split from the original specification and reorganized under a new specification named WebGL. If you are working in three-dimensional space, you will use the "webgl" context, and if you are working in two-dimensional space, you will use the "2d" context. The webgl context is developing quite quickly, and there are some absolutely beautiful examples of using the 3D context on the web. However, its use in HTML5 games lags behind the 2D context by quite a lot. Not only are browsers still working on the implementations and details of the specification for the webgl context, but there are some issues with the API that still need to be developed (e.g., a mouse lock to keep the mouse inside the canvas element for a first-person shooter) in order to make the webgl context a viable option for game development. For our games here in Facebook, I focus on the 2D context, both because it is supported by more browsers and because it is a more mature API for developing games.

Coordinate System

The canvas element uses a Cartesian coordinate system that you may remember from your middle school geometry class. If you are like me, that was a while ago, so here is a brief overview in case you forgot some of this stuff.

The Cartesian coordinate system consists of two planes that are perpendicular to each other (you may remember the term orthogonal). The planes are commonly referred to as the x-axis and y-axis in two-dimensional space, with an *origin* of (0,0) where the x- and y-axes cross. In your middle school geometry, you were most likely introduced to the different sections of the coordinate system, with positive x- and y-values in the top-right quadrant, and positive x and negative y in the bottom-right quadrant. See Figure 3–1.

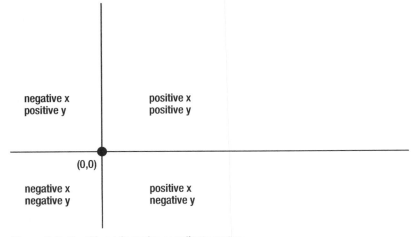

Figure 3–1. *Traditional Cartesian coordinate system*

The canvas element, however, implements a slightly different coordinate system, with the origin being in the upper-left-hand corner, with positive x-values along the x-axis, and positive y-values moving down the y-axis. It is worth pointing out, that the canvas coordinate system, and the coordinate system you used in middle school are actually the same, but the perspective from which you observe the coordinates is changing.

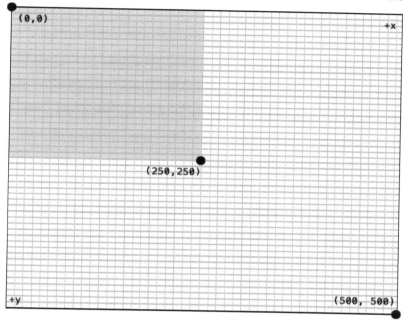

Figure 3–2. *Cartesian coordinate system as implemented in a 500 Í 500 canvas element*

This coordinate system uses conventions most computer programs use in building GUI software. See Figure 3–2. This system fixes the co-ordinate system in the upper-left-hand corner and allows you to resize the window to keep growing without needing to recalculate the contents of the entire window. Although the contents may resize when you expand/contract the window size, the origin point remains fixed. If the origin were moved to the middle of the screen, every point would need to be redrawn if you resized the window.

First Shape

As I stated before, the canvas element is part of the HTML5 specification and provides developers with an API for manipulating pixels on the screen. So what does this look like exactly? Take the code in Listing 3–1 as an example:

Listing 3–1. *Simple Canvas Rectangle*

```
<!DOCTYPE HTML>
<html>
<head>
```

```
    <meta charset="utf-8" />
    <meta name="viewport" content="width=device-width,initial-scale=1">

    <title>A Simple Canvas Square</title>
    <style type="text/css" media="screen">
      #canvas {
        border: 1px solid #c0c0c0;
      }
    </style>

</head>
<body>
  <canvas id="canvas" width="270" height="270"></canvas>

  <script type="text/javascript" charset="utf-8">
    var canvas = document.getElementById('canvas');
    var context = canvas.getContext('2d');

    context.fillStyle = "gray";
    context.fillRect(30, 30, 200, 200);
  </script>
</body>
</html>
```

This code can be split up into different elements. First the HTML declaration tells browsers the code that follows should be treated as HTML, specifically, HTML5 if the browser has implemented any of the features in the specification. The head section contains metadata about the character encoding (utf-8 in this case), the initial viewport (for mobile devices and responsive design), a title (appears either on the tab or across the top of the browser), and a simple style that places a gray border around the canvas element.

Within the body element, you see the actual canvas element, with an id, width, and height. The width and height specify the dimensions of the canvas element. By initializing the size of the canvas, we set the dimensions of the coordinates to be 270 × 270, any co-ordinates outside of this (e.g., 280, 280) will not show up on the canvas.

Lastly, we have the code that actually does something with the canvas. Because the JavaScript block is executed after the canvas element is declared, the code will execute. However, if the code were in the head element, this code would throw an error because of the way in which DOM elements are loaded. Another way to handle loading the JavaScript is with a listener that waits until the page has loaded, or even using a library such as jQuery that will wait until the information on the page is loaded and then execute the script. However, for clarity, I am placing the code at the bottom of the page and executing it there.

The JavaScript creates a new canvas variable that selects the canvas element by using the DOM canvas id. It then creates a context element by declaring the canvas to be two-dimensional. At this point, we have tapped into the Canvas API, and have access to a vast library of items with which to work. In this case, we want to set a fill style (boring "gray" because it prints well), and draw a rectangle that has a margin on each side of 30 pixels, and is 200 pixels wide in both the x-and y-directions. The result, shown in Figure 3–3, is the exciting square in browsers that support the canvas element.

Figure 3–3. *Rendered canvas rectangle*

The canvas API supports a variety of methods to make drawing shapes easier as shown in Figure 3–4.

- arc: For drawing arcs (a segment of a circle).

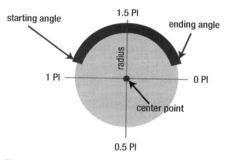

Figure 3–4. *Canvas arc segment*

- **arcTo**: Draws an arc of a fixed radius between two points (or tangents).

- **beginPath**: Creates a new "path" of pixels on the canvas.

- **bezierCurveTo**: Creates a curve based on a set of Bezier co-ordinates.

- **clearRect**: Clears pixels within a given rectangle.

- **clip**: Hides pixels outside a given area.

- **closePath**: Closes the current subpath and starts a new path at the coordinates of the closed subpath.

- **drawImage**: Draws image files to the canvas.

- **fill**: Fills the current path with the fillStyle property.

- **fillRect**: Fills pixels of given dimensions from the `fillStyle` property.

- **fillText**: Fills the canvas with a "text" element at a given coordinate.

- **lineTo**: Draws a line from the current path location to the given coordinate.

- **moveTo**: Creates a new subpath from the given coordinates.

- **quadraticCurveTo**: Connects the last point in the current subpath to a given point using a quadratic Bezier curve.

- **rect**: Creates a subpath rectangle from a given point, and a height and width.

- **restore**: If there is a saved drawing state, it pops the top entry off the drawing state stack; otherwise it does nothing.

- **rotate**: Rotates a path in a clockwise manner by an angle expressed in radians.

- **save**: Pushes a copy of the current drawing state onto the drawing state stack.

- **scale**: Scales a path by a factor along the *x*- and *y*-axes.

- **setTransform**: Resets the current transform to the identity matrix, then invokes a transform with the same arguments.

- **stroke**: Calculates the stroke of all subpaths along the current path, then fills the stroke area using the `strokeStyle` property.

- **strokeRect**: Like stroke, but for a given rectangle.

- **strokeText**: Fills a "text" with the value of the `strokeStyle` property.

- **transform**: Runs a transform matrix on the current path by multiplying the path by the matrix: [[a, c, e],[b, d, f], [0, 0, 1]].

- **translate**: Translates a path to a new location using a transformation matrix.

These methods in the HTML5 specification for the canvas elements allow developers to do some rather amazing things. You can easily render a shape, resize it, move it across the screen, and apply different textures to it. These methods all require a fair amount of math (linear algebra) to calculate, but instead of developing your own routines to do these tasks, browsers provide you with a consistent API for these complex operations. Of all the drawing methods, one that you will use quite often in developing games is drawImage(), which I get into more in depth in future chapters. I give some basic examples of using some of the other methods, but depending on the type of game you envision writing, you may not need to use all of these methods.

Triangles and Lines

There is a lot packed into the previous section, especially if you are not familiar with a lot of the math that sits behind computer graphics. It will probably make a bit more sense if I break down a few more examples and explain what is going on. This example uses the boilerplate HTML from Listing 3–1, and adds a canvas element and code to render a triangle.

Listing 3–2. *Simple Triangle Path*

```
<!DOCTYPE HTML>
<html>
<head>
  <meta http-equiv="content-type" content="text/html; charset=utf-8">

  <title>Triangle</title>
  <style type="text/css" media="screen">
    #canvas {
      border: 1px solid #c0c0c0;
    }
  </style>

</head>
<body>
  <canvas id="canvas" width="500" height="400"></canvas>

  <script type="text/javascript" charset="utf-8">
    var canvas = document.getElementById('canvas');
    var context = canvas.getContext('2d');

    context.fillStyle = "#fa7b08";
    context.beginPath();
    context.moveTo(250, 100);
    context.lineTo(400, 230);
    context.lineTo(100, 230);
    context.closePath();
    context.fill();

    context.strokeStyle = "rgb(168, 8, 0)";
    context.lineWidth = 10.0;
    context.stroke();

    context.beginPath();
    context.moveTo(0, 0);
    context.lineTo(400, 400);
    context.closePath();
```

```
    </script>
  </body>
</html>
```

In this example, I again create a context element with the canvas. However, this time, I declare a path fillStyle of #fa7b08 (a hue of orange), start a new subpath and move its starting location to the pixel coordinates of 250, 100 (right 250 pixels, down 100 pixels). From that point, I draw a line to the point 400, 230, and from there to 100, 230, creating the bottom of the triangle. From there, I close the path (back to 250, 100) and call fill to color the pixels within the triangle subpath to be colored #fa7b08.

I also wanted to have a reddish outline, so I created a new strokeStyle with RGB colors (canvas also accepts hue, saturation, and lightness [HSL] values) with a line width of 10 pixels. Because the current subpath is still the triangle, I call stroke to trace the path with the color.

The result is the triangle shown in Figure 3–5.

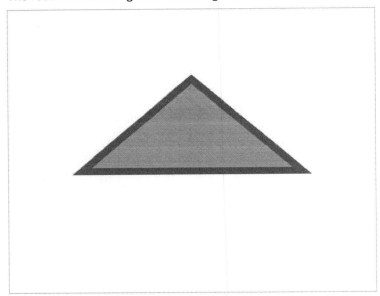

Figure 3–5. *Rendered canvas triangle*

Transparency

Sometimes when you draw a path, you want it to have some opacity (the amount of light that can pass through an object). You can use the globalAlpha channel, but you can also create a fillStyle that takes an RGBA (red, green, blue, alpha) color to control the path's opacity.

> **NOTE:** An alpha channel is a mask that specifies the transparency level for a pixel. You typically do not use the alpha channel at the pixel level, but on an object (e.g., a shape or image) level. The alpha channel is actually a mask that defines how the pixel colors will be mixed when overlaid with another color. Objects with a higher alpha-level are treated as more opaque; those with a lower alpha level are more transparent.

Listing 3–3. *Transparency Example*

```
<!DOCTYPE HTML>
<html>
<head>
  <meta http-equiv="content-type" content="text/html; charset=utf-8">

  <title>Example4: Overlapping Box</title>
  <style type="text/css" media="screen">
    #canvas {
      border: 1px solid #c0c0c0;
    }
  </style>

</head>
<body>
<canvas id="canvas" width="500" height="400"></canvas>

<script type="text/javascript" charset="utf-8">
  function draw(canvasId) {
    "use strict";
    var canvas = document.getElementById(canvasId);
    var context = canvas.getContext("2d");

    context.fillStyle = "#091F5D";
    context.fillRect (10, 10, 160, 150);

    context.fillStyle = "rgba(255, 78, 0, 0.5)";
    context.fillRect (90, 90, 160, 150);

    context.fillStyle = "rgb(255, 78, 0)";
    context.fillRect (170, 160, 160, 150);

  }

  draw('canvas');

</script>
</body>
</html>
```

Notice a few things with this code. First, I refactored the drawing commands into a function that I could apply to multiple canvases on a page. I also combined two lines that created separate canvas and context variables into a single line. After creating the context, I defined three `fillStyle`s and fill rectangles on the canvas with solid blue and orange, with a rectangle overlapping the two rectangles that is the same color as the orange color, but with an alpha channel of 50%. Because the alpha channel defines how the pixels will be mixed, the result is as shown in Figure 3–6.

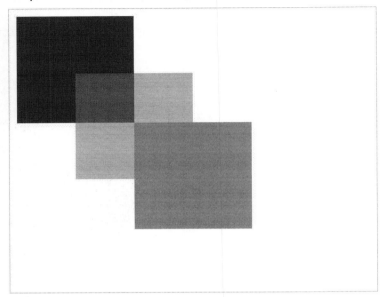

Figure 3–6. *Rendered canvas squares with alpha channel*

Translation and Rotation

Rotating paths on the canvas, as well as translating (shifting) the transformations of the shapes, is something you will spend quite a bit of time on when developing canvas applications.

Listing 3–5. *Translation and Rotation*

```
<!DOCTYPE HTML>
<html>
<head>
  <meta http-equiv="content-type" content="text/html; charset=utf-8">

  <title>Example5: Movement</title>
  <style type="text/css" media="screen">
    #canvas {
      border: 1px solid #c0c0c0;
    }
  </style>

</head>
<body>
<canvas id="canvas" width="500" height="125"></canvas>

<script type="text/javascript" charset="utf-8">
```

```
      function drawRectangle(context, fillStyle) {
        context.fillStyle = fillStyle || "gray";

        context.fillRect(-30, -30, 60, 80);
      }

    function dot(context) {
        context.save();
        context.fillStyle = "black";
        context.fillRect( -2, 8, 4, 4);
        context.restore();
      }


    function draw(canvasId) {
        var context = document.getElementById(canvasId).getContext("2d");

        context.translate(45, 45);
        context.save();

        drawRectangle(context, "red");
        dot(context);
        context.restore();

        context.save();
        context.translate(100, 5);
        context.rotate(45 * Math.PI / 180);
        drawRectangle(context, "green");
        dot(context);
        context.restore();

        context.save();
        context.translate(200, 10);
        context.rotate(90 * Math.PI / 180);
        drawRectangle(context, "blue");
        dot(context);
        context.restore();

        context.save();
        context.translate(300, 20);
        context.rotate(135 * Math.PI / 180);
        drawRectangle(context, "green");
        dot(context);
        context.restore();

        context.save();
        context.translate(400, 0);
        context.rotate(0 * Math.PI / 180);
        drawRectangle(context, "red");
        dot(context);
        context.restore();
      }

    draw('canvas');

</script>
</body>
</html>
```

Listing 3–5 is a bit more complex example using a few different techniques to add items to the canvas. The first function, drawRectangle, takes care of actually drawing a rectangle by creating a 60 × 80 pixel rectangle from the visible canvas with the provided fillStyle (or gray if none is given). The dot function saves the current drawing state, creates a new drawing state with a fillStyle of black, creates a 4 × 4 pixel square, and then restores the previous drawing state.

As before, the draw function takes the id of the canvas element you are attaching the code to, and then begins the translations and rotation. This is achieved by saving the drawing state, applying a transformation to the path, rotating the path, drawing a shape in that perspective, adding a dot, and returning to the base state. Wash, rinse, repeat. Remember, the rotate method takes its parameter in radians (the math works out a bit easier), so be sure you can convert your angles from degrees to radians like a champ. See Figure 3–7.

> **NOTE:** Angles are measured two ways, degrees and radians. Depending on what you are doing, you will need to translate back and forth between these two systems. Remember that to convert to radians, multiply the degree angle by (Math.PI/180) and to convert back, multiply the radian angle by (180/Math.PI).

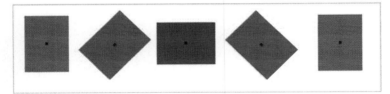

Figure 3–7. *Rendered canvas shapes with rotation*

Simple Motion

In the previous section, I showed how to draw static shapes and change their opacity, and how to rotate and transform paths. But what about moving objects within the canvas? Once the canvas has been rendered, you have an image. What we want to do here is redraw the canvas at a set interval to update the drawing while moving an object in some manner. In grade school you may have drawn flip books where you would draw a picture on a page, then a slightly moved version of the picture on the next. After you had a few of these, you could flip them with your thumb to see a "moving" scene. Working with motion with the canvas element is a programmatic version of this flip book idea. You draw an image, render it, move it slightly, render it, move it slightly, render it . . . you get the idea. See Listing 3–6.

Listing 3–6. *Simple Motion*

```
<!DOCTYPE HTML>
<html>
  <head>
    <meta http-equiv="content-type" content="text/html; charset=utf-8">

    <title>Example3-5</title>
    <style type="text/css" media="screen">
      #fps { clear: both; }
      #canvas {
        clear: both;
        border: 1px solid #c0c0c0;
      }
    </style>

  </head>
  <body>
      <canvas id="canvas" width="800" height="600">
      You need a better browser.
      </canvas>

      <script type="text/javascript" charset="utf-8">
        var context;

        var WIDTH = 800;
        var HEIGHT = 600;
        var x;
        var y;
        var dx = 4;
        var dy = 8;

        var lastTime = new Date();
        var fps = 0;
        var frameCount = 0;

        function randomNumber(max) {
          return Math.floor(Math.random() * max + 1);
        }

        function setXY() {
          x = randomNumber(WIDTH);
          y = randomNumber(HEIGHT);
        }

        function clear() {
          context.clearRect(0, 0, WIDTH, HEIGHT);
        }

        function drawCircle(x, y, radius) {
          context.beginPath();
          context.arc(x, y, radius, 0, Math.PI * 2, true);
          context.fill();
        }

        function draw(canvasId) {
          clear();
```

```
            context.fillStyle = "blue";
            drawCircle(x, y, 75);

            context.fillStyle = "green";
            drawCircle(x, y, 10);

            if (x + dx > WIDTH || x + dx < 0) {
              dx = -dx;
            }

            if (y + dy > HEIGHT || y + dy < 0) {
              dy = -dy;
            }

            x += dx;
            y += dy;

        }

        function init(canvasId) {
          context = document.getElementById(canvasId).getContext('2d');
          setXY();
          return window.setInterval(draw, 10);
        }

        init('canvas');
    </script>
</body>
</html>
```

This example creates a circle that interacts with the bounds (or sides) of the canvas to change direction when it hits a limit of the canvas. Notice the init function call sets a random coordinate on the canvas to start, and then calls a very useful function for the canvas called window.setInterval. This function is useful for working with the canvas and redrawing frames at a set interval as it calls on a function repeatedly with a set delay between each call. In the case of our code here, we call the draw function every 10 milliseconds, which effectively redraws the scene. See Figure 3–8.

Figure 3–8. *Object in motion on the canvas*

The hard work for this routine is actually done in the draw function. The code first needs to clear all the pixels from the canvas. Without this, the canvas would fill with the color of the circle as it is redrawn. By explicitly clearing the entire canvas, we ensure that only the shapes we want are drawn on the canvas.

Recalculating where to draw the circle with its x- and y-coordinates sets movement on the canvas. These values are recalculated in the code by adding or subtracting a delta (change in a variable) constant. In the case of this code, this change in position is four pixels along the x-axis and eight pixels along the y-axis. These were arbitrarily chosen and do not imitate physics (e.g., a decay after an initial acceleration). The "physics" of this example simply checks to see if the next x- and y-coordinates are within the bounds of the canvas. If they are not, it multiplies the offending coordinate(s) by –1, thus reversing the direction of the circle. It is worth noting that the test here checks if the center point of the circle is within the bounds.

As an exercise, how would you refactor the code to take the radius of the circle into account when testing if the shape should reverse its direction?

Keyboard Control

Depending on what you are doing with the canvas element, you may at some point want to control the canvas with keyboard controls. At the abstract level, this involves adding a listener for keyboard strokes from the browser then defining what to do when a specific key is pressed. This example implements a simple WASD and arrow control system.

> **NOTE:** I have seen a lot of games that implement just the arrows for different movement. This is fine if all your actions are taken care of with those four keys, but you may want to reconsider if you have any type of mouse interaction. For right-handed players, this works fine, but it is maddening for left-handed players who have the mouse on the opposite side of their keyboard. With four extra lines of code, you can remove this frustration for more users, as well as give players more options on how they play your game.

Listing 3–7. *Keyboard Control*

```
<!DOCTYPE HTML>
<html>
<head>
  <meta http-equiv="content-type" content="text/html; charset=utf-8">

  <title>Example 3-7: Keyboard Bindings</title>
  <style type="text/css" media="all">
    #canvas {
      border: 1px solid #c0c0c0;
    }
  </style>

</head>
<body>
  <canvas id="canvas" width="500" height="400"></canvas>

  <script type="text/javascript" charset="utf-8">
    var context;
    var x = 100;
    var y = 150;
    var dx = 5;
    var dy = 5;
    const HEIGHT = 400;
    const WIDTH = 500;

    function init(canvasID) {
      context = document.getElementById(canvasID).getContext('2d');
      window.addEventListener('keydown', keyDown, true);
      return setInterval(draw, 10);
    }

    function keyDown(event) {

      switch(event.keyCode) {
        case 87: // w
        case 38: // up arrow
          if (y - dy > 0 ) {
            y -= dy;
          }
          break;
        case 83: // s
        case 40: // down arrow
          if (y + dy < HEIGHT) {
            y += dy;
```

```
        }
        break;
      case 65: // a
      case 37: // left arrow
        if(x - dx > 0) {
          x -= dx;
        }
        break;
      case 68: // d
      case 39: // right arrow
        if(x + dx < WIDTH) {
          x += dx;
        }
        break;
    }
  // console.log(x + ", " + y);
  }

  function clear() {
    context.clearRect(0, 0, WIDTH, HEIGHT);
  }

  function rectangle(x, y, width, height) {
    context.beginPath();
    context.rect(x, y, width, height);
    context.closePath();
    context.fill();
    context.stroke();
  }

  function draw() {
    clear();
    context.fillStyle = "black";
    context.strokeStyle = "blue";
    rectangle(x, y, 30, 50);
  }

  init('canvas');

  </script>

</body>
</html>
```

Listing 3–7 adds a few new tricks to the previous examples. Notice the addition of the
`window.addEventListener` to listen to events from the keyboard, and to react when a
given key is pressed. Using a switch statement, the keyboard inputs for the up, down,
left, and right keys, as well as w, a, s, and d keys (for those who game with those key
bindings) will move the box around on the screen. See Figure 3–9.

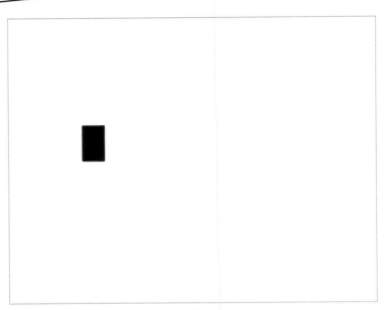

Figure 3–9. *Binding keyboard events to the canvas*

Debugging Tools

Inevitably when working with new APIs you are going to run into situations where your code just is not performing, or behaving, as you intended. This could be the Facebook APIs, browser APIs, or some JavaScript library you are using on a project. When you are working with these technologies, it can be quite frustrating to figure out what is going on at what level of your code. Is it the JavaScript? Is it a response from Facebook? As your codebase grows, finding where bugs are hidden becomes more difficult, but there are some really good tools to help you figure out where your errors are happening. When developing JavaScript for a canvas game, you will want to pay attention to the JavaScript debugging tools. Because, it is hoped, you are doing some experimentation with the JavaScript canvas API, I thought it would be worth going over (briefly) some of the tools that are out there to help you write "better" code and find bugs in your codebase. I cover aspects of these tools in future chapters, but I introduce some of the tools here for the impatient.

- **JSPerf**: If you are running into performance issues, this site may help. It allows you to write code snippets and share them with the world to run on multiple systems in the "real" world. You will want to isolate some segment of your code you believe to be causing the performance issue, then write a test to have others give you numbers of the code's performance.

■ **JSLint**: Like all good lint programs (looks for potential bugs in your code), JSLint will hurt your feelings. Because the code analysis is quite stringent, you will need to be sure to read the output of the analysis before making major changes to your code. Running your code through JSLint, however, can help you catch inadvertent bugs in your code and is generally a good idea. This provides a very opinionated result of what the author (Doug Crockford) believes are the best practices for JavaScript development, although there is a branch of this code (JSHint) that uses more community feedback to produce code results that are based on community best practices.

■ **JSHint**: This is a code quality tool that runs on JSLint, but tweaked to detect errors and alert you to potential issues in your code. There is an online version that allows you to paste in your code (at http://www.jshint.com), and a downloadable version that you can integrate into your workflow. I use this with Rake and Ant, depending on what type of project I am working on to make sure I did not forget some of the best practices for JavaScript as I switch between multiple languages.

■ **Firebug/Chrome Developer Tools**: I use these both on a daily basis. Each of these tools provides a JavaScript console to try out different code, as well as the ability to profile and unravel bits of code to truly see what is going on. Each of these tools has powerful debugging tools for JavaScript, which you will need eventually. Getting comfortable with these tools is important, and although I tend to spend a bit more time with Firebug, the developer tools in Chrome have been growing on me and I routinely switch between the two.

■ **JSFiddle**: There are times when you just want to test out some bit of code, but not write out an entire HTML page, CSS, and JavaScript. The JSFiddle website (http://jsfiddle.net) is a site that allows you to run different bits of code using different frameworks as well as share your code with others. It also has JSLint and code reformatters to help you debug and share your best code.

What About Mobile?

Most vendors of "smart" mobile devices already support many of the HTML5 specification features, and most modern browsers running on mobile devices support the HTML5 canvas element. There is native browser support for the canvas application, so your applications will work. You may need to do some work to dynamically resize your application (media queries are a popular technique for presenting different styles based on the screen size of the requesting device). This is actually one of the strengths of the HTML5 canvas elements; it allows you to deliver rich content natively to your mobile users, without needing to write a native application.

This is good news for you as a game developer. The mobile version of Facebook (either the website or a platform-specific client) will be able to play your game with minimal issues. You may need to rethink some of the controls in your game if you really want to go after the mobile market, but the engine you write to power your game should work with minimal adjustments on the mobile platform. However, it is worth mentioning that mobile browsers are still a bit more limited in their power than their desktop counterparts. You may notice that there is a significant drop in performance when operating on a mobile device, a fact that has had many game developers looking at ways to accelerate their applications by compiling their HTML5 game as a native application. By leveraging these compilers, you ensure that your game uses any operating-system-level hardware acceleration available for graphics.

Summary

The HTML5 canvas element provides web browsers with a powerful tool for drawing and manipulating pixels on the screen. By manipulating subpaths on the canvas, you can draw simple and complex shapes and manipulate their appearance. You can move objects about the canvas with simple (and not so simple) algorithms that simulate (or defy) the laws of physics as well as hook up movements of objects in the canvas to execute keyboard commands. By leveraging the power of the HTML5 canvas element, you can also open your application up to mobile devices without a wholesale rewrite of your codebase.

In the next chapter I get into the design process for a project. Effective planning can make all the difference in the success of a project, and having a process in place can help you make decisions as you go that will help ensure your project's success. The process will also help you codify your expectations, and give you success points along the way where you can celebrate your progression.

Chapter 4

The Plan: Idea to Design

If you are like most developers (myself included), you most likely have opened your favorite editor or IDE and just started developing. You may have had some vague idea of what you wanted your program to do, but you probably just made it up as you went along. Although this can work well for small projects, or learning new techniques, a design-as-you-go approach on a project of a nontrivial size will cause you a lot of headaches. As someone who has started more than one project as an experiment with no plan to grow it into something, I can attest to the fact that you encounter far fewer problems if you spend a little bit of time planning your project out, to understand its scope and anticipate where the hard parts of it will be. This is especially important if you plan to produce an application that is fun and scalable to all the individuals who may install your application on Facebook!

In this chapter I discuss a design process that can help you structure your ideas and build a better application. There are a lot of different formalized discussions of these patterns (e.g., waterfall, Agile, etc.), however, I talk about one that has worked well for me on the projects I have been involved with, taking techniques from several approaches and applying them to my own workflow. I encourage you also to take a look at other approaches and develop one that works best for how you approach problems and does not get in the way of your workflow, but helps streamline your thought process and coding practices.

The Design Process

The word design is overloaded, but for our purposes here I use design to refer to everything from the application idea, code, and the integration of image and sound assets. I cover some top-level steps that you can follow, and if you ascribe to the Agile methodology, you can use these steps to shape your iterations. Remember, for everything you plan, you need to keep the big picture in mind so you do not veer off course and develop a product that does not fit your original vision, or get so bogged down in one particular aspect that the entire project is stymied. For myself, I typically break the design process out into the following areas.

1. Brainstorming ideas.

2. Research potential audiences.

3. Identify the competition.

4. Review the project; figure out what you know, what you need to figure out (and do some research to approach the problem), and develop an overall vision for the application.

5. Decide on an artistic direction for the application.

6. Cull aspects of your project that are not practical for constraints on your time, skill, and computing resources.

7. Plan project milestones.

8. Write your code.

9. Deploy your code.

10. Test your application with users.

11. Launch.

This list is by no means comprehensive, and it simplifies the iterations that you will find yourself doing as you refine your project design, but it does give you a place to start your planning. Let's get into these topics in a bit more detail now.

Brainstorming

Before you can code anything, you need an idea, a novel or interesting concept that you believe some audience will enjoy or find useful. In the brainstorming stage, simple ideas that you can easily explain to others are important. If you come up with a concept that takes a long time to explain, or is confusing when you attempt to explain it to others, it may be time to come up with another concept, or to simplify the one on which you are working.

Once you have a concept, it is a good idea to codify it in a series of steps, which clearly lays out the game or application rules for the end user and clearly defines the objective or purpose of the application.

Idea: Klondike Solitaire.

Objective: Order a deck of 52 playing cards by suit from Ace to King.

Rules:

- This is a single-player game.
- The game of Klondike is played on a table.

- A deck of 52 playing cards is used, consisting of four suits (Hearts, Diamonds, Spades, Clubs) with 13 cards (Ace, 2, 3, 4, 5, 6, 7, 8, 9, 10, Jack, Queen, King) each.

- The cards are "shuffled" to be in random order.

- The player is dealt 28 face-down cards in seven piles in a left-to-right orientation. The first pile has one card, the second two, the third pile has three, and so on, so that the seventh pile has seven cards.

- The last card on each pile is turned over to reveal its suit and value.

- This configuration is referred to as the tableau.

- The remaining cards are placed face down in a pile to the side.

- The remaining cards are referred to as the draw pile.

- Aces form the "foundation" for the ordered piles. Once placed, cards in the foundation cannot be moved.

- Face-up cards in the tableau can have the next lower card with an alternative color.

- A turn consists of turning over a card from the draw pile; then making any legal plays on the tableau.

- A player may only go through the draw pile once.

If you have ever played Klondike on the computer before, this should look quite familiar to you. However, you may have some idea that modifies these rules, or an alternative method for handling some aspect of this application that makes this more compelling for users. Be sure to be as complete as possible to ensure that you have a good understanding of the problem domain you are trying to solve and can communicate this to others.

Identify Your Audience

Who is going to use your application? With more than 800 million users actively using Facebook in over 70 languages, it is important to understand who the intended end user is for the application. This should not be a difficult task, just an exercise in common sense to help you gauge your expectations. For instance, if you are building a set of puzzle games that makes the Sunday New York Times' puzzles look like child's play, it may not hold the attention of 8–10-year olds for long. If you really want to build something enjoyable for the elementary school crowd, you may need to rethink your idea, or shift your thinking in audience to what actually fits your idea.

A big issue you may run across if you are doing contract work is helping guide your clients in identifying their audience. You may get a response such as "Everyone should be able to use this application," but in reality, this is infeasible. You need to be able to help your client refine the "everyone" statement to a specific group of individuals who you want to attract.

Once you identify an audience, how do you know if your idea will resonate with them? This is a difficult question, especially if your idea is similar to other applications. If something exists that is similar, you can see if that application is useful/interesting to your audience. If you have a unique idea, a mockup (storyboards, a quick conversation) can be used to see if the idea gets the response you are expecting. If not, you may need to further refine your idea and ask again. Although there is no way to determine accurately who will like your game, you can check to see if there is any traction within that demographic before you get too far into the design process.

If we were to identify the market for a Klondike Solitaire game, we may want to look at an older demographic who may have played the game with actual cards. They will already be familiar with the rules of the game, and need less convincing to try it out. A younger audience may actually associate this game with something their parents would play on a break at work, and make you as the developer work harder to attract them as an audience.

Depending on the scope of your project, this testing may take on the form of asking your neighbor, or a more formal setup where you bring people into a space and have a set of qualitative questions for respondents to answer. The larger point is to be in conversation with the people you identified as your audience at an early stage.

Identify Your Competition

If there are products similar to yours, you need to make sure that you can differentiate your product in some meaningful way. Is there some piece of gameplay that your idea enhances? Does your idea for some feature make your product more compelling for users? Are you different enough in your look and feel that users do not confuse your product with a competitor's?

Competitors can be both direct (those who offer similar products) and indirect (offerings that are close substitutes). You may find a matrix of your competitors to look something like that shown in Table 4-1.

Table 4-1. *Competitor List*

Questions	Answer
Company	Rovio
URL	http://www.rovio.com/
Product	Angry Birds
Genre	Puzzle action
Target Audience	Casual gamers
Reputation	High
Gameplay	Fire assortment of birds at pigs who are protected by various structures

Questions	Answer
Strengths	Addictive puzzles, low price, fun
Weaknesses	No in-game hints for users stuck on puzzles
Company	XMG Studios
URL	http://www.xmg.com/
Product	Cannon Cadets
Genre	Action
Target Audience	Casual gamers
Reputation	Medium
Gameplay	Rocket Boy shoots cannonballs at structures created by Gordeo the monkey
Strengths	Good physics engine, ability to design your own levels
Weaknesses	A lot of gray in the color palette; can be overly silly

After you have collected several of these (do not go too wild), you will have a good understanding of where your product sits within the competition. This will be a great benefit when you then explain to users how your offering stacks up against the competition.

Artistic Direction

A big decision you will need to make about your project is the overall look and feel of the interface. The interface says something about your project, and deciding what that should be is important. For example, if you were developing a Klondike card came, you may decide that you want to make the game look a bit weathered, as if you have traveled to Alaska in search of gold and are looking for a respite from the tedium of panning for gold. In this case, using an artistic style out of Tron may not work. You would want to use more weathered wood textures, perhaps fade the print on the cards, and perhaps use saloon style music to help set the mood for the game.

A lot of art in games these days is done, or at least starts, as vector art. There are many reasons, but this is done primarily as a way to make resizing images for different devices trivial. Vector graphics are stored as mathematical formulas of the shapes, so resizing the image simply changes the perspective of the shapes, allowing you to resize without distorting the image quality. Although your final image assets may be a more compressed format (such as a png, jpeg, or gif), the "master" images can remain as vectors.

Project Review

Now that you have a good sense of what the project encapsulates, who you are developing the application for, and what differentiates your project from others, you need to take a look at the needs of the project and assess what is needed to complete the project, what skills and abilities you have as a developer, and how to augment and add any skills or resources that you do not possess.

This is a self-reflective step, and it is important that you are honest. Every project has areas that will require you to do some research and develop new skills. New projects are a great time to learn something new, and if you are honest at this point and identify areas that will require more research, it will help you manage your time and help you ship your project. If you haven't learned something new on a project, you probably haven't done it right. Table 4-2 shows a hypothetical checklist for building a Klondike Solitaire game.

Table 4-2. *Project Needs Checklist*

Need	Do I have this skill?	Solution
Proficiency in JavaScript	Yes	You can always get better. Read the articles on the Mozilla Developer Network and the HTML5 Rocks website. Also, read the books back in the "Getting Good with JavaScript" section of Chapter 2.
Understanding of gaming system construction	No	Read this book.
Proficiency with software versioning	No	Learn to use git.
Ability to move cards on the screen	No	Need some type of library to allow a click event to select an image, then follow cursor while clicked.
Access to audio assets	No	Read Chapter 5 on collecting assets.
Ability to create graphic assets	No	Can the neighbor's cousin show me how to use Photoshop or Inkscape? Are there collections that I can download to use?
Access to a text editor	Yes	I have mad vim skills.
Server space to deliver game	Yes	I have a basic hosted web server account.

By identifying the resources you have already developed, and what skills you need to develop to implement your software effectively, you begin to get an idea of the time commitment for your application. One big help in this area is that there are many outlets for getting started in the various aspects of application design. Remember, if there is something on your list that you cannot do yourself, or find someone else to do it, you will need to think of a way to cut it from the project.

If you are a new developer, there will be many things that you do not know how to do. You really need to spend time understanding what your code is doing, and resist the urge to Google-and-paste. Take a few moments before you go to a search engine and find something close to what you are trying to do. If you do, be sure you completely understand what the code is doing; if some concept is unclear, ask a question. With the rise of social coding (Github, Google Code, etc.), it is easier than ever to be in direct contact with the author of the code.

Feature Cull

Now that you have a good idea of what is needed to complete the project, it is time to take a look at these needs and weigh them against a set of project constraints. I generally find the biggest constraints in time (and money), technology, and ability, but there may be others that you encounter. You can ask yourself the following questions to help determine if your project is not only feasible, but a good idea. You at least need to ask about the following for your project.

- Can you meet all of the requirements needed to complete the project (ability)?

- Does feature x affect the overall performance of the game (technology)?

- Is the timeline for completing the project feasible (time)?

You may find that you have some features that are difficult to code initially. Take the Klondike game for instance. Let's say you wanted to add a feature that would automatically stack the cards in the foundations when legal moves permitted. You may run into a situation where the code causes a severe slowdown in the performance of the application. You then need to ask yourself if it is worth the time and effort to find a suitable solution to the performance issue, or if the feature can be scrapped and perhaps added into a future edition of your code.

With a game like Klondike solitaire, you may have wanted to add a feature to the game such as a "versus mode" where two people could compete against each other. The feature would allow each player to play the same game, and the person with the quickest time would win the match. However, as you begin to develop the feature, you realize that it not only is having an adverse effect on your game (the game has slowed down considerably), but it is also pushing you against your deadline to the point that you are now two weeks behind. You need to seriously consider if this feature truly adds enough value to your software, or if you can push this feature to a later release when you have more time to plan for the issues that are popping up.

As I have stated before, it is important that you keep the overall vision of the system in mind when making decisions about what to cut, and what to keep. If there is an element of the plan that does not make sense to the overall vision, it should go. However, if you are cutting elements that change the vision of the project, be sure to refine the vision in a text and be sure that it still makes sense to your audience.

Planning Milestones

Putting dates on milestones helps you gauge where your project is, and if you are ahead of time or behind schedule. You can think of these milestones as places to evaluate where you are in your project cycle, and how good your estimates are in implementing particular components. Some of the hardest things to gauge in any project are the unknowns that accompany a project. Especially when you are working with a third-party system such as the Facebook platform, unknown glitches can pop up (e.g., they remove a particular feature that you are using, or change its behavior), and these milestones can help you evaluate where you are, where you are going, and how well you are sticking to your plan.

- **Feature Freeze:** Set a date to lock in all required features and check that your project review has uncovered no new details. At this point, no new features can be added for this release cycle. OK, so this is a bit harsh, but features added after this point can start to create some real scope creep.

- **Code Freeze:** Implementation of the project features has been completed and the software is functional and believed to be free of software issues.

- **System Test:** Code moves from development environment to "real" hardware. This test is really about testing the software on the systems it will be delivered from, giving systems engineers and developers time to tune the servers and software with any issues that crop up.

- **Beta:** Open your system up to a small number of real users. This allows you to have feedback and observe the systems as they perform under a load. You will also be able to rework any unforeseen issues that have cropped up, clarify any interface issues that arise, and find those weird things that users "shouldn't" be able to do, but figure out/stumble into.

- **Final Product:** You ship a bug-free product to your users. With a website, or game, this is the product launch.

For a small project, you may only have one iteration of this cycle. For larger projects, you may do this repeatedly, with each iteration being a new release of your software.

Recent trends (OK, so this is reasonably mature, but gaining momentum with independent developers) in planning these cycles are to compress portions of your cycles into weekly, or biweekly, iterations. You can develop specific features of your application and deploy them, then reassess what is next. Using this method allows you to address any serious issues that occur that were not anticipated (e.g., this recent fix drops the frame rate from 90 frames per second, to 4), and be more responsive to your user's needs and desires.

Code

At some point, you actually do need to write some code. If you don't already use a source control manager (SCM), I highly suggest you put this book down and download one now! I personally use git on almost all of my projects, but just about any modern SCM will be hugely beneficial to your workflow.

You may ask why this is a good idea; if you work with software for any amount of time, you will inevitably run into a situation where some code you are working on stops working in some catastrophic way. Even worse, your computer stops working in a catastrophic way. With most SCM systems, you not only have an external copy of your code somewhere, you also have a database of your changes that allows you to have point in time (or at least point in commits) access to your code changes. The tools go beyond simple code recovery; SCM systems also provide you with other administrative tools to make working with your code easier.

There are also several online resources you can use with your software to enhance not only your work, but work with clients and the larger open source community. Github, Bitbucket, and Google Code are just some of the services that provide free accounts (and in the case of Github and Bitbucket, paid private accounts), to host your code. There are also wikis, bug trackers, and code visualizations that generally accompany these online platforms, providing you with solid, basic workflow tools for managing your source code.

When developing your code, you also want to pay attention to best practices. Ensuring your code is consistent (consistent indentation, naming functions, executing code, writing tests, and so on, will make it easier for you as your codebase grows. If you are doing work that other developers are contributing to, having these standards will help a lot. Nothing is more maddening (and useless) than a commit from a developer that does nothing other than change the spacing of the code. By codifying the standards in which you write your code, you can ensure that anyone who sits down to your code has a small ramp-up time to get familiar with the code base, and that the code is readable, logical, and functional.

Deployment

Once you have written your software and it is working the way you expect it to, you need to get it onto a server. When I first started doing web work, we would push our code to our servers with an FTP client. With every update of our code, we prayed nothing would go wrong in the transfer (dropped dial-up connection, network switch) and that there was nothing in the code that would cause the server to crash. And, we hoped, we would only need to push the updates to a single machine, otherwise we would need to coordinate getting the updates to the different servers.

I have noticed that if you annoy enough smart people, someone will come up with a better way. Today there are many different methods you can use to deploy your software on servers. I fell in love with Capistrano, "a utility and framework for executing commands in parallel on multiple remote machines," (https://github.com/capistrano/capistrano) when I encountered it several years ago, and use it on many of my projects. Depending on what I am deploying, I may also use rsync, or even use a server callback on Github to push my code when it receives a particular push to a branch (generally master).

For the purposes of this book, we deploy our code to Heroku, a cloud application for deploying web-based software, so our deployments are dead simple (literally just push our git repository to Heroku). However, as your codebase grows, you may find yourself needing to stage your deployments. For example, you may need to push your code to an environment that has the most bleeding edge of your code to test, but want to maintain a stable platform for your users. At this point, you will need to have multiple servers (or at least virtual servers) that can handle your code. Once you are certain that your code runs as expected on the staging servers, you can then push those updates out to the rest of your users on your main production servers. A setup like this, although it can get expensive, helps ensure your users have a good experience, while providing you a platform for testing new features on production-level hardware.

User Testing

After you have the code in a form that you believe is reasonably free of bugs, it is time to get someone to sit down and use it. More than likely your users will find some issues that you had not expected, or try something that just doesn't make sense. This is particularly true in web applications where the different rendering engines in web browsers handle CSS and JavaScript slightly differently. Compounding this are plugins that actually inject (e.g., Greasemonkey) code into yours, or remove certain elements (e.g., noScript). To paraphrase Marco Arment, these aren't necessarily issues with your code, but they are your problem. It can be a slow, sometimes frustrating, process working through some of the issues that arise from your user testing, but having a good idea of how users perceive how to use your software can help you rework your visual interface to ensure a pleasant playing experience for all of your users.

Launch

The launch stage should, it is hoped, be less stressful than many of the others. After you have crafted an announcement, it is time to get the message out. Facebook, Twitter, blog posts, and email campaigns all help you spread the word. You may also want to have a launch party. If you are doing this on a small scale, be sure you invite the right audience and give them a highlight of the project goals and objectives. Be sure that you invite anyone who sponsored the project (including family and friends) and be sure to thank people individually for their contribution in making the project possible. It is often overlooked, but taking a little bit of time to celebrate your success is as important a step in the design process as the rest of the steps.

Summary

The process of developing a project takes a lot of planning. Making sure you fully understand what you are getting yourself into is an important step. If you cannot describe the project to an ideal user rather rapidly, you may need to rethink the project and make sure it quickly makes sense to users. Writing your features, researching your place in the market, and determining what you need to learn to bring your project to fruition are all important parts of the process and I have given you some tools to help get you going. You (I hope) have, or will develop, some of your own. The more tangible aspects of your project—art, code, sound, servers—can be daunting to deal with, but are generally ultimately solvable if you have a clear vision for the project and the experience you are trying to provide your users.

When you are all done, and have taken a break to celebrate your success, it is time to start looking at new features, enhancing current features, and any other improvements that may be needed. Remember, web projects are never truly finished, just abandoned.

In the next chapter, I cover some of the basics of developing the assets that you use for your games: how you actually go about designing not only the visual assets that compose your game play, but also how you can develop sounds. In addition, if you want to leverage the work of others, I show where to go to find assets that can be used, such as royalty-free graphics and sounds, to add to the entire game experience you are developing for your users.

Chapter 5

Essential Game Components

In addition to the code you need to develop, you need to spend time developing other components for your game. This chapter introduces some of the basics of constructing those other components. Although a full treatment of building game components would fill a bookshelf, this chapter does touch on some of the tools and techniques used to develop graphic and audio assets.

Types of Graphics

Graphics for computer systems are grouped into two different approaches that have different strengths and weaknesses. A *raster* graphic is an image composed of a two-dimensional pixel grid. Each pixel of a raster image has a color associated with it, and the mosaic of color creates a digital surrogate of an object. If you have ever taken a picture with a digital camera, you have created a raster image. A vector graphic, by contrast, uses sets of mathematical formulas to represent the different shapes in an image. One of the strengths that a vector-based graphic has over a raster-based graphic is the fact that you can resize a vector image with no loss in the quality of the image. Because vectors use mathematical formulas, resizing the image simply means multiplying these formulas by some number to control the size. With a raster, resizing an image generally means either a loss of information (e.g., removing pixels when creating smaller derivatives) or that the information must be interpolated, which can result in a pixelated image. See Figure 5–1.

So what advantages do raster images have? Vector graphics are generally used when working with solid shapes and colors. And although a real artist who is skilled with a vector-graphics editor can do some amazing things, it is usually "easier" to create more complex graphics in a raster format. Raster images can more easily handle subtle shading and changes in colors that are more difficult to achieve with vector graphics. See Figure 5–2.

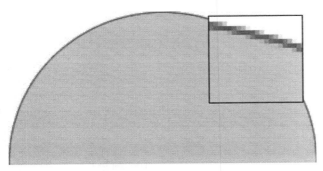

Figure 5–1. *Zoomed-in view of a raster-based circle created in Adobe Fireworks*

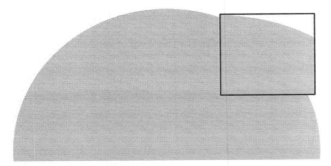

Figure 5–2. *Zoomed-in view of a vector-based circle created in Inkscape*

Depending on your needs, you may use different software and techniques to build up the graphic assets for your game. When using raster graphics, typically you will want either a Portable Network Graphics (.png) or a JPEG (there are others, like gif, but PNG and JPEG are most commonly used). When you are creating these graphics, be sure to optimize them for web delivery. Many of the tools for raster graphic editing contain algorithms to optimize your graphics, but you may also want to use tools like the open source tools opting (http://optipng.sourceforge.net/) and jpegtran (http://jpegclub.org/) to squeeze every bit of optimization you can out of your graphics to ensure the smallest network payload possible. These utilities are also available as part of the HTML 5 Boilerplate package that Paul Irish maintains, and there are scripts in place that use predefined optimizations to get you started.

> **NOTE:** The JPEG format does not have an alpha channel to control opacity. The png format allows you to set an alpha channel, but requires a bit more overhead than a JPEG does, increasing its file size.

Vector graphics typically need to be exported to a raster format for use in HTML games, especially if using the canvas element (remember that the canvas element only supports pixel-level elements; svg is used to render vector graphics). Most vector-based graphics editors have tools to make this export very simple. When deciding on a format, be sure to look not only at the visual aspects of the implementation, but also the technical. If you have awesome graphics that slow your frame rate down by 50% (or more), you probably want to look at some different solutions.

Graphics Tools

Today there are a great number of excellent tools for creating both vector- and raster-based graphics. Choices for selecting the right tool for you depend on your budget, operating system, and requirements for creating your graphics.

- **Acorn:** Acorn is a popular graphics editor for OS X. It has many advanced features for manipulating graphics and a relatively intuitive user interface. Acorn also allows you to do some simple vector graphics, work with PSD (Adobe Photoshop files), and has a nice set of filters for adding components to raster images (e.g., shadows, bevels, etc.). At $49, Acorn comes with support and is significantly less expensive than Adobe Photoshop. You can download a trial of the software at `http://flyingmeat.com/acorn/`.

- **Adobe Fireworks:** This is Adobe's lower-end offering for graphics editing. I personally use this tool for most of my graphics editing, from mocking up web and application designs, to basic image touchups. Fireworks runs on Windows and OS X operating systems and comes in at just under $300 for a full license of the software. Like Acorn, Fireworks allows you to do both pretty sophisticated raster work and also basic vector work, allowing you to mix-and-match your image approach in one piece of software. You can download a 30-day trial of the software from the Adobe Fireworks site (`http://www.adobe.com/products/fireworks.html`).

- **GIMP:** This is an open source project that is closest in comparison to Adobe Photoshop. The software runs on most operating systems and allows you to edit and author raster graphics. GIMP is a very robust image editor and can be a bit intimidating for new users. There is a strong community of support online, with mailing lists and IRC channels where people can answer your questions. The software is freely available at `http://www.gimp.org/`.

- **Inkscape:** Inkscape is an open-source vector graphics editor with capabilities similar to Adobe Illustrator that runs on most operating systems. The software supports advanced SVG features including markers, clones, and alpha blending, and has a very streamlined interface. Inkscape works on many different platforms, in both binary (precompiled) and source formats. There is a thriving community of both users and developers with several lists and IRC channels. Inkscape is freely available for download at `http://inkscape.org/`.

- **Paint.net:** This editor for Windows is a free replacement for the Windows Paint program for Windows. The program has some basic tools for color correction, gradients, and even sports some facilities for creating basic vector graphics. There is a series of community-generated tutorials on the site's forums that will help you get going too. If you find one of these helpful, be sure to write one of your own! Paint.net can be downloaded for free from `http://www.getpaint.net`.

- **Adobe Photoshop:** Photoshop is the 900-pound gorilla of raster graphics editing and runs on Windows and OS X. The tool has sophisticated filters and tooling, which gives you a lot of tools for developing graphics. In the latest version (CS 5.5 at the writing of this book), Adobe has added tools for 3D design and motion editing in its Photoshop CS 5 Extended version. This is a heavyweight tool with a steep learning curve, and at nearly $700 per license, it is also quite a financial investment. However, if you have the time, patience, and budget, you can create amazing graphics with the software in both 2D and 3D. You can download a 30-day trial of the software from Adobe at `http://www.adobe.com/products/photoshop.html`.

- **Adobe Illustrator:** Adobe Illustrator is a professional vector graphics tool that runs on Windows and OS X. Beyond the typical brushes, gradients, and typography elements in vector tools, Illustrator supports turning 2D shapes into 3D objects by extruding and revolving paths. This gives you some amazing possibilities in turning your vector art into 3D models. Like Photoshop, this is a top-of-the-line product that charges a top-of-the-line price. At just under $600, this product is probably out of the price range for most for casual use, but is definitely worth the money if you are creating vector graphics professionally. If you would like to try the software out, Adobe provides a 30-day license at `http://www.adobe.com/products/illustrator.html`.

Knowing what tools are out there, and which fit your specific needs can go a long way in helping you make a good decision about which software package you use. If you are comfortable figuring out software, or using Linux, one of the open source or free offerings may suit your needs. If you want a little more attention paid to the interface you are using, and are willing to spend a little money, Acorn or Fireworks may fit your needs. If you are getting ready to do a lot of production, and need the features, then high-end software is the way to go. One of the really great things about most of this software is that there are passionate individuals blogging, writing books, and participating in various communities that are willing to help others out.

Another tool that may be slightly overlooked is a scanner. Scanners are particularly useful in transferring design sketches to your computer to help you create usable art. Just about any scanner you can buy these days will have a high enough dpi count (should be around 300) to give you a good base image to trace in your graphics editor. You may also find that a good drawing tablet saves you some time and gives you more control of your graphics.

Graphics Design Process

Just as the entire project uses a design process, you should develop the graphics and sounds using a process. Breaking down the development of graphics into discrete stages helps if you are working on a team, but even more generally it will help you keep organized and focused. The following stages are generalized, and will, we hope, get you going until you develop your own workflow. If the entire idea of developing graphics for your game makes you a little uneasy, don't worry: there are a lot of great sites (e.g., OpenGameArt.org) where you can download sprites, tiles, and other graphics for use in your game.

Sketch

In this stage, you will want to draw a lot of versions of everything that will be in the game. If you are like me, I have to stop myself from just jumping into a graphics editor and starting to mock up what I want the application to look like. However, if you are working on a project of any real scale, you really do need to sit down and think through all the necessary assets for your game, and what is needed to implement the overall vision.

As an example, let us say you are developing a game that involves aliens shooting at your spaceship. What do the "enemies" look like? Do they have different states? Can you view them from different angles? Figure 5–3 shows some different designs.

Figure 5–3. *Sketches of alien ship ideas*

Although the enemies are fun, you also need to sketch out different backgrounds for the game, as well as any ships, weapons, explosions (we can ignore the fact that you cannot have an explosion in the vacuum of space), as well as any navigational elements. These can be slightly less fun to sketch, but having a good handle on the different graphic elements that your game requires will stand you in good stead later on.

This is also a good time to start making some decisions on the general color scheme for your game. Because this is a space alien game, the backgrounds will be pretty dark. To contrast the backgrounds, I use brightly colored spaceship sprites so as not to overwhelm users with a sea of gray metal.

A technique I like to employ is making copies of my black-and-white sketches, then experiment with colored pencils. This will let you play with different color palettes, as well as to start seeing what colors work best for the overall look and feel you want to achieve. Remember, these are meant to be a tool to help you work out your ideas and you should not worry about others seeing them; they are more or less tiny experiments to test ideas.

Refine

Once you have finished a set of drawings (remember, the sketching exercise is to help you focus on good ideas), bring out the sketches that best embody the vision that you had of the game and use those to refine the sketches further. Remember, there may be a lot of cool drawings, but you need to be honest and settle on the designs that best encompass the overall theme of the game. Although you will probably not use most of the images you sketch out, you do not need to throw them away. In fact, it's a good idea to keep them around as you never know if they may be right for a future project. Keep them in an idea box, or scan them and keep them in a photo organizer such as Picasa or iPhoto. This way you not only have a nicely organized set of previous art, you have a trove of inspiration.

Figure 5–4. *A refined sketch of alien spaceships*

Once you have decided on an artistic direction, you can start adding detail to the graphics as shown in Figure 5–4. You can continue this process until you have a nearly final version.

Produce

Because this is an iterative process, it is time to add more detailed work. As you worked through this graphic process, you no doubt noticed that you have necessarily needed to drop some of your favorite designs as they did not quite fit the overall look and feel. With all the designs, sketch refinements, and color direction, it is time to get that drawing into the computer. By now you should know which technical direction you want to go in with your graphics and have (we hope) downloaded your favorite editing tool.

You should be able to scan your sketch. A few pointers before diving in: first, be sure to add your scanned base image as its own layer. This will allow you to "draw" on top of the image without actually changing pixels on the scan itself. Second, learn to use the pen or line tool in your editor of choice. If your editor does not have this feature, download GIMP or Inkscape. This will generate a vector shape of your drawing, giving you the ability to change the path of the line more easily, with the fewest vector points possible.

Let's walk through tracing an image in Inkscape. If you are using another editor, your steps may be slightly different.

1. Create a new layer by clicking **Layer ➤ Add Layer** . . . .

2. Give your layer a meaningful name (e.g., sketches) and change the position (see Figure 5–5).

Figure 5–5. *Naming a new layer in Inkscape*

3. Now select **File ➤ Import**… (or ctrl + I).

4. Navigate to the scan of your sketch and click Open (see Figure 5–6).

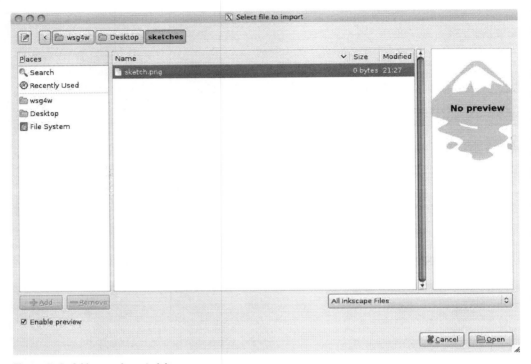

Figure 5–6. *Add a new layer to Inkscape*

5.   Now select the Bezier tool from the tool palette on the left (Figure 5–7).

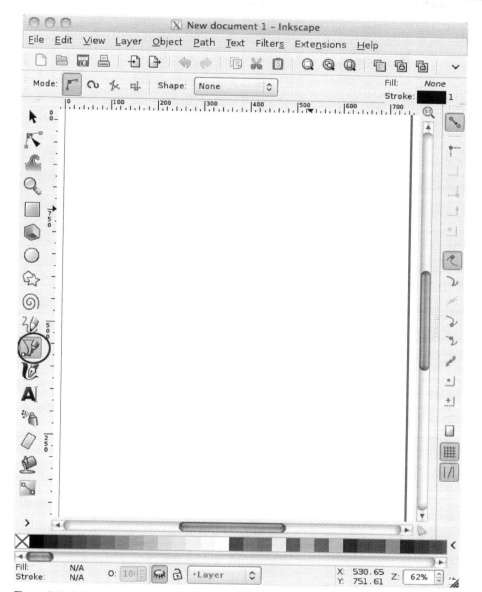

Figure 5–7. *Inkscape Bezier tool*

6. Now change to the layer named "Layer" and trace the graphic carefully.

If you are really in a hurry, there is an automated tool in Inkscape that automates the conversion of bitmap images to vectors.

7. Click **File ➤ Import** and navigate to your sketch.

   8.   Choose "embed" when prompted.

You should now be able to see the entire image. Click on the image to select it and resize the image as necessary to take up the entire document outline.

   9.   Select **Path ➤ Trace Bitmap**.

On the Mode tab, select the different settings until you find one that works best for your sketch. To update the view of the image, click on the Update button. If the outlines are too weak, increase the settings. If they are too strong, decrease the settings.

   10.   Click OK to trace the image.

You can now select the new vector layer and copy and paste it to a new layer.

Techniques

If you are new to graphic design, there are a few techniques that will help you develop better graphics for your game. As with many things in the development cycle, you may find that there are endless possibilities for tweaking the graphics you are developing, so this can take more time than you expect. Remember that you will need to be cognizant of the time you are putting into your graphics. They should be awesome, as this is what everyone sees when they look at your game, but they are one piece, and you do not want to get stalled here.

What is important is to create the effects you want efficiently. This section discusses some techniques to help you create more professional graphics quickly. There are a growing number of integrated environments for producing games in HTML5 that can save you time from jumping back and forth between programs (see Chapter 6 for a discussion of these tools); the examples are in the tool I use most often for creating graphics, Adobe Fireworks. Although many of the freely available graphics have similar abilities, you may need to look around a bit to find the correct menu or option that may be named differently.

Lighting

The human eye is very sensitive to changes in light, and getting lighting effects correct goes a long way in allowing game players to engage in momentary suspension of disbelief. Our brains are very apt at processing subtle changes in shadows and movement and although our games do not get into WebGL (3D graphics for HTML5) we still need to pay attention to lighting effects to produce more realistic professional graphics.

You need to determine where your light source will be coming from in your game. This affects not only the portion of your object that will be illuminated, but also where the shadow will be cast. You can save a lot of time by making a quick sketch, like that in Figure 5–8, of where the light source is located and where the shadow on the object will be.

Figure 5–8. *Shadow location sketch*

After you determine where your light source will be located for your game, be sure to note it so you can be consistent across all of your graphic assets. You do not want to deliver a piece of your game that has some elements with a lighting source from the top-left, and others from the bottom-right. This effect can be disorienting for your players, and lead them not to "believe" pieces of your game.

In computer graphics, there are several different lighting models that one uses to create effects on objects. Ambient light is the level of light around an object. Think of this as the amount of light that you can perceive at a given time of day. As the color of day changes, say observing an object at dusk, the intensity of the ambient light changes. Diffuse light is the reflection of a light source from the surface of an object. Diffuse light does not depend on where the observation of the object is taken (e.g., where you are looking at it), but only from where the light source is located. Specular light, on the other hand, is a reflection of a light source from the perspective of the observer.

In Fireworks, you can simulate these different lighting effects using combinations of different gradients. One technique I employ to add a specular highlight (a bright spot of light on an object) that approximates Phong shading is adding a layer to an object with a complex radial gradient.

> **NOTE:** Phong shading is named after Bui Tong Phong who developed a technique for shading 3D objects using normal-vector interpolation in his 1973 PhD dissertation at the University of Utah. His reflectance model adds ambient, diffuse, and specular lighting effects by calculating pixel colors by linearly interpolating (calculating a straight line between two points) surface normals (a perpendicular vector) for each pixel toward a light source.

Let's look at a quick example of lighting in Fireworks.

1. For this exercise, draw a simple ellipse on the canvas of Fireworks as displayed in Figure 5–9.

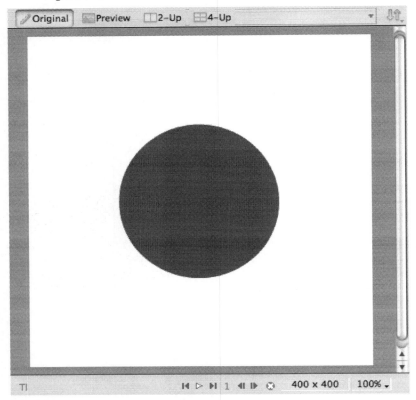

Figure 5–9. *Simple ellipse shape in Fireworks*

2. Now create a new layer on top of the circle.

3. Use the Rectangle tool to draw a rectangle on top of the circle.

4. Set the fill to **Gradient ➤ Radial**.

5. Set the color to go from white to white, and the transparency levels to 100 on the left, and 0 on the right.

In Figure 5–10 I have set the background to black and hidden the layer with the gray circle in it to show what these steps produce.

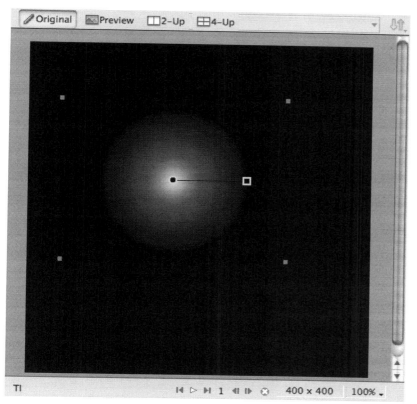

Figure 5–10. *Simple radial gradient in Fireworks. The background has been changed to black to better show the effect.*

Now, move the highlight to where the light source looks correct. The resulting image (shown in Figure 5–11) has more depth than the circle with which we started.

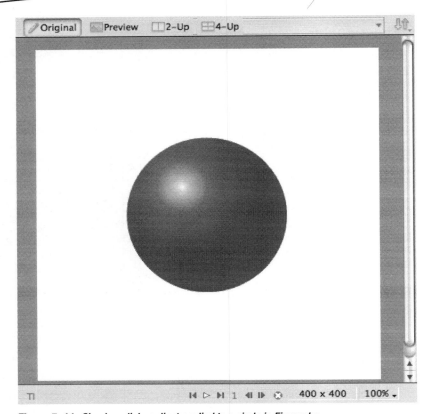

Figure 5–11. *Simple radial gradient applied to a circle in Fireworks*

You can now manipulate the rectangle layer to produce different lighting effects by skewing and distorting the rectangle and manipulating the color of the "light." Remember, light is not precisely white (#ffffff). You should play with the color wheel to make sure that the light looks right for the objects you are creating.

Depth

Adding depth to your graphics is a good way to add a touch of realism. You will want to highlight certain graphic elements such as your main players and mute background elements. Anything you want users to focus on needs to be highlighted with contrasting colors compared to your background graphics. If you play many games on Facebook (or in Chrome, or any other online game system), you may notice that the character you are playing is generally brighter, and visual clues about what you should do in the game have similar colors that stand out from the backgrounds. You want to stay away from having your backgrounds too close to the same color as your main graphics, and choosing subtly muted colors that are still in your color palette will help make the gameplay for your users more compelling.

As an example, Figure 5–12 shows a screenshot of the HTML 5 game VII (`http://www.mattpelham.com/vii/`). Notice that the slight blur for the background graphics, producing a depth that although it still fills the screen, does not detract from the elements on which you need to focus.

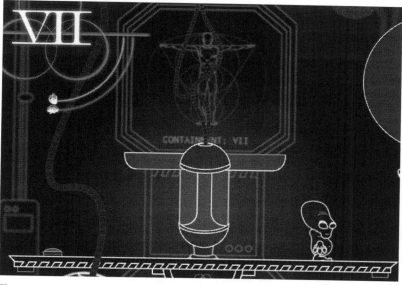

Figure 5–12. *Graphic depth, courtesy of VII*

Color

A good way to differentiate the colors in your backgrounds is to adjust the brightness and contrast settings for the layer. Essentially you adjust these settings to make the layer muted compared to the game objects you want to highlight. Another technique is to add a layer on top of a graphic (generally white) and tweak the opacity level until the desired effect is achieved. Think of this technique as adding fog to the background, allowing you to control how much light is getting through to illuminate the other elements in your scene. Another good idea for differentiating backgrounds from focal items is to be sure to remove any edge lines on background graphics or add a slight blur. Generally there are filters that make these techniques quite simple. In addition, the software you are using may offer alternative methods to massage these graphics that produce better effects. However, if you need a quick-and-dirty way to produce a mock-up, these techniques go a long way in helping convey your intent.

Remember, the farther things are in the background, the darker they will appear. If you have a background element, you can adjust the brightness levels with a filter. You can go further by adding transparency layers and adjusting the layer settings. By combining different filters on an object you can achieve quite compelling effects, even with a limited color palette as the screenshot from VII (Figure 5–12) demonstrates.

Focus and Blur

Because of the way our eyes work, we generally perceive items closer to us as being more in focus than items farther away. We can fake this in games by using different filters on our graphics and stacking these effects on top of one another. Adding a subtle blur filter to your background objects can go a long way in bringing other elements into focus for the player as a way to provide visual cues for the players on what they need to do to complete a level.

You may be developing a side scroller type of game where a spaceship flies and shoots missiles at incoming enemies. The background screens need to allow the player to focus on moving and shooting the aircraft, and not at a highly detailed terrain. As shown in Figure 5–13, any of these background elements can be softened by adding blur filters and playing with the opacity layers.

Figure 5–13. *Subtle background image with blur effects to decrease the resolution in Fireworks*

Movement

You can control the illusion of movement by controlling the speed at which different elements move across the screen. Items in the foreground (e.g., closer to the player) will appear to move faster than objects in the background. Depending on the type of game you are developing, this is something to keep in mind when you begin programming, but I did want to mention it here as a consideration in developing your graphics as many side scrolling games employ this technique to improve the movement mechanics.

Drop Shadow

Drop shadows are a popular effect that makes an element appear to be raised above another object. Score boards, level boards, even components in your game can all have drop shadows to enhance their realism. In Fireworks, the drop shadow is a filter that can be applied to shapes and even text elements (see Figure 5–14).

Figure 5–14. *Simple drop shadows on text and shapes in Fireworks*

In Fireworks, you control the light source angle relative to a two-dimensional circle from 0 to 360 degrees. As you change the angle of the light source, you control where the shadow is cast. This is a simple technique that allows you to add dimension and depth easily for graphics that may need this.

Audio

When developing games, you want to engage as many senses as you can. We want our graphics to engage users' sight senses and reactions to input (sense of touch), but we also want to engage their auditory senses. There has been some recent work in delivering smells through your computer, however, it is not quite there yet, so we are limited to only the sight, touch, and hearing senses.

Sounds evoke emotional responses in players. I remember the first time I played through Resident Evil where the music would actually raise my heartbeat in certain places. When I first played Minecraft, my speakers were not working and it was a much different game when I eventually tried the game with speakers. The eerie music letting me know that nearby were zombies that I would have to fight is a staple of the horror-survival genre. Racing games generally have upbeat music to let you know you must react quickly. Games like World of Warcraft have much different music in the background when you are in a city as compared to fighting through a high-level dungeon against a multistage boss. It is important that you pick music that actually fits your game, and not just choose a random loop from the Internet.

There are different types of sounds that you need to gather for your game. You can use full-length songs that you have created (or licensed). These can range from full-length compositions to shorter pieces that play when some event occurs (e.g., completing a level, the player dies, etc.). Sound loops are shorter bits of sound that repeat. Leveraging loops effectively will allow you to have a smaller payload for your game, and thus will load faster. However, using this technique is not always a possibility for every game.

Sound effects are sound elements that are triggered by some event and are of a relatively short duration. For instance, when you fire a gun in a game, you can fire a gunshot sound effect, or if a character jumps, having some auditory cue for the event goes a long way in engaging the game player.

Rarely have I ever spoken to someone who has commented on the sounds in a game. This is mainly because if the music is doing its job properly, it does not stand out or overpower the game. Think of a soundtrack to a movie. No, not the popular sounds that are on the release for a movie, but the orchestral pieces. You may be able to hum part of the tune from the track *Jaws* "Main Title," theme (du-dum, du-dum . . .), but did you remember that piece is over two minutes long? Out of the context of the movie, it is a rather odd piece, and probably not one that would go on your iPod. However, in the context of the movie, that piece really helps set the mood that something really bad is about to happen. Likewise in games, music plays an important part in alerting players to certain gameplay elements. If your users pay too much attention to the sounds in a game, you most likely have not successfully implemented your sound design: sounds that do not belong tend to stand out to players.

Creating Sounds

Most likely you are not a professional sound engineer, and most likely do not have access to high-end recording equipment. If you have a laptop, you probably have a microphone already, and if you have a desktop, you may have a cheap microphone hanging around somewhere (mine is at the bottom of a box of cables). This should be more than enough equipment to get you started, and I give some tips on creating your own sounds, as well as some places to go online to find more that others have shared.

Software

Most likely you already have some type of audio recording software on your computer. This may suit your needs, or be awful. Depending on the operating system you are running, and how much money you are willing to spend, there are a lot of options available to you, which run the gamut in terms of functionality.

- **GarageBand:** GarageBand is an Apple product for OS X that is often bundled on new computers. The software includes thousands of royalty-free loops that you may compose together as new derivative sounds. GarageBand allows you to record your own multitrack music and master (add effects, adjust equalizers, and add additional effects). There is even a feature that helps teach you how to play guitar and piano, and it also has tutorials by various artists to teach you how to play their songs.

- **Sound Studio:** Sound Studio, made by felt tip, inc., is an intuitive application for sound recording and editing on OS X. Several of the podcasts I listen to swear by this software for recording and mixing their audio. At $30, it will not break the bank, and may provide you with the flexibility and ease of use you need. If you run OS X, you can download a 15–use demo of the software at `http://felttip.com/ss/` or purchase through the Mac App Store.

- **Audacity:** Audacity is a free, cross-platform sound editor. This software does not have many bells or whistles, but if you need a no-frills sound recorder, Audacity is your tool. You can download Audacity from the project's page at `http://audacity.sourceforge.net`. It is worth noting that because this is free software, it cannot encode MP3s without installing another third-party MP3 encoder due to patents on the MP3 ISO reference code. However, Audacity is written to look for other MP3 encoders and you can download LAME to encode your MP3s from `http://lame.sourceforge.net/`.

- **Audition:** Back in the day, this was called Cool Edit Pro before it was bought by Adobe. This is a Windows and OS X software package that is designed to be part of a workflow with powerful video-editing software, but also as a stand-alone, postproduction audio tool. At $350, this software is an investment, but is a professional tool that will help you produce polished results in editing your sounds. You can download a 30-day trial of the software at `http://www.adobe.com/products/audition.html`.

- **Logic Studio:** Logic Studio is Apple's suite of professional sound engineering software. This is professional-level software, with professional-level features and a professional learning curve. At $500, this may be beyond the price range of beginners, but it has expansion packs that include more than 20,000 royalty-free sound loops on over 4,700 instruments, and has over 4,500 presets for plugins. If you need access to a large collection of sounds, this may be worth your money.

- **Cubase:** Cubase is a professional sound editor for Windows and OS X produced by Steinberg. The software has state-of-the-art hardware controllers for editing music, as well as add-ons for additional sounds and effects. Cubase comes in several versions, with its Elements package starting at $99, its middle offering of Artist at $250, and the full Cubase which will run you $500. You can download a 30-day trial at `http://www.steinberg.net/en/products/cubase/trial_version.html`.

- **Sonar:** Cakewalk is a software company owned by the Roland music company. They actually support many different audio-editing software packages, but Sonar is perhaps the most well known. This is Windows-only software, and the various packages start at $99 for the basics, and run up to $400 for the kitchen sink edition. If you are a Windows user, this is worth a look.

- **ProTools:** Protools by Avid runs on both Windows and OS X and is another professional-level sound-editing suite. Beyond the normal suite of tools, Avid also sells a line of customized keyboards to make working with the software more efficient. The software costs $700, and has upgrades for additional instruments to use with the software. If you have high-end needs for sound editing and are on Windows, this software may be right for you.

- **Live:** Ableton's Live sound editor runs on both Windows and OS X. This is popular software for DJs who mix and match their music, but is also used by game studios to master loops. At $450, this software is not cheap, but may fit your needs, especially if you are a Windows user. You can download a free 30-day trial from `http://www.ableton.com/live-8`.

> **NOTE:** Did you know that MP3 is a patented audio format? Software that includes MP3 compression software based on the ISO reference source code must pay the Fraunhofer Institute and Thomas Media a licensing fee. For games, the fee for MP3 is $2,500 per title. This is one of the contributing factors to several browsers not implementing the MP3 codec natively in the browser for the HTML5 specification, and instead working with the Ogg Vorbis standard. This is not to say that in developing a game for delivery on the web you need to obtain a license for MP3, but the software that does the actual encoding does pay a licensing fee.

Hardware

There is a variety of hardware that can help you make better digital recordings. Perhaps one of the most important peripherals you can purchase for improving your sound recordings is an external audio interface. Sound is a weird thing in the wild; it is not digital (sound waves are analog). Audio interfaces have special hardware that various recording software can work with that efficiently converts analog signals from microphones and instruments to digital input. You can think of these interfaces as external, specialized sound cards that only process audio input.

You may find some folks with different preferences, but I have only ever used M-Audio products. They have a range of products, starting with the Fast Track at their entry level (around $150), the Fast Track Pro as their mid-grade (about $250), and their pro-sumer Fast Track Ultra comes in at around $550.

If you are also looking for some recommendations for microphones that are not of the plastic variety, here are several that I have used at a few different levels:

- **Beginner:** The Plantronics Audio 655 DSP is one of my favorite headsets for gaming, Skype, and audio recordings of just my voice. If you are limiting the amount of sounds you are recording, this is a great option as it can serve a few different purposes and at $50 will not break the bank.

- **Entry Level:** Audio-Technica makes some really great microphones. The AT 20 series has a terrific group of entry condenser microphones. These mikes will typically require you to purchase a microphone stand, but the AT2020 Cardioid Condenser Microphone is a solid piece of equipment that lists for $170 (but be sure to search online shopping sites).

- **Mid-Range:** The Rode Procaster is a popular microphone with podcasters even though it is a dynamic microphone (usually dynamic microphones are used on stages). The Procaster has a 10-year warranty and is solidly built.

- **Professional:** Heil makes some of the best microphones on the planet, and the PR40 has a great reputation. Most likely you will want several different rigs for adjusting this microphone, but if you are really committed to recording high-end audio, this is one of the best. The PR40 lists for $375 and ships to you in a cherry box. You may also want to invest in a preamp (take a look at the Joe Meek threeQ) to make sure the audio you are recording is the absolute best quality.

Recording

After you have set up your sound equipment, you can start recording and mixing your own sounds. Remember this from the start: no matter how good you think you have a sound, you never know exactly how it will come out until you put all of the data into the game, and have all the pieces working together. It is really important to have a lot of options as there are many variables when you start mixing audio, so do not be surprised if what you think is the best take initially turns out to be the worst (and vice versa).

When you hit record, make the sound you want repeatedly in various fashions in your recording software. This should be a single file, with "takes" to separate different versions. Then, when you have enough audio, you can trim down the audio to what you need, copying what you do not end up using into separate files to use later.

Remember, the more variations you have, the more material you have to work with and not have to come back and repeat the work later. Record a sound; then move the microphone and do it again.

But how do you create some of these sounds? In its heyday, radio played a vital role in American pop culture and many artists came up with clever ways to simulate real-world noises when needed. Here are a few of the tricks these folks pioneered. If you want to simulate boiling water, you can blow bubbles through a straw into a glass of water. Have horses galloping? Some coconut shells will come in handy (put some cloth on them to simulate running on soft terrain). Need arrows shooting, or swinging fists? Try swinging a stick or wire near the microphone (be careful not to hit it). Jet noises? A hair dryer played at double-speed sounds awesome.

> **NOTE:** Digital audio is measured in negative decibels relative to the full-scale (dBFS) with a maximum of 0 dBFS. Sounds higher than 0 dBFS will experience distortion called clipping when reconstructed to analog output due to the way the digital signals are reconstructed. Be sure you do not go over the 0 dBFS; although the distortion may sound neat on your setup, it does not on anyone else's!

Most professional sound engineers record everyday sounds and change them by altering the speed, reversing the sound, adding reverb, or other filters. If you have ever heard the "Chung Chung" from Law and Order, Mike Post actually includes the "sound of 500 Japanese men stamping their feet on a wooden floor." Experimenting with different sounds will provide you with a lot of different options for adding different audio effects in your game.

Royalty-Free Sounds

You may find that creating all the loops and effects from scratch to be a daunting task. Fortunately there are a lot of websites that host royalty-free (or even paid license) sounds for your game. Royalty-free does not necessarily mean that the sound you get is free of charge: it simply means that once you pay the original author of the piece a licensing fee, you are subject to pay royalties based on the sales of your game. Be sure to read (and understand) any licensing restrictions and fine print before you use any of the sounds that you may find.

- **SoundBible:** This is a great collection of various royalty-free sounds. The website allows you to search for different sounds and play them back on the web page. In addition, they display the license next to the file, so you can filter out items that do not meet your licensing needs. SoundBible can be found at `http://www.soundbible.com/`.

- **Freesound:** This is a nice community-driven site with sounds, forums, and nice filtering abilities to help you find just the right sound. A handy feature of the site is its "packs" where contributors group multiple sounds together to provide you with variations of different sounds as imagined by the contributor. You can get to Freesound at `http://www.freesound.com/`.

■ **Soundsnap:** This site allows sound producers to sell their work to consumers. It works much the same way as many stock photography websites work where you purchase credits and can then download some predetermined number of sounds. The site is reasonably simple to use and provides you as a consumer of sound with the ability to support various contributors who are spending considerable time producing new material. Soundsnap can be found at http://www.soundsnap.com/.

■ **Sound-Effect:** This is another site that allows sound producers to sell their work. Unlike Soundsnap, each sound is sold for a price. The interface is a bit cludgy, but does contain thousands of clips where you may just find the perfect sound or effect you are looking for to complete your game. You can check out the site at http://www.sound-effect.com/.

■ **Other:** If you purchased sound-editing software, the vendor you bought it from may have expansion packs to help you build out your sound library. This is a great way to build a large library of sound quickly that you can remix for your own purposes. Just be sure that the sounds you use are royalty free. Who wants the RIAA coming after them!

Preparing Your Audio

You will eventually need to prepare your audio for your game. Depending on the recording software, it may have a proprietary format that it defaults to when saving a recording that not all of your players will have the correct software to play. There are several formats in which you can deliver your audio to the user.

The WAV has been a mainstay of gaming audio since the 1990s and is a lossless format storing and delivering audio. The format has an issue with large audio files (we hope you are not delivering WAV files in your game that are larger than 4 GB), but is almost universally playable on every platform.

MP3s have been popular since their introduction and have a lossy compression algorithm that affects audio quality to make the file size smaller. This typically is not an issue with an appropriate bitrate, but is a consideration if you choose this output.

Since the introduction of the HTML5 audio specification, and Firefox's adoption of the Ogg Vorbis format for playing native audio elements, I have seen an uptick in this format. Although it does not have a huge amount of the market share compared to MP3, Ogg Vorbis also has a lossy compression algorithm, but has slightly higher fidelity than MP3s.

Generally a bitrate around 128 kbps will produce an adequate sound experience. The higher the bitrate is, the better the audio will sound, but will increase the size of the file. You may also have an option in your editing software to use a variable bitrate (VBR) filter. VBR filters allow you to use a higher bitrate when needed, but drop the bitrate when a less complex sound is occurring. This allows you to encode at a high bitrate, optimizing the size of the resulting file without sacrificing much in the way of quality.

Understanding Copyright

When you start working with assets that you use from other authors, you will need to have a basic understanding of trademark, copyright, and licensing. If you are using elements for your game that you have downloaded from the Internet to use in your game, it is important that you fully understand what it means when you use something that is open source.

Copyright should more accurately be called copyrights, and, in most Western countries expressly provide the holder the following *exclusive* rights.

- The right to produce copies, or reproductions of the work, and to sell those copies
- The right to import and/or export the work
- The right to create derivative works
- The right to perform or display the work publicly
- The right to sell or assign those rights to others
- The right to transmit or display the work by radio or video

In the context of copyrights, the exclusive rights mean that the copyright holder retains the ability to exercise those rights, and all others are prohibited from using the work without permission. So when does something become your copyright? Well, as soon as it meets a minimal standard for originality and is recorded with a verifiable date. Although you are no longer required to expressly use the copyright symbol to claim copyright, it is a good idea to do so should you be unlucky enough to be involved in an infringement lawsuit.

Notice on the different browse menus over at Open Game Art (http://opengameart.org; see Figure 5–15), that you have several licenses in which to filter. If you are unfamiliar with these, the nuances of the different licenses can be a bit confusing, so I thought it would be a good idea to introduce some of the differences here.

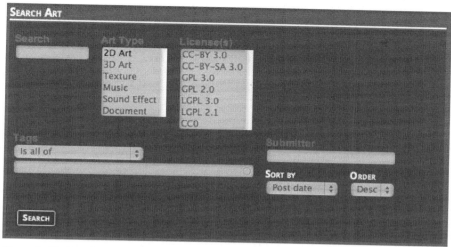

Figure 5–15. *OpenGameArt.org search page*

Creative Commons—BY(CC-BY)

You are free to copy and distribute this work, and adapt (change) it for your own purposes, as well as make commercial use of the work. The one caveat is that you must attribute the piece to the author (or licensor), but not in a manner that suggests they endorse you or your product.

Creative Commons—BY—Share Alike (CC-BY-SA)

This is very close to the Creative Commons BY license in that you are allowed to copy, distribute, and adapt the piece for commercial use with proper attribution. However, this license places an additional condition on the piece's use that any derivative work also be distributed under the same (or similar) license.

Creative Commons 0 (CC0)

The Creative Commons 0 license places items in the public domain. Public domain works are those in which the intellectual property rights have expired, have been forfeited, or not covered at all. Creative Commons 0 waives all copyrights that you have with the work. Essentially you are allowed to use anything with Creative Commons with no restrictions placed on your derivative works.

Gnu General Public License (GPL)

The GPL license is the brainchild of Richard Stallman who is a strong advocate for freely distributable software on the Internet. This license, like the Creative Commons licenses discussed previously, allows you to use the software freely, with the caveat that you freely distribute any code or asset that derives from that software. Unlike other free licenses, the GPL does allow you to charge for your contributions. Essentially, if you use any piece of GPL code, you must either include your source code in a distribution, or a written offer to provide the source upon request. Many commercial software vendors shy away from this license scheme because of this last fact.

Note that this is typically used with software, and not image or sound assets.

Apache 2.0

Apache 2.0 is typically used to license software, but I have seen it attached to other types of media. Unlike the GPL, Apache does not require you to redistribute changes you make to the underlying code. When using the Apache 2.0 license, if there is a NOTICE text file in the original work, all derivative works must also contain the same NOTICE with any of your additions in an addendum. One of the really nice features of this license is that you can have different licensing terms for your modifications. This fact allows software builders to take a core project that is open source, and then build upon the software while retaining intellectual property rights on those modifications. Thus, Apache 2.0 is a nice license to use if you plan on retaining some closed source modifications or improvements to open source code.

MIT

You may occasionally happen upon a project that holds an MIT License. The license permits the use of MIT Licensed software within proprietary software, but restricts you from using the author's name to "endorse" your software in promotional materials without the express written permission of the author. This license is compatible with GPL as it also allows the redistribution and combination of software that uses the MIT License.

Dual/Multi License

You may run into a situation where some software contains two (or more) licenses. Many open source projects use this to allow individuals, and corporations, to choose the license that best fits their needs when redistributing software, and any proprietary improvements. For instance, during the writing of this book, the Ruby 1.9.3 language was released. Previous versions of the software were released under the Ruby license and GPL 2.0. With the 1.9.3 release, the developers changed the licensing to a two-clause (Simplified BSD) license. The change gives developers a bit more free rein in what they are permitted to do with the source code, allowing those with the requisite knowledge the ability to change the underlying source to make a "better" proprietary language, and redistribute it in a binary format.

Summary

This chapter gives you a brief introduction to some of the tools and skills that are required for creating assets for games. If you are lucky, you can specialize in one piece of the development, but it is always advisable to have at least a basic understanding and appreciation of how all the different pieces work together. You will need to work to balance all of the different components that comprise your game, not only in the amount of time that is required to build, but striking the correct balance where no one piece of the game overwhelms any other component.

Because of the trends in the way assets and software are developed and distributed these days, I also wanted to introduce some of the important elements of copyright and licensing. If you are developing software, you really need to have an understanding of what the different licenses mean and how they affect how you deliver your software. If you have concerns about redistributing your source code, make sure you use software with an appropriate license that permits you to keep some of your software private.

In the next chapter I take many of the elements I have discussed in the chapters up to this point and discuss how to put them together to create a playable game.

Chapter 6

Your First Game: Alien Turtle Invasion

The time has come to put everything we have gone over in the previous chapters into practice and see how these all work together to work as a game. I follow the development steps I have laid out, including leveraging some open source graphics and sounds to add to the game experience. There is a lot of code in this chapter, but the game only requires your browser, so there is no server setup involved.

This game could be easily made into a game that you can play on Facebook. Most of the development effort for your HTML games will be on the JavaScript side of the equation, and I have found that segregating the development of a game from integration and deployment on the Facebook platform helps you localize where your bugs are coming from, and write better code much faster. I use many of the techniques discussed in previous chapters for this game, building up the final result.

Defining the Game

If you recall, back in Chapter 4, I discussed the design process. In the Brainstorming section, I laid out a boilerplate for defining the game. For the game we develop in this chapter, here are the objective and rules:

Idea: Alien Turtle Invasion

Objective: Shoot all the turtle invaders before they shoot you.

Rules:

- This is a single-player game.
- The game is played in space.
- There are 10 enemy ships.
- There is one spaceship to defend earth.

- Invaders will move back and forth across the screen.
- Invaders will fire missiles at a set interval.
- The spaceship is controlled by the player.
- The defender can shoot lasers at the turtle invaders.
- The game is over if the player's spaceship is hit by a missile.
- The level is over if all the turtle invader ships are destroyed.

Define the Audience

This game is targeted at casual gamers who enjoy action games. This game is not intended to be very difficult, but something people can pick up and play for short periods of time.

Identify the Competition

Quite honestly, there are a lot of Space Invader clones out there.

Table 6–1. *Competition List*

Info	Answer
Company	Free Space Invaders
URL	`http://www.freespaceinvaders.org`
Genre	Action Game
Target Audience	Late-teens and up; people who play classic video games
Reputation	Really high; Space Invaders is a pop-culture icon
Gameplay	Invaders scroll across the screen shooting at the player; object is to shoot all invaders before they reach your base.
Strengths	Online version has brand recognition; gameplay straight out of 1978
Weaknesses	Flash-based, will not work on mobile devices

Now that we have a good idea where our game fits in the game ecosystem, we can start building it with confidence.

Boilerplate

There is some boilerplate code that we need to get out of the way before we begin coding our game. This includes setting up the directory structure for the game, as well as some HTML and CSS code that we refine throughout this chapter to make this an engaging game. Although my personal development platform is OS X, I provide the Windows equivalent of any commands I mention. My editor of choice is vim (well, macvim), which is shown in my screenshots, but all you really need is a text editor.

> **TIP:** There are a growing number of Cloud-based integrated development environments (IDE) that allow you to code in your browser. Cloud9 (`http://c9.io`), EtherPad (`http://etherpad.com/`) and codr.cc (`http://codr.cc`) all provide online editing services. If you are looking for a more traditional IDE, you can take a look at the Eclipse IDE for JavaScript Web Developers and Aptana Studio. Both of these IDEs are robust platforms designed to help ease development roadblocks, and make you a more effective developer.

We first need to add some structure. When I am coding, I put all of my code in a projects directory. In the terminal/command prompt, you can create new directories with the `mkdir` (make directory) command. See Listing 6–1.

Listing 6–1. *Creating the Projects Directory.*

```
mkdir -p ~/projects # OS X
md projects # Windows
```

This will create a new directory in your home directory named `projects`. Now, while still in the terminal or command prompt, change in to the projects directory and create a new directory (named `turtlegame`) that will contain the files for your game (see Listing 6–2).

Listing 6–2. *Setting up the Game Directory*

```
cd projects
mkdir turtlegame
cd turtlegame
```

You should now be in the `turtlegame` directory. Now it is time to add a file with some content. Create a new file named "index.html" in the `turtlegame` directory and open it with your editor of choice. I use a stripped-down version of Paul Irish's HTML5 Boilerplate HTML here. You may want to check the official website (`http://html5boilerplate.com/`) to see if there are any updates. In your `index.html` file, type Listing 6–3.

Listing 6–3. *HTML Boilerplate*

```
<!DOCTYPE html>
<html lang="en">
<head>
  <meta charset="utf-8">
  <title>Alien Turtle Invasion</title>
  <meta name="description" content="Alien Turtle Invasion Canvas Game">
```

```
    <meta name="author" content="Your Name">
    <meta name="viewport" content="width=device-width,initial-scale=1">
    <link rel="stylesheet" href="css/style.css">
</head>

<body>
  <header>

  </header>
  <div id="main" role="main">
    <canvas id="game" width="600" height="400"></canvas>
  </div>
  <footer>

  </footer>

  <!-- Prompt IE 6 users to install Chrome Frame. Remove this if you want to support
IE 6.
        chromium.org/developers/how-tos/chrome-frame-getting-started -->
  <!--[if lt IE 7 ]>
    <script defer src="//ajax.googleapis.com/ajax/libs/chrome-frame/1.0.3
/CFInstall.min.js"></script>
    <script defer>window.attachEvent('onload',function(){CFInstall.check
({mode:'overlay'})})</script>
  <![endif]-->

</body>
</html>
```

> **NOTE:** You may notice at the bottom of the HTML code there is code that prompts users of IE6 to install the Chrome Frame plugin. Essentially this plugin runs Chrome inside Internet Explorer to provide a more consistent browsing experience. Microsoft has officially declared IE6 a dead browser and no longer supports it, but the number of users using IE 6 to look at various websites I monitor the analytics of constantly shocks me. Although I personally do not make much effort to support old versions of Internet Explorer, adding this code to the bottom of your page prompts the users of your content to install Chrome Frame, where you at least will have some fighting chance of your code actually functioning!

This page is the basis that we use for our game, and it contains the <canvas> element that we use to render our game. It also contains a hack for folks who have not yet made the move, for whatever reason, to a more recent version of Internet Explorer to prompt them to install the Google Chrome Frame extension. This extension actually runs the requested content through Google Chrome to allow users of Internet Explorer to experience modern web content without launching a new browser.

At this point, the page is unstyled, but has a link to a CSS file. In the main turtlegame directory, create a new directory named "css" and add a file "style.css." Open style.css up in a text editor, and add a few styles that will make the display a little easier to view.

Listing 6–4. *Game CSS*

```
#main {
  width: 61em;
  max-width: 100%;
  *zoom: 1;
  margin: auto;
}

#game {
  margin: auto;
  display: block;
  border: 1px solid #ccc;
}
```

The first block of CSS (Listing 6–4) matches the content block `<div id="main"
role="main">` and sets a width of 61 ems (976 pixels) and then centers itself in the
browser window. The second block matches the `<canvas>` element's identifier, placing a
one-pixel border around the element and centering the element on the page. The result,
although not much, gives us the base we need to build up the game we are developing.

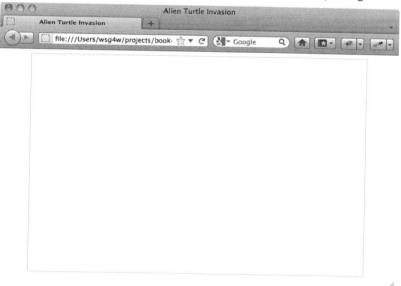

Figure 6–1. *Basic boilerplate HTML for Alien Turtle Invasion*

Note that the gray line is not needed (Figure 6–1), but I generally put a border around the
canvas to help me keep track of things happening inside the canvas as opposed to the
things happening in the page (specifically in the DOM).

Coding the Engine

I take an iterative approach to writing this game, adding layers to the game to build and hone it to a working game. With the scaffold out of the way, the first thing I want to do is create some variables that will store the canvas DOM element, as well as create a context for the game. Below the <footer>, add a <script> element with Listing 6–5.

Listing 6–5. *Defining the canvas Element*

```
<script>
var canvas = document.getElementById('game');
var context = canvas.getContext('2d');
</script>
```

I am placing the script at the bottom of the page to ensure that all the page content loads before the code for the game loads into the browser's memory. Next, I want to stub out a gameLoop function that will handle all the drawing on the canvas as well as add a call to the setInterval function to redraw the canvas. See Listing 6–6.

Listing 6–6. *Defining the Game Loop*

```
function gameLoop() {
    // update and draw functions called here
}

setInterval(gameLoop, 1000/60);
```

Because the setInterval function is called at the bottom of the HTML file, it will execute after the page content is loaded.

> **NOTE:** Determining an optimal refresh rate can be a bit tricky. You want the movement of your objects to appear smooth, and not jumpy. With a monitor refresh rate of 60 Hz, your screen refreshes once every 17 milliseconds (16.66667 to be a bit more precise). In order to ensure you have smooth movements in your game, you want to match that targeted refresh rate. In my example, I use 1,000/60 (the number of milliseconds divided by the Hertz rate) to give me the desired 16.66667 redraw rate. You may find in your game development that a refresh loop of 60 frames per second is overkill. A lot of games can easily drop down to 30 frames per second without players noticing a drastic change. There are techniques in some game engines that dynamically test the frame rate the browser is capable of and dynamically adjust the frame rate for the game loop. This allows you to take advantage of hardware acceleration offered by different browser implementations easily, while providing consistent game play for less powerful browsers and computers.

Now that we have the canvas redrawing itself, the next thing to do is write a function that will draw the background (Listing 6–7). Because this is a space game, we can get away with a black background. As an element of coding style, I always define functions before they are called, so this function should be positioned above the gameLoop() function in your code.

Listing 6–7. *Drawing the Background*

```
function drawBackground() {
    context.fillStyle = "#000000";
    context.fillRect(0, 0, canvas.width, canvas.height);
}
```

This function uses the declared 2D context and canvas element to redraw a black canvas background. Now we can call it from the main gameLoop function (Listing 6–8).

Listing 6–8. *Updating the Gameloop Function*

```
function gameLoop() {
    drawBackground();
}
```

Now if you refresh the page in your browser, you should see a black rectangle in the middle of the page as in Figure 6–2.

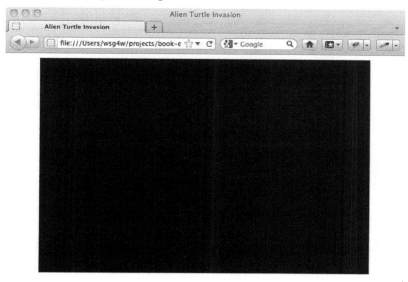

Figure 6–2. *Canvas background redrawn about every 17ms*

Now, let's work on building our spacecraft. In the early stages, we use an easy-to-code rectangle in place of a spacecraft sprite, just to get a sense of the movement and gameplay. We need to create a structure that can store information about our spaceship, specifically, its *x* and *y* position on the canvas, as well as its width and height. Do this just under the declarations for the canvas and context variables, as shown in Listing 6–9.

Listing 6–9. *Creating the Spaceship Object*

```
var canvas = document.getElementById('game');
var context = canvas.getContext('2d');

var spaceship = {
    x: 100,
    y: 300,
    width: 50,
    height: 50,
    counter: 0
};
```

We now have a spaceship object we can pass around in our code, so let's write a method to draw the spaceship, and call it from the main game loop (Listing 6–10).

Listing 6–10. *Drawing the Spaceship*

```
function drawSpaceship() {
    context.fillStyle = "white";
    context.fillRect(spaceship.x, spaceship.y, spaceship.width, spaceship.height);
}
...
function gameLoop() {
    drawBackground();
    drawSpaceship();
}
```

Refreshing the page (Figure 6–3), you will see a white rectangle that is standing in for our eventual spaceship.

Figure 6–3. *Canvas with stand-in shape for the spaceship*

Great, now let's add some code to allow the player to move the ship across the screen. We add an event listener, and a function to update the player position. The game will need to have several types of events, so it is a good idea to abstract this out into a few different functions to make it easier to work with, as well as create an empty structure to hold our keyboard elements (Listing 6–11).

Listing 6–11. *Defining the Keyboard Events*

```
var keyboard = {};

function addKeyboardEvents() {
        addEvent(document, "keydown", function(e) {
          keyboard[e.keyCode] = true;
        });

        addEvent(document, "keyup", function(e) {
          keyboard[e.keyCode] = false;
        });
}

function addEvent(node, name, func) {
        if(node.addEventListener) {
          node.addEventListener(name, func, false);
        } else if(node.attachEvent) {
          // handle Microsoft browsers too
          node.attachEvent(name, func);
        }
}
```

Because this does not need to be redrawn, we can call the addKeyboardEvents function outside the gameLoop. However, it needs to be called before the setInterval call to ensure we have the events for our keydown and keyup listeners.

```
addKeyboardEvents();

setInterval(gameLoop, 1000 / 60);
```

Now that the eventListener for the keyboard events has been written, we need to actually tell the spaceship how to update its position (Listing 6–12).

Listing 6–12. *Updating the Spaceship's Position*

```
function updateSpaceship() {
        // move left
        if(keyboard[37]) {
          spaceship.x -= 10;
          if(spaceship.x < 0) {
            spaceship.x = 0;
          }
        }

        // move right
        if(keyboard[39]) {
          spaceship.x += 10;
          var right = canvas.width - spaceship.width;
          if(spaceship.x > right) {
            spaceship.x = right;
          }
        }
}
```

Next, we need to execute this code in the gameLoop before we draw the ship (Listing 6–13).

Listing 6–13. *Drawing the Ship in the Game Loop*

```
function gameLoop() {
    updateSpaceship();

    drawBackground();
    drawSpaceship();
}
```

You should now be able to move the ship using the left and right arrow keys on your keyboard.

> **NOTE:** A new feature that is still much in flux at the writing of this book for handling animations in the browser (including DOM, canvas, and WebGL) is requestAnimationFrame(). Using this function will allow for smoother graphics and allow the browser to optimize concurrent animations into a single repaint cycle. If the code is running in a hidden tab, the loop will not execute until the tab is brought back into focus, greatly decreasing CPU, GPU, and memory consumption, thus increasing battery life for mobile devices. The requestAnimationFrame function (there are slight browser-specific variances of this) helps actually scheduling at a known interval in the browser execution queue, whereas functions such as setInterval and setTimeout only queue the functions for possible execution (which can lead to issues if timing is important).

With the most basic interaction between the player and the game board, we can begin to layer on top of this gameplay interaction. For our next step, we add in the ability to fire a powerful laser capable of downing multiple alien ships. As with everything we have coded to this point, we need an update and draw function for the laser, then call both from gameLoop(), as well as add an event to listen for the spacebar being pressed. See Listing 6–14.

Listing 6–14. *Drawing the Lasers*

```
var lasers = []; // array holding the lasers

function drawLasers() {
    context.fillStyle = "white";
    for(var iter in lasers) {
      var laser = lasers[iter];
      context.fillRect(laser.x, laser.y, laser.width, laser.height);
    }
}

function updateLasers() {
    // move the laser
    for(var iter in lasers) {
      var laser = lasers[iter];
      laser.y -= 2;
      laser.counter++;
    }

    // remove lasers that are off the screen
```

```
        lasers = lasers.filter(function(laser) {
          return laser.y > 0;
        });
}

function fireLaser() {
      lasers.push ({
        x: spaceship.x + 20, //offset
        y: spaceship.y - 10,
        width: 10,
        height: 30
      });
}

function updateSpaceship() {
      // move left
      if(keyboard[37]) {
        spaceship.x -= 10;
        if(spaceship.x < 0) {
          spaceship.x = 0;
        }
      }

      // move right
      if(keyboard[39]) {
        spaceship.x += 10;
        var right = canvas.width - spaceship.width;
        if(spaceship.x > right) {
          spaceship.x = right;
        }
      }

      // spacebar pressed
      if(keyboard[32]) {
        // only fire one laser
        if(!keyboard.fired) {
          fireLaser();
          keyboard.fired = true;
        } else {
          keyboard.fired = false;
        }
      }
   }
}
```

The fireLaser() function adds a new laser to the array container lasers. Each laser has its own coordinate system, as well as a width and height used to draw the "laser" on the canvas. Add a call to updateLasers() and drawLasers() in the gameLoop() function and when you reload the webpage, you should now be able to fire the lasers by pressing the spacebar. See Figure 6–4.

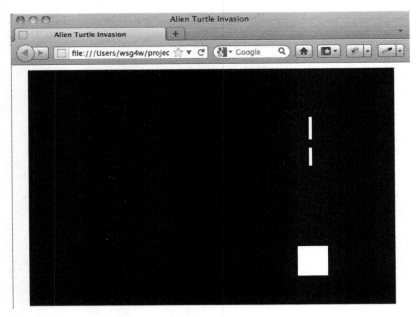

Figure 6–4. *Spaceship can fire projectiles*

We are still missing the ships for the invading turtles, so we block these into the game in a similar method as the player ship. However, because there are more of them, and we want the targets to move, we need to code these in a slightly different manner. This is also a good point to start concerning ourselves with the state of the game. There are several states that this game can enter into, the start, playing, lost, and won are a few, and depending on what state the game is in, we want interactions to behave slightly differently. For instance, we want the spacebar to start the game as well as fire the lasers. We can track this as a game object literal, as in Listing 6–15.

Listing 6–15. *Setting the Game State*

```
var game = {
      state: "start"
};
```

Changing the game status is now simply a matter of calling game.state = 'newstate';. We now just need to code our draw and update functions for the invaders (Listing 6–16).

Listing 6–16. *Drawing Invaders*

```
var invaders = [];

function drawInvaders() {
      for(var iter in invaders) {
        var invader = invaders[iter];
        context.fillStyle = "red";
        context.fillRect(invader.x, invader.y, invader.width, invader.height);
      }
}
```

The updateInvaders function is a bit more complicated. We need to make the invaders move back and forth on the screen. If you remember back to your high school geometry, you may recall that there are a few math functions that do this oscillation (sine and cosine). For our purposes, we use the sine, with some padding to control the amount of oscillation on the screen (Listing 6–17).

Listing 6–17. *Updating Invader Position*

```
function updateInvaders() {
      // populate invaders array
      if(game.state === "start") {
        for(var iter = 0; iter < 10; iter++) {
          invaders.push({
            x: 10 + iter * 50,
            y: 10,
            height: 40,
            width: 40,
            phase: Math.floor(Math.random() * 50),
            counter: 0,
            state: "alive"
          });
        }
        game.state = "playing"
      }

      for(var iter in invaders) {
        var invader = invaders[iter];

          if(!invader) {
            continue;
          }

          if(invader && invader.state == "alive") {
            invader.counter++;
            invader.x += Math.sin(invader.counter * Math.PI * 2 / 100) * 3;
          }

      }
}
```

After adding the calls to `updateInvaders()` and `drawInvaders()` to the `gameLoop()` function, you should now have red blocks oscillating across the top of the canvas. See Listing 6–18 and Figure 6–5.

Listing 6–18. *Updated gameLoop*

```
function gameLoop() {

  updateInvaders();
  updateSpaceship();

  drawSpaceship();
  drawInvaders();

drawLasers();
}
```

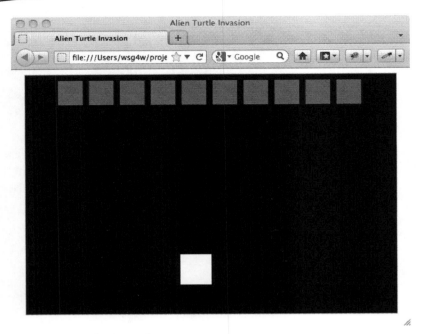

Figure 6–5. *Alien Turtle Invasion*

Although you can now fire "lasers" at the invaders, nothing happens. We need to write a couple of functions that will check if objects have hit one another. There are many different nuanced algorithms for detecting collisions between objects, but we use a simple method that places a "hitbox" around different objects to make the math faster. Again, these functions need to be added to the gameLoop() function, as in Listing 6–19.

Listing 6–19. *Hit Detection*

```
function checkHits() {
    for(var iter in lasers) {
      var laser = lasers[iter];
      for(var inv in invaders) {
        var invader = invaders[inv];

        if(hit(laser, invader)) {
          laser.state = "hit";
          invader.state = "hit";
          invader.counter = 0;
        }
      }
    }

    // check for enemy hits on the player
  }

  function hit(a, b) {
    var hit = false;
    // horizontal collisions
```

```
    if(b.x + b.width >= a.x && b.x < a.x + a.width) {
      // vertical collision
      if(b.y + b.height >= a.y && b.y < a.y + a.height) {
        hit = true;
      }
    }

    // a in b
    if(b.x <= a.x && b.x + b.width >= a.x + a.width) {
      if(b.y <= a.y && b.y + b.height >= a.y + a.height) {
        hit = true;
      }
    }

    // b in a
    if(a.x <= b.x && a.x + a.width >= b.x + b.width) {
      if(a.y <= b.y && a.y + a.height >= b.y + b.height) {
        hit = true;
      }
    }

    return hit;
}
```

We also need to update the `drawInvaders()` function to check for the invader's state and change its fill, and we need to update the `updateSpaceship()` function so it does not draw the spaceship if the ship's state is "dead." See Listing 6–20.

Listing 6–20. *Updating Invader Position and Checking for Collisions*

```
function drawInvaders() {
      for(var iter in invaders) {
        var invader = invaders[iter];

        if(invader.state == "alive") {
          context.fillStyle = "red";
        }

        if(invader.state == "hit") {
          context.fillStyle = "purple";
        }

        if(invader.state == "dead") {
          context.fillStyle = "black";
        }

        context.fillRect(invader.x, invader.y, invader.width, invader.height);
      }
}

function updateSpaceship() {
      if (spaceship.state === 'dead') {
          return;
      }
      // move left
      if(keyboard[37]) {
        spaceship.x -= 10;
        if(spaceship.x < 0) {
```

```
        spaceship.x = 0;
      }
    }

    // move right
    if(keyboard[39]) {
      spaceship.x += 10;
      var right = canvas.width - spaceship.width;
      if(spaceship.x > right) {
        spaceship.x = right;
      }
    }

    // spacebar pressed
    if(keyboard[32]) {
      // only fire one laser
      if(!keyboard.fired) {
        fireLaser();
        keyboard.fired = true;
      } else {
        keyboard.fired = false;
      }
    }
  }
}
```

Now that we can successfully shoot the invaders, it is time to add a bit more of a challenge and have the invaders fire at the player. Each invader needs its own intelligence to know when to fire. We do not need anything too smart, just the ability to randomly fire a projectile. We also need to check if the spaceship has been hit by any of the invaders' projectiles. With the invader's missiles defined, we also need to define when the missiles are fired in the updateInvaders() function. See Listing 6–21.

Listing 6–21. *Spaceship Firing at Random Intervals*

```
var invaderMissiles = [];

function addInvaderMissile(invader){
    return {
      x: invader.x,
      y: invader.y,
      width: 10,
      height: 33,
      counter: 0
    }
}

function drawInvaderMissiles() {
    for(var iter in invaderMissiles) {
      var laser = invaderMissiles[iter];
      var xoffset = (laser.counter % 9) * 12 + 1;
      var yoffset = 1;
      context.fillStyle = "yellow";
      context.fillRect(laser.x, laser.y, laser.width, laser.height);
    }
}
```

```
function updateInvaderMissiles() {
    for(var iter in invaderMissiles) {
      var laser = invaderMissiles[iter];
      laser.y += 3;
      laser.counter++;
    }
}
    continue;
  }

  if(invader && invader.state === "alive") {
    invader.counter++;
    invader.x += Math.sin(invader.counter * Math.PI * 2 / 100) * 3;

    // fire every
    if((invader.counter + invader.phase) % 200 === 0) {
      invaderMissiles.push(addInvaderMissle(invader));
    }
  }

  if(invader && invader.state === "hit") {
    invader.counter++;

    // change state to dead to be cleaned up
    if(invader.counter >= 20) {
      invader.state = "dead";
      invader.counter = 0;
    }
  }

}

invaders = invaders.filter(function(event) {
  if(event && event.state !== "dead") { return true; }
  return false;
});

}
```

We also need to update the checkHits function to check for collisions on the spaceship, as well as test for a new state for the spaceship, as in Listing 6–22.

Listing 6–22. *Checking if the Spaceship Has Been Hit*

```
function checkHits() {
  for(var iter in lasers) {
    var laser = lasers[iter];
    for(var inv in invaders) {
      var invader = invaders[inv];

      if(hit(laser, invader)) {
        laser.state = "hit";
        invader.state = "hit";
        invader.counter = 0;
      }
    }
  }
}
```

```
    // check for enemy hits on the spaceship
    if(spaceship.state == "hit" || spaceship.state == "dead") {
      return;
    }

    for(var iter in invaderMissiles) {
      var missle = invaderMissiles[iter];
      if(hit(missle, spaceship)) {
        missle.state = "hit";
        spaceship.state = "hit";
        spaceship.counter = 0;
      }
    }
  }
```

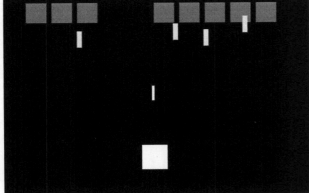

Figure 6–6. *Turtle Invaders and spaceship can shoot at each other*

Now the invaders can shoot back in waves (Figure 6–6), and our spaceship can shoot at the invaders, but there is not anything that happens after the screen has been cleared. The next thing we work on is providing some feedback to the player. For this, we want an initial game state that tells the player to press the spacebar to start the game, and a playing state where the player shoots the invading turtles, as well as a level won state, and a game over state (Listing 6–23).

Listing 6–23. *Updating the Game State*

```
var textOverlay = {
  counter: -1,
  title: "",
  subtitle: ""
};

function updateGameState() {
  //console.log('updateGameState');
  if(game.state == "playing" && invaders.length == 0) {
    game.state = "won";
    textOverlay.title = "Turtles Defeated";
    textOverlay.subtitle = "press space bar to play again";
    textOverlay.counter = 0;
  }
```

```
  if(game.state == "over" && keyboard[32]) {
    game.state = "start";
    spaceship.state = "alive";
    textOverlay.counter = -1;
  }

  if(game.state =="won" && keyboard[32]) {
    game.state = "start";
    spaceship.state = "alive";
    textOverlay.counter = -1;
  }

  if(textOverlay.counter >= 0 ) {
    textOverlay.counter++;
  }
}

function updateSpaceship() {
  if(spaceship.state == "dead") {
    return;
  }

  // move left
  if(keyboard[37]) {
    spaceship.x -= 10;
    if(spaceship.x < 0) {
      spaceship.x = 0;
    }
  }

  // move right
  if(keyboard[39]) {
    spaceship.x += 10;
    var right = canvas.width - spaceship.width;
    if(spaceship.x > right) {
      spaceship.x = right;
    }
  }

  if(keyboard[32]) {
    // only fire one laser
    if(!keyboard.fired) {
      fireLaser();
      keyboard.fired = true;
    } else {
      keyboard.fired = false;
    }
  }

  if(spaceship.state == "hit") {
    spaceship.counter++;
    if(spaceship.counter >= 40) {
      spaceship.counter = 0;
      spaceship.state = "dead";
      game.state = "over";
      textOverlay.title = "Game Over";
```

```
        textOverlay.subtitle = "press space to play again";
        textOverlay.counter = 0;
      }
    }
}

function drawTextOverlay() {
  if(textOverlay.counter == -1) {
    return;
  }

  var alpha = textOverlay.counter / 50.0;

  if(alpha > 1 ) {
    alpha = 1;
  }

  context.globalAlpha = alpha;
  context.save();

  if(game.state == "over") {
    context.fillStyle = "white";
    context.font = "Bold 40pt Arial";
    context.fillText(textOverlay.title, 140, 200);
    context.font = "14pt Helvectica";
    context.fillText(textOverlay.subtitle, 190, 250);
  }

  if(game.state == "won") {
    context.fillStyle = "white";
    context.font = "Bold 40pt Arial";
    context.fillText(textOverlay.title, 50, 200);
    context.font = "14pt Helvectica";
    context.fillText(textOverlay.subtitle, 190, 250);
  }

  context.restore();

}
function gameLoop() {

  updateGameState();
  updateBackground();
  updateInvaders();
  updateSpaceship();

  updateLasers();
  updateInvaderMissiles();

  checkHits();

  drawBackground();
  drawSpaceship();
  drawInvaders();

  drawInvaderMissiles();
  drawLasers();
```

```
  drawTextOverlay();
}
```

Congratulations, you now have all the pieces working together for the game. Just in case something is not working correctly, Listing 6–24 shows the JavaScript code to this point.

Listing 6–24. *Full Game Code*

```
"use strict";

var canvas = document.getElementById('game');
var context = canvas.getContext('2d');

var spaceship = {
  x: 100,
  y: 300,
  width: 50,
  height: 50,
  counter: 0
};

var game = {
  state: "start"
};

var keyboard = {};

var lasers = [];
var invaders = [];
var invaderMissiles = [];

var spaceship_image;
var missle_image;
var laser_sound;

var textOverlay = {
  counter: -1,
  title: "",
  subtitle: ""
};

function updateGameState() {
  if(game.state === "playing" && invaders.length === 0) {
    game.state = "won";
    textOverlay.title = "Turtles Defeated";
    textOverlay.subtitle = "press space bar to play again";
    textOverlay.counter = 0;
  }

  if(game.state === "over" && keyboard[32]) {
    game.state = "start";
    spaceship.state = "alive";
    textOverlay.counter = -1;
  }

  if(game.state === "won" && keyboard[32]) {
    game.state = "start";
```

```
      spaceship.state = "alive";
      textOverlay.counter = -1;
    }

    if(textOverlay.counter >= 0 ) {
      textOverlay.counter++;
    }
}

function updateBackground() {
    // do nothing
}

function addInvaderMissle(invader){
    return {
      x: invader.x,
      y: invader.y,
      width: 10,
      height: 33,
      counter: 0
    };
}

function drawInvaderMissiles() {
    for(var iter in invaderMissiles) {
      var laser = invaderMissiles[iter];
      var xoffset = (laser.counter % 9) * 12 + 1;
      var yoffset = 1;
      context.fillStyle = "yellow";
      context.fillRect(laser.x, laser.y, laser.width, laser.height);
    }
}

function updateInvaderMissiles() {
    for(var iter in invaderMissiles) {
      var laser = invaderMissiles[iter];
      laser.y += 3;
      laser.counter++;
    }
}

function updateInvaders() {
    // populate invaders array
    if(game.state === "start") {

      invaders = []; // be sure to reset the invaders array when starting a new game

      for(var iter = 0; iter < 10; iter++) {
        invaders.push({
          x: 10 + iter * 50,
          y: 10,
          height: 40,
          width: 40,
          phase: Math.floor(Math.random() * 50),
          counter: 0,
          state: "alive"
        });
```

```
      }
      game.state = "playing";
    }

    // invaders float back and forth
    for(var iter2 in invaders) {
      var invader = invaders[iter2];

      if(!invader) {
        continue;
      }

      if(invader && invader.state === "alive") {
        invader.counter++;
        invader.x += Math.sin(invader.counter * Math.PI * 2 / 100) * 3;

        // fire every
        if((invader.counter + invader.phase) % 200 === 0) {
          invaderMissiles.push(addInvaderMissle(invader));
        }
      }

      if(invader && invader.state === "hit") {
        invader.counter++;

        // change state to dead to be cleaned up
        if(invader.counter >= 20) {
          invader.state = "dead";
          invader.counter = 0;
        }
      }
    }

    invaders = invaders.filter(function(event) {
      if(event && event.state !== "dead") { return true; }
      return false;
    });

}

function drawInvaders() {
  for(var iter in invaders) {
    var invader = invaders[iter];

    if(invader.state === "alive") {
      context.fillStyle = "red";
    }

    if(invader.state === "hit") {
      context.fillStyle = "purple";
    }

    if(invader.state === "dead") {
      context.fillStyle = "black";
    }
```

```javascript
        context.fillRect(invader.x, invader.y, invader.width, invader.height);
    }
}

function drawBackground() {
  context.fillStyle = "#000000";
  context.fillRect(0, 0, canvas.width, canvas.height);
}

function updateLasers() {
  // move the laser
  for(var iter in lasers) {
    var laser = lasers[iter];
    laser.y -= 2;
    laser.counter++;
  }

  // remove lasers that are off the screen
  lasers = lasers.filter(function(laser) {
    return laser.y > 0;
  });

}

function fireLaser() {
  lasers.push ({
    x: spaceship.x + 20, //offset
    y: spaceship.y - 10,
    width: 5,
    height: 30
  });

  //playSound('laser');
}

function updateSpaceship() {
  if(spaceship.state === "dead") {
    return;
  }

  // move left
  if(keyboard[37]) {
    spaceship.x -= 10;
    if(spaceship.x < 0) {
      spaceship.x = 0;
    }
  }

  // move right
  if(keyboard[39]) {
    spaceship.x += 10;
    var right = canvas.width - spaceship.width;
    if(spaceship.x > right) {
      spaceship.x = right;
    }
  }
```

```
    if(keyboard[32]) {
      // only fire one laser
      if(!keyboard.fired) {
        fireLaser();
        keyboard.fired = true;
      } else {
        keyboard.fired = false;
      }
    }

    if(spaceship.state === "hit") {
      spaceship.counter++;
      if(spaceship.counter >= 40) {
        spaceship.counter = 0;
        spaceship.state = "dead";
        game.state = "over";
        textOverlay.title = "Game Over";
        textOverlay.subtitle = "press space to play again";
        textOverlay.counter = 0;
      }
    }
  }

function drawSpaceship() {
  if(spaceship.state === "dead") {
    return;
  }

  if(spaceship.state === "hit") {
    context.fillStyle = "blue";
    context.fillRect(spaceship.x, spaceship.y, spaceship.width, spaceship.height);
    return;
  }

  context.fillStyle = "white";
  context.fillRect(spaceship.x, spaceship.y, spaceship.width, spaceship.height);
}

function drawLasers() {
  context.fillStyle = "white";
  for(var iter in lasers) {
    var laser = lasers[iter];
    context.fillRect(laser.x, laser.y, laser.width, laser.height);
  }
}

function hit(a, b) {
  var ahit = false;
  // horizontal collisions
  if(b.x + b.width >= a.x && b.x < a.x + a.width) {
    // vertical collision
    if(b.y + b.height >= a.y && b.y < a.y + a.height) {
      ahit = true;
    }
  }

  // a in b
```

```javascript
    if(b.x <= a.x && b.x + b.width >= a.x + a.width) {
      if(b.y <= a.y && b.y + b.height >= a.y + a.height) {
        ahit = true;
      }
    }

    // b in a
    if(a.x <= b.x && a.x + a.width >- b.x + b.width) {
      if(a.y <= b.y && a.y + a.height >= b.y + b.height) {
        ahit = true;
      }
    }

    return ahit;
}
function checkHits() {
  for(var iter in lasers) {
    var laser = lasers[iter];
    for(var inv in invaders) {
      var invader = invaders[inv];

      if(hit(laser, invader)) {
        laser.state = "hit";
        invader.state = "hit";
        invader.counter = 0;
      }
    }
  }

  // check for enemy hits on the spaceship
  if(spaceship.state === "hit" || spaceship.state === "dead") {
    return;
  }

  for(var iter2 in invaderMissiles) {
    var missle = invaderMissiles[iter2];
    if(hit(missle, spaceship)) {
      missle.state = "hit";
      spaceship.state = "hit";
      spaceship.counter = 0;
    }
  }
}

function addEvent(node, name, func) {
  if(node.addEventListener) {
    node.addEventListener(name, func, false);
  } else if(node.attachEvent) {
    // handle Microsoft browsers too
    node.attachEvent(name, func);
  }
}

function addKeyboardEvents() {
  addEvent(document, "keydown", function(e) {
    keyboard[e.keyCode] = true;
```

```javascript
    });

    addEvent(document, "keyup", function(e) {
      keyboard[e.keyCode] = false;
    });

}

function drawTextOverlay() {
  if(textOverlay.counter === -1) {
    return;
  }

  var alpha = textOverlay.counter / 50.0;

  if(alpha > 1 ) {
    alpha = 1;
  }

  context.globalAlpha = alpha;
  context.save();

  if(game.state === "over") {
    context.fillStyle = "white";
    context.font = "Bold 40pt Arial";
    context.fillText(textOverlay.title, 140, 200);
    context.font = "14pt Helvectica";
    context.fillText(textOverlay.subtitle, 190, 250);
  }

  if(game.state === "won") {
    context.fillStyle = "white";
    context.font = "Bold 40pt Arial";
    context.fillText(textOverlay.title, 100, 200);
    context.font = "14pt Helvectica";
    context.fillText(textOverlay.subtitle, 190, 250);
  }

  context.restore();

}

function gameLoop() {

  updateGameState();
  updateBackground();
  updateInvaders();
  updateSpaceship();

  updateLasers();
  updateInvaderMissiles();

  checkHits();

  drawBackground();
  drawSpaceship();
  drawInvaders();
```

```
    drawInvaderMissiles();
    drawLasers();
    drawTextOverlay();
}

addKeyboardEvents();
setInterval(gameLoop, 1000 / 60);
```

You have now done most of the heavy lifting for the game, but it still looks pretty lame and probably would not get played much. In the next section, we focus on gathering the graphical assets to give this game more polish.

Adding Textures

Games need graphics that look good for the game. Right now the Alien Turtle Invasion game is a set of blocks that interact with one another. We could use graphics that we build from scratch, but instead we take a bit of a shortcut and use some premade assets for our game. Fortunately there are several communities of game developers that share their work with one another. After some searching on the Open Game Art website, I came across a great set of graphics for our game.

You can download the great public domain "Space Starter Kit" by CruzR at `http://opengameart.org/content/space-starter-kit`. The kit contains two flags, and two color variations of a spaceship, UFO, missiles, laser beam, asteroid, and flags. We do not use all of these graphics, but will use the spaceship, lasers, missiles, and UFOs for our initial game.

Download and unzip the files in a convenient location. Notice that these are SVG files, and the canvas element cannot work with an SVG image, only raster-based images. We need to manipulate the files to get them to the proper dimension and format we need for the game. Open the 'starship.svg' file in Inkscape (or your favorite SVG editor). If you remember from the previous section, the size of our spaceship is 50 × 50 pixels. We can export the vector graphic to a bitmap in Inkscape by selecting **File ➤ Export Bitmap** (Shift + Ctrl + E). The starfighter is slightly wider than it is tall, so we can set the width of the bitmap to 50 pixels, which should reset the height to 51 pixels. See Figure 6–7.

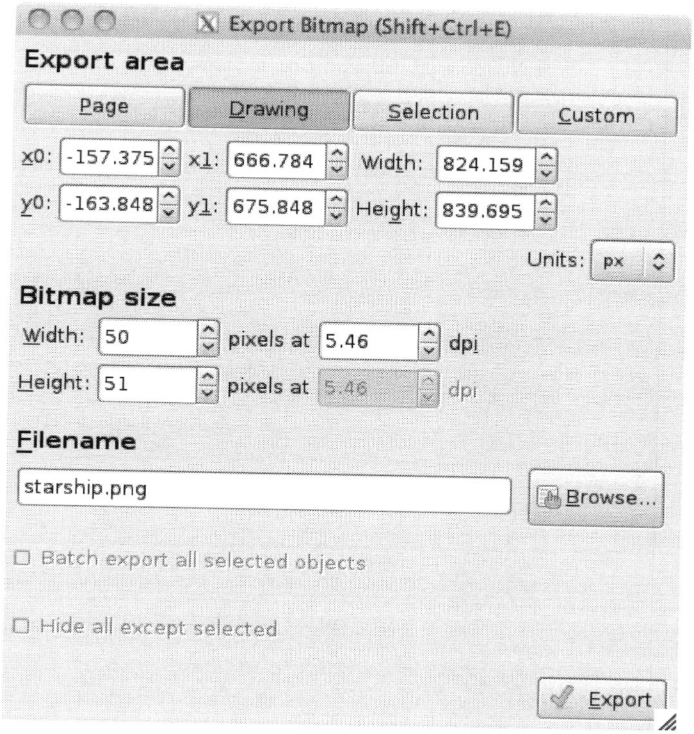

Figure 6–7. *Inkscape export of the starship.svg*

Create an images subdirectory in your project directory (e.g., `mkdir images`) and place the resulting file there. Next, export `projectile1.svg`, `torpedo.svg`, and `ufo.svg` with the following dimensions.

- projectile1.svg: 5 × 30 px; rename to "laser.png"

- starship.svg: 50 × 51 px; rename to "spaceship.png"

- torpedo.svg: 10 × 33 px; rotate the image 180 degrees; rename to "torpedo.png"

- ufo.svg: 40 × 40 px; rename to invader.png

In your images directory, you should now have the following files: `invader.png`, `laser.png`, `spaceship.png`, `torpedo.png`. Now we need to edit our JavaScript to load these resources and draw them on the canvas instead of the rectangles we have been using.

Listing 6–25 shows a function we can write that will load our image resources for us to use in the game.

Listing 6–25. *Loading Image Resources*

```
var invader_image;
var laser_image;

...

function loadResources() {
  spaceship_image = new Image();
  spaceship_image.src = 'images/spaceship.png';

  missle_image = new Image();
  missle_image.src = 'images/torpedo.png';

  invader_image = new Image();
  invader_image.src = 'images/invader.png';

  laser_image = new Image();
  laser_image.src = 'images/laser.png';
}
```

We also need to call this before we call the setInterval function (Listing 6–26).

Listing 6–26. *Loading Resources for the Game*

```
addKeyboardEvents();
loadResources();
setInterval(gameLoop, 1000 / 60);
```

Now it is just a matter of updating the draw functions for the spaceship, missiles, lasers, and invaders (Listing 6–27).

Listing 6–27. *Updating the Draw Functions*

```
function drawInvaderMissiles() {
  for(var iter in invaderMissiles) {
    var missle = invaderMissiles[iter];

    context.drawImage(
      missle_image,
      missle.x, missle.y, missle.width, missle.height
    );
  }
}

function drawInvaders() {
  for(var iter in invaders) {
    var invader = invaders[iter];

    if(invader.state === "alive") {
      context.fillStyle = "red";

      context.drawImage(
        invader_image,
        invader.x, invader.y, invader.width, invader.height
      );
    }

    if(invader.state === "hit") {
```

```
        context.fillStyle = "purple";
      }

    if(invader.state === "dead") {
      context.fillStyle = "black";
      context.fillRect(invader.x, invader.y, invader.width, invader.height);
    }

  }
}

function drawSpaceship() {
  if(spaceship.state === "dead") {
    return;
  }

  if(spaceship.state === "hit") {
    context.fillStyle = "blue";
    context.fillRect(spaceship.x, spaceship.y, spaceship.width, spaceship.height);
    return;
  }

  context.drawImage(
    spaceship_image,
    0, 0, 50, 50,
    spaceship.x, spaceship.y, spaceship.width, spaceship.height
  );
}

function drawLasers() {
  context.fillStyle = "white";

  for(var iter in lasers) {
    var laser = lasers[iter];

    context.drawImage(
      laser_image,
      laser.x, laser.y, laser.width, laser.height
    );
  }
}
```

When you have all the code working, you will see a screen that looks like that in
Figure 6–8.

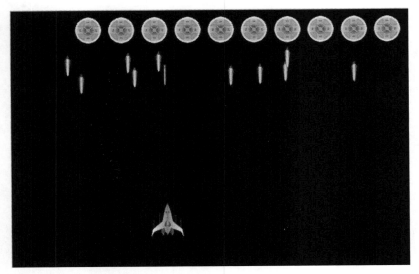

Figure 6–8. *Alien Turtle Invasion game*

The game is really starting to look good now with the invaders firing missiles, and our spaceship firing lasers. Now we need to make this sound as good as it looks.

Adding Sound

Although we could certainly build the sounds we need from scratch, you can get quite far down the road using stock, or community-contributed sounds for your game. What I wanted to do for this game is have sounds for when the spaceship explodes, when the spaceship fires a laser, when a ship fires a missile, and when a ship explodes. I spent some time browsing the SoundBible.com and OpenGameArt websites and settled on the following sounds for my version of the game. If you find something that you like better, by all means use that sound instead!

- Invader Explosion: File 15 from HorrorPen's "41 Random Sound Effects" (http://opengameart.org/content/41-random-sound-effects).

- Invader Missile: Bottle Rocket (http://soundbible.com/709-Bottle-Rocket.html).

- Spaceship Explosion: Grenade (http://soundbible.com/696-Grenade.html).

- Laser: Laser Blasts (http://soundbible.com/472-Laser-Blasts.html).

I chose the explosions and missile firing for the aliens because I wanted a short sound that alerts the player to the fact that either the missiles are firing, or they have scored a hit on the Turtle Invaders, but not detract from the fact that they still need to get out of the way of the incoming barrage of missiles. The grenade explosion was a nice concussive sound that I thought felt good for ending the game. I also was very close to using a catapult sound for the sound of the Turtle Ships firing on the player's spaceship as it had a nice "whoosh" effect.

Now that you have the sounds you want to use, we need to do a little prep work to get the files to be played in the browser natively. If the sound you have is in a format other than wav, we need to convert the file to an appropriate format. This is quite easy to do with the freely downloadable Audacity program (http://audacity.sourceforge.net/). Simply select **File ➤ Export** and select "WAV (Microsoft) signed 16 bit PCM" from the format options. Create a sounds directory in your project (e.g., mkdir sounds) and save the different formats of the sound as the same name (e.g., laser, rocket, missile, explosion, etc.), but with a different extension (e.g., mp3 and wav).

Once you have all of your sounds converted to wav format, place them in the sounds subdirectory within your main project folder. We can now create a few variables for our sound and use the HTML 5 <audio> element on the DOM to hold our sounds. See Listing 6–28.

Listing 6–28. *Loading Audio*

```
var laser_sound;
var missle_sound;
var explosion_sound;
var invader_explosion_sound;

function loadResources() {
  spaceship_image = new Image();
  spaceship_image.src = 'images/spaceship.png';

  missle_image = new Image();
  missle_image.src = 'images/torpedo.png';

  invader_image = new Image();
  invader_image.src = 'images/invader.png';

  laser_image = new Image();
  laser_image.src = 'images/laser.png';

  missle_sound = document.createElement("audio");
  document.body.appendChild(missle_sound);
  missle_sound.setAttribute("src", "sounds/rocket.wav");

  laser_sound = document.createElement("audio");
  document.body.appendChild(laser_sound);
  laser_sound.setAttribute("src", "sounds/laser.wav");

  explosion_sound = document.createElement("audio");
  document.body.appendChild(explosion_sound);
  explosion_sound.setAttribute("src", "sounds/explosion.wav");

  invader_explosion_sound = document.createElement("audio");
  document.body.appendChild(invader_explosion_sound);
  invader_explosion_sound.setAttribute("src", "sounds/invader_explosion.wav");
}
```

With the code in place, we just need to play the appropriate sounds in the update functions, as shown in Listing 6–29.

Listing 6–29. *Playing Sounds*

```
function addInvaderMissle(invader){

  missle_sound.play();

  return {
    x: invader.x,
    y: invader.y,
    width: 10,
    height: 33,
    counter: 0
  };
}

function fireLaser() {

  laser_sound.play();

  lasers.push ({
    x: spaceship.x + 20, //offset
    y: spaceship.y - 10,
    width: 5,
    height: 30,
    counter: 0
  });
}

function drawSpaceship() {
  if(spaceship.state === "dead") {
    return;
  }

  if(spaceship.state === "hit") {
    explosion_sound.play();
    context.fillStyle = "black";
    context.fillRect(spaceship.x, spaceship.y, spaceship.width, spaceship.height);
    return;
  }

  context.drawImage(
    spaceship_image,
    0, 0, 50, 50,
    spaceship.x, spaceship.y, spaceship.width, spaceship.height
  );
}

function checkHits() {
  for(var iter in lasers) {
    var laser = lasers[iter];
    for(var inv in invaders) {
      var invader = invaders[inv];

      if(hit(laser, invader)) {
        laser.state = "hit";
```

```
          invader.state = "hit";
          invader.counter = 0;
          invader_explosion_sound.play();
        }
      }
    }

    // check for enemy hits on the spaceship
    if(spaceship.state === "hit" || spaceship.state === "dead") {
      return;
    }

    for(var iter2 in invaderMissiles) {
      var missle = invaderMissiles[iter2];
      if(hit(missle, spaceship)) {
        missle.state = "hit";
        spaceship.state = "hit";
        spaceship.counter = 0;
      }
    }
}
```

Now when you reload the game and play, you should have sound effects that happen when you interact with the game. This layer of the game does provide the player with more immersion in the game, and although admittedly short, does polish off more of the rough edges in your first game.

Summary

This chapter put everything we have discussed up to this point into practice. The idea for the game was codified, and then the engine was built iteratively. At first, the game had stand-in shapes for our eventual sprites as we added functionality. This allows you, as a developer, to keep the number of moving parts you need to keep track of to a minimum while you are adding functionality.

Having a clear game plan helps you remain focused through the development process. There may be some feature you had not considered, but which becomes very evident that it is needed once the game starts to come together. Or, as is more common, you may find that there is a feature that would be nice, but is taking far too long to implement. Every time you begin to add a feature, always ask yourself if it is within the original specification of your project. If it is not, write it down as a new feature for a future release.

Lastly, working with royalty-free resources, both graphic and audio, helps free you up to spend more time working on other pieces of your game. You do not need to be an expert in all areas of game development to build a good game, but you do need to rely on the kindness of strangers, and their passion for releasing their work to the world. If you find yourself in a position to give back to the community, be it a contribution of your own, a few dollars for server maintenance, something off a developer's wish-list, or even a quick note of thanks, you go a long way to help encourage individuals to continue to develop open-source material.

In the next chapter, I start discussing the trend toward social gaming, and components that make up this genre of games. To keep up the practice of developing games, and providing exposure to different techniques, I also walk through the development of a Tic-Tac-Toe game that has some artificial intelligence built in as an example of the minigames that often accompany games on social platforms.

Chapter 7

Social Components and HTML5 Games

Games are designed to distract us from our daily routines and allow us to engage in a world that would otherwise be impossible. A game that you play with others is, by definition, social. I fondly remember sitting around a table with friends playing board games. I also remember sitting around a living room with friends watching one of them play a game like *Mike Tyson's Punch-Out!!* Friends that were not actively playing the game would also sit around, either yelling at the players that they were doing it wrong, or engaging in some type of competition for dibs on the next game. I admit here, probably for the first time, these nongaming interactions while gaming were responsible for more than one piece of broken furniture (sorry, Mrs. Jabbar).

This style of sitting around a one- or two-player game was arguably the first generation of social gaming. These were mainly due to hardware constraints. The hardware running games in this era was limited, not only in the number of bits it could produce on the screen, but the number of control inputs the device could handle. Even today, most console gaming devices are limited to four controllers, not so much because of the physical constraints of the hardware, but because there is no good way to split the screen up in such a manner that allows for the effective use of the television or monitor screen real estate. In the late 1990s, as the Internet was gaining more steam, you started seeing more games where each computer was a player on a local area network which all worked together for a better multiplayer game.

Players also began seeing a modern spin on the chess- (and other games) by-mail scenario: the play-by-email (PBeM) game. I recall some epic PBeM rounds of *Civilization* back in the day, but they always felt quite constrained. If you started some strategy, there could be several days before you would have the opportunity to make your next move. I recall trying to play several of these games where it just fizzled out due to some competing time requirement by one of the players. That is why when the game *Everquest* came out, which dealt with the social aspects of the game by building a world where you could experience the game content with anyone that was playing, game companies essentially took over the role of LAN organizer, and began to shift some game mechanics to encourage individuals to interact with each other more.

Perhaps one of the best examples of this has been the recent changes by Blizzard in their *World of Warcraft*. To encourage players to join guilds, they introduced a perk system for guilds to make leveling easier. There is a built-in channel for chatting with your guild members, and a hosting industry that sprung up to host guild-specific websites dedicated to conversations about playing the game.

All of this has been going on in what you might consider the traditional gaming marketplace, however, big changes in the online social spaces over the last decade have transformed many attitudes toward games and gaming. After MySpace and Facebook first opened their platforms to outside developers, games quickly found their way into user profile pages. Companies such as Zynga, developers of the wildly popular *Farmville*, have not only created a new class of social gamers, but new models for monetizing their games with microtransactions. Although games from publishers including Zynga are missing some of the elements of a AAA-level game, startups such as Rumble Entertainment (with veterans from EA, BioWare, and Activision) hope to develop top-level content for social and mobile platforms. Rumble Entertainment's $15 million first-round funding, and Zynga's $1 billion IPO, shows that investors see strong potential for gaming on social platforms.

Social Mechanics in Games

Beyond the basics of the gameplay mechanics, social games leverage mechanics to emphasize, or expand, portions of the game play. In *Farmville*, to keep you coming back to the game, Zynga implemented the *harvest* gameplay mechanic. The player plants some seeds, and needs to come back to the game to harvest the crops. As the player levels through game play, items are then available for "Farm cash," which can be purchased through leveling, or for real money. To encourage you to play with others, players are encouraged to visit each other's farms, performing up to five tasks for experience points, or provide gifts.

Neopets utilizes a slightly more sophisticated gameplay mechanic. As a player travels across the site, she is presented with random events from pet modifications, to losing/gaining money, to opening new areas to explore. To get people "hooked," the early stages drop a lot more of these bonuses, gradually tailing off as the player progresses. The *Neopets* world is also massive, which seems to be a common feature of these games. Coupling massive content to explore in random progressions (many with minigames) engages many players in the social arena in a sustainable way.

Tic-Tac-Toe

Building a massive world can take months even with an army of engineers. However, the minigames that one plays in these systems are far simpler to dissect and explain. Because there are different tricks and techniques in all of these, getting a feel for how to put these together is important. For our social gaming minigame, we create a version of Tic-Tac-Toe that you have to play against the computer. We add some storyline to the cycles to play the game to make it a bit more engaging.

As in Chapter 6, the first thing to set up is the HTML and the project directories. I use the same directory structure as the last project in Chapter 6, so if you need help setting that up, check out the "Boilerplate" section (Listing 7–1), with a couple of minor differences here. First, I am making a call to the Google Font API to use a font named "Permanent Marker."

> **NOTE:** The Google Font API (http://www.google.com/webfonts) is a great place to find fonts for your web designs. Although adding new fonts every day, it still does not contain the number of fonts that services such as Font Squirrel (http://www.fontsquirrel.com/) or Typekit (https://typekit.com/) offer to their users. All of these services are worth exploring to help you find web-friendly fonts that are consistent across platforms and browsers.

Listing 7–1. *HTML Boilerplate*

```
<!doctype html>
<!--[if lt IE 7]> <html class="no-js lt-ie9 lt-ie8 lt-ie7" lang="en"> <![endif]-->
<!--[if IE 7]>    <html class="no-js lt-ie9 lt-ie8" lang="en"> <![endif]-->
<!--[if IE 8]>    <html class="no-js lt-ie9" lang="en"> <![endif]-->
<!--[if gt IE 8]><!--> <html class="no-js" lang="en"> <!--<![endif]-->
<head>
  <meta charset="utf-8">

  <title>Tic-Tac-Toe</title>

  <meta name="viewport" content="width=device-width,initial-scale=1">
  <link href='http://fonts.googleapis.com/css?family=Permanent+Marker' rel='stylesheet'
type='text/css'>
  <link rel="stylesheet" href="css/style.css">
  <script src="js/libs/modernizr-2.0.6.min.js"></script>
</head>

<body>

  <div id="main" role="main">
    <h1>Tic-Tac-Toe</h1>
    <canvas id="game" width="300" height="300"></canvas>
  </div>

  <script src="js/tictactoe.js"></script>

  <!--[if lt IE 7 ]>
    <script defer src="//ajax.googleapis.com/ajax/libs/chrome-
frame/1.0.3/CFInstall.min.js"></script>
    <script defer>
    window.attachEvent('onload',function(){CFInstall.check({mode:'overlay'})})
    </script>
  <![endif]-->
</body>
</html>
```

In addition to the stylesheet used in Chapter 6, add a definition to the stylesheet (css/style.css) for the header containing the words "Tic-Tac-Toe" to use the font "Permanent Marker" and center the text as in Listing 7–2.

Listing 7–2. *Game CSS Using Google Font*

```css
#main {
  width: 61em;
  max-width: 100%;
  *zoom: 1;
  margin: auto;
}

#main h1 {
  font-family: 'Permanent Marker', cursive;
  font-size: 4em;
  text-align: center;
}

#game {
  margin: auto;
  display: block;
  border: 1px solid #ccc;
}
```

The new header selector (h1) tells the browser to use the "Permanent Marker" font from the Google API and center it across the page at a size of 4 em.

> **NOTE:** An *em* is a unit of measure in typography. When type was manually set using metal type (sometimes called "hot metal" typesetting), font sizes were measured by the height of the metal body from which the letter rose. The capital M was used as the standard of measurement as it was normally cast (or carved) using the entire square block for that point size.
>
> As digital typography has replaced physical typesetting, the em has taken on a new definition. In digital type (e.g., with browsers), using an *em* scales a font to a specified point size. Rather than use a fixed measurement such as a pixel or point (both are valid in CSS), many designers use this scalable font measurement to create more robust designs in their sites. It is, however, worth noting that a browser scales fonts defined using pixels and ems the same. The only difference is in how many pixels a whitespace character has. If you define the font using a pixel size, whitespace is fixed; with ems, whitespace is included in the font as part of the design.

Figure 7–1. *Boilerplate code rendered with fonts from Google Font API*

As you can see in Figure 7–1, the font changes the look and feel of the page with only a few lines of code.

The Rules

You have probably played tic-tac-toe, but it is worth laying out the rules of the game to codify how the game interactions will occur.

- Tic-Tac-Toe is played on a 3 × 3 grid of squares.

- Two players play this game; one team uses the X mark, the other an O mark.

- Players win by placing three of their marks in a straight line, horizontal, diagonal, or vertical.

- A tie occurs if either player is unsuccessful in obtaining a straight line of their marks.

This game was originally designed for two players. Because we want to design a game experience for a single user, we develop an algorithm to simulate a second player. This artificial intelligence (AI) evaluates the board and calculates a "best" move given the current state of the board. Although not impossible to beat, it uses logic to determine the best move against the player. With a bit of randomness built in, we can help the game seem more random and engaging to the player.

The Board

The first thing needed for the game is the board. Look at the code for the canvas element in our boilerplate, and notice I set the width and height to 300 pixels. However, not knowing the exact dimensions of what I eventually will need, I want to give some flexibility to the program. Thus, it is a good idea to calculate the size of the canvas from the `<canvas>` element in the DOM. I do this by creating variables in the script to hold references to these values, and set these values in my `init` function.

To calculate where the grid lines should be, we need to do some math to determine where each line should be located. We need three boxes segmented by two lines, so we need to split the box into thirds. The first line starts one-third of the way through our canvas, and the second at two-thirds of the way through. Although our 300 × 300 pixel grid results in a nice round number when we divide it by three, other potential sizes of the canvas give us fractional results (e.g., 500 × 500 pixel sets the grid at 166.666667 and 333.333333). We need to stay away from these subpixel calculations as this can cause a performance issue in some browsers, so we use JavaScript's math rounding to avoid the browser needing to take additional steps to produce the same result. At this point, I have two functions and some variables in my script, as in Listing 7–3.

Listing 7–3. *Starting JavaScript*

```
var canvas;
var context;
var width;
var height;
```

```
function drawBoard() {

    context.beginPath();
    context.strokeStyle = 'black';
    context.lineWidth = 4;

    var vLine1 = Math.round(width / 3);
    var vLine2 = Math.round(vLine1 * 2);

    var hLine1 = Math.round(height / 3);
    var hLine2 = Math.round(hLine1 * 2);

    context.moveTo(vLine1, 0);
    context.lineTo(vLine1, height);

    context.moveTo(vLine2, 0);
    context.lineTo(vLine2, height);

    context.moveTo(0, hLine1);
    context.lineTo(width, hLine1);

    context.moveTo(0, hLine2);
    context.lineTo(width, hLine2);

    context.stroke();
    context.closePath();

}

function init(canvasID) {

    canvas = document.getElementById(canvasID);
    context = canvas.getContext('2d');

    width = canvas.width;
    height = canvas.height;

    drawBoard();
}
```

Make a new script element in your `index.html` file, call the `init()` function to initialize the game, and draw the grid on the canvas, as shown in Listing 7–4.

Listing 7–4. *Adding tictactoe.js to the Web Page*

```
<script src="js/tictactoe.js"></script>
<script>
    init('game');
</script>
```

When you refresh the page, you now see the grid drawn nicely for you. See Figure 7–2.

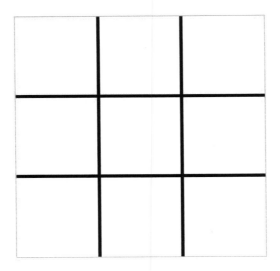

Figure 7–2. *Tic-tac-toe game board with grid lines*

You can now change the size of the canvas element and the code will automatically resize itself to calculate the grid areas. Try out the page with different values for the canvas element.

Keeping Track

Now that we have the visual basics set up, we need to develop a method to keep track of the plays on the board. In order to optimize the performance of our game, we make use of bitwise operations to shift bits to keep track of our game. We could keep track of the data in an array, but speed is a big factor in game development, so we need to be able to evaluate the game table and I do so through pushing bits onto the X and O boards. Treating these boards (and the potential wins) as bitmasks, we use significantly less memory in the browser application (a factor of 32) to hold our information. Less memory needed to run the application can greatly improve the performance of the application as browsers can bloat memory usage quite quickly (I routinely have Firefox running using over a gigabyte of memory). Comparisons and mathematical operations are also generally faster using bit-shifts than arrays and numbers, increasing the performance of your application.

We also need to keep track of the game state. Unlike our spaceship game in Chapter 6, we have a much less complex state machine; essentially we only need to keep track of when the game has started and when it is being played. To save a couple of milliseconds, we just use a Boolean variable for this check, stored in a variable.

We start this piece with Listing 7–5, by creating some variables to hold our information, the xBoard and yBoard to hold the information for which tiles are selected, and a Boolean variable (begin) that records the board state.

Listing 7–5. *Initializing X and O Boards and Game State*

```
var xBoard = 0;
var oBoard = 0;
var begin = true;
```

With the variables initialized, we now need to think about where on the board the individual has clicked. The grid system we have created has a visual segmentation through the lines drawn by the drawBoard() function, but how does one translate these areas to know where a player has clicked? We need to develop a method that listens for the "click" event from the browser, translating the *x*- and *y*-co-ordinates of the mouse into the sections.

If you take the *x*-axis of a 300-pixel grid, co-ordinates 0–99 are in the top-left grid, 101–200 in the top middle, and 201–300 are in the third. You calculate in the code of the clickHandler() function by taking the pixel co-ordinate of the click and dividing it by the width (height in the case of the Y-axis). This gives you a decimal representation of the grid you are in. The code simplifies the number by calling the floor method that rounds a number down to the nearest integer. See Figure 7–3.

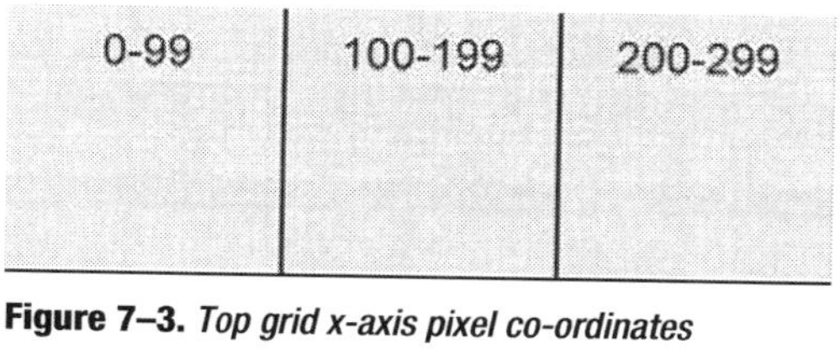

0-99	100-199	200-299

Figure 7–3. *Top grid x-axis pixel co-ordinates*

For example, if I clicked in a box that had an *x*-co-ordinate, of say 203 in a 300-pixel grid, applying the above algorithm we would find that the *x*-co-ordinate is in grid 2.

```
203 / (300 / 3) = 2.03
|2.03| = 2
```

Those funny symbols around the 2.03 are the formal mathematical symbols for the floor function. The same technique works across the Y-axis, but you use the height of the grid instead of the width. Once the x- and y-grids have been calculated, you save this as a bit, using a left shift. This shift produces a new binary number that will store "moves" in the game.

> **NOTE:** Bitwise operations work on binary numbers. The left shift (<<) shifts the first operand the specific number of bits to the left, filling 0 bits on the right.
>
> 1 (base 10): 00000001 (base 2)
> 1 << 3 (base 10): 00001000 (base 2)
>
> The result of this operation **produces** a decimal value of 8.

In using these bit operations, we can later evaluate the bitmask (data stored for bitwise operations) to evaluate the state of the board more efficiently (e.g., has any player achieved a win state).

We also need to be able to calculate if a given grid is available (e.g., not on either the xBoard or yBoard) to be marked, as well as place the grid on the player's board. We also need a function to handle clicks in the canvas (clickHandler()) that is initialized in the init() function to determine what block has been clicked on. See Listing 7–6.

Listing 7–6. *Checking and Drawing the Board*

```
function isEmpty(xBoard, oBoard, bit) {
  return (((xBoard & bit) == 0) && ((oBoard & bit) == 0));
}

function drawX(x, y) {
  context.beginPath();

  context.strokeStyle = '#ff0000';
  context.lineWidth = 4;

  var offsetX = (width / 3) * 0.1;
  var offsetY = (height / 3) * 0.1;

  var beginX = x * (width / 3) + offsetX;
  var beginY = y * (height / 3) + offsetY;

  var endX = (x + 1) * (width / 3) - offsetX;
  var endY = (y + 1) * (height / 3) - offsetY;

  context.moveTo(beginX, beginY);
  context.lineTo(endX, endY);

  context.moveTo(beginX, endY);
  context.lineTo(endX, beginY);

  context.stroke();
  context.closePath();
}
```

```
function markBit(markBit, player) {
  var bit = 1;
  var x = 0;
  var y = 0;

  while((markBit & bit) == 0) {
    bit = bit << 1;
    x++;
    if(x > 2) {
      x = 0;
      y++;
    }
  }

  xBoard = xBoard | bit;
  drawX(x,y);
}


function clickHandler(event) {

  var x = Math.floor((event.clientX - canvas.offsetLeft) / (width/ 3));
  var y = Math.floor((event.clientY - canvas.offsetTop) / (height/ 3));

  var bit = (1 << x + (y * 3));

  if (isEmpty(xBoard, oBoard, bit)) {

    markBit(bit, 'X');

  } else {
    alert ('That grid is already taken');
  }
}

function init(canvasID) {

  canvas = document.getElementById(canvasID);
  context = canvas.getContext('2d');

  width = canvas.width;
  height = canvas.height;

  canvas.addEventListener('click', clickHandler);

  drawBoard();
}
```

If you refresh your web page now, you should be able to click on any of the grids and place an X mark in the grid, as shown in Figure 7–4.

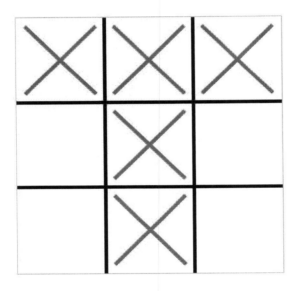

Figure 7–4. *Tic-tac-toe game board with X marks*

The X mark is calculated using an offset pixel to start and end, with diagonal lines. This could just as easily (perhaps more so) be implemented using an image marker of some type. However, for our purposes here, I use the drawing facilities in canvas to show off some of the drawing capabilities.

Adding Some Intelligence

Right now, the game is not that compelling inasmuch as all a player can do is place a mark on the game. We could just alternate between X player and O player marks, but the player is just playing himself or herself and will lose interest quickly. What we need to make this game a bit more engaging is an algorithm to make a computer opponent that evaluates the game board and plays a "best" move.

Because this is a relatively small grid, and computers are fast, we can write an algorithm that walks through each grid, checking for a "win," or whether that grid has the best ratio for a win. The way this will work is by precalculating the different win states (there are eight combinations possible for a win). The code needs to look at each possible move on the board, and calculate a "best" move, either to block the opponent, or win. The code then simulates placing a tile in each of the available spaces, choosing the best position for the move and drawing the tile there, as in Listing 7–7.

Listing 7–7. *Tic-Tac-Toe Artificial Intelligence*

```
function checkWinner(board) {
  var winState = false;

    if (
      ((board | 0x1C0) === board) ||
      ((board | 0x38 ) === board) ||
      ((board | 0x7) === board) ||
      ((board | 0x124) === board) ||
      ((board | 0x92) === board) ||
      ((board | 0x49) === board) ||
      ((board | 0x111) === board) ||
      ((board | 0x54) === board)){
      winState = true;
  }

  return winState;
}

function calculateRatio(oBoard, xBoard, player, bit, ratio) {
  var best;

  if(player === 'O') {
    oBoard = oBoard | bit;
  } else {
    xBoard = xBoard | bit;
  }

  if(checkWinner(oBoard)) {
    ratio *= 1.1;
    best = ratio;
  } else if (checkWinner(xBoard)) {
    ratio *= 0.7;
    best = ratio;
  } else {
    best = 0;
    ratio *= 0.6;

    for(var iter = 0; iter < 9; iter++) {
      if(isEmpty(xBoard, oBoard, 1 << iter)) {
        var newPlayer = player == 'O' ? 'X' : 'O';
        var newRatio = calculateRatio(oBoard, xBoard, newPlayer, 1 << iter, ratio);
```

```
            if(best === 0 || best < newRatio) {
              best = newRatio;
            }
          }
        }
      }
    }

    return best;
}

function simulate(oBoard, xBoard) {

  var ratio = 0;

  var bit = 0;
  for (var i= 0; i < 9; i++) {

    var checkBit = 1 << i;

    if (isEmpty(xBoard, oBoard, checkBit)) {

      if (checkWinner(oBoard | checkBit)) {
        bit = checkBit;
        break;
      } else if (checkWinner(xBoard | checkBit)) {
        bit = checkBit;
      }
    }
  }

  if (bit === 0) {
    for (var i= 0; i < 9; i++) {
      var checkBit = 1 << i;

      if (isEmpty(xBoard, oBoard, checkBit)) {
        var result = calculateRatio(oBoard, xBoard, 'X', 0, 1);
        if (ratio === 0 || ratio < result) {
          ratio = result;
          bit = checkBit;
        }
      }
    }
  }
  return bit;
}
```

OK, that was a lot of code, and I made heavy use of bit shifts and bit operators, as well as a programming structure called *recursion* in the calculateRatio() function. Recursion in programming is a handy feature that allows you to define a function and then call it from within the function text. In the case here, we keep calculating a ratio for the best move until we find the best move to make. By simulating all the possible moves by the computer and the player, we develop an artificial intelligence where the game has a consistent strategy for selecting which grid to choose for its play in the game.

With the calculations for choosing a best move, we now need to draw the mark on the <canvas>, and start/restart the game. See Listing 7–8.

Listing 7–8. *Evaluate Answers and Draw Guess on the Board.*

```
function restart() {
  incrementScores();
  context.clearRect(0, 0, width, height);
  xBoard = 0;
  oBoard = 0;
  drawBoard();
}

function checkTie() {
  var tie = false;

  if((xBoard | oBoard) === 0x1FF) {
    alert('We tied...');
    restart();
    tie = true;
  }
  return tie;
}

function play(){
  var bestPlay = simulate(oBoard, xBoard);
  markBit(bestPlay, 'O');
}

function drawO(x, y) {
  context.beginPath();

  context.strokStyle = '#0000ff';
  context.lineWidth = 10;

  var offsetX = (width / 3) * 0.1;
  var offsetY = (height / 3) * 0.1;

  var beginX = x * (width / 3) + offsetX;
  var beginY = y * (height / 3) + offsetY;

  var endX = (x + 1) * (width / 3) - offsetX * 2;
  var endY = (y + 1) * (height / 3) - offsetY * 2;

  context.arc(
    beginX + ((endX - beginX) / 2),
    beginY + ((endY - beginY) / 2),
    (endX - beginX) / 2 ,
    0,
    Math.PI * 2,
    true
  );

  context.stroke();
  context.closePath();

}

function clickHandler(event) {

  var x = Math.floor((event.clientX - canvas.offsetLeft) / (width / 3));
```

```
var y = Math.floor((event.clientY - canvas.offsetTop) / (height / 3));

var bit = (1 << x + (y * 3));

if (isEmpty(xBoard, oBoard, bit)) {

  markBit(bit, 'X');

  if (!checkTie()) {
    if (checkWinner(xBoard)) {

      alert('You Win!!');

      score.win++;

      restart();

    } else {

      play();
      if (!checkTie()) {

        if (checkWinner(oBoard)) {
          alert('You Lost!!');
          score.lost++;
          restart();
        }
      }
    }
  }
}
}
```

The O mark is drawn with an arc in much the same way the X mark is created, with a beginning and ending X and Y location. This is not a *real* letter, just a mark, so any two shapes would work nicely here. See Figure 7–5.

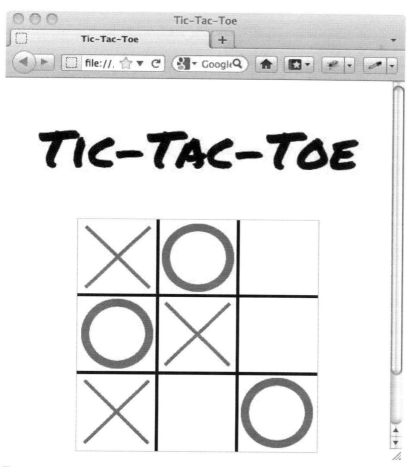

Figure 7–5. *Tic-tac-toe game board with X marks*

Going Further

After you play around with this for a while, you may find that you want to keep score, or have a slightly more sophisticated "You Won/Lost/Tied" message than a JavaScript alert box; you may even want to add sounds for each of the players. That is just what we build in this section.

Scoreboard

For the scoreboard, we can create a structure to keep track of our wins and losses, as in Listing 7–9.

Listing 7–9. *Score Object*

```
var score = {
  win: 0,
  lost: 0,
  tie: 0
};
```

You will find yourself needing to interact with other components on a web page quite often, so we add the scores (and update) them on a DOM element. To do this, we need to add a function to update elements in our DOM when the restart function is called, as in Listing 7–10.

Listing 7–10. *Incrementing Scores*

```
function incrementScores() {
  document.getElementById('wins').innerHTML = score.win;
  document.getElementById('losses').innerHTML = score.lost;
  document.getElementById('ties').innerHTML = score.tie;
}

function restart() {
  incrementScores();
  context.clearRect (0, 0, width , height);
  xBoard = 0;
  oBoard = 0;
  drawBoard();
}
```

We can add Listing 7–11 to your HTML page to display the scores:

Listing 7–11. *Displaying Scores*

```
<div id="scores">
    <ul>
        <li><strong>Wins:</strong> <span id="wins">0</span></li>
        <li><strong>Losses:</strong> <span id="losses">0</span></li>
        <li><strong>Ties:</strong> <span id="ties">0</span>
    </ul>
</div>
```

Now when you play the game, you will have a score at the bottom of the page, as shown in Figure 7–6.

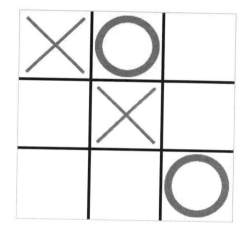

- **Wins:** 4
- **Losses:** 1
- **Ties** 2

Figure 7–6. *Tic-tac-toe game with scoreboard*

Sound

For the sound, I spent some time looking at the OpenGameArt.org site and came across some public domain clicks by Paulius Jurgelevičius (`http://opengameart.org/content/click-sounds6`). I am using `click_sound_1` as my xSound, and `click_sound_4` as my oSound. As in the previous chapter, these need to be converted to wav format for more browser support. For my purposes, I converted the files with Audacity and named them xSound.wav and oSound.wav in my `sounds` directory. I added two variables to hold references to the `audio` tags in the DOM as in the last chapter, and reused the `loadResources` function. See Listing 7–12.

Listing 7–12. *Adding Sound*

```
var xSound;
var oSound;

function loadResources () {
  xSound = document.createElement("audio");
  document.body.appendChild(xSound);
  xSound.setAttribute('src', 'sounds/xSound.wav');

  oSound = document.createElement("audio");
  document.body.appendChild(oSound);
  oSound.setAttribute('src', 'sounds/oSound.wav');
}
```

The last thing to do is to call the loadResources() function from the init function, as in Listing 7–13.

Listing 7–13. *Calling loadResources()*

```
function init(canvasID) {

  canvas = document.getElementById(canvasID);
  context = canvas.getContext('2d');

  width = canvas.width;
  height = canvas.height;


  canvas.addEventListener('click', clickHandler);

  drawBoard();

  loadResources();
}
```

Now that the entire file is working together, when you play the game, you should hear sounds when each marker is played. Just for clarification, the entire script should now look like that shown in Listing 7–14.

Listing 7–14. *Code for Tic-Tac-Toe Game*

```
var canvas;
var context;
var width;
var height;

var xBoard = 0;
var oBoard = 0;
var begin = true;

var xSound;
var oSound;

var score = {
  win: 0,
  lost: 0,
  tie: 0
};
```

```javascript
function loadResources() {
  xSound = document.createElement('audio');
  document.body.appendChild(xSound);
  xSound.setAttribute('src', 'sounds/xSound.wav');

  oSound = document.createElement('audio');
  document.body.appendChild(oSound);
  oSound.setAttribute('src', 'sounds/oSound.wav');

}

function incrementScores() {
  document.getElementById('wins').innerHTML = score.win;
  document.getElementById('losses').innerHTML = score.lost;
  document.getElementById('ties').innerHTML = score.tie;
}

function drawBoard() {

  context.beginPath();

  context.strokeStyle = 'black';
  context.lineWidth = 4;

  var vLine1 = Math.round(width / 3);
  var vLine2 = Math.round(vLine1 * 2);

  var hLine1 = Math.round(height / 3);
  var hLine2 = Math.round(hLine1 * 2);

  context.moveTo(vLine1, 0);
  context.lineTo(vLine1, height);

  context.moveTo(vLine2, 0);
  context.lineTo(vLine2, height);

  context.moveTo(0, hLine1);
  context.lineTo(width, hLine1);

  context.moveTo(0, hLine2);
  context.lineTo(width, hLine2);

  context.stroke();
  context.closePath();

}

function isEmpty(xBoard, oBoard, bit) {
  return (((xBoard & bit) === 0) && ((oBoard & bit) === 0));
}

function drawX(x, y) {
  context.beginPath();

  context.strokeStyle = '#ff0000';
  context.lineWidth = 4;
```

```
    var offsetX = (width / 3) * 0.1;
    var offsetY = (height / 3) * 0.1;

    var beginX = x * (width / 3) + offsetX;
    var beginY = y * (height / 3) + offsetY;

    var endX = (x + 1) * (width / 3) - offsetX;
    var endY = (y + 1) * (height / 3) - offsetY;

    context.moveTo(beginX, beginY);
    context.lineTo(endX, endY);

    context.moveTo(beginX, endY);
    context.lineTo(endX, beginY);

    context.stroke();
    context.closePath();

    xSound.play();
}

function drawO(x, y) {

    context.beginPath();

    context.strokStyle = '#0000ff';
    context.lineWidth = 10;

    var offsetX = (width / 3) * 0.1;
    var offsetY = (height / 3) * 0.1;

    var beginX = x * (width / 3) + offsetX;
    var beginY = y * (height / 3) + offsetY;

    var endX = (x + 1) * (width / 3) - offsetX;
    var endY = (y + 1) * (height / 3) - offsetY;

    context.arc(
      beginX + ((endX - beginX) / 2),
      beginY + ((endY - beginY) / 2),
      (endX - beginX) / 2 ,
      0,
      Math.PI * 2,
      true
    );

    context.stroke();
    context.closePath();

    oSound.play();

}

function restart() {
    incrementScores();
    context.clearRect(0, 0, width, height);
```

```
    xBoard = 0;
    oBoard = 0;
    drawBoard();
}

function checkTie() {
  var tie = false;

  if ((xBoard | oBoard) === 0x1FF) {
    alert('We tied...');
    score.tie++;
    restart();
    tie = true;
  }
  return tie;
}

function markBit(bitMask, player) {
  var bit = 1;
  var x = 0;
  var y = 0;

  while ((bitMask & bit) === 0) {
    bit = bit << 1;
    x++;
    if (x > 2) {
      x = 0;
      y++;
    }
  }

  if (player === 'O') {
    oBoard = oBoard | bit;
    drawO(x, y);
  } else {
    xBoard = xBoard | bit;
    drawX(x, y);
  }
}


function checkWinner(board) {
  var winState = false;

    if (
      ((board | 0x1C0) === board) ||
      ((board | 0x38) === board) ||
      ((board | 0x7) === board) ||
      ((board | 0x124) === board) ||
      ((board | 0x92) === board) ||
      ((board | 0x49) === board) ||
      ((board | 0x111) === board) ||
      ((board | 0x54) === board)) {
      winState = true;
    }

  return winState;
```

```
  }

  function calculateRatio(oBoard, xBoard, player, bit, ratio) {
    var best;

    if (player === 'O') {
      oBoard = oBoard | bit;
    } else {
      xBoard = xBoard | bit;
    }

    if (checkWinner(oBoard)) {
      ratio *= 1.1;
      best = ratio;
    } else if (checkWinner(xBoard)) {
      ratio *= 0.7;
      best = ratio;
    } else {
      best = 0;
      ratio *= 0.6;

      for (var iter = 0; iter < 9; iter++) {
        if (isEmpty(xBoard, oBoard, 1 << iter)) {
          var newPlayer = player === 'O' ? 'X' : 'O';
          var newRatio = calculateRatio(oBoard, xBoard, newPlayer, 1 << iter, ratio);

          if (best === 0 || best < newRatio) {
            best = newRatio;
          }
        }
      }
    }
    return best;
  }

  function simulate(oBoard, xBoard) {

    var ratio = 0;

    var bit = 0;
    var checkbit;

    for (var i = 0; i < 9; i++) {

      checkBit = 1 << i;

      if (isEmpty(xBoard, oBoard, checkBit)) {

        if (checkWinner(oBoard | checkBit)) {
          bit = checkBit;
          break;
        } else if (checkWinner(xBoard | checkBit)) {
          bit = checkBit;
        }
      }
    }
```

```
    if (bit === 0) {
      for (var j = 0; j < 9; j++) {
        checkBit = 1 << j;

        if (isEmpty(xBoard, oBoard, checkBit)) {
          var result = calculateRatio(oBoard, xBoard, 'X', 0, 1);
          if (ratio === 0 || ratio < result) {
            ratio = result;
            bit = checkBit;
          }
        }
      }
    }
    return bit;
}

function play() {
  var bestPlay = simulate(oBoard, xBoard);
  markBit(bestPlay, 'O');
}

function clickHandler(event) {

  var x = Math.floor((event.clientX - canvas.offsetLeft) / (width / 3));
  var y = Math.floor((event.clientY - canvas.offsetTop) / (height / 3));

  var bit = (1 << x + (y * 3));

  if (isEmpty(xBoard, oBoard, bit)) {

    markBit(bit, 'X');

    if (!checkTie()) {
      if (checkWinner(xBoard)) {

        alert('You Win!!');

        score.win++;

        restart();

      } else {

        play();
        if (!checkTie()) {

          if (checkWinner(oBoard)) {
            alert('You Lost!!');
            score.lost++;
            restart();
          }
        }
      }
    }
  }
}
```

```
function init(canvasID) {

  canvas = document.getElementById(canvasID);
  context = canvas.getContext('2d');

  width = canvas.width;
  height = canvas.height;

  canvas.addEventListener('click', clickHandler);

  drawBoard();

  loadResources();
}
```

Next Steps

Now that the game functions and all the components are on the page, you can really start working on the look and feel of your page. The styles for the scoreboard could be on a single line, and centered directly under the board. You could remove the gray border from around the canvas element, and add a nice texture background to the entire page to give it a finished look.

Summary

This chapter talked about mechanics that work in the social gaming arena. How you go about designing your game play to encourage people to come back and play your game on a regular basis is your special sauce, but some winning recipes include random progression, asynchronous play, and a reward system that allows you to earn new perks in the game, either through game play or purchase (or both).

One of the mainstays of the social gaming genre is the minigame, and in this chapter we worked through the development of the Tic-Tac-Toe game. This game introduced some new concepts, namely the use of artificial intelligence to enhance game play, as well as using bitmasks to optimize performance.

So far this book has spent a lot of time talking about different aspects of HTML5 game development, going over the fundamentals and techniques that you will use developing games. In the next chapter, I shift gears and start discussing the Facebook Platform as it pertains to game development. There are a number of APIs and services supported by Facebook that will help you easily integrate your game application into the Facebook ecosphere.

Chapter 8

Introducing the Facebook Platform

When I first started writing the *Facebook API Developer's Guide* back in 2007, I was contending with two big issues. First, the documentation for everything was spotty at best. The engineers at Facebook had put up a wiki, which at the time was mostly just an outline naming the different methods available. The real reason for this was the second issue I had to deal with, the application programming interface (API) was changing on an almost weekly basis. In fact, large portions of the example code I wrote for that book had to be scrapped as different pieces of the API were significantly changed, or worse, silently dropped.

Over the last five years, Facebook has continued to make improvements to the API, and major changes to how you access different information has slowed greatly, and it is much easier to keep up with changes. This chapter focuses on how you can use the Facebook API to interact with the platform, use the tools Facebook provides, and develop a simple application that utilizes these techniques.

You may find it odd that in a book about writing games for the Facebook platform that it is not until Chapter 8 that there is much discussion of Facebook. Developing any browser-based game is difficult, and where you will spend the majority of your development cycles. The engineers at Facebook have spent a great deal of time and effort creating a set of APIs that allows you to enrich your application on their platform without it feeling like a burden. They have some APIs specifically useful for game development (e.g., achievements, scores, etc.), and this chapter introduces you to some of the basics of how the platform works.

The Facebook Development Platform

When Facebook first rolled out, it was a relatively simple web application for sharing information. The site was intended for college students, and for the first several years of its existence you had to have an email address that ended with "edu" to create a

Facebook account. As the service began to grow, Facebook engineers began to think of ways that they could allow developers outside the organization to use their platform to help engage more users.

What came out of this project was the first Facebook API. At the time, Facebook users numbered around 22 million, and the engineers needed to develop a system that allowed developers access to pieces of their users' information, isolate server security issues, not dictate a workflow for developers, and yet integrate all of the code into the existing Facebook look-and-feel.

What the engineers designed was a rather ingenious mix of technologies that allowed them to separate the online user interface of Facebook from your code. At the time, Facebook was touting this as a platform, where there was a superset of HTML (FBML) that you could use on your pages to display content, a REST API for retrieving information about users for your application, an SQL-style language to help you filter information, a JavaScript library to give you access to Facebook "actions," and a set of programming languages.

The way Facebook solved the issue of not serving everyone's code was by setting up a proxy on their servers that would pass requests and views of your application back and forth among your users.

Every time a Facebook user interacted with your application, their request was passed to your server (see Figure 8–1). From your server, you would then ask for information through the REST API from Facebook's servers, and with that response object, you constructed your FBML template to send back to Facebook. The Facebook servers would process the FBML on the page and convert it to HTML to deliver to your user.

On top of this language stack that Facebook was developing, the company continued to expand developer access to its underlying technologies. There were storage APIs for uploading images to Facebook, and even a database system for your data that Facebook would host. As these capabilities grew, so did the complexity of the API. Facebook also needed to find better ways to communicate with the developers who were building client libraries for various Facebook APIs that were not in the list of officially supported languages. These community contributions allowed developers in languages such as ColdFusion, Ruby, or Flash to work with the Facebook APIs, but major changes, and additions, meant that these libraries were difficult (at best) to maintain.

Realizing that a large audience of their users could easily get confused with the growing list of parameterized REST functions, intermediate languages, and a growing realization that mobile computing is here to stay, Facebook began working on rebranding their development platform to make some of the more commonly used things far easier to implement, and change the way in which developers talk about using the Facebook platform.

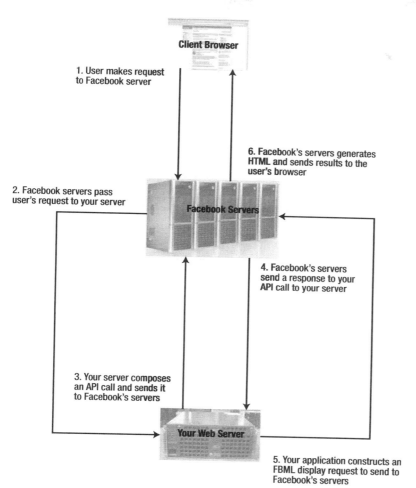

Figure 8–1. *Basic Facebook application request architecture*

When you visit the Facebook Developers pages these days, you will notice that the language centers on the concept of social connections. In fact, when you visit the Developers website (http://developers.facebook.com), you are funneled to information for integrating Facebook features for websites, building mobile, and building applications.

Creating Applications with the Facebook Platform

Before you can do much with the Facebook platform, you first need to "register" a new application (assuming you have a Facebook account). You access this form from the Facebook Developers site (https://developers.facebook.com/apps). Simply click on the "Create New App" button and fill out at least an "App Display Name" in the modal window. You do not need to fill out the App Namespace option at this point, but only a short unique name (no punctuation allowed) that allows you to create custom elements when using the Open Graph protocol (discussed later). For now, you can just click on the Continue button (see Figure 8–2).

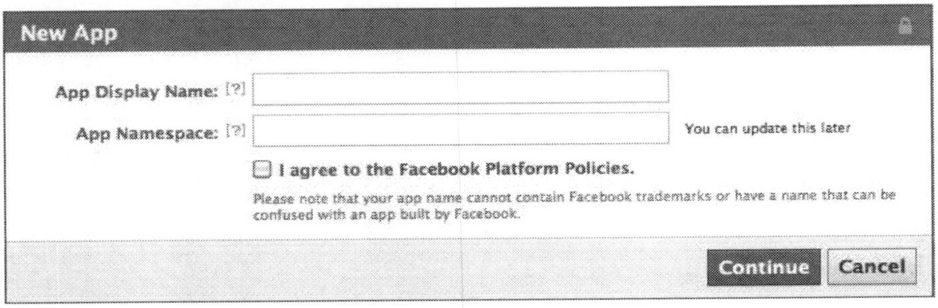

Figure 8–2. *New Facebook Platform application form*

In case you chose to just tick the "Agree to the Policies," here are some of the highlights, abridged for brevity:

- Don't break the law.
- Don't collect usernames or passwords.
- Only request the data you need.
- Users have to be able to "log out" of your application.
- Don't play media without a user clicking on something.
- Games that are apps on Facebook (or mobile web) must use Facebook Credits as their sole source of payment.
- Apps on Facebook cannot integrate with or redirect to a competitor's site.
- There is a list of Ad providers that you can use in your application (https://developers.facebook.com/adproviders/); make sure you do not use a provider that is not on the list if you are going to include ads!

> **NOTE:** Facebook Platform Policies change on a regular basis, and you really need to be aware of what the current revision states that you are agreeing to for the privilege of running your application on Facebook's Platform with its users. It is worth making a habit of heading to their policy site (https://developers.facebook.com/policy/) and reading over any changes that may have occurred to people.

You will be asked to fill out a reCaptcha (to help verify you are a human), and you may also be asked to verify your Facebook account. Facebook allows you to either verify by mobile phone where they will SMS you a special code, or by verifying a credit card.

Once you have created the basic application (Figure 8–3), Facebook creates an application ID and a secret that is specific for your application, as well as a page to fill out more information about your application. The application ID is used to identify your project on the Facebook graph, and the application secret is a hash generated specifically for your application, which allows Facebook to authenticate that it is your specific application making the API requests. It may help to think of these values as your application's username and password to interact with the Facebook API servers.

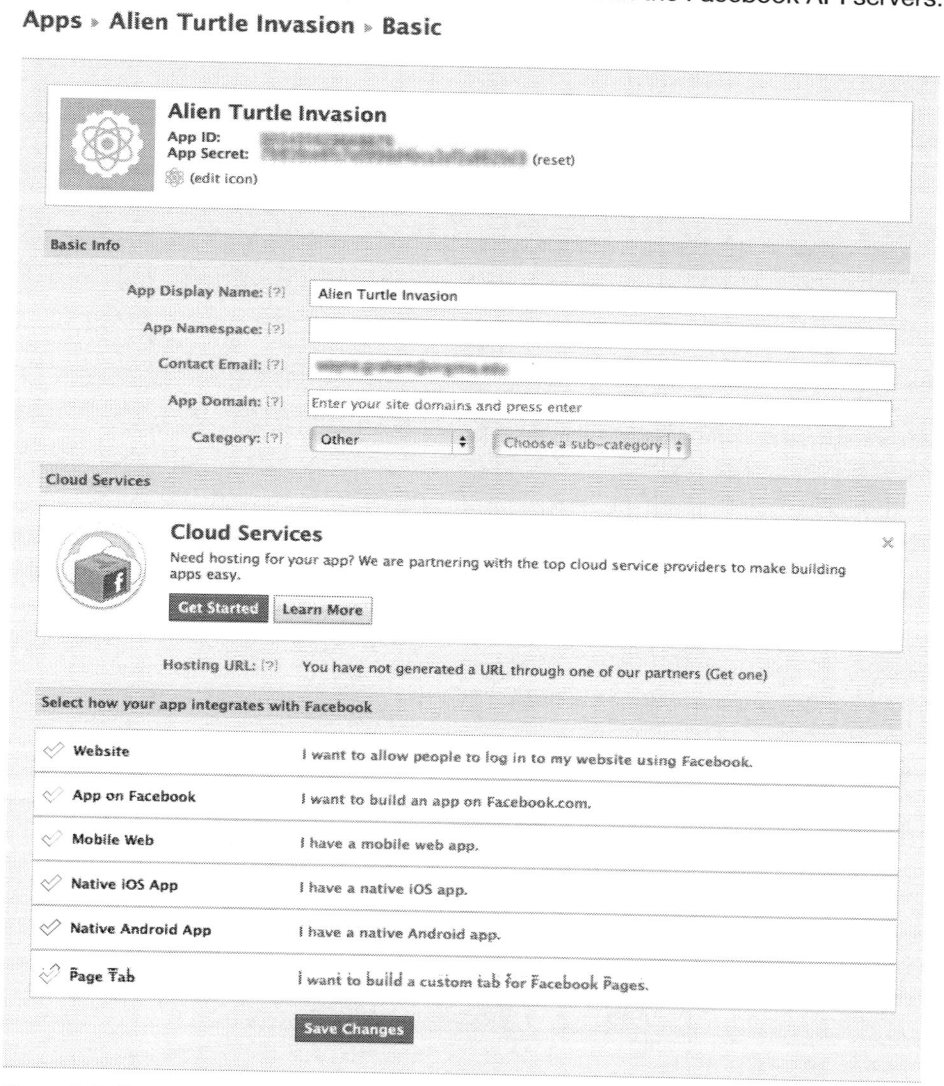

Apps ▸ Alien Turtle Invasion ▸ Basic

Figure 8–3. *New Facebook Platform application*

There are a few sections to this page, so let's take a look at what some of this means.

Basic Info

- App Display Name: The name of your application that will be displayed to users. There is some validation for this so that no one else has the application name (you will see an error that Facebook trademarks are prohibited).

- App Namespace: This is for when you are using the Open Graph API or creating Canvas pages. If you have dealt with the Facebook platform before, this was previously referred to as the `canvas_name`. If not, Facebook allows you to declare a namespace that allows you to qualify elements and attributes for use in FBML views.

- Contact Email: The primary email for communications regarding your application. You may want to set up a separate email (that you will need to check) to separate email from Facebook regarding your application. This is an important (required) piece of information should something happen and you need to be contacted.

- App Domain: If you are using Facebook for authentication, you need to let Facebook know where this traffic is originating. This is a wildcard, so `example.com` will enable authentication traffic from all subdomains (`*.example.com`) for `example.com`. If you need to restrain this, be more specific (e.g., `game.example.com`).

- Category: Assuming you are reading this book to create a game, select "Games" from the category select box. You can further categorize your game (see Chapter 1, "Game Genres" if you need some assistance categorizing your game).

Cloud Services

Facebook recently partnered with Heroku, a cloud hosting company. In my day job, I do quite a bit of development with Ruby and have been using Heroku for several years now. The great thing about Heroku is that they allow you to deploy small applications to their services for free. In the development stages, this has been a real boost to my productivity. I can whip up a quick proof-of-concept and show it to someone quickly and reliably.

Although Heroku started as a company hosting Ruby projects (Sinatra and Rails), they have greatly expanded their offerings to include Node.js, Clojure, Java, Python, and Scala. You do need to have Ruby installed on your local system with the languages package manager (gem), but the workflow makes deployment dead simple.

I am a fan of Heroku, but you may find you have needs that are not met by Heroku, especially if you have your own infrastructure to which you will be deploying your software. Although the form layout leads you to believe you need an account, do not worry, this is not actually necessary to set up, but it does speed setting up a new project a bit, at least for the development stage.

Facebook Integration

Lastly, you need to tell Facebook how your application will be interacting with the platform. Your application may have multiple integration points and this section allows you to manage all of the information in a single location.

- Website: The Site URL is the URL of your site using Facebook data. This is the only URL Facebook will redirect users to after authenticating, so make sure this URL is correct.

- App on Facebook: At the time of the writing of this book, there are two options for defining the Canvas URL: a secure and "normal" URL. If you have the option, use a *secure* URL (https) for your canvas URL as new policies will be enforcing the use of secure connections for web traffic. I get into more detail on how to use the Facebook canvas (not to be confused with the HTML 5 canvas element).

- Mobile Web: Like the Website section, but a URL for the content you have optimized for mobile browsing. If you are using advanced techniques in your main website to do media queries for mobile devices, this may be the same URL that you list as the Site URL in the Website section.

- Native iOS App: Facebook has a software development kit (SDK) in Objective-C for iOS development. If you are doing iOS development, you will need to provide Facebook with your bundle ID, iPhone and iPad App Store ID, if you will be using Single Sign On (SSO), as well as a list of scheme suffixes if you are using the same Facebook App ID across multiple iOS applications. Developing applications for Facebook on iOS is a book in itself, however, if this is an area that interests you, you will need to join the iOS Developer program (http://developer.apple.com/) to develop any code for iPads/iPods and submit iOS apps to iTunes.

- Native Android App: For applications on the Android platform (Facebook does provide an official SDK for developing Java applications on Android), you need to provide Facebook with your public key. You can read more information about developing for the Android platform at http://developer.android.com/.

■ Page Tab: You may find that you want to allow your application to be used within the context of a Facebook Page (e.g., create a link on the page). These are called Page Tabs on a Facebook Page, and you configure how this will work on the Page Tab section of the developer app. You will need to provide a Tab Name (the label for your tab), a secure URL (https) for the content page for your application, and a link for admins of your application to edit the page tabs.

Software Development Kits

Once you have registered your application with Facebook, it is time to start working with the data. Although Facebook leverages PHP for its development, they provide "official" SDKs for C#, JavaScript, PHP, Python, iOS (Objective C), and Android (Java). There are also numerous unsupported libraries for just about any language imaginable. You have a lot of options when picking a server-side language to work with; if you are already comfortable with a server-side language, using the various SDKs should be simple.

Your First Facebook Application

As I mentioned earlier in this chapter, Heroku has partnered with Facebook to provide a hosting platform. Here I show you how to get a new application up and running easily using Heroku, Git, and the PHP SDK.

Prerequisites

In order to work with Heroku, you will need to have a few things installed on your computer. Essentially you need a few software components installed and the instructions for each vary slightly depending on what platform you are running. The two requirements for using Heroku are `git` and the `heroku` Ruby gem.

Git

Git is an open source distributed version control system for source code. I cover more about using Git in the next chapter, but for the impatient, Git allows you to create a workflow for managing your source code. For our purposes here, Git will not only allow us to keep track of changes to our sources, but also is the primary method of deploying the software to Heroku.

You can download the Git client for both Windows and OS X from the Git project page (http://git-scm.com/). There is one caveat for Windows: during the installer process, when you get to the screen for "Adjusting your PATH environment," I generally suggest changing the option to run Git from the Windows Command Prompt. Git on Windows runs a couple of different ways, and sometimes I forget to launch the special Git prompt (Git Bash) and this saves me the frustration of launching another application should I accidentally launch the Command Prompt. See Figure 8–4.

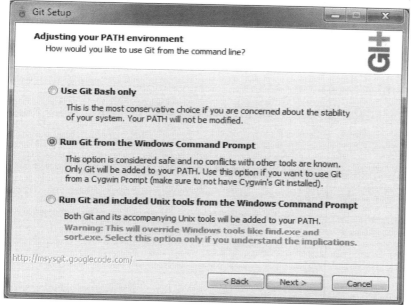

Figure 8–4. *RubyInstaller for Windows*

All of the other defaults for the Windows installer should be fine.

For OS X users, just download the disk image that is appropriate for your OS version, and click through the installer.

> **NOTE:** If you use OS X, I highly recommend using a package manager for installing open source software packages such as Git. I use a manager called Homebrew (`http://mxcl.github.com/homebrew/`), which does an excellent job of managing this software, as well as upgrades. Other package managers you may want to try are fink and macports, although each of these has its own headaches associated with it.

Ruby

When Heroku first came on the scene, it was built to allow developers to quickly deploy Ruby-based projects. Ruby packages its libraries in a system called Gems, and Heroku used this to develop a command-line tool to manage your Heroku deployments. You do not need Ruby for anything other than installing the Heroku management application.

Windows

The easiest way to get Ruby and RubyGems installed on your computer is with the RubyInstaller (`http://rubyinstaller.org/`) project. Just grab the latest release, and walk through the installer. By default, the installer puts the interpreter in the root partition (C:), and when prompted, be sure to check the box next to the option "Add Ruby executables to your PATH" (see Figure 8–5). This will allow you to use Ruby (and the heroku tool) from the Command Prompt. If you do not click this, you will only be able to use the terminal that the installer adds with Ruby (**Start ➤ All Programs ➤ Ruby version ➤ Start Command Prompt with Ruby**).

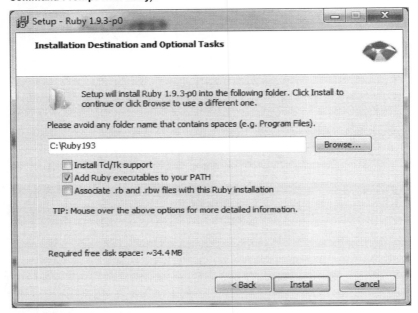

Figure 8–5. *RubyInstaller for Windows*

OS X

OS X ships with Ruby preinstalled, so you are done! You can install an updated version, but it is unnecessary for our purposes here.

> **NOTE:** If you are doing much with Ruby, you may want to investigate either RVM (http://beginrescueend.com/) or rbenv (https://github.com/sstephenson/rbenv) to manage your Ruby environment. These tools allow you to switch quickly between versions of Ruby, as well as segregate collections of gems. I personally use RVM (it allows me to script some things such as pull the latest revisions from my Github project when I enter a project directory), however, both of these are great tools that will make it simpler to test your code against multiple versions of Ruby.

Heroku

Heroku allows you to control your Heroku applications through a command-line client it provides through Ruby's rubygems package manager. As long as you have a recent version of Ruby, which includes the rubygems manager, this is a simple matter of typing a single command on the Terminal or Command Prompt.

In Windows, you can enter either the Command Prompt (**Start ➤ All Programs ➤ Accessories ➤ Command Prompt**) or the Ruby Command Prompt. To install the gem, simply issue the gem command to install the heroku gem, as shown in Listing 8–1.

Listing 8–1. *Installing the Heroku Gem (Windows)*

```
gem install heroku
```

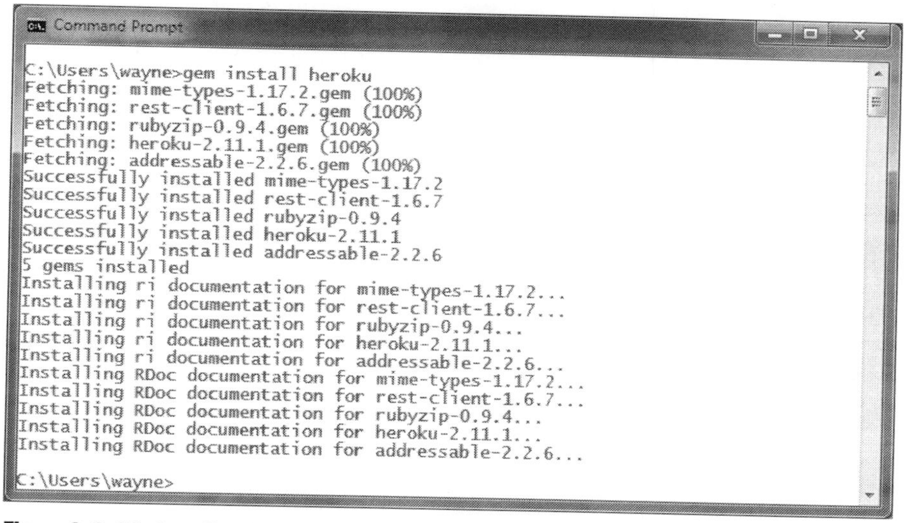

```
Command Prompt

C:\Users\wayne>gem install heroku
Fetching: mime-types-1.17.2.gem (100%)
Fetching: rest-client-1.6.7.gem (100%)
Fetching: rubyzip-0.9.4.gem (100%)
Fetching: heroku-2.11.1.gem (100%)
Fetching: addressable-2.2.6.gem (100%)
Successfully installed mime-types-1.17.2
Successfully installed rest-client-1.6.7
Successfully installed rubyzip-0.9.4
Successfully installed heroku-2.11.1
Successfully installed addressable-2.2.6
5 gems installed
Installing ri documentation for mime-types-1.17.2...
Installing ri documentation for rest-client-1.6.7...
Installing ri documentation for rubyzip-0.9.4...
Installing ri documentation for heroku-2.11.1...
Installing ri documentation for addressable-2.2.6...
Installing RDoc documentation for mime-types-1.17.2...
Installing RDoc documentation for rest-client-1.6.7...
Installing RDoc documentation for rubyzip-0.9.4...
Installing RDoc documentation for heroku-2.11.1...
Installing RDoc documentation for addressable-2.2.6...

C:\Users\wayne>
```

Figure 8–6. *Windows Heroku gem installation output*

This will take a few moments, and will install the necessary libraries, as well as documentation (see Figure 8–6).

In OS X, simply open the Terminal and install the gem, as shown in Listing 8–2.

Listing 8–2. *Installing the Heroku Gem (OS X)*

```
sudo gem install heroku
```

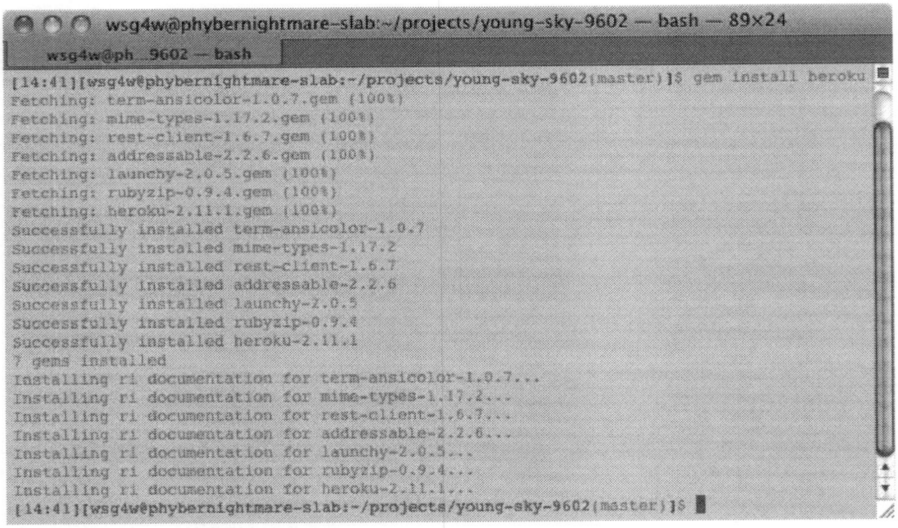

Figure 8–7. *OS X Heroku gem output*

If everything goes as expected (Figure 8–7), you should see that the rubygems package manager has installed the heroku gem library for you, as well as its library dependencies and documentation.

You can test out the heroku command-line tool by typing "heroku" at the prompt. Without any additional parameters the tool returns a help screen listing the various commands that you can issue to the Heroku platform. See Figure 8–8.

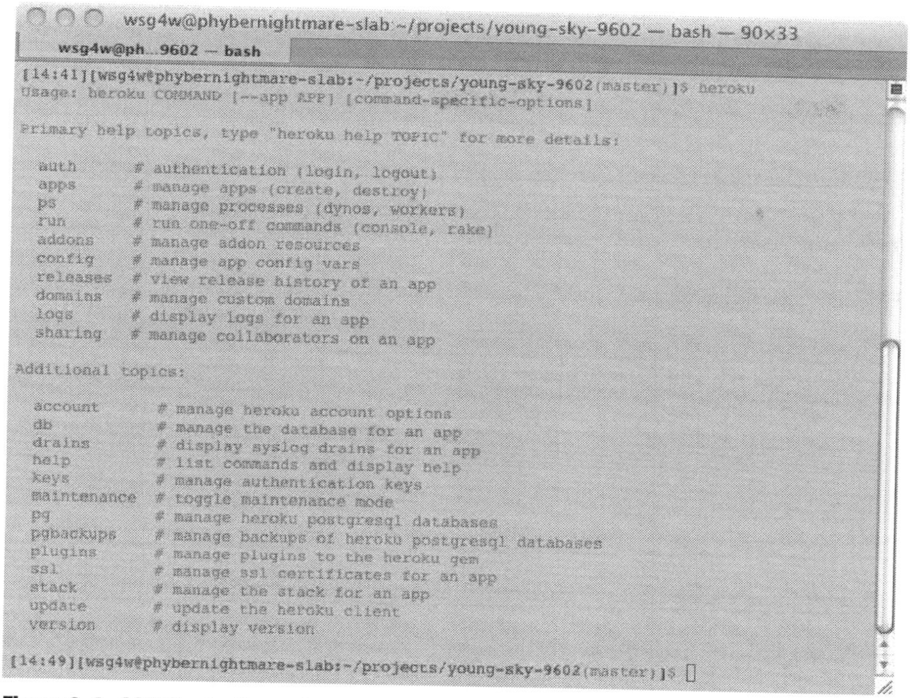

Figure 8–8. *OS X Heroku Gem output*

At this point, we have everything we need on our client machine to start creating a simple Facebook application.

Facebook Setup

Head to the Facebook Developer App and create a new application. You can name this anything you wish, but this will be in the list of applications you manage. After you get through the reCaptcha screen, you should be redirected to a screen that contains the basic information about your application; your app id, secret, and your application's name, as well as your email address should be filled out. Look under the Cloud Services section, and you should see a prompt that "You have not generated a URL through one of our partners (Get one)." See Figure 8–9.

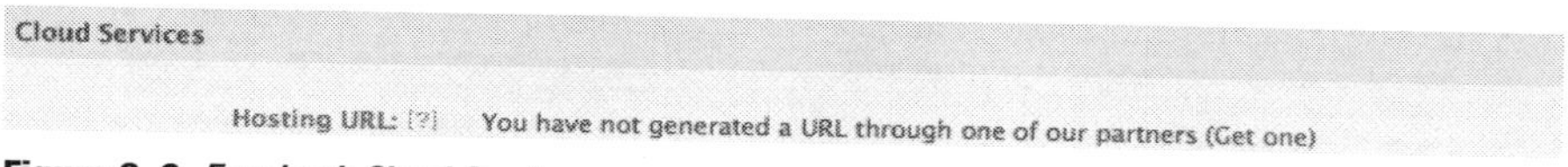

Figure 8–9. *Facebook Cloud Services*

When you click on the "Get One" link, a modal window will launch to walk you through the process of setting up a project on Heroku.

The first screen prompts you for the programming environment you want to use and the email address that you use for Heroku (if you do not have one, they will automatically create one for you with the email address you provide; see Figure 8–10). The default is to create a new PHP application, and will be what I show throughout the book for the server-side examples. If you select another language, you may not be able to follow some of the examples later on.

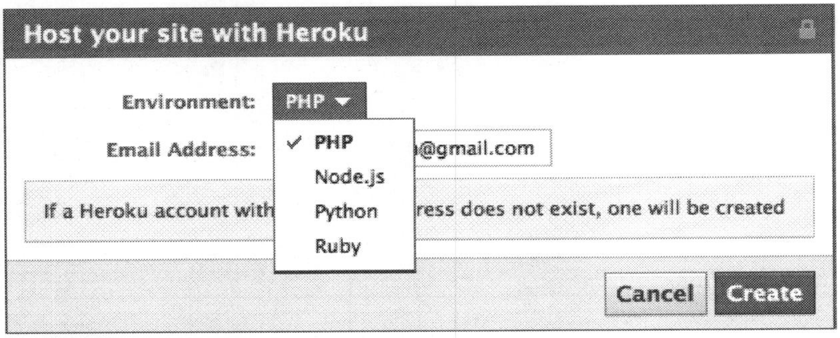

Host your site with Heroku

Environment: PHP ▼

✓ PHP

Email Address: @gmail.com

Node.js

Python

If a Heroku account with

ress does not exist, one will be created

Ruby

Cancel   Create

Figure 8–10. *Facebook Heroku setup*

As soon as the application has been created on Heroku, you will see a confirmation dialog, as in Figure 8–11, that has a link to take to you the application.

Success

Your app has been set up! Your provider will send you an email with instructions for how to manage your app environment

Go to app

Figure 8–11. *Facebook Heroku confirmation*

If you visit the application at this point, you will be prompted to log on to the site (Figure 8–12).

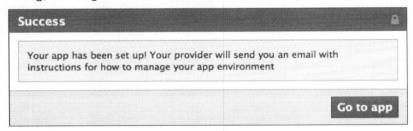

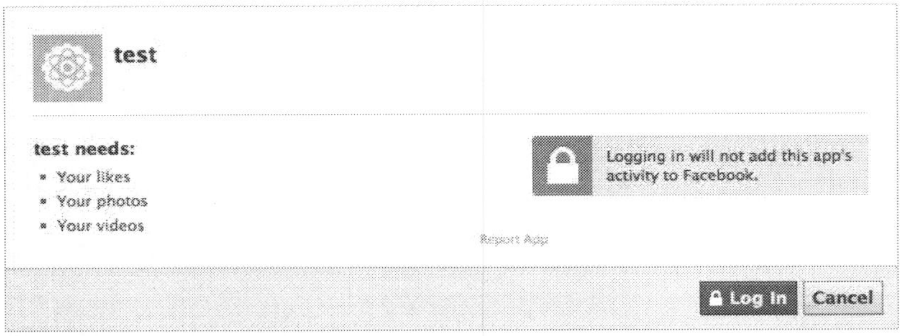

test

test needs:

* Your likes
* Your photos
* Your videos

Logging in will not add this app's activity to Facebook.

Report App

🔒 Log In   Cancel

Figure 8–12. *Facebook login*

Once logged in, you will be redirected to the URL that Heroku generated for you with some dummy code for a basic Facebook website (see Figure 8–13).

Figure 8–13. *Basic Facebook application*

You now have a functioning webpage using the Facebook platform! In the next sections I talk about how to use some of the capabilities of the platform to develop a slightly more sophisticated application. However, you may notice that you have some crazy generated URL (e.g., falling-water-5412). You can rename this on the Heroku admin interface if you log on to the Heroku site (http://www.heroku.com/) and click on the crazy URL prefix for your site (e.g., falling-water-5412; see Figure 8–14). Pick a saner name (e.g., facebook-test-app) and update the URL.

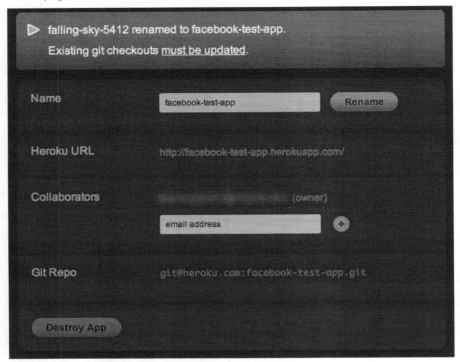

Figure 8–14. *Heroku Rename Application screen*

If you update the URL for your application on Heroku, also be sure to update the URL for your application in the Facebook Developer App or your application will stop working!

You can now clone the application to your local machine to work on the code. Simply open the Terminal or Command prompt, and check out the Git repository URL (git clone <your git repo url>. For my application, I would type the following, shown in Listing 8–3.

Listing 8–3. *Cloning the Heroku Application.*

```
git clone git@heroku.com:facebook-test-app.git
```

If this is the first time you are accessing a Git repository, there is a little setup you need to do, but the Heroku command-line tool will walk you through the process. Git uses encryption keys to identify users, and you need to generate a key pair (a public and private key).

On Windows, you will need to make sure you launch the Git Bash prompt (**Start ➤ All Programs ➤ Git ➤ Git Bash**). If you are using OS X, you only need to open the Terminal. To generate the key-pair, issue the `ssh-keygen` command, as in Listing 8–4.

Listing 8–4. *Generating SSH Keys.*

```
$ ssh-keygen
```

This will walk you through generating the keys you need to work with Git.

You can let Heroku know about the keys for your computer by issuing the `keys:add` command, as in Listing 8–5.

Listing 8–5. *Add your SSH Key to Heroku.*

```
heroku keys:add
```

This will upload your keys to Heroku. However, you may find that these instructions do not work (especially if you are a Windows user). If you find yourself spinning your wheels trying to get this working, head over to Heroku's Windows documentation (`http://devcenter.heroku.com/articles/windows`) to read the latest on setting up Heroku in a Windows environment.

So what did all of this do? Well, Heroku cloned a working application for you, added environmental variables that store your Facebook App ID and secret, and gave you some well-commented boilerplate PHP code, as well as a free hosting environment where you can deploy by simply pushing your code with Git!

Using the Graph API

Now that we have a bit of code to work with, it is actually time to take a look at one of the main components of the Facebook platform, the Graph API. To understand the rhetoric behind a lot of the terminology used, it is worth pointing out that a lot of the concepts are based on the discipline of *graph theory*. Graph theory is a branch of discrete mathematics that studies the mathematics of relationship modeling between objects in a collection. These objects are referred to as *nodes* (or vertices) with connections between them named *edges*.

With the Graph API, the nodes are the photos, events, comments, friends, tags, groups, pages: anything to which Facebook gives developers access. Each of these objects has a unique identifier that allows you to fetch that specific node from the graph. The edges of the graphs are your friends, likes, or notes; all of the different ways in which Facebook allows you to express connections to others.

The Graph API responds to requests in the JSON format (a key value pair) with the requested information. Depending on privacy policies, you may have more (but generally less) information than you may like, but understanding how the Graph API works will let you function effectively to integrate Facebook in just about any application. Because everything in the graph has a unique ID, it makes working with the API exceptionally simple for elements where you know the ID. The base Graph URL is `https://graph.facebook.com/`, and when you know the ID of an object (or node), you just pass the ID.

As an example, look up the `App ID` that you created in the previous section. Mine was 172642759492488; if I pass that to the Graph API, I construct a URL that looks like that shown in Listing 8–6.

Listing 8–6. *Facebook Graph Request.*

```
https://graph.facebook.com/172642759492488
```

The resulting JSON response will provide you with all of the information that a Facebook user has allowed you access to in the response (Listing 8–7).

Listing 8–7. *Unauthenticated Facebook Graph API Response.*

```
{
  "id": "172642759492488",
  "name": "test",
  "link": "http://www.facebook.com/apps/application.php?id=172642759492488"
  "icon_url": "https://static.ak.fbcdn.net/rsrc.php/v1/yT/r/4QVMqOjUhcd.gif",
  "logo_url": "https://static.ak.fbcdn.net/rsrc.php/v1/yq/r/IobSBNz4FuT.gif"
}
```

Depending on the language you are running on your server, you can then use these data to build up information for a web page. Notice in the response from Facebook's servers, that you are provided with the application id, the name you entered in the platform administration, and a direct link to the application, as well as an icon and logo URL. These are the default data returned by Facebook if you have not authenticated in Facebook. If you have (and you are looking at the application you created), you will see two additional pieces of information, the weekly active user and monthly active user counts as shown in Listing 8–8..

Listing 8–8. *Authenticated Facebook Graph API Response.*

```
{
  "id": "172642759492488",
  "name": "test",
  "link": "http://www.facebook.com/apps/application.php?id=172642759492488"
  "icon_url": "https://static.ak.fbcdn.net/rsrc.php/v1/yT/r/4QVMqOjUhcd.gif",
  "logo_url": "https://static.ak.fbcdn.net/rsrc.php/v1/yq/r/IobSBNz4FuT.gif"
  "weekly_active_users": "256",
  "montly_active_users": "512"
}
```

So what are the objects in the graph to which you have access? Think of the objects in Facebook: users, pages, events, groups, and so on. Here you still need to know the ID or name of the resource, but you can explore some of these different types with the following URLs.

- User: The publicly available information for a user (e.g., `https://graph.facebook.com/7608007`)

- Page: `https://graph.facebook.com/scholarslab`

- Event: `https://graph.facebook.com/140518646048907`

- Groups: `https://graph.facebook.com/2389758281`

- Apps: `https://graph.facebook.com/FarmVille`

- Photos: `https://graph.facebook.com/172349956185394`

- Profile Picture: `https://graph.facebook.com/phybernightmare/picture`

- Videos: `https://graph.facebook.com/817129783203`

This is not an exhaustive list of the objects in the graph, but it gives you an idea of what is available to you as actual objects. Because these are all objects in the graph sense, there are connections that you can make through *relationships* (edges, if you want to use the mathematical terminology). See Listings 8–9 and 8–10.

> **NOTE:** You can retrieve extra metadata about the graph object by appending an additional URL parameter (metadata) and setting it to true (e.g., `https://graph.facebook.com/phybernightmare?metadata=1`). This is useful if you need to look at the different relationships (edges) a user has, as well as the permissions those relationships require at the application level.

Listing 8–9. *Basic Facebook Graph Request (Without Metadata Parameter)*

```
{
    "id": "7608007",
    "name": "Wayne Graham",
    "first_name": "Wayne",
    "last_name": "Graham",
    "link": "https://www.facebook.com/phybernightmare",
    "username": "phybernightmare",
    "gender": "male",
    "locale": "en_US"
}
```

Listing 8–10. *Abridged Facebook Graph Request with Metadata Parameter*

```
{
    "id": "7608007",
    "name": "Wayne Graham",
    "first_name": "Wayne",
    "last_name": "Graham",
    "link": "https://www.facebook.com/phybernightmare",
    "username": "phybernightmare",
    "gender": "male",
    "locale": "en_US",
    "metadata": {
        "connections": {
            "home": "https://graph.facebook.com/phybernightmare/home",
            "feed": "https://graph.facebook.com/phybernightmare/feed",
            "friends": "https://graph.facebook.com/phybernightmare/friends",
            "mutualfriends": "https://graph.facebook.com/phybernightmare/mutualfriends",
            "family": https://graph.facebook.com/phybernightmare/family
...
```

```
    },
    "fields": [
    {
      "name": "id",
      "description": "The user's Facebook ID. No `access_token` required. `string`."
    },
    {
      "name": "name",
      "description": "The user's full name. No `access_token` required. `string`."
    },
    {
      "name": "first_name",
      "description": "The user's first name. No `access_token` required. `string`."
    },
    {
      "name": "middle_name",
      "description": "The user's middle name. No `access_token` required.  `string`."
    },
    {
      "name": "last_name",
      "description": "The user's last name. No `access_token` required.  `string`."
    }
...
    ]
  },
  "type": "user"
}
```

The way the Graph API structures these is much the same way that a graph works. An object has connections, which have endpoints. You will need an access token (authentication) to access the information on these relationships, but these edges allow you access to elements including a user's friends, news feed, photo tags, and the like. The basic URL structure for these objects is shown in Listing 8–11.

Listing 8–11. *Facebook Graph API URL Structure*

```
https://graph.facebook.com/me/<object>
```

If you had an application that needed to display the events that the current authenticated user was attending, you would simply construct the call in Listing 8–12 to the Graph.

Listing 8–12. *Facebook Graph API Events Request*

```
https://graph.facebook.com/me/events
```

These links will not work if you paste them into the browser as the authentication for the user (using Facebook's OAuth service) needs to take place, but will work in the PHP code you have created with your PHP application on Heroku. If you are authenticated and make this request, Facebook will return a structure of your events that includes the event name, start time, end time, the event description, location, and privacy type (for the event), as shown in Listing 8–13.

Listing 8–13. *Facebook Event Response*

```
{

    "id": "185180044923536",
    "owner": {
        "name": "Wayne Graham",
        "id": "7608007"
    },
    "name": "Book Launch",
    "description": "Join me as I celebrate the launch of my new book, Beginning↵
Facebook Game Apps Development.",
    "start_time": "2012-03-26T12:00:00",
    "end_time": "2012-03-26T15:00:00",
    "privacy": "OPEN",
    "updated_time": "2012-02-04T20:40:15+0000"

}
```

> **NOTE:** The "me" in Facebook is important. The events in your life and how your friends interact with you in the online setting are what make Facebook, well, Facebook. Throughout the different Facebook APIs, "me" refers to the authenticated user accessing some piece of information, with different relationship edges spanning from that node. As an application developer, just think of "me" as an easier way to code the current user's ID into your application.

When reading the Facebook documentation, you will see that the objects you have access to are listed first with the fields of information to which you have access. Below that are the different connection types that object can have, along with the permissions that the user will need to grant to your application to ensure your code works properly. It takes a little getting used to, but having all of the objects, and knowing there are more "connections" available for that object (as well as hyperlinks to that object's documentation) is very convenient.

Status message

Core Concepts › Graph API › Status message

A status message on a user's wall as represented in the Graph API.

Example

A status message on the Facebook Page:

https://graph.facebook.com/10150224661566729

Fields

A Status message has the following fields.

Name	Description	Permissions	Returns
id	The status message ID	Requires access_token	string
from	The user who posted the message	Requires access_token	object containing id and name fields
message	The status message content	Requires access_token	string
updated_time	The time the message was published	Requires access_token	string containing ISO-8601 date-time
type	The object type which is set to status	Requires access_token	string

Update

You cannot edit any of the fields in the status message object.

Connections

A Status message has the following connections.

Figure 8–15. *Facebook API documentation*

There are many different objects that you have access to in the Graph API. Be sure to check the Facebook Developer's documentation (http://developers.facebook.com/docs/reference/api/) to ensure you are reading the latest version (see Figure 8–15).

Searching

The Graph API has a nice facility for searching objects. This API allows you to look up public (and private, with appropriate privileges) information in the graph. Search can be "everything" (default) or specific objects. To search, simply append search to the Graph API URL and pass a query URL parameter as in Listing 8–14.

Listing 8–14. *Basic Facebook Search*

```
https://graph.facebook.com/search?q=wayne
```

Because this is unspecified as to what to search for, you will get back links for anything that matches "wayne:" any concerts, videos, images, anything. If you were searching for me, well, this may not be the best way to go about doing it. Inasmuch as I am a user, you would want to limit the search to "user." See Listing 8–15.

Listing 8–15. *Facebook Type Search*

```
https://graph.facebook.com/search?q=wayne&type=user
```

Again, the type is just the object used to limit the search. For example, you could imagine someone, say at work, or even traveling, who might want to see where he might be able to get a cup of coffee. If you know your location (in longitude, latitude co-ordinates), you can pass this information to do geospatial searches. Say you want to search for coffee near your location; you simply pass in a location, and a maximum search radius. When I am in my office, I would generate a request that looks like that shown in Listing 8–16.

Listing 8–16. *Search Facebook Graph for Coffee Shops*

```
https://graph.facebook.com/search?q=coffee&type=place&center=↵
38.037783,-78.505297&distance=1000
```

This produces a response with the results of a query of *coffee* of object type *place* with a centroid (a fancy word for center point) from my browser, and limits results to a radius of 1,000 meters from my location. Because this a geospatial search, you also get some extra information, the latitude and longitude of the result as in Listing 8–17.

Listing 8–17. *Facebook Search Response*

```
{
  "data": [
  {
    "name": "Para Coffee",
      "category": "Restaurant/cafe",
      "location": {
        "street": "19 Elliewood Ave",
        "city": "Charlottesville",
        "state": "VA",
        "country": "United States",
        "zip": "22903",
        "latitude": 38.036498035768,
        "longitude": -78.500138726843
    },
      "id": "179370586840"
```

```
  },
  {
    "name": "The Prism Coffeehouse",
    "category": "Concert venue",
    "location": {
      "street": "Formerly 214 Rugby Road, Now Memories and Archives",
      "city": "Charlottesville",
      "state": "VA",
      "country": "United States",
      "latitude": 38.0407,
      "longitude": -78.50107
    },
    "id": "200545076623316"
  },
  {
    "name": "Mermaid Express Coffee Shop",
    "category": "Restaurant/cafe",
    "location": {
      "street": "2121 Ivy Road",
      "city": "Charlottesville",
      "state": "VA",
      "country": "United States",
      "zip": "22903",
      "latitude": 38.04293,
      "longitude": -78.51211
    },
    "id": "223612891001370"
  },
  {
    "name": "Common Grounds Coffee",
    "category": "Restaurant/cafe",
    "location": {
      "street": "480 Rugby Road",
      "city": "Charlottesville",
      "state": "VA",
      "country": "United States",
      "zip": "22903",
      "latitude": 38.04066,
      "longitude": -78.50109
    },
    "id": "202680563086598"
  }
  ],
    "paging": {
      "next": "https://graph.facebook.com/search?q=coffee&type=place&center↵
=38.037783\u00252C-78.505297&distance=1000&format=json&limit=25&offset↵
=25&__after_id=202680563086598"
    }
}
```

Using this geospatial searching capability in conjunction with the HTML5 Geolocation API gives you a very rich toolset to interact with the users of your application. This actually just takes a few lines of JavaScript to do. If you open the project Heroku generated for you and open the index.php page, you will see a lot of PHP code before hitting the actual HTML. Since jQuery is already included on the index.php page, all we need to do is add the logic to access the Geolocation API. Just after the line that loads jQuery (line 107), we need to add a check to see if the browser supports the geolocation API, then get data back on coffee houses near our location. On a new line (after the jQuery call), add Listing 8–18 to search Facebook for coffee shops near your current position:

Listing 8–18. *Search Facebook Graph for Coffee Shops*

```
<script>
$(document).ready(function() {
  if (navigator.geolocation) {
    navigator.geolocation.getCurrentPosition(
      function(position) {
      var centroid = position.coords.latitude + ',' + position.coords.longitude;
      var url = 'https://graph.facebook.com/search';
      var coffeeShops = [];

      $.getJSON(
        url,
        {
          q: 'coffee',
          type: 'place',
          center: centroid,
          access_token: '<?php echo $facebook->getAccessToken();?>',
          distance: 1000 // search radius in meters
        },

        function(data) {
          $.each(data.data, function(i, item) {
            coffeeShops.push('<li id="' + item.id + '">' + item.name + '</li>');
          });

          $('<ul/>', {
            'class': 'coffee-list',
            html: coffeeShops.join('')
          }).prependTo('body');

        }); // getJSON
    }); // getCurrentPosition
  } // navigator check
});
</script>
```

This script is not sophisticated, just meant to show off a simple interaction with an HTML 5 browser API and the Facebook Graph API. All it does is check if the browser supports the Geolocation API, then constructs a URL to pull in the JSON response for places with the term coffee within 1000 meters of your location from the Facebook Search API using the jQuery functions. If the getJSON method returns data, it creates a new ordered list with the elements from the API and pushes those on the HTML body element. If everything went well, you should see a list of nearby coffee shops if you reload the index page for your application, as in Figure 8–16.

Para Coffee
The Prism Coffeehouse
Mermaid Express Coffee Shop
Common Grounds Coffee

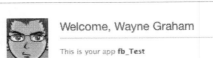

Welcome, Wayne Graham

This is your app **fb_Test**

Figure 8–16. *Local coffee shops returned from geospatial place search in the Graph API*

Facebook Query Language

Facebook developed its own language that allows you to select user information from an API called Facebook Query Language (FQL). If you have worked with SQL before, FQL will be quite familiar to you. When the Facebook platform first launched, there were a total of nine tables that you could query to return information for your application, now there are 60! If you find yourself making multiple Graph API calls in order to get the data needed for your application, the FQL API will help you decrease the number of calls to the Graph API and get you the specific information you need for your application.

At a very simple level, you select elements from the object table. For example, if you want to query the Event table for information about a particular event, you may write something along the lines of Listing 8–20 as your FQL:

Listing 8–19. *FQL for Selecting Elements*

```
SELECT name, host, pic_small FROM event WHERE eid = 140518646048907
```

You can pass this string directly to the FQL API as a query. The above URL would look like that in Listing 8–21.

Listing 8–20. *URL Containing FQL Query*

```
https://graph.facebook.com/fql?q=SELECT name, host, pic_small FROM event WHERE eid =↵
140518646048907
```

And the response from Facebook (Listing 8–22) would produce a JSON object with the name, host, and URL to the small, resized picture used for the event.

Listing 8–21. *Facebook's Response to FQL Query*

```
{
  "data": [
    {
      "name": "Speaker Series: Joe Gilbert",
      "host": "Scholars' Lab",
      "pic_small": "https://fbcdn-profile-a.akamaihd.net/hprofile-ak-snc4/↵
372800_140518646048907_541019902_t.jpg"
    }
  ]
}
```

Unlike SQL, FQL only allows you to perform simple selects of data from a single table. Although you can only query a single table at a time, you can pass multiple queries to the API in order to retrieve the information you need. However, one of the really cool features in the FQL language is that it allows you to perform subqueries. You can build a query that is dependent on the data of another query to return some limiting information back to your first query. Take the code generated when you created your application on Heroku. To determine which of your friends are using the application you "wrote," the author uses the FQL query in Listing 8–23.

Listing 8–22. *FQL to Select Friends from Facebook Graph*

```
SELECT uid, name, is_app_user, pic_square FROM user WHERE uid in (SELECT uid2 FROM⏎
    friend WHERE uid1 = me()) AND is_app_user = 1
```

Because the Graph API does not include a method `friends_using_app`, you would need to make a few different requests to the Graph API, and then merge the data in the logic of your program. If you have been forced to do this in the past, you know what kind of nightmare this can become to manage. Fortunately Facebook allows you to have much cleaner code by allowing you to nest a second query (`SELECT uid2 FROM friend WHERE uid1 = me()`) in the FQL request. This second query limits the elements Facebook returns from the User table to just those who are the friends of the user requesting the information.

Once you begin to do much work with the Facebook Platform, you will find yourself using the FQL queries to get the information you need. I cover this in more detail in the next chapter, but Facebook provides a wonderful tool for testing interactions with the Facebook graph called the Graph API Explorer (Figure 8–17). This tool is invaluable for testing FQL queries, as well as constructing calls to the Graph API. You can access the tool at `https://developers.facebook.com/tools/explorer` and pass any elements that are valid for the Graph API, including FQL statements. One of the nice features of this tool is that it allows you to navigate an object's connections, as well as alerting you to the fields that the current object has available to it.

Figure 8–17. *Facebook Graph API Explorer*

Exploring the Graph with this tool is a great way to get familiar with the Graph API and knowing what kind of information is returned (and not returned) for the different objects you have available.

Facebook SDKs

You will most likely be working with the Facebook platform from a server installation for deploying your game. There are several libraries for programming environments that are developed by Facebook for PHP, Java, JavaScript, Python, and iOS. Depending on your proficiency (and the environment on which you will ultimately deploy your software), all of these libraries help you work with the Facebook Platform in ways that are natural to the way that particular language works with external web APIs.

All of the official libraries are quite good, but I did want to take a few moments to talk about Ruby. There is not currently an "official" Ruby library maintained by Facebook, and there are quite a few libraries out there. Some have not been updated to work with the new Graph API, so when evaluating gems, be sure to stay away from these. The two libraries that I have seen a lot of developers use when interacting with the Facebook Platform are mainly Koala and Mogli.

Of the two, the one I have come to like most is Koala (https://github.com/arsduo/koala). If you use the default Sinatra application that runs off Heroku, it uses *mogli* for working with Graph API. Mogli is a decent Graph client, but my critique of the library is that they attempt to hard-code every call to the API, and there are edge cases where you can potentially lose data in certain circumstances. Koala has much better documentation and rspec tests. It also has the advantage of being able to work in conjunction with the "official" JavaScript SDK to parse the OAuth cookies, giving you a lot of flexibility when working with the platform.

Setting up a Development Environment

In your work with the Facebook platform, you may find that pushing your changes to your remote server to check if a particular new feature is working can get in the way and slow down your development cycle. What you will need to do is set up a local development environment.

Depending on your operating system, you have a few different options available for running PHP on your computer. As an OS X user, I use a package named MAMP (http://www.mamp.info/) when writing PHP applications. For Windows users, there is a nice package named WampServer (http://www.wampserver.com/) which is roughly the same as the MAMP server. Once installed (see the documentation on the respective sites), you can edit your project locally without needing to deploy your code to a production server. You will need to create a new application in the Facebook Developer app, and use the loopback address your web server uses (generally 127.0.0.1) and port. For example, if you are a MAMP user, the site URL for your local development environment would be http://127.0.0.1:8888.

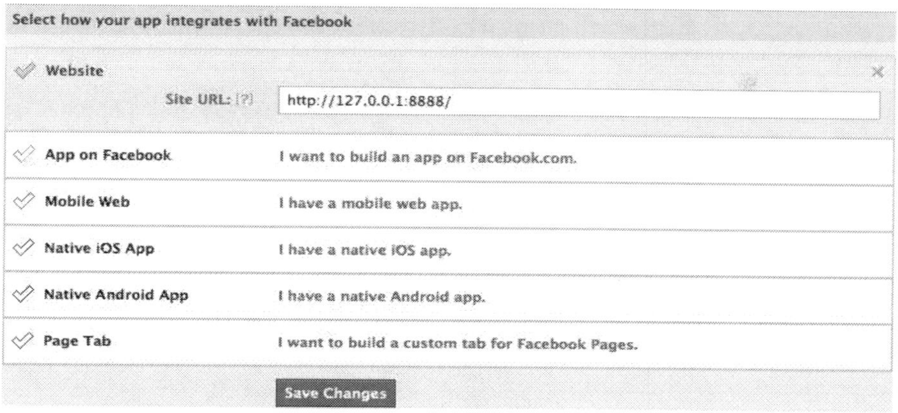

Figure 8–18. *Facebook Graph API response*

You do not need to add any cloud services (the code is running locally), but I have found that setting the app URL to a top-level directory (e.g., `http://127.0.0.1:8888/`) to mimic what Facebook sees can save a few headaches, especially if there are authentication requests (see Figure 8–18).

If you are working with Heroku, it is also a good idea to install the PostgreSQL server that Heroku utilizes to have a local instance running to debug any SQL issues that can pop up. You can download an installer package for your operating system from the PostgreSQL website (`http://www.postgresql.org/download/`) which will walk you through the installation. Another very useful tool to have for working with PostgreSQL development is pgAdmin (`http://www.pgadmin.org/`), which provides a graphical user interface (GUI) for working with the database system.

There is an edit to the Apache web server that you will need to make in order to enable the code template generated by Heroku to determine your Facebook appID and appSecret. Heroku saves these as environmental variables on the server, so you can do the same locally. In the Apache configuration file, you will need two values. In your `httpd.conf` file (see documentation that comes with your version of MAMP/WAMP), you will need to set a FACEBOOK_APP_ID and FACEBOOK_SECRET value. Find the line that defines DocumentRoot in the file, and add Listing 8–24 under it (replace the 0s with your appID and secret for the Facebook application you set to run locally):

Listing 8–23. *Set Facebook Env Variables in Apache*

```
DocumentRoot "/Applications/MAMP/htdocs"
SetEnv FACEBOOK_APP_ID 00000000000000000000
SetEnv FACEBOOK_SECRET 00000000000000000000
```

After you restart the Apache server on your local machine, your code will use the correct appID and secret for the Facebook application you set up in the Facebook Developer app to point at your local machine. The nice thing is that when you deploy your code to the Heroku server, your code will use the appropriate appID and secret for your production application.

Summary

This chapter has focused on some of the conceptual basics of working with the Facebook Platform's Graph API. It covered how the calls to this service are structured, how the platform works with your application, and the great hosting service that Heroku provides for getting you up and running with your development needs quickly.

Working with Web APIs can be challenging, but fortunately Facebook supports "official" clients for many popular languages, and there are many community-driven extensions in many other languages. One of the big things to remember if you are working with a server-side language that does not have an "official" SDK library, is to be sure that it supports the Graph API, as well as SSL, which is required for production-level applications.

In the next chapter, I go into more detail on the various tools Facebook provides for developers to debug, manage, and promote their applications. Defining how your application interacts with your users is important in attracting new users. Equally important is analyzing those who are using your application, and what content they are using. These are all tools that Facebook provides for developers, and provide invaluable information for analyzing the usage of your application.

Chapter 9

Facebook Developer Tools

Now that we have covered the very barest of basics of setting up the infrastructure for a Facebook application, I turn attention in this chapter to leveraging the Facebook platform, with special attention to their developer tools. Developing complex applications for Facebook is perhaps more difficult than other platforms because of all the moving parts. Being able to quickly determine what piece is broken, from your server code that interacts with Facebook's APIs, to issues with your JavaScript, to issues with the Facebook Platform itself, will go a long way to help you quickly determine what is going on with your application.

Developer App

The central tool that developers use to manage their applications is the Facebook Developer App. This is the central place to manage all of your applications and can be accessed at `http://developer.facebook.com/apps/`. This gateway lists all of the applications you have registered with Facebook, as well as the place to start with creating Facebook applications. We covered some of the basics of the tool in Chapter 8, but I go into more depth with several aspects of the tool in this chapter, including using the Open Graph Protocol (for adding objects to the graph), Facebook Credits (for selling virtual goods), and Insights (for managing application analytics).

Open Graph Protocol

The Open Graph protocol is a new feature that Facebook announced at the f8 Conference in 2011. Facebook announced a shift to a new interface for its users called Timeline, designed to take the elements you interact with on Facebook and tell your story. In the announcement, Mark Zuckerberg framed this shift to using your data to create a digital scrapbook of your life, allowing you to scroll back easily and see what your friends were doing, and saying, in previous years. With the shift to the Timeline interface, Facebook wanted to provide developers with a mechanism to add content to the streams. The mechanism they introduced to allow developers to integrate content into the *graph* is through leveraging a set of HTML metadata elements. This allows developers to add specific information to the head element that tells the Facebook platform how to treat your application and ultimately display on the Timeline.

The Open Graph protocol requires four pieces of information: the title that should appear in the graph, a type (e.g., game), a thumbnail, and a URL reference for your application. It is also a good idea to include a site name and a brief description of what is on the page. These are expressed through the HTML meta tags that live in the head of your HTML. See Listing 9–1.

Listing 9–1. *Example Open Graph Metadata*

```html
<!DOCTYPE HTML>
<html>
  <head>
    <meta charset="utf-8">

    <title>My Awesome Game</title>

    <meta property="og:title" content="teka-teki">
    <meta property="og:type" content="game">
    <meta property="og:url" content="http://www.yourdomain.com/game/slug">
    <meta property="og:image" content="http://www.yourdomain.com/images/timeline-
thumb.png">
    <meta property="og.site_name" content="LiquidFoot Games">
    <meta property="og:description" content="A puzzle game that creates a puzzle
        game out of your Facebook friend's photos.">
    <meta property="fb:app_id" content="[YOUR FACEBOOK APP ID]">
  </head>
  <body>
    ...
  </body>
</html>
```

The meta element in HTML takes several different attributes, and in the case of the Open Graph, we use the property and content attributes. The property attributes have a slightly off-putting syntax (e.g., og:title). This method provides context for the metadata values and is referred to as *namespace*. If you have used XHTML before, you may have seen explicit declarations for a namespace in the html element (e.g., <html xmlns:og="http://ogp.me/ns#">). However, the HTML5 specification does not have a real syntax for namespaces (this is only a feature of the XHTML specification) and you are permitted to use just a namespace without explicitly declaring the namespace.

The Open Graph Protocol at a technical level is what is known as a *resource description framework in attributes* (RDFa). This technique allows content developers to add rich metadata to their web content, and the design that was implemented in the Open Graph Protocol had goals to make the content useful outside the Facebook context. To this end, the protocol actually includes many other useful details for specific web content.

As an example of this, the IMDb.com site uses the open graph tags to describe individual titles, and actually has Graph IDs. For example, the movie *Serenity* (http://www.imdb.com/title/tt0379786/) has open graph data associated on the web page. Search engines such as Google (outside the Facebook domain) use this information to help generate result views. You see how Google parses the Open Graph data by accessing their

Rich Snippets Testing Tooll (http://www.google.com/webmasters/tools/richsnippets; see Figure 9–1) and pasting in the link to *Serenity*. You will see a familiar search result, with the rating, thumbnail, and movie description in the result.

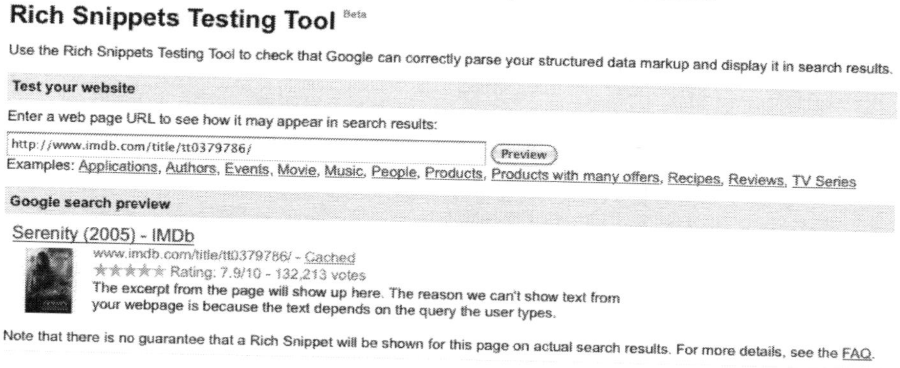

Rich Snippets Testing Tool ^{Beta}

Use the Rich Snippets Testing Tool to check that Google can correctly parse your structured data markup and display it in search results.

Test your website

Enter a web page URL to see how it may appear in search results:

`http://www.imdb.com/title/tt0379786/`   (Preview)

Examples: Applications, Authors, Events, Movie, Music, People, Products, Products with many offers, Recipes, Reviews, TV Series

Google search preview

Serenity (2005) - IMDb
www.imdb.com/title/tt0379786/ - Cached
★★★★★ Rating: 7.9/10 - 132,213 votes
The excerpt from the page will show up here. The reason we can't show text from your webpage is because the text depends on the query the user types.

Note that there is no guarantee that a Rich Snippet will be shown for this page on actual search results. For more details, see the FAQ.

Figure 9–1. *Google Rich Snippet Testing Tool*

Open Graph Types

The Open Graph protocol uses a type specification to help determine how the object you are describing will be represented. There are several broad categories that can be represented in the graph. Each `type` then can have additional metadata associated with it, which further explains the resource that is specific to that type, separated by a period. For example, if you had a site that had a song that a Facebook user could play, you could use the `type` attributes in Listing 9–2 to further describe the song.

Listing 9–2. *Example Song Open Graph Metadata*

```
<!DOCTYPE html>
<html>
  <head>
    <meta property="og:title" content="Scary Monsters and Nice Sprites">
    <meta property="og:type" content="song">
    <meta property="og:url" content="http://www.skrillex.com/music/307f76-scary-
monsters-and-nice-sprites/">
    <meta property="og:image" content="http://www.domain.com/path/to/image.png" />
    <meta property="og:locale" content="en_US">

    <meta property="fb:app_id" content="123456">

    <meta property="music:duration" content="243">
    <meta property="music:album" content="Scary Monsters and Nice Sprites">
    <meta property="music:musician" content="Skrillex">

  </head>
  <body>
    ...
  </body>
</html>
```

Notice the addition of the `music:duration`, `music:album`, and `music:musician` values in the `meta` elements. These provide Facebook with additional information describing the content on the page for use on the Timeline. When looking at the documentation, these are referred to as "verticals," referring to their vertical alignment in the code.

Facebook Types

Facebook supports a number of Open Graph object types by default. If you find there is a type to describe your content type more accurately, you can create a new namespace (e.g., your domain name would work nicely) and create a custom content type. However, this list will handle most use cases for describing the content on your page.

Activities

- activity
- sport

Businesses

- bar
- company
- cafe
- hotel
- restaurant

Groups

- cause
- sports_league
- sports_team

Organizations

- band
- government
- non_profit
- school
- university

People

- city
- country
- landmark

- state_province

Products and Entertainment

- album

- book

- drink

- food

- game

- product

- song

- movie

- tv_show

Websites

- blog

- website

- article

You can also specify your own types if there is not one that suits your needs. To do this, just choose a namespace (your domain name is a good one) and add your suffix. For instance, if I wanted to mark a page on my site as awesome, I could add the type shown in Listing 9–3 to it:

Listing 9–3. *Custom Open Graph Type Metadata*

```
<!DOCTYPE html>
<html>
  <head>
    …
    <meta property="og:type" content="liquidfoot:awesome">
```

Facebook is actually monitoring these values, and as one becomes more popular, they will add it to the list.

> **NOTE:** Types in the Open Graph protocol are designed to support real-life objects (not virtual ones). If you are describing an online news article, photo, or video on your web page, you should use the `article` type. The article will not show up on the user's Timeline, as it has no publishing rights on the Facebook platform and should be used as these are not real-world objects.

Open Graph Stories

In the previous section I covered how to add the Open Graph metadata to a web page, which is great for letting Facebook and Google know about how to handle this content. This information is also used in Facebook's Timeline interface to help tell "stories" about what you are up to online. Facebook loves metaphors, and the story metaphor follows the vision of using Facebook to create a digital scrapbook of your online social interactions (e.g., posts, likes, pictures, etc.).

In order for you, as a developer, to interact with the storyline of the Timeline, there are a few steps you need to take in order to define how an event in your application becomes a story. You configure these interactions through the Facebook Developer Application. Using the project we created in Chapter 8, we can explore how to add and customize the stories that will appear in the Facebook Timeline.

After logging in to the Facebook Developer Application, click on your application and you will see a section for Open Graph, as shown in Figure 9–2.

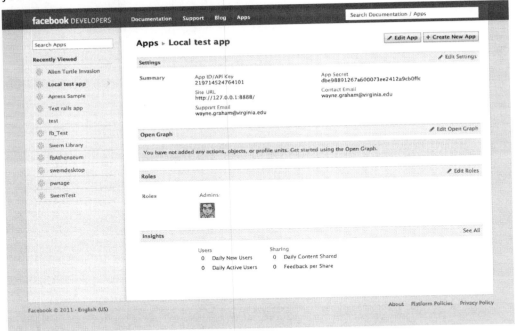

Figure 9–2. *Facebook application dashboard*

Assuming you have created a namespace for your application (your domain name is a really good one) in the *Open Graph* settings for your application, you will be able to start the story (Figure 9–3). Because we are building games for Facebook, you will fill out the sentence, "People can play a game."

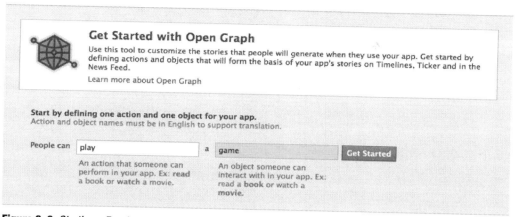

Figure 9–3. *Starting a Facebook Open Graph Story*

You are now on the screen where you can define what actions your application has so you can register them with Facebook. This is a three-step process designed to define objects (in our case "games"), actions (playing a game), and aggregations (showcasing of actions in an interesting way on Facebook).

The web form is relatively straightforward, and for the most part does not need to be edited for our purposes. Do make sure that if you are doing something clever in the use of verbs that the present and past tenses are correct, but for our purposes, the examples that "Wayne played" and "Wayne is playing" do a good job explaining what is going on. When you are happy with the screen, click "Save Changes and Next." See Figure 9–4.

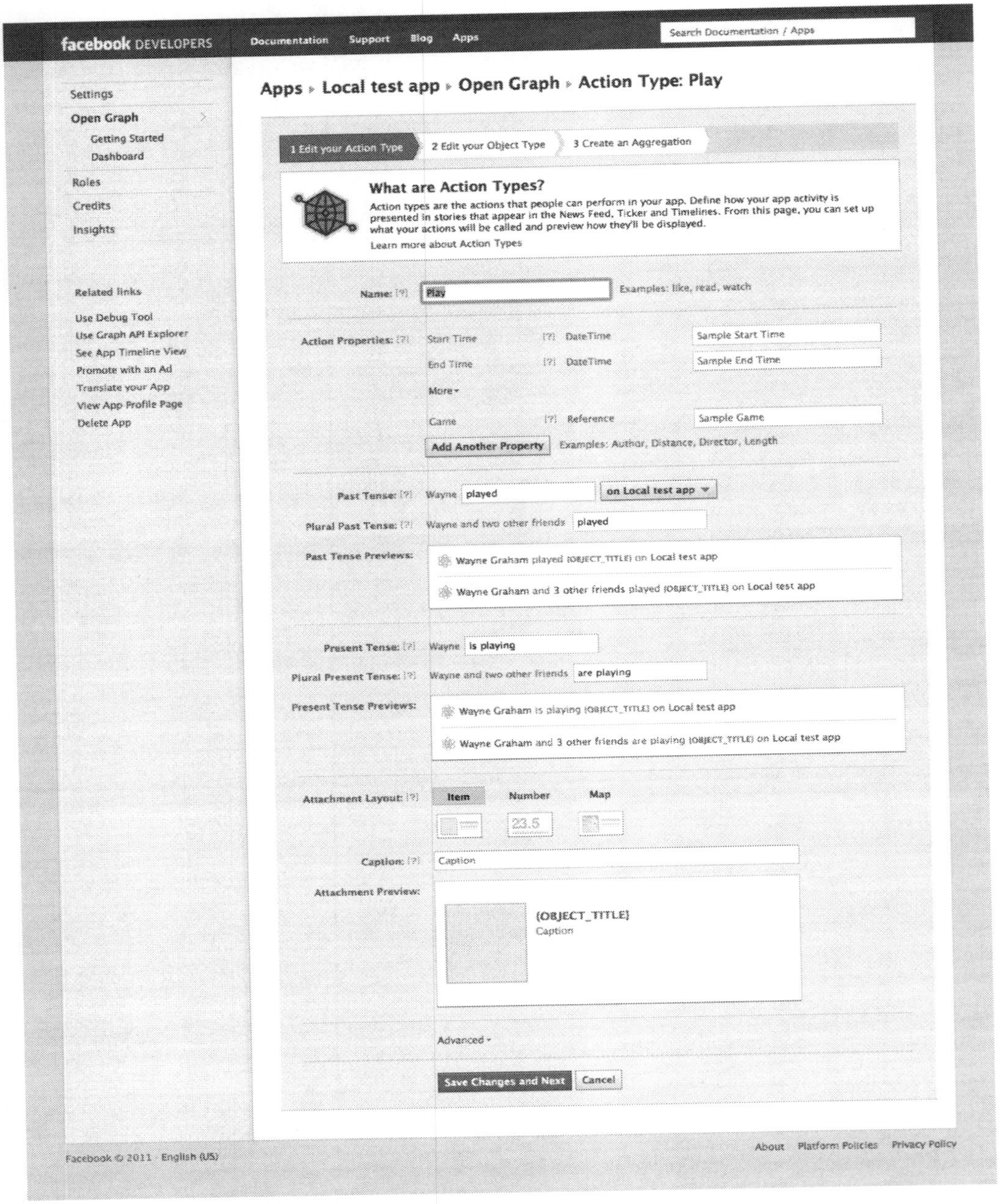

Figure 9–4. *Open Graph action configuration*

Aggregations

Aggregations let you tell Facebook how you want to showcase your content on a user's Timeline. Certain content becomes eligible to be displayed on the Timeline based on two factors:

- There are sufficient data available to generate a full story showcasing the user's action in a structured and interesting way.

- User feedback based on how users have engaged with your application, both positive (likes, commenting, and pinning) and negative (removal of the aggregation and/or the application).

> **NOTE:** You can make use of the Analytics Tool (covered later) to understand user feedback and use that information to optimize your application. Understanding how (and when) people are using your application is important for making new features (and knowing when to cut others). If you find users really like a particular feature, you can use that input to create complementary elements that more people will enjoy.

If you define several aggregations, they may appear on the Timeline as a report and are shown for each period that has activity in the Open Graph to make the viewing experience consistent (and readable). See Figure 9–5.

 Wayne Graham drank a beverage at Social Cafe.

 Iced Mocha

Like · Comment · Unfollow Post · 5 seconds ago via Social Cafe

Figure 9–5. *Simple story aggregation*

When you configure multiple aggregations, just make certain that the most important ones are listed first. For instance, users should have their high scores higher up on the list than when signing up for a new account.

For this aggregation, I used the *List* layout style and changed the *Aggregation Title* to "Games I've Played." The *Caption Lines* section allows you to use a template from the Open Graph elements, so I opted to show the game.title and the game.description to display that information on the Timeline preview, as in Figure 9–6.

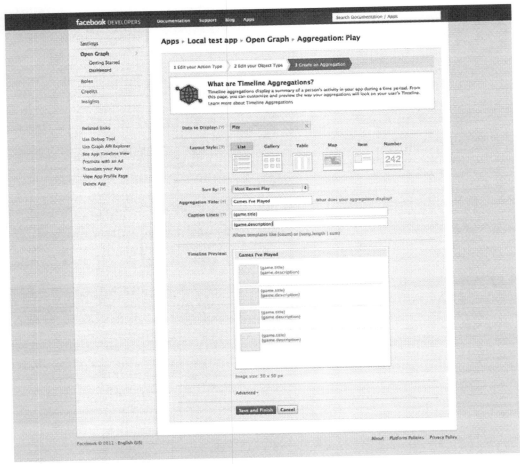

Figure 9-6. *Open Graph aggregation configuration*

Achievements

One popular option for social interactions has been the inclusion of an achievement system. From consoles (Xbox 360 and PlayStation 3) to the development in games such as *World of Warcraft*, achievements provide players with the ability to play your game in different ways. This is such a prevalent game device that Facebook implemented an achievement system in the Graph API.

The achievement system in Facebook provides you with 1,000 total points to divide into specific achievements. You can have up to 1,000 achievements (I suggest against it; your achievements need to be meaningful to game players), but the more points associated with a particular achievement, and hence increasing its rarity, will receive a higher rank in the user's Timeline. Achievements with less than 10 points will receive almost recognition. It is a good idea to have a mix of achievements that range between

10 and 50 points; 50-point achievements being difficult to achieve, 25-point achievements of medium difficulty, and 10-point achievements being easy. You could theoretically have only one achievement worth 1,000 points, but I would recommend against that. In addition, once an achievement has been earned, it cannot be revoked and a particular achievement can only be obtained once.

Each achievement needs to have its own unique URL using the Open Graph protocol metadata to describe it, as in Listing 9–4.

Listing 9–4. *Example HTML with Open Graph Metadata*

```
<!DOCTYPE HTML>
<html>
<head>
  <meta charset="utf-8">

  <title>Achievement | Exterminator</title>

  <meta property="og:type" content="game.achievement">
  <meta property="og.title" content="The Exterminator">
  <meta property="og:url" content="http://www.yourdomain.com/path/to/achievement.html">
  <meta property="og:description" content="Beat entire game in under 30 seconds">
  <meta property="og:image"
content="http://www.yourdomain.com/path/to/exterminator.png">
  <meta property="game.points" content="50">
  <meta property="fb:app_id" content="[appId]">
</head>
<body>
  <img src="images/exterminator.png" alt="The Exterminator">
</body>
</html>
```

Now that you have an example achievement, you need to tell Facebook how to tell the story. You do this by creating a new aggregation. I created a new action called Earn. See Figure 9–7.

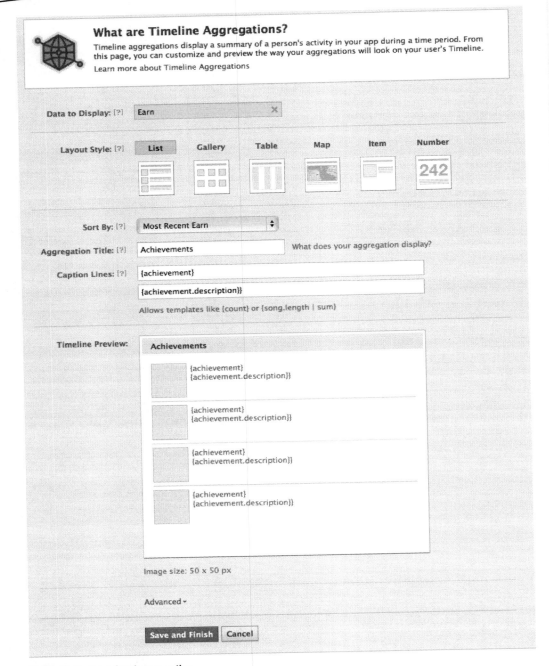

Figure 9–7. *Open Graph earn action*

Now with an achievement defined, we can preview what this will look like for users. In the Open Graph Dashboard (on the left-hand side), you will be able to edit/add to your achievement under the aggregations. As shown in Figure 9–8, I added the Game Achievement for the *Data to Display*, selected Item for the layout, then changed the *Aggregation Title* to "Achievements" and changed the caption to the {achievement} template.

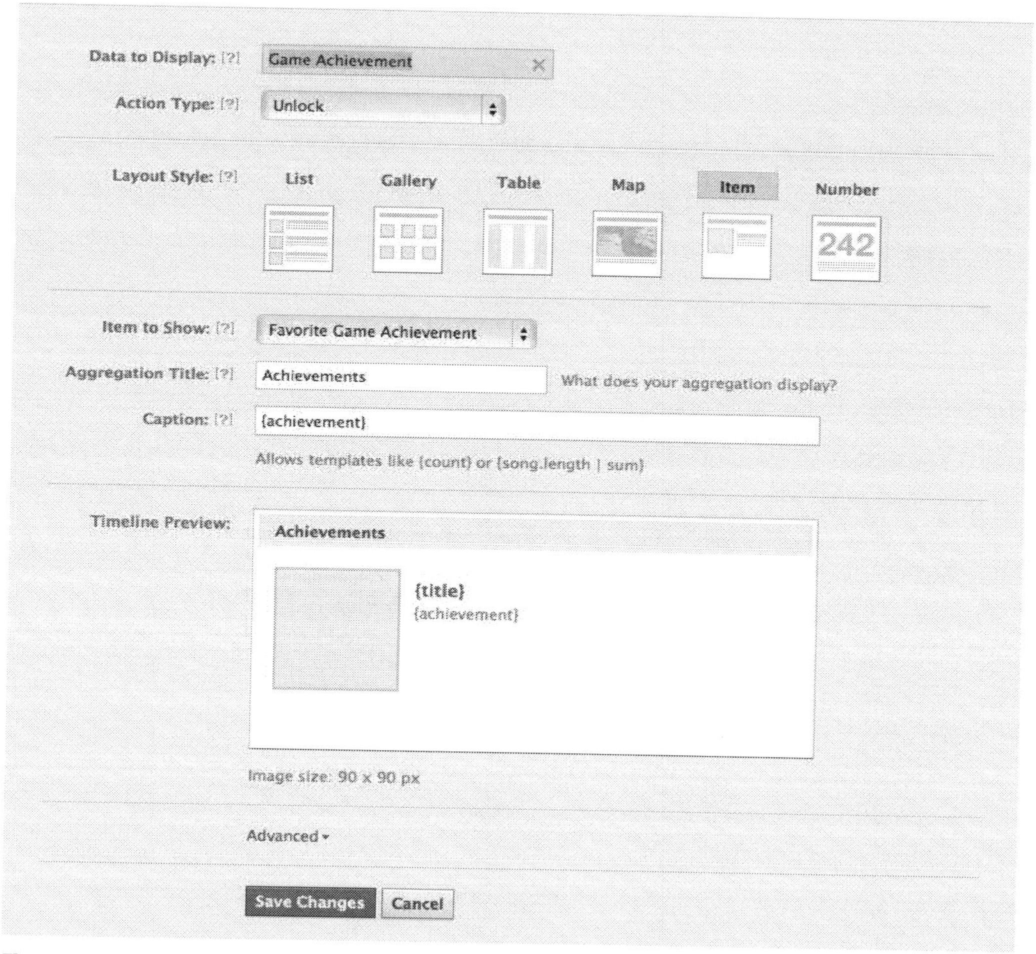

Figure 9–8. *Open Graph achievement description*

After saving your changes, preview how your achievement will display to users by clicking on the "Preview" link next to the Achievement aggregation. This will bring up a window with a preview of what users will see, as in Figure 9–9.

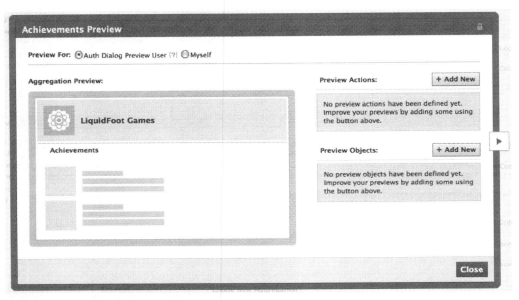

Figure 9–9. *Open Graph achievement preview*

You can also create dummy objects (in this case, achievements) for your application (as well as actions). After you have filled out the form, you will be able to preview the objects (as well as debug the request and view the expected Open Graph protocol data). See Figure 9–10.

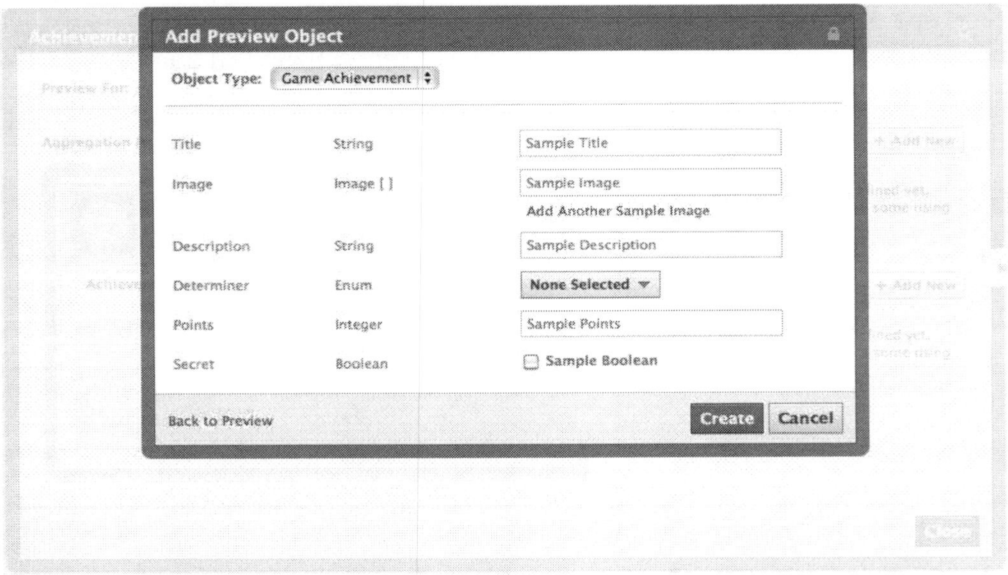

Figure 9–10. *Open Graph achievement dummy objects*

So how are these achievement "stories" integrated into your application? You could implement a very simple example of adding an achievement to the Timeline as shown in Listing 9–5.

Listing 9–5. *Adding an Achievement as a Timeline Story*

```
<!DOCTYPE HTML>
<html>
<head>
  <meta http-equiv="content-type" content="text/html; charset=utf-8" />

  <title>Add Achievement</title>

  <meta property="fb:app_id" content="APP_ID">
  <meta property="og:type" content="game.achievement">
  <meta property="og:title" content="Dummy Achievement">
  <meta property="og:url" content="http://www.yourdomain.com/path/to/achievement.html">
  <meta property="og:description" content="Power up. I clicked on something.">
  <meta property="og:image" content="http://placekitten.com/g/100/100">
  <meta property="game.points" content="1">

  <style>
    h3 { font-size: 30px; font-family: verdana, sans-serif; color: gray; }
  </style>
</head>
<body>
  <div id="fb-root"></div>

  <fb:add-to-timeline></fb:add-to-timeline>

  <h3>Dummy Achievement</h3>

  <p><img title="Dummy Achievement" src="http://placekitten.com/g/550/400" /></p>

  <form>
    <input type="button" value="Get Achievement" onclick="postAchievement();" />
  </form>

  <script src="https://connect.facebook.net/en_US/all.js"></script>
  <script>
    FB.init({
      app_id: 'your app id',
      cookie: true,
      statue: true,
      xfbml: true, // parse xfbml tags like fb:add-to-timeline
      oauth: true
    });
  </script>

  <script>
    function postAchievement() {
      FB.api('/me/YOUR_NAMESPACE:earn' +
        '?achievement=http://yourdomain.com/add_achievement.html',
        'post',
        function(response) {
          if (!response || response.error) {
            alert('Oh no, something went wrong.');
```

```
        } else {
          alert('Sucess! Action ID: ' + response.id);
        }
      });
    }
  </script>

</body>
</html>
```

This example makes use of the fb:add-to-timeline code in the FBML markup language to parse the timeline command. When viewed through the Facebook application, Facebook will replace this custom tag with the appropriate code to add the element to the user's Timeline.

Credits

Facebook runs its own payment system called Facebook Credits that developers must use for any virtual goods in your game. They support over 80 payment methods in over 50 countries, making it easy for Facebook users to purchase virtual goods from you. You have two options for dealing with credits with your users, either a direct payment for goods (e.g., $0.99 for a pink pony) or to purchase in-app currency to purchase other goods ($5.00 for 50 credits). If you design a game that has a store, it may make sense to leverage the "credits as currency" option as you can push some of the management of your in-game currency onto Facebook. For this service, Facebook retains a 30% cut of all transactions, which is on par with what Apple retains with both its mobile (iTunes) and desktop (App Store) software stores.

If you have not already done so, you will need to register yourself (or company) with Facebook to process payments. On your application, click on the *Credits* tab on the left, shown in Figure 9–11.

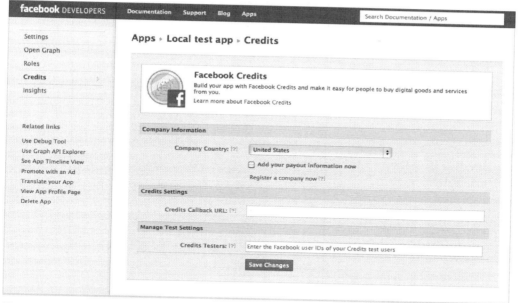

Figure 9–11. *Facebook Credits configuration*

After clicking on the "Register a company now" link, you will be able to fill out information about your company (see Figure 9–12). You will need to provide information on your business location, as well as additional contact information. If you do not already have a dedicated email address, now is a good time to get one. If you do not have a dedicated line for the phone number, Google Voice (http://voice.google.com) provides a free telephony service to help manage your incoming calls.

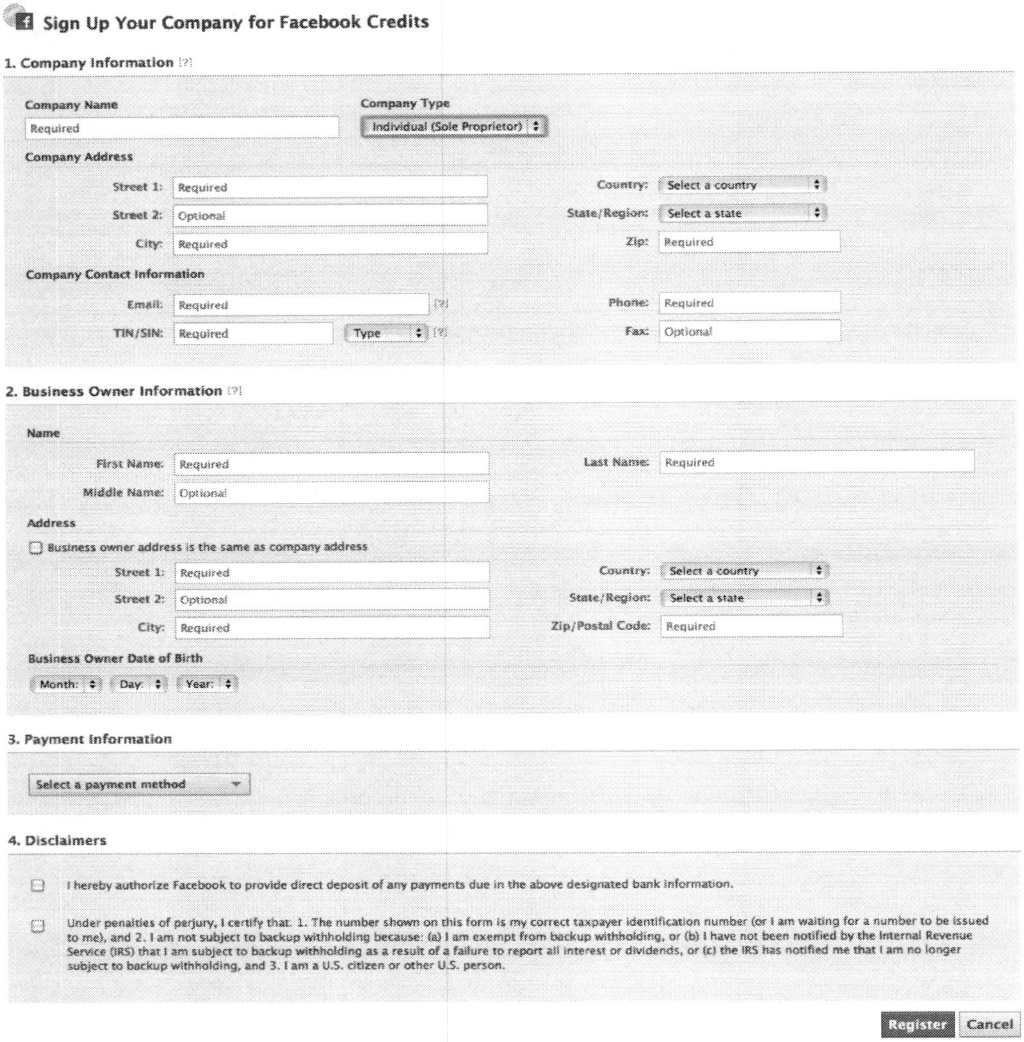

Sign Up Your Company for Facebook Credits

1. Company Information [?]

Company Name
[Required]

Company Type
[Individual (Sole Proprietor) ⇕]

Company Address

Street 1:	[Required]	Country:	[Select a country ⇕]
Street 2:	[Optional]	State/Region:	[Select a state ⇕]
City:	[Required]	Zip:	[Required]

Company Contact Information

Email:	[Required] [?]	Phone:	[Required]
TIN/SIN:	[Required] [Type ⇕] [?]	Fax:	[Optional]

2. Business Owner Information [?]

Name

First Name:	[Required]	Last Name:	[Required]
Middle Name:	[Optional]		

Address

☐ Business owner address is the same as company address

Street 1:	[Required]	Country:	[Select a country ⇕]
Street 2:	[Optional]	State/Region:	[Select a state ⇕]
City:	[Required]	Zip/Postal Code:	[Required]

Business Owner Date of Birth

[Month: ⇕] [Day: ⇕] [Year: ⇕]

3. Payment Information

[Select a payment method ▾]

4. Disclaimers

☐ I hereby authorize Facebook to provide direct deposit of any payments due in the above designated bank information.

☐ Under penalties of perjury, I certify that: 1. The number shown on this form is my correct taxpayer identification number (or I am waiting for a number to be issued to me), and 2. I am not subject to backup withholding because: (a) I am exempt from backup withholding, or (b) I have not been notified by the Internal Revenue Service (IRS) that I am subject to backup withholding as a result of a failure to report all interest or dividends, or (c) the IRS has notified me that I am no longer subject to backup withholding, and 3. I am a U.S. citizen or other U.S. person.

[Register] [Cancel]

Figure 9-12. *Facebook Credits company registration*

One important decision to make is how Facebook should pay you. You can choose either a bank account or the PayPal service. If you choose to use a bank account, I would suggest setting up a special account at your bank to receive these payments to make it easier to manage revenue generated from your application. PayPal is the other option, but be aware that there are additional fees associated with the transfers ($0.30 USD + (1.9–2.9% of the total transaction)).

Another issue that will surface quite quickly is differences in international tax codes and rates. Because you have the potential for raising revenue from individuals in more than one country, you may have to remit taxes in more than one country. For US-based developers, you will receive an IRS form 1099K should you receive more than $20,000 and more than 200 transactions. If you are having any type of success with your Facebook game, the advice of a good tax accountant is invaluable. Finding someone good with international law will also go a long way in determining which countries you may be responsible for paying taxes in as trade treaties change often.

After registering your company, you will need to register a callback URL for payments. This is the URL that users are redirected to after they initiate a payment. If you are using PHP on the server (as we set up in Chapter 8), then your callback code will look something like that shown in Listing 9–6.

Listing 9–6. *Facebook Callback Processing Template*

```php
<?php

require_once('FBUtils.php');
require_once('AppInfo.php');
require_once('utils.php');

function base64_url_decode($input) {
  return base64_decode(strtr($input, '-_', '+/'));
}

function parse_signed_request($signed_request, $app_secret) {
  list($encoded_sig, $payload) = explode('.', $signed_request, 2);

  // Decode the data
  $sig = base64_url_decode($encoded_sig);
  $data = json_decode(base64_url_decode($payload), true);

  if (strtoupper($data['algorithm']) !== 'HMAC-SHA256') {
    error_log('Unknown algorithm. Expected HMAC-SHA256');
    return null;
  }

  // Check signature
  $expected_sig = hash_hmac('sha256', $payload, $app_secret, $raw = true);

  if ($sig !== $expected_sig) {
    error_log('Bad Signed JSON signature!');
    return null;
  }

  return $data;
}

$appSecret = AppInfo::appSecret();

$data = array('content' => array());

// ensure the signed request is from Facebook
$request = parse_signed_request($_REQUEST['signed_request'], $appSecret);

if($request == NULL) {
  // handle unauthenticated request
```

```php
}


$payload = $request['credits'];

$func = $_REQUEST['method'];
$order_id = $payload['order_id'];

if($func == 'payments_status_update') {
  $status = $payload['status'];

  // Add logic for validating and recording a purchase for your game here

  // move state from placed to settled to grant in-game item
  if($status == 'placed') {
    $next_state = 'settled';
    $data['content']['status'] = $next_state;
  }

  // compose returning data
  $data['content']['order_id'] = $next_state;

} else if ($func == 'payments_get_items') {
  // remove escape characters
  $order_info = stripcslashes($payload['order_info']);
  $item_info = json_decode($order_info, true);

  // look up the item in the database, should return a title, price,
  // description, image_url and product_url
  //
  // For this example, the item array is manually set

  $item['title'] = 'Sword of Bludgeoning';
  $item['price'] = 5;
  $item['description'] = '+5 Hit';
  $item['image_url'] =
'http://www.yourdomain.com/images/fdb7a414a96660add08c40636e34b4fd.jpg';
  $item['product_url'] =
'http://www.yourdomain.com/images/fdb7a414a96660add08c40636e34b4fd.jpg';

  $data['content'] = array($item);
}

// required by api_fetch_reponse;
$data['method'] = $func;

echo json_decode($data);
```

This is just basic code to process data responses that you will need to integrate into your application later on, but should give you a good outline for processing your purchasable items. Once you have this page up on a server (e.g., https://www.yourdomain.com/credits_callback.php), fill out its URL in the Callback URL in the Facebook Developer app.

The parts you will need to really edit are handling unauthenticated requests (e.g., redirect or send an "Unauthorized" response back to the browser). After moving the state of your item, you need to update your database with the user's information (e.g., the item they have just purchased) and return the entire response as a JSON object to the JavaScript page that made the request to purchase the item. The sample code in Figure 9–4 manually creates a structure containing the information needed to create a single item, but this is more typically done with database lookups. We work a bit more with databases in future chapters, but you have the basic framework to implement your own store with whatever database backend your system has on the platform your game (or application) is running.

But before you release this into the wild, you need to do some testing to make sure everything is running properly. You can actually add Facebook IDs to the Credits tool for testers to not be charged, but allow people to test out the process. Definitely a good idea to add your own!

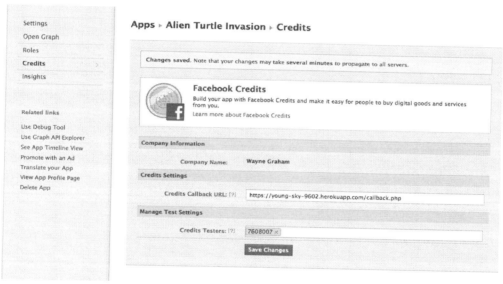

Figure 9–13. *Facebook application credits configuration*

Now when you interact with a page that creates a request to purchase credits, and your ID is on the Credit Testers page, you will see a dialog box, minus the ability to actually purchase credits, as in Figure 9–13.

We can see how this is actually implemented by looking at an example using the Facebook JavaScript SDK. On the Heroku system, this code will produce a button that when clicked on, will initiate the purchase of the Facebook credits (see Listing 9–7).

Listing 9–7. *Purchase Credits with Callback Example*

```php
<?php
  require_once('FBUtils.php');
  require_once('AppInfo.php');
  require_once('utils.php');
?>
<!doctype html>
<html>
<head>
  <meta charset="utf-8">

  <title>Purchase Credits</title>
  <meta name="viewport" content="width=device-width,initial-scale=1">
</head>
<body>

  <div id="fb-root"></div>

  <p><a onclick="purchaseCredits(); return false;">Purchase Credits</a></p>

  <script src='http://connect.facebook.net/en_US/all.js'></script>
  <script>
    var app_id = '<?php echo AppInfo::appId(); ?>';

    FB.init({appId: app_id, status: true, cookie: true});

    function purchaseCredits() {
      var obj = {
        method: 'pay',
        credits_purchase: true
      };
      FB.ui(obj, callback);
    }

    var callback = function(data) {
      if (data['order_id']) {
        return true;
      } else {
        //handle errors here
        return false;
      }
    };

  </script>

</body>
</html>
```

This will handle all of the purchasing of credits for your application. The callback code
(Listing 9–6) can also be updated to handle the purchase of credits, updating the user's
account accordingly within your application.

Credit Callback

To really understand the process of the credit callback, I want to get a bit more in-depth with how Facebook interacts with your application to process payments. Specifically, your application must track the state of a payment, and receive confirmation from the Facebook servers once the payment has been authorized (as opposed to canceled).

Order statuses can have the values shown in Table 9–1.

Table 9–1. *Facebook Credit Callback Status Values*

Status	Description	Set By	Next Status
placed	This is the initial state set once the user initiates and approves a transaction. Facebook sends your application a payments_status_update call to your system that should then grant a user an item before moving the order to the settled state.	Facebook	settled or cancelled
settled	After the order has been processed and funds transferred, the state should be updated to settled. This is typically the end of the processing, however, the account can enter into a refunded or disputed state later on.	Developer	refunded or disputed
refunded	The user has been refunded the purchase amount for the credits he purchased. There are numerous reasons that a purchase may be refunded, and should things escalate, Facebook has the final say in resolving conflicts.	Facebook or Developer	None
disputed	A user has disputed a purchase that requires your attention. This has either been initiated through a complaint to Facebook which they will forward to you, or directly from the customer.	User	settled or refunded
cancelled	The user has cancelled the transaction and no funds were transferred.	Developer	None

Keeping track of these states is the responsibility of your application logic, so be sure to test this out extensively. Again, the logic for handling this can be with the callback code example (Listing 9–6), with the logic for handling

Troubleshooting

Once you have signed up for Credits, Facebook will send you a daily report of your transactions. The format is tab-separated values (tsv), so programs such as Excel or OpenOffice will have no problem opening the files. This is a good way to keep up with what is going on with your credits, but what if something has gone wrong? You are getting warnings, or notice something not going as you expected; the best place to go to start to resolve the issue is the Facebook Help Center (`http://www.facebook.com/help`). There are many resources here that will help you quickly understand what is happening, and how to resolve the issue quickly. Another great resource for more technical issues is the Facebook StackOverflow page (`http://facebook.stackoverflow.com/`). Here you will find a forum to ask and answer technical questions surrounding the Facebook platform. This is a great place (as is all of StackOverflow) to add to the technical discussion (and learn a few things) around developing Facebook applications.

Another resource to have handy is the Platform Status. Facebook is a large company, and sometimes things happen. From networking issues, to hardware issues, to even more nefarious attacks from outside (e.g., denial of service attacks), there may be times when the Facebook platform is unavailable. I will say that Facebook does an excellent job in keeping its platform online, but it is a good idea to check the platform status to make sure Facebook is not reporting any issues when you notice yours. See Figure 9–14.

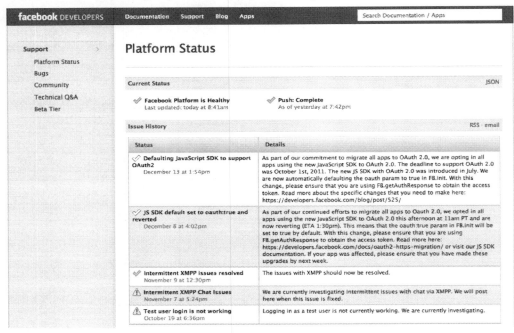

Figure 9–14. *Facebook platform status*

Roles

The Roles (Figure 9–15) for your application allow you to manage who has access to your application, and what rights they have. Administrators have full rights to edit the application (including deleting it). Developers have the ability to change their requests to include debug information, and Testers can use the application without information displaying on their Timeline; users listed under Insights will be able to view the analytics of the application.

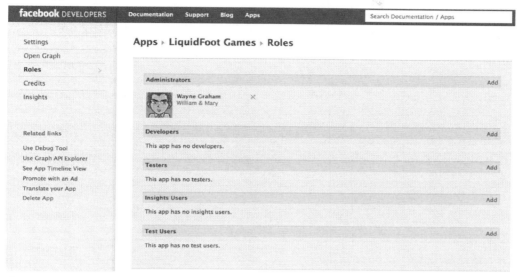

Figure 9–15. *Facebook Application roles*

Not only can you manage actual people and their roles in the project, you can also generate "test user" accounts to help you walk through how users will view your content. Simply click on the "add" on the Test Users line and you can select the number of accounts to generate as well as if the accounts should authorize your application by default. I always find it useful to create at least one account that has authorization and one that does not so I can experience the installation process too. You can then log out of Facebook as your real user, and log in as an avatar by clicking on the Switch To.

You will be launched into a new session as the new user with dummy data filled into the profile, as in Figure 9–16.

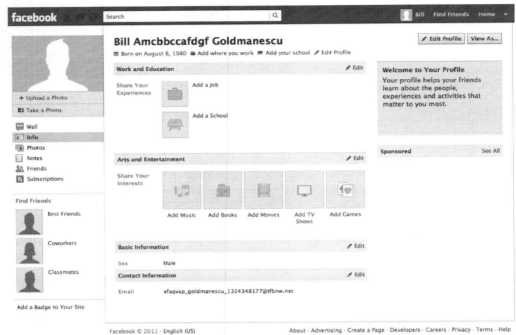

Figure 9–16. *Facebook Application test user*

You can now test your application as the generated user. I have to say this was a welcome addition as I ran through a bunch of bogus email accounts setting up test users when the Facebook Platform first came out.

Insights

Facebook Insights provides metrics around your content. Understanding how users are consuming your content (and specifically what content) as well as demographics and growth patterns help you make decisions about what pieces of your application to work on next. With the Insights for applications, you will receive feedback for stream stories, referral traffic, a breakdown of user actions, and demographics on authorized users. You will also receive feedback on API errors as well as throttling information. The Insights are accessed on the Insights tab for your application. See Figure 9–17.

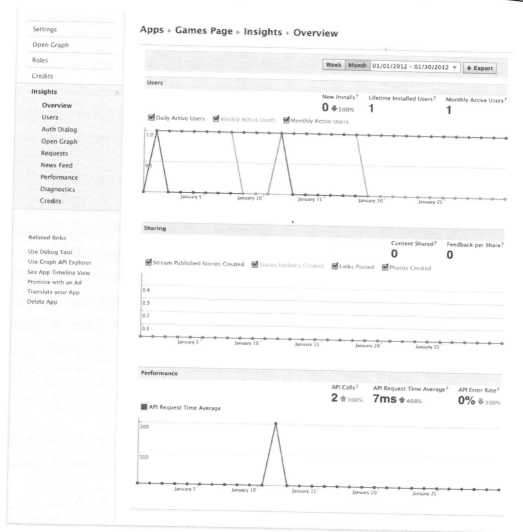

Figure 9–17. *Facebook Insights*

As this was a new application (with no users), the metrics here are not very robust. However, over time, the information visualized on this page will help you know more about your users.

To do more in-depth analysis of your analytics data, Facebook allows you to export the data, or access them through the Open Data protocol. To export the data, click on Export button (top-right corner), and select a date range from the dialog box (see Figure 9–18).

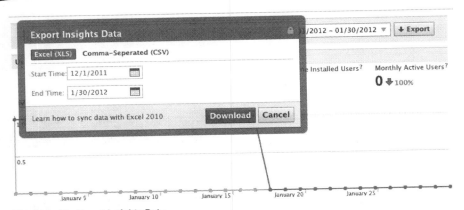

Figure 9–18. *Export Insights Data*

The resulting report gives you access to raw data to perform more in-depth analysis of who is using your site. You have access to a lot of different data to look at, including demographics, location, and top referrers. Access to these raw data will allow you to perform much deeper analysis and create custom charts and graphs of your data for presentations, and when looking at whom to target your advertising to (Figure 9–19) is an invaluable resource.

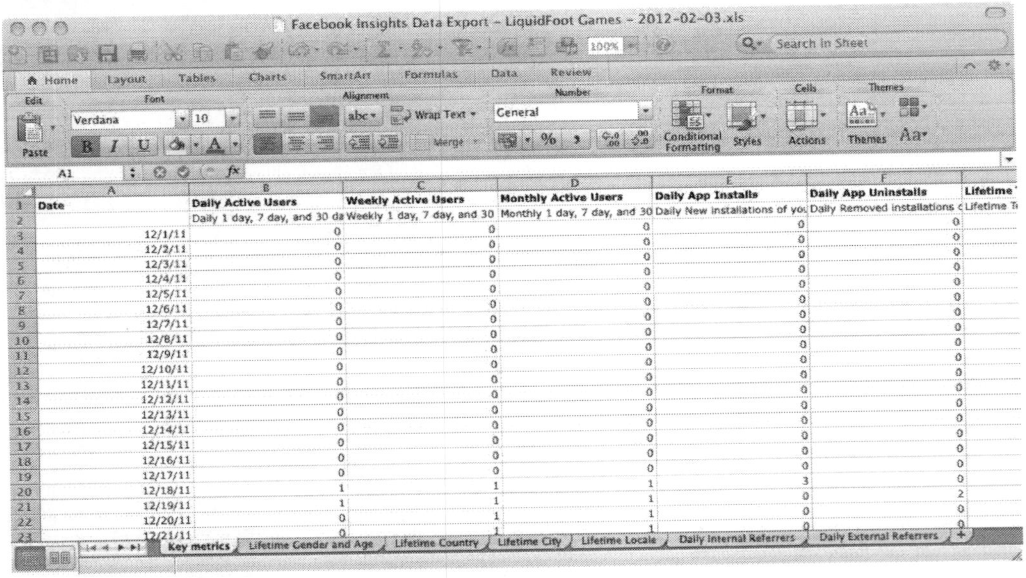

Figure 9–19. *Insights data in Excel*

Summary

This chapter went into a lot of detail on using the tools the Facebook Platform provides developers to manage and promote their applications. The Open Graph protocol is a vitally important aspect of the Facebook Platform as it provides not only the identification of objects on the web, but the Facebook API leverages the Open Graph to provide its content back to your application. I also discussed how Open Graph stories can be generated, how the Facebook Credits system works (and how to change the state to process credits) to help you monetize your game.

In the next chapter, we put together everything we have gone over to this point to launch a game on the Facebook platform. There will be some new elements (working directly with the PHP SDK on the Heroku platform), and some familiar ones (HTML 5 canvas).

Chapter 10

Creating Your First Facebook Game

With all the moving parts that compose a game, especially when dealing with a third-party platform like Facebook, learning which pieces go where can be a little overwhelming. Hopefully, you now have a good idea of the different components needed for a game and how the individual components work. In this chapter, we will put those together to build and deploy a game to the Facebook platform. I will revisit many of the steps I covered in Chapter 6 when I walked through the development of a simple game, but this time, we will follow some additional steps for deploying to the Facebook platform, as well as using some of the Facebook API calls to add an important game play component.

Project Planning

Facebook makes sharing pictures with your friends very simple. For example, some pretty sophisticated tools allow you to "tag" people in a photograph. Other tools create albums, add captions and locations to images, and let people comment on what was going on in the photograph. Since photo sharing is such a big feature, I started brainstorming on ways to integrate a feature like this in to a game. What if a puzzle game took images from your friend's photo albums and created a slider puzzle for you? People could do a set number of puzzles per day and purchase credits to do more if they'd like. With estimates of around 200 million images uploaded per day, there is a lot of content to make the game different every time you play!

Define the Rules

Just like I have done before, I want to write down the rules for the game. This helps me not only formalize the constraints for the game but also explain it to people.

Idea: Facebook Image Puzzle

Objective: Reconstruct the original image.

Rules:

- This is a single-player game played on Facebook.

- The application picks a random image from your Facebook images.

- That image is divided in to a grid.

- Grid pieces are jumbled, and one piece is removed from the top-left corner.

- A level system will increase the difficulty by creating smaller grids.

Identify Your Audience

Although there are a lot of potential users of this application, most likely the people most interested in this are uploading a lot of pictures and interacting with their friends often on albums. Facebook users that are most likely to use this game are out of their teen years and looking for a quick game to play on a break.

Competition

There are a lot of puzzle games on Facebook, though surprisingly few picture puzzles. From my initial research, four applications could be considered competition: Cute Puppy Drag and Drop Picture Puzzle Game, Naruto, and Play Make Your Own Puzzle Game. These applications are detailed in Table 10–1.

Table 10–1. *Competitors List*

Questions	Answers
Project	Cute Puppy Drag and Drop Picture Puzzle Game
URL	`http://www.fupa.com/game/Jigsaw-flash-games/cute-puppy-drag-and-drop-puzzle.html`
Genre	Puzzle game
Target Audience	Dog lovers
Reputation	Average
Gameplay	Drag-and-drop puzzle to reconstruct pictures of cute puppies
Strengths	Available from a site called Fupa.com, which has over 800 games to play
Weaknesses	Only pictures of cute puppies

Questions	Answers
Project	Naruto
URL	http://play3.games123.info
Genre	Puzzle game
Target Audience	Manga lovers
Reputation	Average
Gameplay	Drag-and-drop puzzle to reconstruct a manga scene
Strengths	Available on a site with a lot of different games to play
Weaknesses	Only one picture available
Project	Play Make Your Own Puzzle Game
URL	http://games.practiceone.co.uk
Genre	Puzzle game
Target Audience	Puzzle lovers
Reputation	Average
Gameplay	Slide puzzle of different colored shapes
Strengths	Eight levels of difficulty, with the easiest being a 3×3 grid and the most difficult being a 10×10 grid; can add an arbitrary image URL to make your own picture puzzle
Weaknesses	The geometric shapes can be difficult to reconstruct at the higher levels. The color palette is jarring. It's written in Flash.

After evaluating each of these competitors, we can clearly see that our project is unique in that it has access to a much larger selection of images for its puzzles. Most of these games, despite being Facebook applications, do not seem to do much with the platform other than use Facebook for authentication and to collect profile information. None seem to have much of a connection back to Facebook to engage users; all of these games appear to get you to a site and keep you there by offering an array of other distractions.

Developing the HTML Game

Now that I have a good understanding of the project I want to develop, have taken a look at the competition, and have an audience in mind, it is time to start developing the actual game. This first iteration will implement the actual game, ensuring that this component works before adding in a layer to interact with the Facebook platform. Developing in phases like this helps you compartmentalize your bugs and provides you with a couple of good milestones to reach.

Project Setup

As I covered in Chapter 6, we need to do a little project setup to get the ball rolling. I know I need an HTML page, and I want to organize my files in to JavaScript, style sheet, image, and sound directories, so I will create those on the command line as follows:

```
mkdir -p ~/projects/game
cd ~/projects/game
mkdir -p images javascript css sounds
```

This will create a directory in your projects directory named puzzle_game, and add directories named images, javascript, css, and sounds. Now, you can create some boilerplate HTML to hold your game (see Listing 10–1).

Listing 10–1. *HTML Container Boilerplate*

```html
<!doctype html>
<html lang="en">
<head>
  <meta charset="utf-8">

  <title>Picture Game</title>
  <meta name="description" content="Sliding Picture puzzle game">

  <meta name="viewport" content="width=device-width,initial-scale=1">

  <link rel="stylesheet" href="css/style.css">
</head>

<body>
  <header>

  </header>
  <div role="main">
    <canvas id="game" width="600" height="600"></canvas>
  </div>
  <footer>

  </footer>

  <script src="javascript/puzzle.js"></script>

  <!-- Prompt IE 6 users to install Chrome Frame. Remove this if you want to support
  IE 6.
```

```
        chromium.org/developers/how-tos/chrome-frame-getting-started -->
    <!--[if lt IE 7 ]>
        <script defer src="//ajax.googleapis.com/ajax/libs/chrome-frame/1.0.3↵
/CFInstall.min.js"></script>
        <script defer>window.attachEvent('onload',function(){CFInstall.check↵
({mode:'overlay'})})</script>
    <![endif]-->

</body>
</html>
```

This HTML includes most of what we will need to implement our game. This code will not produce anything in the web browser if you looked at the page, but it does contain the components ultimately needed display our game.

Game Code

With the HTML out of the way, we can focus on the code to actually play the game. Since this game relies on images, and we are holding off on the Facebook integration for a little bit, I need a test image that I can use as the filler image. I did some looking around and found an image on Flickr that was under a Creative Commons BY license (for a refresher on licenses, see Chapter 5). The photo that struck me was posted by the user gnuckx (available at http://www.flickr.com/photos/gnuckx/5544439526/). I downloaded the large image in to my project's images directory and gave it the more meaningful file name of island.jpg. Ultimately, we want to load the image on to the canvas to make the original image that looks like Figure 10–1.

Figure 10–1. *Original image by gnuckx loaded onto a canvas*

And then we need to transform it in to a jumbled set of tiles with the top-left tile missing, as shown in Figure 10–2.

Figure 10–2. *Image processed through code to generate tiles*

First things first, though—we need to set up a method to instantiate the canvas and hold our information. In other words, we need to create a canvas element and set its context, as shown in Listing 10–2.

Listing 10–2. *Setting Up the Canvas in puzzle.js*

```
var canvas;
var context;

function init(canvasId) {
  canvas = document.getElementById(canvasId);
  context = canvas.getContext('2d');
}

init('game');
```

Our code now has access to a `canvas` DOM element as well as the 2D `context` for our game set up as in previous chapters. Now, we need to add the actual image that we will manipulate in the game. As you recall, in Chapter 6, I discussed changing the code to make the spaceships use an image and explained that `canvas` has several methods that make working with images relatively easy. The method that I will use here is `drawImage`, which actually takes a few different sets of attributes (see Listing 10–3). At its simplest, drawImage takes an image object and x and y coordinates to display an image on the canvas. You can also add in additional arguments to resize the image with width and height attributes.

Listing 10–3. *drawImage Method for Resizing Image on Canvas*

```
drawImage(image, x, y, width, height);
```

If you look at the drawImage() documentation (see http://www.whatwg.org/specs/web-apps/current-work/multipage/the-canvas-element.html), the method actually takes up to nine arguments, as shown in Listing 10–4.

Listing 10–4. *Full drawImage Method for Resizing Image on Canvas*

```
drawImage(image, source_x, source_y, source_width, source_height, destination_x,↵
 destination_y, destination_width, destination_height);
```

This method takes an original image and allows you to resize it on the canvas element. This version of drawImage() will allow our code to break up the image and deal with it in a grid. The basic premise here is that we want to take an image and generate a sprite sheet based on the grid size for the image.

Next, we want to load our image but add an eventListener() to ensure that only after the image is loaded will it be broken in to tiles. This is an important step, because drawImage() will throw an exception if the image being drawn is not fully loaded. By adding an event listener to fire once the image has been loaded, we ensure that we will not run into problems with this particular method. To handle this, we add a couple of functions to the code, as shown in Listing 10–5.

Listing 10–5. *Loading the Image for the Canvas*

```
var image;
function drawTiles() {
  context.drawImage(image, 0, 0);
}

function setImage(imagePath) {
  image = new Image();
  image.src = imagePath;
  image.addEventListener('load', drawTiles, false);
}
```

There is now a container for the image to pass around in the code, as well as the ability to set the path to the image. With a small change to the init method and the code to instantiate the game, this code (see Listing 10–6) should now actually draw the image on the canvas of the index.html page in your browser. The loaded image is shown in Figure 10–3.

Listing 10–6. *Loading the Image for the Canvas*

```
function init(canvasId, imagePath) {
  canvas = document.getElementById(canvasId);
  context = canvas.getContext('2d');

  setImage(imagePath);
}

init('game', 'images/island.jpg');
```

Figure 10–3. *Image rendered on canvas*

To add the tiles to the game, we need to calculate a few elements. First, we need to determine the width of the canvas element we are working with. You could hard-code this information (e.g., var gameSize = 600;), but a time may come when you want or need to change this in the HTML code. To get around making a change in two different places, I will just calculate the width by calculating the width of the canvas DOM element. Second, we need to store the desired grid coordinates. We are dealing with a square grid, so we need to store only one value that we can pass in when we initialized the game. Listing 10–7 contains the calculation code.

Listing 10–7. *Calculating Tile Size*

```
var gameSize;
var gridSize;
var tileSize;

function init(canvasId, imagePath, gridCount) {
  canvas = document.getElementById(canvasId);
  context = canvas.getContext('2d');

  setImage(imagePath);
```

```
        gameSize = canvas.width;
        gridSize = gridCount;
        tileSize = gameSize / gridSize;

    }

    init('game', 'images/island.jpg', 3);
```

This code calculates the width of the canvas (600), sets a grid count (3) and calculates how wide (and tall) each grid will be. For this example, each image in the 3 × 3 grid will be 200 × 200 pixels large.

With the size of the tiles set, we can work on actually generating the tiles. Since we are taking an image and manipulating it, we need to create a container to hold our game pieces:

```
var boardParts = {};
function setBoard() {};
```

The setBoard() function will set up the tiles for us. An easy way to hold the information on the board is in an array that contains the x and y coordinates of the top-left corner of each image piece. Unfortunately, the code to do this in JavaScript is a little gnarly. You first need to create an array, and within the array, create a container that holds the x and y properties. This effectively provides two sets of coordinates: the position of the tile in the array and its x and y coordinates on the canvas. When a tile's position in the array matches the board's position, you know that the tile is correctly placed.

A lot of information was packed in to that last sentence, which may make more sense with an image. If we take the image, split it in to a 200 × 200 pixel grid, and label those grids 0 to 8, you will see the correct order for each tile to be in (see Figure 10–4).

Figure 10–4. *Image tile positions*

We also want to have a special tile that is empty and give it an initial location of (0,0) (the top-left corner). We can take care of this with Listing 10–8.

Listing 10–8. *Calculating Tile Positions*

```
var solved = false;
var boardParts = {};
var emptyLoc = {
  x: 0,
  y: 0
};

function setBoard() {
  boardParts = new Array(gridSize);

  for (var i = 0; i < gridSize; ++i) {

    boardParts[i] = new Array(gridSize);

    for (var j = 0; j < gridSize; ++j) {
      boardParts[i][j] = new Object;
      boardParts[i][j].x = (gridSize - 1) - i;
```

```
      boardParts[i][j].y = (gridSize - 1) - j;
    }

  }
  emptyLoc.x = boardParts[gridSize - 1][gridSize - 1].x;
  emptyLoc.y = boardParts[gridSize - 1][gridSize - 1].y;

  solved = false;
}
```

We also need to keep track of the x and y coordinates of the location where a user clicks; this is also just stored in a container with an initial x and y coordinate set to (0, 0). Listing 10–9 shows our click container.

Listing 10–9. *Click Location Container*

```
var clickLoc = {
  x: 0,
  y: 0
};
```

To calculate if a click location has a valid move (e.g., there is an open space next to the clicked tile), we can use a geometry trick. We need to calculate the total difference in the x and y coordinates between the clicked tile and the open tile; this is effectively the distance between the two points. If they equal 1, the move is valid. The distance calculation code is shown in Listing 10–10.

Listing 10–10. *Distance Calculation*

```
function distance(x1, y1, x2, y2) {
  return Math.abs(x1 - x2) + Math.abs(y1 - y2);
}
```

> **NOTE:** This distance formula is actually derived from Euclidean geometry. If you treat an array as a Euclidean plane (a two-dimensional surface), the distance between two points is formally defined as
>
> $$d(p, q) = \sqrt{(p_1 - q_1)^2 + (p_2 - q_2)^2}$$
>
> We use a trick in the function to calculate the absolute value of the difference between the two numbers to ensure that they are positive. If JavaScript did not have a predefined absolute value function, we would need to step back to squaring each value, adding them together, and then taking that value's square root to calculate the distance.

We now need to be able to move the tiles and check if the board is solved. Moving a tile consists of switching the tile coordinates of the tile that was clicked with those of the empty tile. After the swap, we can check if the tiles are in the correct positions in the array. To slide the tile, we need to check if the puzzle has been solved. If it has not, we need to shift the x and y coordinates for the tile with the empty tile location. We then check to see if the move solved the board by iterating through all of the tiles and checking to see if they are in the correct order (see Listing 10–11).

Listing 10–11. *Moving Tiles and Checking the Board*

```
function slideTile(toLoc, fromLoc) {
  if (!solved) {
    boardParts[toLoc.x][toLoc.y].x = boardParts[fromLoc.x][fromLoc.y].x;
    boardParts[toLoc.x][toLoc.y].y = boardParts[fromLoc.x][fromLoc.y].y;
    boardParts[fromLoc.x][fromLoc.y].x = gridSize - 1;
    boardParts[fromLoc.x][fromLoc.y].y = gridSize - 1;
    toLoc.x = fromLoc.x;
    toLoc.y = fromLoc.y;
    checkSolved();
  }
}

function checkSolved() {
  for (var i = 0; i < gridSize; ++i) {
    for (var j = 0; j < gridSize; ++j) {
      if (boardParts[i][j].x != i || boardParts[i][j].y != j) {
        solved = false;
      }
    }
  }
  solved = true;
}
```

Now, to actually update the drawing of the tiles, we will add event handlers to listen to the canvas and redraw the tiles when the mouse position has been moved or the mouse has clicked an object (see Listing 10–12).

Listing 10–12. *Game Click Events and Tile Drawing*

```
function addEvents(canvas) {
  canvas.onmousemove = function(event) {
    clickLoc.x = Math.floor((event.pageX - this.offsetLeft) / tileSize);
    clickLoc.y = Math.floor((event.pageY - this.offsetTop) / tileSize);
  };

  canvas.onclick = function() {
    if (distance(clickLoc.x, clickLoc.y, emptyLoc.x, emptyLoc.y) === 1) {
      slideTile(emptyLoc, clickLoc);
      drawTiles();
    }
    if (solved) {
      setTimeout(function() {alert("You solved it!");}, 500);
    }
  };
}

function drawTiles() {
  context.clearRect ( 0 , 0 , gameSize , gameSize );
  for (var i = 0; i < gridSize; ++i) {
    for (var j = 0; j < gridSize; ++j) {
      var x = boardParts[i][j].x;
      var y = boardParts[i][j].y;
      if(i !== emptyLoc.x || j !== emptyLoc.y || solved === true) {
        context.drawImage(image, x * tileSize, y * tileSize, tileSize, tileSize,
                          i * tileSize, j * tileSize, tileSize, tileSize);
      }
```

```
        }
      }
    }
```

For the time being, when you solve the puzzle, you get an alert box that you have solved it. You should now be able to play the game with the JavaScript in the javascript/puzzle.js file, which is shown in Listing 10–13.

Listing 10–13. *Complete Game Code*

```
var canvas;
var context;

var image;

var solved;

var gameSize;
var gridSize;
var tileSize;
var boardParts = {};

var clickLoc = {
  x: 0,
  y: 0
};

var emptyLoc = {
  x: 0,
  y: 0
};

function setImage(imagePath) {
  image = new Image();
  image.src = imagePath;
  image.addEventListener('load', drawTiles, false);
}

function addEvents(canvas) {
  canvas.onmousemove = function(event) {
    clickLoc.x = Math.floor((event.pageX - this.offsetLeft) / tileSize);
    clickLoc.y = Math.floor((event.pageY - this.offsetTop) / tileSize);
  };

  canvas.onclick = function() {
    if (distance(clickLoc.x, clickLoc.y, emptyLoc.x, emptyLoc.y) === 1) {
      slideTile(emptyLoc, clickLoc);
      drawTiles();
    }
    if (solved) {
      setTimeout(function() {alert("You solved it!");}, 500);
    }
  };
}

function setBoard() {
  boardParts = new Array(gridSize);
  for (var i = 0; i < gridSize; ++i) {
```

```
      boardParts[i] = new Array(gridSize);
      for (var j = 0; j < gridSize; ++j) {
        boardParts[i][j] = {
          x: (gridSize - 1) - i,
          y: (gridSize - 1) - j
        };
      }
    }
    emptyLoc.x = boardParts[gridSize - 1][gridSize - 1].x;
    emptyLoc.y = boardParts[gridSize - 1][gridSize - 1].y;
    solved = false;
  }

  function drawTiles() {
    context.clearRect ( 0 , 0 , gameSize , gameSize );
    for (var i = 0; i < gridSize; ++i) {
      for (var j = 0; j < gridSize; ++j) {
        var x = boardParts[i][j].x;
        var y = boardParts[i][j].y;
        if(i != emptyLoc.x || j != emptyLoc.y || solved === true) {
          context.drawImage(image, x * tileSize, y * tileSize, tileSize, tileSize,
                            i * tileSize, j * tileSize, tileSize, tileSize);
        }
      }
    }
  }

  function distance(x1, y1, x2, y2) {
    return Math.abs(x1 - x2) + Math.abs(y1 - y2);
  }

  function slideTile(toLoc, fromLoc) {
    if (!solved) {
      boardParts[toLoc.x][toLoc.y].x = boardParts[fromLoc.x][fromLoc.y].x;
      boardParts[toLoc.x][toLoc.y].y = boardParts[fromLoc.x][fromLoc.y].y;
      boardParts[fromLoc.x][fromLoc.y].x = gridSize - 1;
      boardParts[fromLoc.x][fromLoc.y].y = gridSize - 1;
      toLoc.x = fromLoc.x;
      toLoc.y = fromLoc.y;
      checkSolved();
    }
  }

  function checkSolved() {
    var flag = true;
    for (var i = 0; i < gridSize; ++i) {
      for (var j = 0; j < gridSize; ++j) {
        if (boardParts[i][j].x != i || boardParts[i][j].y != j) {
          flag = false;
        }
      }
    }
    solved = flag;
  }

  function init(canvasId, imagePath, gridCount) {
    canvas = document.getElementById(canvasId);
```

```
    context = canvas.getContext('2d');

    gameSize = canvas.width;

    gridSize = gridCount;

    tileSize = gameSize / gridSize;

    setImage(imagePath);
    addEvents(canvas);

    solved = false;

    setBoard();
}

init('game', 'images/island.jpg', 3);
```

When you load the game in the browser, you should now have a playable game. Take some time to grab some other images and play with the game, as well as to manipulate the number of grids by changing the values passed to the init function. Figure 10–5 shows my example image, using a grid size of 7.

Figure 10–5. *Image game initialized with a 7 × 7 grid*

Because of the way we wrote the code, adding levels of difficulty to this game is as trivial as changing the initialization parameter.

Adding Music

Although we now have a functioning puzzle game, we can give it a little more polish by adding a sound loop in the background. For this, I headed over to the No Soap Radio (http://www.nosoapradio.us) to find a loop. After listening to everything in the Platform/Puzzle section, I decided the song Rialto suited my needs quite nicely, but you may find that another is better for your game. The process to download a song (which is not readily self-evident) is to select the song to start the preview, right-click, and select "Download this song." This will redirect you to a page with an MP3 file that you can then download.

To play the MP3 in our game using the HTML5 audio element, we need to create an Ogg Vorbis version of the song. Just open the MP3 file for your song in Audacity and select **File ➤ Export** and change the format to Ogg Vorbis (see Figure 10–6).

Figure 10–6. *Export the MP3 in Ogg Vorbis format.*

After you have completed the export, you should have both an MP3 and Ogg Vorbis version of the song in your sounds directory (e.g., DST-Rialto.mp3 and DST-Rialto.ogg). We will implement a slightly more sophisticated method of determining which file to use than we have previously. Here, we will write code that will ask the browser what type of <audio> element it supports natively, attach the appropriate file to the HTML DOM, and play the sound (see Listing 10–14).

Listing 10–14. *Adding Background Music*

```
var music;

function playMusic(musicPath, filename) {
  music = new Audio;
  var soundStub = musicPath + "/" + filename;

  if(music.canPlayType('audio/ogg')) {
    music = new Audio(soundStub + '.ogg');
  } else if(music.canPlayType('audio/mp3')) {
    music = new Audio(soundStub + '.mp3');
  }

  music.load();
  music.play();
}

init('game', 'images/island.jpg', 3);

playMusic('sounds', 'DST-Rialto');
```

The function playMusic creates an empty Audio element and tests the browser to see if it can play an Ogg Vorbis or MP3 file. The format the browser can play natively will determine which file is served. While you still need to create both MP3 and Ogg Vorbis formats for the foreseeable future, this technique at least provides a convenient way to add only a single file stub for the music file you want to play.

Some people may be playing their own music in the background and find your music annoying. You can easily create a control for the music that will pause and play the song by calling the audio element's pause() and play() functions.

If you add a div in the index.html with an id of 'pause', you can add an eventHandler() to your JavaScript that will listen for clicks. If the element is clicked, you can pause the music with Listing 10–15.

Listing 10–15. *JavaScript code to pause/play background music.*

```
document.getElementById('pause').onclick = (function(event) {
  music.pause();
});

document.getElementById('play').onclick = function(event) {
  music.play();
});
```

Listing 10–16. *HTML code to display play/pause controls.*

```
<div id="pause">pause music</div>
<div id="play">play music</div>
```

If you reload your page, you should now be able to click the text "pause music" to effectively pause and "play music" to resume. This will give the game players some ability to control the music associated with your game. There is nothing worse than a game where you do not have some control over the audio settings.

Facebook Integration

Now that the game is working as expected and should be bug free, we can turn our attention to integrating the game with the Facebook platform. The major thing we will accomplish here is the code needed to select an image from the user's Facebook albums. As I have explained previously (see Chapter 8), we will set up a new application (though you can certainly use one that already exists) to deploy the application.

For my purposes here, I will create a new application named Facebook Image Puzzle and set the category to Games with a subcategory of Puzzle. I will connect this to the Heroku cloud using the PHP SDK. Most of the code you need to interact with the Facebook platform will already be in the project that is generated for you when you create the project on Heroku. On the main index.php page, the graph call to pictures provides most of the data that we will need for our application (see Listing 10–17).

Listing 10–17. *Pulling your photos from Facebook.*

```
$photos = idx($facebook->api('/me/photos?limit=16'), 'data', array());
```

The code in Listing 10–17 will grab 16 of the most recent photos that you have. The Image Puzzle application needs only one, so to randomize this a bit, we can write a quick PHP function that picks a random element from the pictures array (see Listing 10–18).

Listing 10–18. *Random image function in PHP.*

```
function randomPicture($photos)
{
  $random = rand(0, count($photos));
  return $photos[$random];
}
```

This function takes the array of pictures returned by the API call and picks a random number between 0 and the number of items in the array (16 in our case). The function then returns a single, specific array containing information about one random image from all of the images returned in the $photos array. The result is a PHP array with the information Facebook provides you about your image, its graph ID, the person who uploaded the image, people who have been tagged in the photo, as well as the different sizes of images that Facebook maintains. Listing 10–19 shows the response for a picture from a trip I took with friends to the Football Hall of Fame induction with the Washington Redskins Monks.

Listing 10–19. *PHP image array data from randomPicture function*

```
Array
(
    [id] => 532397154747
    [from] => Array
        (
            [name] => Wayne Graham
            [id] => 7608007
        )
```

```
[tags] => Array
    (
        [data] => Array
            (

                [0] => Array
                    (
                        [id] => 7608007
                        [name] => Wayne Graham
                        [x] => 41.6667
                        [y] => 34.8148
                        [created_time] => 2008-08-04T14:07:29+0000
                    )

            )

    )

[picture] => https://fbcdn-photos-a.akamaihd.net/photos-ak-ash1/v208/234/113/↵
7608007/s7608007_33004207_9773.jpg
[source] => https://fbcdn-sphotos-a.akamaihd.net/photos-ak-ash1/v208/234/113/↵
7608007/n7608007_33004207_9773.jpg
[height] => 453
[width] => 604
[images] => Array
    (
        [0] => Array
            (
                [height] => 453
                [width] => 604
                [source] => https://fbcdn-sphotos-a.akamaihd.net/photos-ak-ash1/↵
v208/234/113/7608007/n7608007_33004207_9773.jpg
            )

        [1] => Array
            (
                [height] => 135
                [width] => 180
                [source] => https://fbcdn-photos-a.akamaihd.net/photos-ak-ash1/↵
v208/234/113/7608007/a7608007_33004207_9773.jpg
            )

        [2] => Array
            (
                [height] => 97
                [width] => 130
                [source] => https://fbcdn-photos-a.akamaihd.net/photos-ak-ash1/↵
v208/234/113/7608007/s7608007_33004207_9773.jpg
            )

        [3] => Array
            (
                [height] => 56
                [width] => 75
                [source] => https://fbcdn-photos-a.akamaihd.net/photos-ak-ash1/↵
v208/234/113/7608007/t7608007_33004207_9773.jpg
            )
```

```
        )
        [link] => http://www.facebook.com/photo.php?pid=33004207&id=7608007
        [icon] => https://s-static.ak.facebook.com/rsrc.php/v1/yz/r/StEh3RhPvjk.gif
        [created_time] => 2008-08-04T14:01:22+0000
        [position] => 19
        [updated_time] => 2008-08-04T14:01:22+0000
)
```

What is really nice about this response is that the image we need for our application can be accessed in the 'source' key location. We can store a reference to the image in PHP quite simply, as shown in Listing 10–20.

Listing 10–20. *Picking a Random Image and Setting Its Image Source*

```php
$photos = idx($facebook->api('/me/photos?limit=16'), 'data', array());

$image = randomPicture($photos);
$src = $image['source'];
```

When we need the image to initialize the game, there is a variable holding the information the code will need.

I stripped out much of the unneeded code in the index.php file after adding these additions, and now my PHP block looks like Listing 10–21.

Listing 10–21. *PHP Block for game application.*

```php
<?php

// Provides access to app specific values such as your app id and app secret.
// Defined in 'AppInfo.php'
require_once('AppInfo.php');

// Enforce https on production
if (substr(AppInfo::getUrl(), 0, 8) != 'https://' && $_SERVER['REMOTE_ADDR'] !=
  '127.0.0.1') {
  header('Location: https://'. $_SERVER['HTTP_HOST'] . $_SERVER['REQUEST_URI']);
  exit();
}

// This provides access to helper functions defined in 'utils.php'
require_once('utils.php');

function randomPicture($photos)
{
  $random = rand(0, count($photos));
  return $photos[$random];
}

require_once('sdk/src/facebook.php');

$facebook = new Facebook(array(
  'appId'  => AppInfo::appID(),
  'secret' => AppInfo::appSecret(),
));
```

```php
$user_id = $facebook->getUser();
if ($user_id) {
  try {
    // Fetch the viewer's basic information
    $basic = $facebook->api('/me');
  } catch (FacebookApiException $e) {
    // If the call fails we check if we still have a user. The user will be
    // cleared if the error is because of an invalid accesstoken
    if (!$facebook->getUser()) {
      header('Location: '. AppInfo::getUrl($_SERVER['REQUEST_URI']));
      exit();
    }
  }

  // And this returns 16 of your photos.
  $photos = idx($facebook->api('/me/photos?limit=16'), 'data', array());

  $image = randomPicture($photos);
  $src = $image['source'];

}

// Fetch the basic info of the app that they are using
$app_info = $facebook->api('/'. AppInfo::appID());

$app_name = idx($app_info, 'name', '');
?>
```

For the actual page content, most of the HTML code can be deleted. The most important thing is to add a canvas element and a link to the JavaScript we created earlier (javascript/puzzle.js) and instantiate the puzzle from this page instead of the JavaScript page.

After the header section, I pretty much removed all of the template data and added the code in Listing 10–22 to hold my canvas.

Listing 10–22. *Main Content for Image Puzzle*

```html
<section id="main" class="clearfix">
    <canvas id="game" width="400" height="400"></canvas>
</section>
```

Above the closing body tag (</body>) I add in my JavaScript and instantiate it with the code in Listing 10–23.

Listing 10–23. *Script tag to initialize puzzle game.*

```html
<script>
        var imagePath = '<?php echo $src ?>';
        init('game', imagePath, 3);
</script>
```

I created a JavaScript variable here to echo the PHP variable $src that was set earlier. You can do this in the init() function, but I tend to do it this way to make certain my intention is clear for the next person who needs to sit down at my code—especially if that person is me, six months from now!

I updated the Open Graph metadata for the page, and the result of the HTML portion of
index.php is shown in Listing 10–24.

Listing 10–24. *HTML Code for Puzzle Game*

```
<!DOCTYPE html>
<html xmlns:fb="http://ogp.me/ns/fb#" lang="en">
  <head>
    <meta charset="utf-8" />
    <meta name="viewport" content="width=device-width, initial-scale=1.0,↵
maximum-scale=2.0, user-scalable=yes" />

    <title><?php echo he($app_name); ?></title>
    <link rel="stylesheet" href="stylesheets/screen.css" media="Screen"↵
type="text/css" />
      <link rel="stylesheet" href="stylesheets/mobile.css"
        media="handheld, only screen and (max-width: 480px), only screen and↵
(max-device-width: 480px)"
        type="text/css" />

    <!--[if IEMobile]>
    <link rel="stylesheet" href="mobile.css" media="screen" type="text/css"  />
    <![endif]-->

    <meta property="og:title" content="<?php echo he($app_name); ?>" />
    <meta property="og:type" content="game" />
    <meta property="og:url" content="<?php echo AppInfo::getUrl(); ?>" />
    <meta property="og:image" content="<?php echo AppInfo::getUrl('/logo.png'); ?>" />
    <meta property="og:site_name" content="<?php echo he($app_name); ?>" />
    <meta property="og:description" content="Facebook Image Puzzle Game" />
    <meta property="fb:app_id" content="<?php echo AppInfo::appID(); ?>" />

    <script type="text/javascript" src="/javascript/jquery-1.7.1.min.js"></script>


<script type="text/javascript">
function logResponse(response) {
  if (console && console.log) {
    console.log('The response was', response);
  }
}

$(function(){
  // Set up so we handle click on the buttons
  $('#postToWall').click(function() {
    FB.ui({
      method : 'feed',
        link   : $(this).attr('data-url')
    },
    function (response) {
      // If response is null the user canceled the dialog
      if (response != null) {
        logResponse(response);
      }
    });
  });
```

```
    $('#sendToFriends').click(function() {
      FB.ui({
        method : 'send',
          link   : $(this).attr('data-url')
      },
      function (response) {
        // If response is null the user canceled the dialog
        if (response != null) {
          logResponse(response);
        }
      }
          );
    });

    $('#sendRequest').click(function() {
      FB.ui(
        {
          method  : 'apprequests',
            message : $(this).attr('data-message')
        },
      function (response) {
        // If response is null the user canceled the dialog
        if (response != null) {
          logResponse(response);
        }
      }
        );
      });
    });


    </script>

        <!--[if IE]>
    <script type="text/javascript">
    var tags = ['header', 'section'];
    while(tags.length)
      document.createElement(tags.pop());
    </script>
        <![endif]-->
      </head>
      <body>
        <div id="fb-root"></div>
    <script type="text/javascript">
    window.fbAsyncInit = function() {
      FB.init({
        appId     : '<?php echo AppInfo::appID(); ?>', // App ID
          channelUrl : '//<?php echo $_SERVER["HTTP_HOST"]; ?>/channel.html', // Channel↩
      File
        status    : true, // check login status
        cookie    : true, // enable cookies to allow the server to access the session
        xfbml     : true // parse XFBML
          });

          // Listen to the auth.login which will be called when the user logs in
          // using the Login button
          FB.Event.subscribe('auth.login', function(response) {
```

```
        // We want to reload the page now so PHP can read the cookie that the
        // Javascript SDK sat. But we don't want to use
        // window.location.reload() because if this is in a canvas there was a
        // post made to this page and a reload will trigger a message to the
        // user asking if they want to send data again.
        window.location = window.location;
      });

      FB.Canvas.setAutoGrow();
    };

    // Load the SDK Asynchronously
    (function(d, s, id) {
      var js, fjs = d.getElementsByTagName(s)[0];
      if (d.getElementById(id)) return;
      js = d.createElement(s); js.id = id;
      js.src = "//connect.facebook.net/en_US/all.js";
      fjs.parentNode.insertBefore(js, fjs);
    }(document, 'script', 'facebook-jssdk'));
  </script>

<header class="clearfix">
  <?php if (isset($basic)) { ?>
  <p id="picture" style="background-image: url(https://graph.facebook.com/<?php
echo he($user_id); ?>/picture?type=normal)"></p>

  <div>
    <h1>Welcome, <strong><?php echo he(idx($basic, 'name')); ?></strong></h1>
    <p class="tagline">
      This is your app
      <a href="<?php echo he(idx($app_info, 'link'));?>" target="_top"><?php
echo he($app_name); ?></a>
    </p>

    <div id="share-app">
      <p>Share your app:</p>
      <ul>
        <li>
          <a href="#" class="facebook-button" id="postToWall" data-url="<?php
echo AppInfo::getUrl(); ?>">
            <span class="plus">Post to Wall</span>
          </a>
        </li>
        <li>
          <a href="#" class="facebook-button speech-bubble" id="sendToFriends"
data-url="<?php echo AppInfo::getUrl(); ?>">
            <span class="speech-bubble">Send Message</span>
          </a>
        </li>
        <li>
          <a href="#" class="facebook-button apprequests" id="sendRequest"
data-message="Test this awesome app">
            <span class="apprequests">Send Requests</span>
          </a>
        </li>
      </ul>
    </div>
```

```
        </div>
        <?php
} else {
    ?>
        <div>
           <h1>Welcome</h1>
           <div class="fb-login-button" data-scope="user_likes,user_photos"></div>
        </div>
        <?php
}
    ?>
    </header>

    <?php
if ($user_id) {
    ?>

    <section id="main" class="clearfix">
      <canvas id="game" width="400" height="400"></canvas>
    </section>

    <?php
}
    ?>

  <script src="javascript/puzzle.js"></script>

  <script>
    var imagePath = '<?php echo $src; ?>';
    init('game', imagePath, 3);
  </script>
  </body>
</html>
```

Everything should be in order now, and when you commit the changes to your code (git commit -am "Added initial code for game with Facebook integration") and deploy the code to Heroku (git push origin master), you will see something along the lines of Figure 10–7, after giving permission for the application to access your images.

Figure 10–7. *Image Puzzle using a random image*

This game is great, but you will notice that in the previous examples, I used a 600 × 600 grid, but when I went to the Facebook example, I changed this to a 400 × 400 grid. This size change actually masks an issue that pops up. The default size of the images served by Facebook is about 600 × 400 pixels. With a 600 × 600 grid, you introduce whitespace into the game. Since the background of the canvas is also white, extra whitespace can make the game almost unplayable. The quickest solution to the problem is to restrict the canvas element to a 400 × 400 size. However, this crops about 200 pixels off the right side of the image—not an acceptable solution.

A better solution is to recalculate the size of the tiles by separating the tile width and height instead of using the single `tileSize` variable. This refactoring will allow the code to handle nearly any aspect ratio for images (provided you have an appropriately sized image). The first thing to do here is create a topic branch in your Git repository, as shown in Listing 10–25.

Listing 10–25. *Creating a New Branch in Your Git Repository*

```
cd path/to/code
git branch refactor
git checkout refactor
```

The new branch in your Git repository will keep your edits separate while you develop the fix. Now, you can add the fixes to `javascript/puzzle.js` (see Listing 10–26). The first step is to add a variable to hold the `tileWidth` and `tileHeight` values. Then, set those values in the `init()` function.

Listing 10–26. *Initializing the tileHeight and tileWidth variables.*

```
var tileWidth;
var tileHeight;
var gridWidth;
var gridHeight;

function init(canvasId, imagePath, gridCount) {
  canvas = document.getElementById(canvasId);
  context = canvas.getContext('2d');

  gameSize = canvas.width;

  gridWidth = canvas.width;
  gridHeight = canvas.height;

  gridSize = gridCount;

  //tileSize = gameSize / gridSize;

  tileWidth = Math.floor(gridWidth / gridSize);
  tileHeight = Math.floor(gridHeight / gridSize);


  setImage(imagePath);
  addEvents(canvas);

  solved = false;

  setBoard();
}
```

I commented out the `tileSize` variable and used the `Math.floor()` function to eliminate subpixel values (e.g., 400 / 3 = 133.333 . . .). Now, we can update other functions in the code that use the `tileSize` in its calculations, substituting the appropriate width and height for the x and y values.

```
function addEvents(canvas) {
  canvas.onmousemove = function(event) {
    clickLoc.x = Math.floor((event.pageX - this.offsetLeft) / tileWidth);
    clickLoc.y = Math.floor((event.pageY - this.offsetTop) / tileHeight);
  };

  canvas.onclick = function() {
    if (distance(clickLoc.x, clickLoc.y, emptyLoc.x, emptyLoc.y) === 1) {
      slideTile(emptyLoc, clickLoc);
      drawTiles();
    }
    if (solved) {
      setTimeout(function() {alert("You solved it!");}, 500);
    }
  };
}

function drawTiles() {
  context.clearRect ( 0 , 0 , gameSize , gameSize );
  for (var i = 0; i < gridSize; ++i) {
```

```
    for (var j = 0; j < gridSize; ++j) {
      var x = boardParts[i][j].x;
      var y = boardParts[i][j].y;
      if(i !== emptyLoc.x || j !== emptyLoc.y || solved === true) {

        context.drawImage(image, x * tileWidth, y * tileHeight, tileWidth, tileHeight,
                          i * tileWidth, j * tileHeight, tileWidth, tileHeight);
      }
    }
  }
}
```

With this refactor, the grid is now properly applied to the image at a 600 × 400 size, allowing the users to play the puzzle game on the full-sized image delivered by Facebook. The entire puzzle.js file should now look like this:

Listing 10–27. *Initializing the tileHeight and tileWidth variables.*

```
var canvas;
var context;

var image;

var solved;

var music;

var gameSize;
var gridSize;

var tileWidth;
var tileHeight;

var tileSize;
var boardParts = {};

var clickLoc = {
  x: 0,
  y: 0
};

var emptyLoc = {
  x: 0,
  y: 0
};

function setImage(imagePath) {
  image = new Image();
  image.src = imagePath;
  image.addEventListener('load', drawTiles, false);
}

function addEvents(canvas) {
  canvas.onmousemove = function(event) {
    clickLoc.x = Math.floor((event.pageX - this.offsetLeft) / tileWidth);
    clickLoc.y = Math.floor((event.pageY - this.offsetTop) / tileHeight);
  };
```

```
     canvas.onclick = function() {
       if (distance(clickLoc.x, clickLoc.y, emptyLoc.x, emptyLoc.y) === 1) {
         slideTile(emptyLoc, clickLoc);
         drawTiles();
       }
       if (solved) {
         setTimeout(function() {alert('You solved it!');}, 500);
       }
     };
   }

   function setBoard() {
     boardParts = new Array(gridSize);
     for (var i = 0; i < gridSize; ++i) {
       boardParts[i] = new Array(gridSize);
       for (var j = 0; j < gridSize; ++j) {
         boardParts[i][j] = {
           x: (gridSize - 1) - i,
           y: (gridSize - 1) - j
         };
       }
     }
     emptyLoc.x = boardParts[gridSize - 1][gridSize - 1].x;
     emptyLoc.y = boardParts[gridSize - 1][gridSize - 1].y;
     solved = false;
   }

   function drawTiles() {
     context.clearRect(0, 0, gameSize, gameSize);
     for (var i = 0; i < gridSize; ++i) {
       for (var j = 0; j < gridSize; ++j) {
         var x = boardParts[i][j].x;
         var y = boardParts[i][j].y;
         if (i !== emptyLoc.x || j !== emptyLoc.y || solved === true) {

           context.drawImage(image, x * tileWidth, y * tileHeight, tileWidth,
                             tileHeight, i * tileWidth, j * tileHeight,
                             tileWidth, tileHeight);
         }
       }
     }
   }

   function distance(x1, y1, x2, y2) {
     return Math.abs(x1 - x2) + Math.abs(y1 - y2);
   }

   function slideTile(toLoc, fromLoc) {
     if (!solved) {
       boardParts[toLoc.x][toLoc.y].x = boardParts[fromLoc.x][fromLoc.y].x;
       boardParts[toLoc.x][toLoc.y].y = boardParts[fromLoc.x][fromLoc.y].y;
       boardParts[fromLoc.x][fromLoc.y].x = gridSize - 1;
       boardParts[fromLoc.x][fromLoc.y].y = gridSize - 1;
       toLoc.x = fromLoc.x;
       toLoc.y = fromLoc.y;
       checkSolved();
     }
```

```
}

function checkSolved() {
  var flag = true;
  for (var i = 0; i < gridSize; ++i) {
    for (var j = 0; j < gridSize; ++j) {
      if (boardParts[i][j].x !== i || boardParts[i][j].y !== j) {
        flag = false;
      }
    }
  }
  solved = flag;
}

function init(canvasId, imagePath, gridCount) {
  canvas = document.getElementById(canvasId);
  context = canvas.getContext('2d');

  gameSize = canvas.width;

  gridWidth = canvas.width;
  gridHeight = canvas.height;

  gridSize = gridCount;

  tileSize = gameSize / gridSize;

  tileWidth = Math.floor(gridWidth / gridSize);
  tileHeight = Math.floor(gridHeight / gridSize);


  setImage(imagePath);
  addEvents(canvas);

  solved = false;

  setBoard();
}


function playMusic(musicPath, filename) {
  music = new Audio();
  var soundStub = musicPath + '/' + filename;

  if (music.canPlayType('audio/ogg')) {
    music = new Audio(soundStub + '.ogg');
  } else if (music.canPlayType('audio/mp3')) {
    music = new Audio(soundStub + '.mp3');
  }

  music.load();
  music.play();

}
```

Once you have this code functioning, it is time to merge your code back in to the `master` branch that you are deploying the code from. First, make sure your changes are committed to the `refactor` branch.

```
git commit -am "Fixes issue in calculating size of grid"
```

Now, merge the refactor branch in to master:

```
git checkout master
git merge refactor
```

Your changes are now in your `master` branch, and you can now deploy the code by pushing your changes to Heroku.

```
git push origin master
```

If you point your browser to the page with your code pushed to Heroku, you should see a correctly rendered image puzzle, like the one shown in Figure 10–8.

Figure 10–8. *Corrected image puzzle using the default width from Facebook images*

2.0 Ideas

This implementation of an image slider puzzle is relatively simple, and there is a lot of room for improvements to make the game more exciting. You could add in a better algorithm for randomizing the image tiles; instead of shifting the tiles and rows, you could build a randomized mosaic of images. You could implement a time-based component that would make players race against the clock to finish. You may also want to expand the locations images come from to include your friends' photo albums or even implement a feature that would allow players to select the pictures they want to use. These are just a few ideas I came up with to improve the overall gameplay, but perhaps a good question to ask here is, "What you would do to make this a better game?"

Summary

This chapter walked through the creation of a game and using the Facebook API to personalize it. We walked through the development of a game first, without using the Facebook integration, and then layered on calls to the Facebook graph. This technique helps you focus on problems as they arise, enabling you deal with them independently from other aspects of your code (e.g. is it a problem in the response data from Facebook, or how my game code initializes a certain parameter). I also walked through an issue that came up in the code that was outside of the planning going in to the game. Thinking about your code and coming up with an acceptable solution is something you will encounter again and again, no matter if you are developing games for Facebook or any other type of platform.

In the next chapter, I will cover how to more tightly integrate the game with Facebook features, getting in to deploying the Credits and Achievements APIs, as well as working with databases on the Heroku platform.

Chapter 11

Adding Facebook Components

In the previous chapter, we walked through using the Facebook Graph API to provide the data for a puzzle game. Now that we have a game people can play, it is time to take it to the next level. We'll leverage some of the other Facebook APIs to recognize achievements for playing the game and track the fastest times for completing a puzzle. To do this, we need to interact with the Heroku system and its database backend.

I will also cover some of the basics for deployment, including minifying your codebase, dealing with cheaters, and protecting your game from theft. If you move your game to a platform other than Heroku, you may need to adjust some of the database commands, but you should be able to port this code to other platforms.

Adding Levels

If you recall, the code in the last chapter was written to allow you to dynamically generate a grid. The examples in that chapter defaulted to a 3 × 3–grid, but by changing the instantiation parameter, you can easily change this to 4 × 4, 5 × 5, and so on. Each time you add a grid column and row, you add a magnitude of complexity and challenge to the game. Not only does the number of tiles grow exponentially but picking out details to properly order the tiles becomes more difficult. We can use this fact to implement a level system, though some thought needs to go in to capping the maximum number of tiles that are playable as a maximum level. For instance, while technically possible, a 400 × 400–grid would give us a total of 160,000 tiles, with each tile being 1 × 2 pixels. While this grid may provide some interesting art, the game would be nearly impossible to play.

After some experimentation at passing different values to the grid generation, the game (at least for me) was impossible with a grid larger than 5 × 5 (25 tiles). Although there are people out there who could not only do but enjoy more complex puzzles, I do want to place some limits on the top level to ensure that a majority of people can finish in a reasonable time period. I also want to have easy, intermediate, and hard levels for the game; each level of difficulty corresponds to a grid value: 3 × 3–grid is easy, 4 × 4 intermediate, and 5 × 5 hard. In your game, and depending on feedback you get from your players, you may want to adjust this and maybe allow the hard mode to go up to even a 10 × 10–grid (100 tiles). However, for the purposes of this chapter, I will constrain each level to one grid size.

For the first iteration of the code, I will let people choose the levels they want to try. Feedback from the user will then be used to instantiate the puzzle with the appropriate number of grids. Since this is an HTML application, we can use both DOM and canvas elements to easily add this effect. We want to present the player with a screen that first prompts the user to select a level. The technique that I will employ here will create a DOM element on the page that is the same size as the canvas and then add an event listener with jQuery that will instantiate the game and show the canvas element.

Open the index.php file for your project, and add a new DOM element with an id of "splash". We also need to hide the canvas element with a CSS element that sets its initial display to "none". The revised code is shown in Listing 11–1.

Listing 11–1. *Adding a Splash Screen*

```
<div id="main">
    <div id="splash">
      <h1>Image Puzzle</h1>
      <ul id="level">
        <li data-level="3">Easy</li>
        <li data-level="4">Medium</li>
        <li data-level="5">Hard</li>
      </ul>
    </div>

      <canvas id="game" width="600" height="400" style="display:none;"></canvas>
    </div>
  </section>
```

The result of this will now produce an unordered list on the screen, and the game no longer appears (see Figure 11–1).

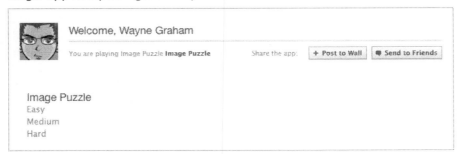

Figure 11–1. *Initial splash screen*

The HTML5 specification has the ability to embed custom data attributes in HTML elements. You do this by creating an attribute prefixed with "data-" and giving it a value.

In the case of the levels, I attached the data level to each of the list items to make working with the information easier in JavaScript.

When working with the DOM, there are a lot of different nuances in the implementation of different specifications. To smooth out these differences, JavaScript frameworks like jQuery help you develop to a common API to take care of the implementation details on the different browsers. Right now, jQuery is one of the more commonly used methods for dealing with these differences, and using it here with the splash screen makes good sense.

To bring jQuery into the project, we pull it from a content delivery network (CDN). Most likely, the version of jQuery you will be using will already be cached on the user's computer, and if not, you can ensure that the browser gets a copy from a server that is geographically close to the user. I use Google's CDN, but the jQuery libraries are also maintained on Microsoft's Bing network, CDNjs, and jQuery's own CDN network. After calling in the jQuery library, I can attach a click listener to the list items in the level list (see Listing 11–2).

Listing 11–2. *Hiding the game*

```
<script src="https://ajax.googleapis.com/ajax/libs/jquery/1.7/jquery.min.js"></script>

<script>
     var imagePath = '<?php echo $src ?>';

     $('#level li').click(function() {
       $('#splash').hide();

         var level = $(this).attr('data-level');

         init('game', imagePath, level);

         $('#game').show();
     });

   </script>
```

This is a relatively minor change to the code. This code listens for any clicks on a list item that is contained in the 'level' container. When it registers a click, it hides the #splash container, reads the data-level attribute from the list item that was clicked, initializes the game, and displays the game canvas. When you click one of the values, you should now be able to have different levels to play.

However, the initial splash screen does not look very good with the default styling. Because these are DOM elements, we can change these easily with CSS in the stylesheets/base.css file. The first pass of the effect just makes the splash screen hold the same dimensions as the canvas element and makes the text look a bit nicer. I centered the main header, resized the list items, and changed the cursor when a user hovers over a list item, as well as giving a little padding to the bottom of the game space (see Listing 11–3).

Listing 11–3. *Splash Screen CSS*

```css
#main {
  width: 92%;
  max-width: 100%;
  *zoom: 1;
  margin: auto;
  padding-top: 2em;
  padding-bottom: 1.3em;
}

#game {
  margin: auto;
  display: block;
}

#splash {
  width: 600px;
  height: 400px;
  margin: auto;
  display: block;
  text-align: center;
  border: 1px solid #c0c0c0;
  padding-top: 2em;
}

#splash h1 {
  font-size: 3em;
}

#splash ul {
  margin-top: 2.2em;
  text-align: left;
  margin-left: 8em;
  font-size: 2em;
}

#splash li {
  line-height: 1.4em;
}

#splash li:hover {
  color: # 656565;
  cursor: pointer;
}
```

Now, when you look at the page, it should look much better (see Figure 11–2).

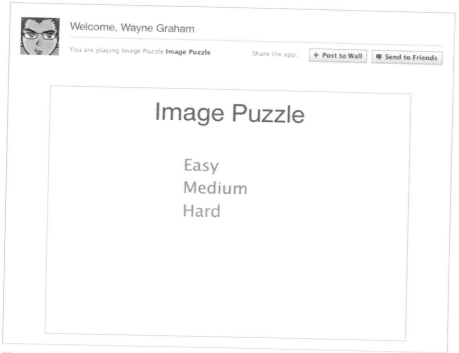

Figure 11–2. *Styled splash screen*

This is a good first step, but we can do better with some of the new CSS features supported in different browsers with a few tricks. First, I want to use a different font for this to make it look more like a game. After spending some time browsing the Google Font directory, I decided to use a font named Slackey. We need to tell our web page about this font before we can use it. The simplest method to use this web font is by including the link Google provides to define the font (see Listing 11–4).

Listing 11–4. *Incorporating a Google Font*

```
<link href='http://fonts.googleapis.com/css?family=Slackey' rel='stylesheet'
  type='text/css'>
```

It is important to add this font before your default style sheet to make sure that the fonts are defined before they are used. After defining this font, we can use it in the main style sheet (stylesheets/base.css). For the splash screen, I want to use a blue background, have an orange banner across the top with the Image Puzzle logo, and have a drop shadow on all the text (see Listing 11–5).

Listing 11–5. *Updated CSS for the splash screen*

```
#splash {
  width: 600px;
  height: 400px;
  margin: auto;
  display: block;
```

```
    text-align: center;
    border: 1px solid #c0c0c0;
    padding-top: 2em;
    background: #77D5FB;
}

#splash h1 {
    background: none repeat scroll 0 0 #E5592E;
    border-radius: 2px 2px 2px 2px;
    box-shadow: 0 0 4px rgba(0, 0, 0, 0.55);
    color: #FFFFFF;
    font-family: 'Slackey',serif;
    font-size: 3em;
    height: 1.2em;
    padding-top: 25px;
    position: relative;
    text-shadow: 0 2px 1px rgba(0, 0, 0, 0.5);
}

#splash ul {
    margin-top: 2.2em;
    text-align: left;
    margin-left: 8em;
    font-size: 2em;
}

#splash li {
    line-height: 1.4em;
    font-family: 'Slackey', serif;
    color: #fff;
    text-shadow: 0 2px 1px rgba(0, 0, 0, 0.5);
}

#splash li:hover {
    color: #E5D9D5;
    cursor: pointer;
}
```

Now when you reload the page, you should see a much better looking splash screen (see Figure 11–3).

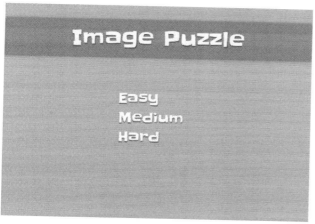

Figure 11-3. *Styled splash screen*

This looks more like a game now. The nice thing about this is that I did not need to produce any artwork for this screen. In fact, it is just text with a few fancy decorations added. But what happens if you are looking at this in a browser that does not support some of the drop shadow and border radius? The fallback version just has white text on a blue or orange background. While the effect does look better in a modern browser, the style degrades quite nicely for browsers without these features enabled.

Adding a Timer

People like to see how they are doing on a game compared to others. One way we may be able to provide some type of metric is by calculating the amount of time a given puzzle takes to solve. Doing so is reasonably straightforward in JavaScript. Essentially, we want to store the time the game starts and set another variable for when the game is completed. A few small changes to the `javascripts/puzzle.js` will make this happen.

First, we need to define some variables to hold when the game was started, when it will end, and the total time taken (see Listing 11–6).

Listing 11–6. *Adding a Timer*

```
var start, stopped, totalTime;

function startTimer() {
  start = new Date().getTime();
}

function stopTimer() {
  stopped = new Date().getTime();
}

function calcTime() {
  totalTime = stopped - start;
}
```

```
function formatTime() {
  return totalTime / 1000;
}
```

In the `index.php` file shown in Listing 11–7, we want to start the timer after the canvas has been revealed to the user.

Listing 11–7. *Starting the Timer*

```
$('#level li').click(function() {
    $('#splash').hide();

    var level = $(this).attr('data-level');

    init('game', imagePath, 2);

    $('#game').show();
    startTimer();
});
```

The `addEvents` method that fires when the game state changes to `solved` also needs to be updated to stop the timer and display the amount of time it takes to solve the puzzle (see Listing 11–8).

Listing 11–8. *Stopping the Timer*

```
function addEvents(canvas) {
  canvas.onmousemove = function(event) {
    clickLoc.x = Math.floor((event.pageX - this.offsetLeft) / tileWidth);
    clickLoc.y = Math.floor((event.pageY - this.offsetTop) / tileHeight);
  };

  canvas.onclick = function() {
    if (distance(clickLoc.x, clickLoc.y, emptyLoc.x, emptyLoc.y) === 1) {
      slideTile(emptyLoc, clickLoc);
      drawTiles();
    }
    if (solved) {
      stopTimer();
      calcTime();
      setTimeout(function() {alert("You solved it! And it only took you " +
formatTime() + " seconds.");}, 500);
    }
  };
}
```

Now a player who has solved the puzzle is presented with the amount of time it took to solve the puzzle in a dialog box like the one shown in Figure 11–4.

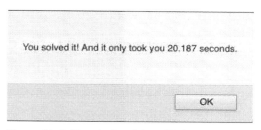

Figure 11–4. *The winning dialog with time taken feedback*

The game will feel a lot more like a game now that you have given players a time to beat for their personal bests. You could also implement a timer, giving players a time to beat, or even assign a score to the time (e.g., beat the easy level in 60 seconds for 500 points, or beat it in 30 seconds for 1,000 points). Another idea for the game play would be to use a count-down timer as a component of game play. Complete the first level in 60 seconds and move to the next puzzle. There are a lot of possibilities for different types of game play.

As the game stands now with the timer display, players need to remember what their best times were. Our application could really use a leader board and some feedback on the average time it takes to finish a puzzle. To implement these features, we need to be able to persist some data that will keep track of this information for us. Fortunately for us, the Heroku platform to which we have deployed our Facebook application has a very powerful database backing it; we just need to enable a few things to unleash its power.

Working with Databases on Heroku

Heroku uses a relational database management system (RDBMS) name PostgreSQL for its projects. Unfortunately, there is not a lot of documentation on how to use Heroku's databases with a PHP application (though there is a lot for using Ruby and nodeJS). Fortunately, I have worked through some of the issues that will come up in using PostgreSQL on Heroku with a PHP application.

By default, PHP applications do not get a database automatically created when the project is initiated (Rails projects do). The first step is to create a shared-database with the heroku command-line interface, as shown in Listing 11–9.

Listing 11–9. *Adding a Database to a Heroku Project*

```
heroku addons:add shared-database
-----> Adding shared-database to [project name]... done, v25 (free)
```

Heroku enforces a best practice of not having passwords in text files for your databases. Instead, it uses a set of environmental variables to store these values. Don't worry; you don't need to know your database username and password are for your application, you can let the server take care of managing this for you. To connect to the database, you will, however, need to establish a database connection by reading these environmental variables and passing them to the database connection, as shown in Listing 11–10.

Listing 11–10. *PHP to Read the Database Connection URL*

```php
function pg_connection_string_from_database_url()
{
    extract(parse_url($_ENV["DATABASE_URL"]));
    $db = substr($path, 1);
    return "user=$user password=$pass host=$host sslmode=require dbname=" . $db;
}
```

This bit of code actually took a while to suss out. However, with the proper PostgreSQL connection string, we can use PostgreSQL drivers for PHP to build our connections. To help manage the connections, I wrote a small PHP class that I placed in a new `libs` directory in the project in a file named `db_manager.php` (see Listing 11–11).

Listing 11–11. *PHP Database Manager for Heroku*

```php
<?php

class DB_Manager
{
  var $dbconn;

  function __construct()
  {
    $this->dbconn = pg_connect(self::pg_connection_string_from_database_url());
  }

  function pg_connection_string_from_database_url()
  {
    extract(parse_url($_ENV["DATABASE_URL"]));
    $db = substr($path, 1);
    return "user=$user password=$pass host=$host sslmode=require dbname=" . $db;
  }

  function open()
  {
    $this->dbconn = pg_pconnect(
      "host=$host port=$port dbname=$dbname user=$user password=$password"
    );
  }

  function close()
  {
    return pg_close($this->dbconn);
  }

  function query($sql)
  {
    return pg_query($this->dbconn, $sql);
  }

  function numrows($query)
  {
    return pg_numrows($query);
  }

  function fetch_array($query, $row = NULL)
  {
```

```
    return pg_fetch_array($query, $row);
  }

  function fetch_object($query, $row = NULL)
  {
    return pg_fetch_object($query, $row);
  }
}
```

This PHP class will give us some easy helper methods to not only manage the database connection (opening and closing it) but also interact with the data in the database by returning the raw data from the database server and converting it in to a format that is easier to work with.

Unfortunately, getting deep in to the PostgreSQL implementation of the ANSI-SQL specification is beyond the scope of this book. However, if you have worked with MySQL before, making the jump to PostgreSQL is not that difficult, especially if you have used an abstraction library like PDO or MDB2. However, for the purposes of this book, I will just manage the connection and queries directly.

To track our players, we need to keep track of a few things: their Facebook user IDs, the levels they completed, the time it took them to complete puzzles, and timestamps of when the users completed their puzzles. The SQL statement, sometimes called a data definition language (DDL) file, for creating this table would look like Listing 11–12.

Listing 11–12. *PostgreSQL DDL for the puzzle_tracker table*

```
DROP TABLE IF EXISTS puzzle_tracker;

CREATE TABLE puzzle_tracker
(
  id serial NOT NULL, -- auto-incremented id
  uid bigint, -- Facebook user id
  level integer, -- level completed
  completion_time int, -- time taken to complete puzzle
  date_added timestamp with time zone DEFAULT now(),
  CONSTRAINT id PRIMARY KEY (id)
);

CREATE INDEX puzzle_tracker_uid_idx
  ON puzzle_tracker USING btree (uid);
```

These commands are somewhat dangerous, especially the first line. As you might guess, this statement is all it takes to drop the table (and its information) from the database. Dropping a table is convenient in development mode if you are changing data (or table definitions) and need to quickly re-create a table and you do not have any "real" data to lose. If you need to add a field to a database after the initial table creation, you will want to use an ALTER TABLE statement to add the field as shown in Listing 11–13, instead of dropping the entire table.

Listing 11–13. *PostgreSQL puzzle_tracker ALTER TABLE Definition*

```
ALTER TABLE puzzle_tracker
ADD COLUMN new_field character varying;
```

The `CREATE TABLE` statement creates the `puzzle_tracker` table and sets an auto-generated ID field that will increment itself to ensure that each record has a unique identifier. The `uid` field is the user ID field associated with a given user's Facebook account, and because Facebook defines this as a `bigint` field, I did the same here. The level is just an integer to record the level that was completed (e.g., 3, 4, or 5), and the `completion_time` records the milliseconds taken to complete the puzzle. To keep track of when the puzzle record was submitted, I created a timestamp (with time zone information) and set the default value to the time when the record is created. Each of these fields has a comment that describes the field for the developer (in SQL, comments are two hyphens followed by the comment).

A lot of lookups for this data will depend on the `uid` field. The number of puzzles completed, average time taken on the puzzles, and fastest/slowest completion times can all be calculated from this single table. To speed up these calculations, I added an index on the `uid` field to ensure these lookups happen as quickly as possible.

To actually build this table on Heroku, I created a new file in the `libs` directory named `setup.php`. I include the database manager created earlier and execute the SQL statements to build the database. To make sure the table gets created, I query the table that keeps track of all the tables in the database and then print them out on the screen (see Listing 11–14).

Listing 11–14. *PostgreSQL DDL for puzzle_tracker Table*

```php
<?php

require_once('db_manager.php');

$db = new DB_Manager();

$sql = <<<'SQL'

DROP TABLE IF EXISTS puzzle_tracker;

CREATE TABLE puzzle_tracker
(
   id serial NOT NULL, -- auto-incremented id
   uid bigint, -- Facebook user id
   level integer, -- level completed
   completion_time int, -- time taken to complete puzzle
   date_added timestamp with time zone DEFAULT now(),
   CONSTRAINT id PRIMARY KEY (id)
);

CREATE INDEX puzzle_tracker_uid_idx
   ON puzzle_tracker USING btree (uid);
SQL;

$add_table = $db->query($sql);

$query = "SELECT relname FROM pg_stat_user_tables WHERE schemaname='public'";
$tables = $db->query($query);

print "<pre>\n";
```

```
if (!pg_num_rows($tables)) {
    print("Your connection is working, but your database is empty.\n
        Fret not. This is expected for new apps.\n");
} else {
    print "Tables in your database:\n";
    while ($row = pg_fetch_row($tables)) { print("- $row[0]\n"); }
}
print "\n";

$db->close();
```

Add the new files in your Git repository (`git add`), commit the changes (`git commit -am` `"Adding database components"`), and deploy (`git push origin master`). Now, you should be able visit your project and add the URL for the setup code (e.g., `http://your-application-name.heroku.com/libs/setup.php`).

After the database has been set up, you will see the text shown in Figure 11–5 on the web page.

```
Tables in your database:
- puzzle_tracker
```

Figure 11–5. *Successfully created database*

Since this is dangerous (you do not want people accidentally dropping all of your tables and data), it is a good idea to go in to the `setup.php` file and comment out the code that actually drops and creates the database, as shown in Listing 11–15.

Listing 11–15. *Comment Out Dangerous Parts*

```php
<?php

require_once('db_manager.php');

$db = new DB_Manager();
/*
$sql = <<<'SQL'

DROP TABLE IF EXISTS puzzle_tracker;

CREATE TABLE puzzle_tracker
(
    id serial NOT NULL, -- auto-incremented id
    uid bigint, -- Facebook user id
    level integer, -- level completed
    completion_time int, -- time taken to complete puzzle
    date_added timestamp with time zone DEFAULT now(),
    CONSTRAINT id PRIMARY KEY (id)
);

CREATE INDEX puzzle_tracker_uid_idx
    ON puzzle_tracker USING btree (uid);
SQL;

$add_table = $db->query($sql);
*/
$query = "SELECT relname FROM pg_stat_user_tables WHERE schemaname='public'";
```

```
$tables = $db->query($query);

print "<pre>\n";
if (!pg_num_rows($tables)) {
  print("Your connection is working, but your database is empty.\n
    Fret not. This is expected for new apps.\n");
} else {
  print "Tables in your database:\n";
  while ($row = pg_fetch_row($tables)) { print("- $row[0]\n"); }
}
print "\n";

$db->close();
```

Now, commit the changes (git commit -am "removed dangerous drop table and create table statement"), and push this code to Heroku (git push origin master). The last thing in the world you want to do is accidentally delete your tables. Speaking as someone who has accidentally dropped the wrong table in a production environment, I can assure you there is no worse feeling in the world. You can recover from this, but it is horribly embarrassing and does take some time (and you will most likely lose some of your user's data).

Recording Puzzle Information

Now that we have created a table to record our information, we need to work on saving data from the puzzle to it. Because we want this to feel like an application, we can take care of the posting of scores to the server with AJAX. Since we already have jQuery included for this project, this is a really simple refactor. As with any AJAX code, there are two pieces: the server-side code that processes the request and the client side that initiates it. I will start with the JavaScript to build the AJAX request and send it to the server and then implement the server side response.

Passing data in AJAX can be quite simple. For our purposes, I am creating a new object in the javascripts/puzzle.js file to hold the data the server side will need. This is named score, and it will hold the values of the current player's Facebook ID, the puzzle level, and the time it took to complete the puzzle (see Listing 11–16).

Listing 11–16. *Score Object*

```
var score = {};
```

Now we need to add some information to the addEvents method to handle submitting the data to the server when the puzzle is solved (see Listing 11–17).

Listing 11–17. *Passing the score Object via AJAX to score.php*

```
function addEvents(canvas) {
  canvas.onmousemove = function(event) {
    clickLoc.x = Math.floor((event.pageX - this.offsetLeft) / tileWidth);
    clickLoc.y = Math.floor((event.pageY - this.offsetTop) / tileHeight);
  };

  canvas.onclick = function() {
    if (distance(clickLoc.x, clickLoc.y, emptyLoc.x, emptyLoc.y) === 1) {
```

```
      slideTile(emptyLoc, clickLoc);
      drawTiles();
    }
    if (solved) {
      stopTimer();
      calcTime();
      setTimeout(function() {
        alert("You solved it! And it only took you " + formatTime() + " seconds.");
        score.level = gridSize;
        score.completion_time = totalTime;
        $.ajax({
          url: 'score.php',
          data: score,
          type: 'POST'
        });
      }, 500);
    }
  };
}
```

This update expands the setTimeout() function and sets the level and completion_time to pass to the server. The jQuery ajax method is used to pass the data to score.php as a post. However, one other piece of data needs to be set—the Facebook user ID. This can be set in the index.php file after the game has been initialized by using the $my_id variable that was set in the PHP code (see Listing 11–18).

Listing 11–18. *Setting the score.uid Value from a PHP Variable*

```
var imagePath = '<?php echo $src ?>';

$('#level li').click(function() {
        $('#splash').hide();

        var level = $(this).attr('data-level');

        init('game', imagePath, level);

        score.uid = <?php echo $my_id; ?>;

        $('#game').show();
        startTimer();
});
```

Now, let's set up the code on the server to process the score object. In the top level of your project directory, create a new file named score.php. This will be where we handle adding scores for the game. In the first pass, we just want to insert the information that is passed from the puzzle.js AJAX call, as shown in Listing 11–19.

Listing 11–19. *Adding Scores*

```
<?php
require_once("libs/db_manager.php");

// make sure only numbers are being passed
$uid = intval($_POST['uid']);
$level = intval($_POST['level']);
$completion_time = intval($_POST['completion_time']);
```

```
$sql = <<<SQL
INSERT INTO puzzle_tracker(uid, level, completion_time)
VALUES($uid, $level, $completion_time);
SQL;

$db = new DB_Manager();

$add_puzzle = $db->query($sql);

print_r($add_puzzle);

$db->close();
```

This code reads the values passed to it via a POST request and parses the values to ensure that they are integers. The SQL is a simple insert statement, which is passed to the database manager. For debugging purposes, the result of the database query is written to the screen (you can see the value in FireBug or Chrome Developer Tools), and the database connection is then closed.

Although this game will now work, we need to a few more things to make it more difficult to cheat. Right now, this code accepts three numbers from anywhere and inserts them in to the database. However, this is an issue as a player who wants to cheat can figure out what where to post their scores (they have downloaded the source code after all) and post their own scores. To combat this a bit, we need to do a little more work on the server side to parse the values and determine where they are coming from. These are some very basic protections against people "cheating" the system. These checks should be made before the insert is made in the score.php file, as shown in Listing 11–20.

Listing 11–20. *Protecting Inserts*

```
// protect from get requests
if (!isset($_POST['uid']) || ! isset($_POST['level']) ||↵
 ! isset($_POST['completion_time'])) {
  header('HTTP/1.1 403 Forbidden');
  die;
}

// check server referrer
if (! strpos($_SERVER['HTTP_REFERER'], $_SERVER['SERVER_NAME'])) {
  header('HTTP/1.1 403 Forbidden');
  die;
}
```

Now that there is some data being recorded, we can add some feedback for users to let them know their best, worst, and average completion times. For this, I just whipped up a quick page that shows the high scores that are recorded. I created a new file named highscore.php with the code in Listing 11–21.

Listing 11–21. *High Score Code (highscore.php)*

```
<?php

require_once("libs/db_manager.php");
```

```php
$db = new DB_Manager();

$high_scores = <<<SQL
  SELECT * FROM puzzle_tracker ORDER BY completion_time LIMIT 10;
SQL;

$time_query = <<<SQL
SELECT avg(completion_time) as average,
  min(completion_time) as min,
  max(completion_time) as max
FROM puzzle_tracker;
SQL;

$high_scores_result = $db->query($high_scores);
$time_result = $db->query($time_query);
$time = $db->fetch_array($time_result);

$counter = 1;

$db->close();
?>
<!DOCTYPE html>
<html lang="en">
  <head>
    <meta charset="utf-8">

    <title>Image Puzzle Hall of Fame</title>

    <link rel="stylesheet" href="stylesheets/screen.css" media="screen">
  </head>
  <body>
    <h1>Image Puzzle Hall of Fame</h1>

    <ul>
      <li>
        <strong>Average Time:</strong>
        <?php echo format_milliseconds($time['average']); ?>
      </li>
      <li>
          <strong>Fastest Time:</strong>
          <?php echo format_milliseconds($time['min']); ?>
      </li>
      <li>
          <strong>Slowest Time:</strong>
          <?php echo format_milliseconds($time['max']); ?>
      </li>
    </ul>

    <table>
      <tr>
        <th>Rank</th>
        <th>Time Taken</th>
        <th>Level</th>
        <th>Player</th>
      </tr>
      <?php while($row = pg_fetch_array($high_scores_result)): ?>
```

```
          <tr>
          <td><?php echo $counter ?></td>
              <td><?php echo $row['completion_time'];?></td>
              <td><?php echo $row['level']; ?></td>
              <td><?php echo $row['uid']; ?></td>
          </tr><?php $counter++; ?>
        <?php endwhile; ?>
      </table>
    </body>
</html>
```

I use SQL to calculate the average, minimum, and maximum times taken for the puzzles using aliases to differentiate the return values. The high scores query orders the table by the `completion_time` field and limits the results of the query to 10. The data is then placed in to a table.

The time format here displays the total milliseconds taken to finish. Although a convenient way for computers to track time, this number is not very meaningful to most people. The typical way to format the time is with the various `date` functions built in to PHP. Unfortunately, a new "feature" in PHP requires the server to set a default time zone to use these functions, and this setting is not configured (currently) on the Heroku servers—not a big deal, we just need to write our own date formatter and use it on the values (see Listing 11–22).

Listing 11–22. *Formatting Milliseconds*

```
function format_milliseconds($ms)
{
   $minutes = floor($ms / 60000);
   $seconds = floor(($ms % 60000) / 1000);
   $milliseconds = str_pad(floor($ms % 1000), 3, '0', STR_PAD_LEFT);
   return $minutes . ':' . $seconds . '.' . $milliseconds;
}
```

This function can be added to the main `index.php` file (or the `utils.php` file to be used in other places in your code base) and used to format the time taken to complete the puzzle in to the format of `minutes:seconds.milliseconds` and limit the millisecond value to three decimal places. Applying this to the time formats will provide more reasonable time output, as shown in Figure 11–6.

Image Puzzle Hall of Fame
Average Time: 693:47.395
Fastest Time: 0:0.000
Slowest Time: 7266:36.443

Rank	Time Taken	Level	Player
1	0:0.000	2	7608007
2	0:0.000	2	1234567
3	0:2.372	2	7608007
4	0:2.418	2	7608007
5	0:2.518	2	7608007
6	0:2.894	2	7608007
7	0:2.916	2	7608007
8	0:3.164	2	7608007
9	0:3.403	2	7608007
10	0:3.647	2	7608007

Figure 11–6. *Hall of Fame*

The style on this page can use some refinement, but you can tinker with the CSS to integrate this into the overall look and feel of your application. You can take this example further and use the data in the database and make requests to the Facebook Graph API to get a user's profile picture. In this case, it is a simple matter of requesting the profile image from the graph using the player_id field:

Listing 11–23. *Requesting a profile image from the Graph API*

```
http://graph.facebook.com/<?php echo $row['uid']; ?>/picture?type=small
```

Tracking Achievements

Facebook has an achievement system that is quite similar to what you see on Xbox and PlayStation games. Your game has access to 1,000 points and up to 1,000 achievements. Each achievement needs its own page, which has a title, description, image, and a number of points. With these constraints in mind, we can build a quick system to try out the Facebook achievements system with the achievements stored in a database, and served from our application.

Setting up achievements involves creating a table that holds the information Facebook uses in the Open Graph protocol to define the achievements for the application. To set up, I created a new directory named achievements, and the first file I created in that directory is setup.php. In this file, I define a new database table and add some achievements. While you may modify how you manage the data in your application (e.g., build an administrative interface to add and edit the achievements), the code in Listing 11–23 will get you started. Listing 11–23 assumes that you have a directory in your projects images subdirectory named achievements (i.e., images/achievements) containing the images for each achievement.

Listing 11–24. *Creating the achievements Database Table*

```php
<?php

require_once('../libs/db_manager.php');

$setup = <<<SQL
CREATE TABLE achievements
(
  id serial NOT NULL,
  title character varying(50),
  description character varying(255),
  image character varying(50),
  points integer,
  CONSTRAINT primary_key PRIMARY KEY (id)
);
SQL;

$easy = <<<SQL
INSERT INTO achievements(title, description, image, points)
VALUES(
  'Easy Mode Complete',
  'Finish an image puzzle on easy mode',
  '/images/achievements/easy.png',
  10
);
SQL;

$medium = <<<SQL
INSERT INTO achievements(title, description, image, points)
VALUES(
  'Intermedia Mode Complete',
  'Finish an image puzzle on intermediate mode',
  '/images/achievements/intermediate.png',
  20
);
SQL;

$hard = <<<SQL
INSERT INTO achievements(title, description, image, points)
VALUES(
  'Hard Mode Complete',
  'Finish an image puzzle on hard mode',
  '/images/achievements/hard.png',
  30
);
SQL;

$db = new DB_Manager();

$db->query("DROP TABLE achievements;");

$db->query($setup);
$db->query($easy);
$db->query($medium);
$db->query($hard);

$records = "SELECT * FROM achievements";
```

```php
$results = $db->query($records);

echo '<pre>';
while($row = pg_fetch_array($results)) {
  print_r($row);
}
echo '</pre>';
```

Now that we have some valid achievements, it is time to create a page that will display the Open Graph data for the achievement. I created this file (show.php) in the achievements directory (see Listing 11–24). This page is responsible for querying the database for the achievement passed in the URL (e.g., http://yourdomain.com/achievements/show.php?achievement=1). The page will generate an appropriate HTML response for Facebook with the appropriate Open Graph metadata for the achievement.

Listing 11–25. *Displaying Achievements (achievements/show.php)*

```php
<?php

require_once('../libs/db_manager.php');
require_once('../AppInfo.php');

if(!isset($_GET['achievement'])) {
  header('Location: /');
  exit();
}

$achievement_id = intval($_GET['achievement']);

$sql = <<<SQL
SELECT *
FROM achievements
WHERE id = $achievement_id;
SQL;

$db = new DB_Manager();
$results = $db->query($sql);
$achievement = pg_fetch_array($results);

if(!sizeof($achievement) === 1) {
  header('Location: /');
  exit();
}

$url = 'http://' . $_SERVER['SERVER_NAME'] . $_SERVER['REQUEST_URI'];
$image_url = 'http://' . $_SERVER['SERVER_NAME'] . $achievement['image'];
?>
<!doctype html>
<html lang="en">
<head>
<title><?php echo $achievement['title']; ?></title>
<meta property="og:type" content="game.achievement">
<meta property="og:url" content="<?php echo $url ?>">
<meta property="og:title" content="<?php echo $achievement['title']; ?>">
<meta property="og:locale" content="en_US">
<meta property="og:description" content="<?php echo $achievement['description']; ?>">
```

```
<meta property="og:image" content="<?php echo $image_url; ?>">
<meta property="game:points" content="<?php echo $achievement['points']; ?>">
<meta property="fb:app_id" content="<?php echo AppInfo::appID();?>">
</head>
<body>
<?php echo $achievement['description']; ?>
</body>
</html>
```

This page will query the database for the appropriate achievement (passed with the `id` URL parameter) and construct the appropriate Facebook Achievement content for the Open Graph protocol. There is also a check to make sure that if the id is not passed in the URL, or if the database did not find the associated achievement, it redirects the browser to the main game. This just adds a little more security, and prevents some

For each of the achievements, you will need to create a 50 × 50–pixel image that represents the achievement. I created a few circular images with stars in them with slightly different colors for the three achievements. You can go nuts with these, but remember, these will be displayed to Facebook users in a 50 ×50–square, and only so much detail looks good at that size.

You can test the achievements to make sure that the data is correct in the Facebook Object Debugger (`https://developers.facebook.com/tools/debug`). When you put in the URL for the specific achievement (e.g., `http://yourdomain.com/achievements/show.php?id=1`), you will see any errors that exist and an output of the raw data under the Object Properties, as shown in Figure 11–7.

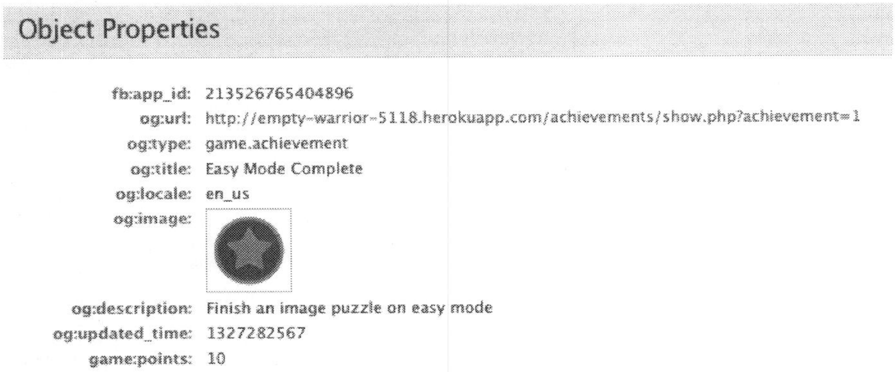

Object Properties

fb:app_id:	213526765404896
og:url:	http://empty-warrior-5118.herokuapp.com/achievements/show.php?achievement=1
og:type:	game.achievement
og:title:	Easy Mode Complete
og:locale:	en_us
og:image:	
og:description:	Finish an image puzzle on easy mode
og:updated_time:	1327282567
game:points:	10

Figure 11–7. *Open Graph debugging tool*

This is one of the easiest ways to register an achievement. At the bottom of the page in the URL section, you will see a link to the Facebook Graph with an ID (see Figure 11–8).

URLs

Graph API: https://graph.facebook.com/10150754321563298
Scraped URL: See exactly what our scraper sees for your URL

Figure 11–8. *Achievement as seen by the Facebook Graph API*

If you click the Graph API link, you will see that Facebook has collected information about the achievement and registered it in the graph; this code is shown in Listing 11–25.

Listing 11–26. *Facebook Achievement Registration Response*

```
{
    "url": "http://empty-warrior-5118.herokuapp.com/achievements/show.php?id=1",
    "type": "game.achievement",
    "title": "Easy Mode Complete",
    "locale": {
        "locale": "en_us"
    },
    "image": [
        {
            "url": "http://empty-warrior-5118.herokuapp.com/images/achievements/easy.png"
        }
    ],
    "description": "Finish an image puzzle on easy mode",
    "data": {
        "points": 10
    },
    "updated_time": "2011-01-29T15:28:30+0000",
    "id": "10150754321563298",
    "application": {
        "id": "213526765404896",
        "name": "Image Puzzle",
        "url": "https://www.facebook.com/apps/application.php?id=213526765404896"
    }
}
```

Assigning Achievements

To assign achievements for your game, you need to request the `publish_actions` permissions. In the `index.php` file, we need to change the scope of the permissions requested for the game to include this permission. This is done in the HTML block which passes the login request to Facebook. Find the 'fb-login-button' and add `publish_actions` to the `data-scope` attribute (see Listing 11–26).

Listing 11–27. *Requesting publish_action permissions*

```
<div class="fb-login-button" data-scope="user_likes,user_photos,publish_actions"></div>
```

Now, when the users log into the application, they will be prompted to give permission to allow applications to publish scores and achievements.

> **NOTE:** An application needs to be listed in the Game category in the Facebook Developer application to use `publish_actions` extended permissions shown in Listing 11–27.

With a bit of logic to determine if the player has unlocked an achievement, you can then post the achievement URL to the Facebook graph. We do this by using the POST method to add the achievement to the user's profile, passing the achievement earned to the Facebook graph, as shown in Listing 11–28.

Listing 11–28. *Assigning an Achievement*

```
$access_token = AppInfo::appID() . '|' . AppInfo::appSecret();

$payload = array(
   'achievement' => 'http://yourapplication.com/achivements/show.php?id=1',
   'access_token' => $access_token
);

$response = $facebook->api('/' . $user_id . '/achievements', 'POST', $payload);
```

Customizing the Authorization Dialog

Before your game goes live, take some time to customize the authorization dialog box that users will see when they install your game. The form to do this is located in the Auth Dialog section in your application's settings in the Facebook Developer application, as shown in Figure 11–9.

The logo file is a thumbnail for your application. The final size of this image is 75 × 75 pixels, so if you use a larger size, Facebook will resize the image. For my example, I created an image at a size of 150 ×150 to make the file easier to work with. I created a quick puzzle piece by drawing a rectangle and then three ellipses on it. I then punched out two of the ellipses and took the union of the third to create a puzzle-piece effect. I put the puzzle piece on a circle and then added some linear gradients and a drop shadow—nothing fancy here, just some basic shapes to make the no default icon shown in Figure 11–10.

Apps ▸ Image Puzzle ▸ Auth Dialog

The New Auth Dialog

Customize your auth dialog and preview the new permissions system before it goes live to all users. You'll be able to configure authenticated referrals, provide a headline, and highlight your app's timeline integrations.

Learn more about Auth

Customize

Preview Dialog

Logo:

Headline: [?]

Description: [?]

Privacy Policy URL:

Terms of Service URL:

Add Data to Profile URL: [?]

Explanation for Permissions: [?]

Default Activity Privacy: [?]   ✿ None (User Default) ▾

Configure how Facebook refers users to your app

✓ **Authenticated Referrals**   Request permissions when users on Facebook click on links to your app

Figure 11–9. *Facebook Auth Dialog form*

Figure 11–10. *Puzzle icon*

The headline for you application needs to be description of your application with 30 characters or fewer and will be located directly below the title of the application; this value is optional, so it does not need to be filled in. The description field can contain up to 140 characters and should give people playing the game a short blurb about the game itself.

These fields should be quite straightforward for your application. However, the privacy policy, terms of service, and explanation of permissions can be new for a lot of developers. Having and adhering to a privacy policy for your application is a really good idea; it establishes your terms of service for the application as well as helps in the transparency of what your site is about, and how you handle your user's information.

Creating Your Privacy Policy

As you may have read in the news, Facebook recently settled with the Federal Trade Commission to have regular audits of its privacy policies until 2031. While the Facebook terms of service allow you to record only information about your users that your game depends on, it is a good idea to have a policy in place that states what information you are recording from users and how you intend to use it. This policy does not typically need to be reviewed by a lawyer but should state clearly what you are doing. An example policy might look something like the following section.

A SAMPLE PRIVACY POLICY

Your privacy is very important to us. Accordingly, we have developed this policy to help you understand how we collect, use, communicate, disclose, and make use of personal information. The following outlines our privacy policy.

- Before, or at the time of, collecting personal information, we will identify the purposes for which information is being collected.

- We will collect and use personal information with the sole objective of fulfilling those purposes specified by us and for other compatible purposes.

- We will retain personal information only as long as necessary for the fulfillment of these purposes.

- We will collect personal information by lawful and fair means, where appropriate, with the express knowledge or consent of the individual concerned.

- Personal data should be relevant to the purposes for which it is to be used, and, to the extent necessary for those purposes, should be accurate, complete, and up to date.

- We will protect personal information by reasonable security safeguards against loss or theft, as well as unauthorized access, disclosure, copying, use, or modification.

- We will make readily available to individuals information about our policies and practices relating to the management of personal information.

We are committed to conducting our business in accordance with these principals to ensure that the confidentiality of personal information is protected and maintained.

Defining Your Terms of Service

A terms of service agreement lists the rights and limitations of a site's users and defines the relationship between your users and your content. While big companies like Facebook have very in-depth terms of service agreements that are written by lawyers, you can get started with some basic text that covers a few aspects of people using your site. The terms of service agreement in the following section is loosely based on several boilerplate terms of service agreements available on the Internet.

A SAMPLE TERMS OF SERVICE AGREEMENT

Terms

By accessing this web site, are you are agreeing to be bound by this site's Terms and Conditions of Use, all applicable laws and regulations, and agree that you are responsible for compliance with any applicable local laws. If you do not agree with any of these terms, you are prohibited from using or accessing this site's content. Materials contained in this site are protected by applicable copyright and trade mark law.

Use License

Permission is granted to temporarily download one copy of the materials (information or software) on this web site for personal, noncommercial transitory viewing only. This is the grant of a license, not a transfer of title, and under this license you may not

- Modify or copy the materials.
- Use the materials for any commercial purpose or for any public display (commercial or noncommercial).
- Attempt to decompile or reverse engineer any software contained on this web site.
- Remove any copyright or other proprietary notations from the materials.
- Transfer the materials to another person or "mirror" the materials on any other server.

This license shall automatically terminate if you violate any of these restrictions and may be terminated by the operator of this web site at any time. Upon terminating your viewing of these materials or upon the termination of this license, you must destroy any downloaded materials in your possession, whether in electronic or print format.

Disclaimer

The materials on this web site are provided "as is." The author of the site makes no warranties, expressed or implied, and hereby disclaims and negates all other warranties, including without limitation, implied warranties or conditions of merchantability, fitness for a particular use, or non-infringement of intellectual property or other violation of rights. Further, the site's maintainer does not warrant or make any representations concerning the accuracy, likely results, or reliability of the use of the materials on this Internet web site or otherwise relating to such materials or on any sites linked to this site.

Limitations

In no event shall the site's maintainer or its suppliers be liable for any damages (including, without limitation, damages for loss of data or profit, or due to business interruption) arising out of the use or inability to use the materials on this Internet site, even if the site's maintainer or the site's authorized representative has been notified orally or in writing of the possibility of such damage. Because some jurisdictions do not allow limitations on implied warranties, or limitations of liability for consequential or incidental damages, these limitations may not apply to you.

Revisions and Errata

The materials appearing on this web site could include technical, typographical, or photographic errors. The site's maintainer does not warrant that any of the materials on its web site are accurate, complete, or current. The site's maintainer may make changes to the materials contained on its web site at any time without notice. The site's maintainer does not, however, make any commitment to update the materials.

Links

The site's maintainer has not reviewed all of the sites linked to its Internet web site and is not responsible for the contents of any such linked site. The inclusion of any link does not imply endorsement by the maintainer of the site. Use of any such linked web site is at the user's own risk.

Site Terms of Use Modifications

The site's maintainer may revise these terms of use for its web site at any time without notice. By using this web site you are agreeing to be bound by the then current version of these Terms and Conditions of Use.

Governing Law

Any claim relating to this web site shall be governed by the laws of the State of [Your State] without regard to its conflict of law provisions.

General Terms and Conditions applicable to Use of a Web Site.

Adding Your Terms of Service Policy

You can add the terms of service and privacy policy on the same page and provide links to the policies on the Auth Dialog. For the game I walked through in this chapter, we did use some extended permissions to use the Facebook Achievements API. It is worth noting in the explanation for permissions that you are using the permissions to publish achievements. When you have filled out the form, you can preview what users will see by clicking the Preview Dialog link in the right-hand corner of the form (see Figure 11–11).

Figure 11–11. *Facebook Auth Dialog Preview*

Remember that this dialog is the first thing your users will encounter in your application. Although it may not seem like a big detail, the first impression can be lasting. Paying attention to details like this helps make the case to your users that your application has been crafted by someone passionate about the application you are sharing with the world.

Deployment Concerns

I hear a lot of people worry, often prematurely, about cheaters and people stealing the code for their games. I feel that the primary concern for your game is developing something that people want to play and that going too far down the rabbit hole of code obfuscation to keep people from stealing your code can lead you in to a false sense of security. A lot of talented developers are out there, and given enough time and interest, they can figure out what you are doing with your code.

However, there are some advantages to using a few techniques to obfuscate your code in production. When you minify you code, you create a file that is not human friendly, but the browser can still handle readily. At a basic level, minifying tools strip out unneeded whitespace that is typically in place to make the code easy for developers to work with. Removing the whitespace can provide a huge reduction in the bandwidth required to get your code to the browser, making your application load faster and saving money on your bandwidth. The magnification libraries also generally include advanced features that help removed unused code, rename variables (to be shorter), and even rewrite certain functions to be more efficient. These advanced features make the JavaScript code you are writing much more difficult to read and thus make tracking what the code is doing more difficult as well. As your codebase grows for your different levels, you can reduce the size of the code you deliver by a substantial amount using these minification libraries.

The goal here is to work this in as part of your workflow, working with an uncompressed version of the JavaScript code while developing your game, and delivering a compressed version of the code when you deploy your game to Heroku. There are a lot of ways to manage this: Paul Irish's HTML5 Boilerplate project (http://html5boilerplate.com/) comes with a set of Java ANT tasks to manage minifying not only your JavaScript code but also your static HTML and CSS using several open source projects. Rakefiles (a set of automated tasks written in Ruby) help a lot, so does using a bash or Windows batch file to automate the generation of these files. Depending on the tools you are most comfortable with (and operating system), you should pick an automation framework that works for you.

Because the HTML5 Boilerplate is being actively maintained and provides tools for several different operating systems, it makes a good tool to start from. I will simplify the build process; HTML5 Boilerplate has quite a few tools to assist in the compression of JavaScript, images, and CSS. However, if you find that you require a more complex build process, I encourage you to read the source of the ant-build-script repository very closely (https://github.com/h5bp/ant-build-script), and customize to your needs.

The first step is to download the latest Boilerplate code (from https://github.com/h5bp/ant-build-script/zipball/master). We will not need everything from the decompressed package, so just copy its contents directory into a new 'build' directory in your game project. This directory will contain an ANT script (build.xml), a configuration directory, scripts to start new Boilerplate projects, and a tools directory with the tools necessary to automate the compression of CSS, JavaScript, and different image assets. For right now, we will only be using the tools directory, so feel free to delete the other files (everything but build/tools) in your project.

In the top level of your project, you can create a new ANT script named build.xml. ANT is a Java-based tool that allows you to build up automation tasks with XML. In the build.xml file, we will add some tasks to automate our compression of our assets, appending "-min" to the filenames to ensure we do not overwrite something we will need to edit (see Listing 11–29).

Listing 11–29. *ANT Tasks for Optimizing Code for Web Delivery*

```
<?xml version="1.0"?>
<!DOCTYPE project>
<project name="Game Project" default="build" basedir=".">

  <property environment="ENV" />

  <!-- Load the Ant-contrib to give us access to some very useful tasks! -->
  <!-- the .jar file is located in the tools directory -->
  <taskdef resource="net/sf/antcontrib/antlib.xml">
    <classpath>
      <pathelement location="${basedir}/build/tools/ant-contrib-1.0b3.jar"/>
    </classpath>
  </taskdef>

<target name="setup">
    <echo message="Creating directory structure..." />
```

```xml
        <mkdir dir="${basedir}/images/optimized/" />
    </target>

    <target name="clean">

    </target>

    <target name="minify-js" description="Minifies JavaScript using Google's Closure↵
Compiler">
        <echo message="Minifying JavaScript" />

        <apply executable="java" parallel="false">
            <fileset dir="${basedir}/javascripts/" excludes="**/*.min.js"↵
includes="**/*.js" />
            <arg line="-jar" />
            <arg path="${basedir}/build/tools/closure-compiler-v1346.jar" />
            <arg line="--js" />
            <srcfile/>
            <arg line="--compilation_level" />
            <arg value="SIMPLE_OPTIMIZATIONS" />
            <arg line="--js_output_file" />
            <mapper type="glob" from="*.js" to="*.min.js" />
            <targetfile/>
        </apply>
    </target>

    <target name="minify-css" description="Minifies CSS">
        <echo message="Minifying CSS" />

        <apply executable="java" parallel="false">
            <fileset dir="${basedir}/stylesheets/" excludes="**/*.min.css"↵
includes="**/*.css"/>
            <arg line="-jar" />
            <arg path="${basedir}/build/tools/yuicompressor-2.4.5.jar" />
            <srcfile/>
            <arg line="-o" />
            <mapper type="glob" from="*.css" to="*.min.css" />
            <targetfile />
        </apply>
    </target>

    <target name="optimize-png" description="Optimizes .png images with optipng">
        <echo message="Optimizing images..."/>
        <echo message="This may take a while, but everything else is already done."/>
        <echo message=" " />

        <echo message="Running optipng on the .png files..." />
        <!-- osfamily=unix is actually true on OS X as well -->
        <!-- On *nix's and OS X, check for optipng and give a helpful message if it's↵
not installed -->
        <if>
          <and>
            <os family="unix" />
            <available file="optipng" filepath="${ENV.PATH}" />
          </and>
          <then>
            <!-- work around https://sourceforge.net/tracker/?func=detail&aid↵
```

```
=2671422&group_id=151404&atid=780916 -->
       <delete>
         <fileset dir="${basedir}/images/optimized/">
           <include name="**/*.png"/>
         </fileset>
       </delete>
       <apply executable="optipng" dest="${basedir}/images/optimized/" osfamily="unix">
         <fileset dir="${basedir}/images/" includes="**/*.png" />
         <arg value="-quiet"/>
         <arg value="-o7"/>
         <arg value="-out"/>
         <targetfile/>
         <srcfile/>
         <mapper type="identity"/>
       </apply>
     </then>
     <elseif>
       <os family="unix" />
       <then>
         <echo message="*** optipng NOT INSTALLED. SKIPPING OPTIMIZATION OF PNGs." />
         <echo message="*** Install optipng to enable png optimization." />
         <echo message="*** For instructions see 'Dependencies' at:↵
  http://html5boilerplate.com/docs/#Build-script#dependencies" />
       </then>
     </elseif>
     <elseif>
       <os family="windows" />
       <!-- work around https://sourceforge.net/tracker/?func=detail&aid↵
=2671422&group_id=151404&atid=780916 -->
       <then>
         <delete>
           <fileset dir="${basedir}/images/optimized/">
             <include name="**/*.png"/>
           </fileset>
         </delete>
         <apply executable="${basedir}/build/tools/optipng-0.6.4-exe/optipng.exe"
           dest="${basedir}/images/optimized/" osfamily="windows">
           <fileset dir="${basedir}/images/" includes="**/*.png" />
           <arg value="-quiet"/>
           <arg value="-o7"/>
           <arg value="-out"/>
           <targetfile/>
           <srcfile/>
           <mapper type="identity"/>
         </apply>
       </then>
     </elseif>
   </if>

 </target>

 <target name="optimize-jpeg" description="Optimizes .jpg images using jpegtan">
   <echo message="Optimizing jpegs..." />

   <var name="strip-meta-tags" value="all" />

   <!-- On *nix's and OS X, check for jpegtran and give a helpful message if it's↵
```

```
not installed -->
    <if>
      <and>
        <os family="unix" />
        <available file="jpegtran" filepath="${ENV.PATH}" />
      </and>
      <then>
        <apply executable="jpegtran" dest="${basedir}/images/optimized" osfamily="unix">
          <fileset dir="${basedir}/images/" includes="**/*.jpg" />
          <arg value="-copy"/>
          <arg value="${strip-meta-tags}"/>
          <arg value="-optimize"/>
          <arg value="-outfile"/>
          <targetfile/>
          <srcfile/>
          <mapper type="identity"/>
          <!-- you may want to flag optimized images. If so, uncomment the line
below -->
          <!--<mapper type="glob" from="*.jpg" to="*.jpg"/>-->
        </apply>
      </then>
      <elseif>
        <os family="unix" />
        <then>
          <echo message="*** jpegtran NOT INSTALLED. SKIPPING OPTIMIZATION OF JPEGs." />
          <echo message="*** Install jpegtran to enable jpeg optimization." />
          <echo message="*** For instructions see 'Dependencies' at:
http://html5boilerplate.com/docs/#Build-script#dependencies" />
        </then>
      </elseif>
    </if>

    <apply executable="${basedir}/build/tools/jpegtran.exe"
      dest="./images/optimized" osfamily="windows">
      <fileset dir="${basedir}/images" includes="**/*.jpg" />
      <arg value="-copy"/>
      <arg value="${strip-meta-tags}"/>
      <arg value="-optimize"/>
      <arg value="-outfile"/>
      <targetfile/>
      <srcfile/>
      <mapper type="identity"/>
      <!-- you may want to flag optimized images. If so, do it here. -->
      <!--<mapper type="glob" from="*.jpg" to="*.jpg"/>-->
    </apply>

  </target>


  <target name="build" depends="minify-js, minify-css, optimize-png, optimize-jpeg" />
</project>
```

When you run the command ant from your project directory, you will generate minified versions of your JavaScript and CSS code, as well as generate new, optimized files (see Listing 11–30).

Listing 11–30. *ANT Tasks Output*

```
Buildfile: [path-to-project]/puzzle-game/build.xml

minify-js:
    [echo] Minifying JavaScript

minify-css:
    [echo] Minifying CSS

setup:
    [echo] Creating directory structure...
    [mkdir] Created dir: [path-to-project]/puzzle-game/images/optimized

optimize-png:
    [echo] Optimizing images...
    [echo] This may take a while, but everything else is already done.
    [echo]
    [echo] Running optipng on the .png files...
    [apply] Result: 1
    [apply] Result: 1
    [apply] Result: 1

optimize-jpeg:
    [echo] Optimizing jpegs...

build:

BUILD SUCCESSFUL
Total time: 13 seconds
```

My workflow for development uses Git, with my local development done on a develop branch, and deployments from the master branch. I run the optimizations on the master branch when I am ready to deploy. Listing 11–31 shows the commands I typically issue to deploy my code (assumes you are on the develop branch).

Listing 11–31. *Git-Heroku Deployment Workflow*

```
git co master
git merge develop
ant
git commit -am "Optimized css, javascript, and images; adds xyz features for production"
git push origin master
```

Git allows me to organize my code in to what I am working on, and bringing ANT in to the picture on the master branch allows me to optimize my code before pushing it on to the servers for Facebook users to use with optimizations to minimize the amount of bandwidth needed to view the game on the web.

Summary

This chapter stepped through adding features from the Facebook APIs to polish the game we developed in the previous chapter. We added additional features to allow players to play the game at different levels, refined the interface, added achievements, and improved the Authorization dialog. I briefly covered creating a terms of service agreement and a privacy statement and finished up with optimizing your CSS, image files, and JavaScript for delivery on the web.

In the next chapter, I will cover some of the basics of launching your game, including setting up a WordPress site to talk about your game, Facebook Pages, advertising, and some tips to help drive users to your game.

Chapter 12

Launching Your Game

Once you have finished your game and have tested it on the Facebook Platform, you next need to get people to play the game. This chapter walks you through a cycle that will help you leverage the power of Facebook to gain players for your game.

The process of launching a game has several different phases, all of them aimed at increasing the visibility and accessibility of your game online.

- Building a Website: Build a web presence for your game outside of Facebook.

- Creating a Facebook Page: Build a Facebook Page to promote your game and provide a platform for interacting with your "fans."

- Advertising: Get your game in front of more people.

- Driving Traffic: Get people to "Like" your content to get your content in front of your fan's friends.

This chapter is dedicated to walking you through the process of setting up your web presence and driving users to your game.

Website

One of the first things you will want to do to get people playing your game is to make it findable not only on Facebook, but also through search engines. If you have multiple games, this is also a good way to show off all your content at once. Creating a website is not very difficult these days (compared to the energy that goes into creating a full-fledged game), and there are a lot of tools out there to make this as simple as possible. The most difficult decision is probably the first one: how you want to handle your content. The decision basically comes down to how much you yourself want to manage. You may find that you want a content management system (CMS) that can manage your content, or may find that a CMS is too much for your content and choose another method that has been gaining popularity with something such as Jekyll, a static site generation tool built by Github's co-founder, Tom Preston-Werner. No matter what technical decisions you make in how you want to manage your content, the design of your site should tell your users something about your content in a clear concise way.

There are a few things to consider when you begin designing your site. First, keep the design simple. You want your users to come to your site and know immediately where to go to play your game, without having to read too much text. You also need to make a few decisions on how you want to handle adding content.

WordPress

The WordPress blogging platform is a popular option for managing web content, and there are a lot of plugins already written that allow you to integrate the platform with Facebook. Setting up an instance of WordPress is usually a very simple task with most web hosts, as the software required to run WordPress (PHP and MySQL) is usually installed. If you are running your own server, you generally will not need to install additional software to run WordPress, although you may need to take additional steps to configure an instance of the MySQL database system to run the backend of WordPress. Your hosting provider should have good documentation on getting up and running quickly, though, as it is quite popular.

Perhaps one of the biggest issues you will run into when setting up your website is where to host. Unfortunately, the Heroku service we set up in Chapter 8 cannot run WordPress without some hacks (Heroku uses a database system called PostgreSQL for its backend and does not allow applications to write files directly to its file system). There are, however, some alternatives.

One option is to pick a web host. Companies such as Dreamhost (http://www.dreamhost.com), bluehost (http://www.bluehost.com), LaughingSquid (http://www.laughingsquid.com), and MediaTemple (http://www.mediatemple.com) all provide decent hosting for WordPress blogs at a reasonable price. What you really want to do is find a host that has a good panel for managing your content. There is nothing more frustrating than setting up a new site and not being able to find the button you need to push in order to get things up and running.

A shared hosting solution will get you pretty far down the road, but you may find (eventually) that the performance is not what you would like. At this point, it is time to investigate running your own server(s) to host your WordPress installation. Although this is outside the scope of this book, I provide some very general advice. Set up separate database and web servers. On your web server, make sure you cache everything you can (Varnish Cache https://www.varnish-cache.org/ is a great help with caching web content) and make sure you tune your MySQL server parameters to handle your web load. Also, make certain you have a good backup policy. Should something go wrong, this will help you get back up and running quickly, minimizing any bad feelings your users may have toward you.

Another emerging method of deploying websites is through cloud services. One service, which allows you to develop PHP applications with a Git workflow much like Heroku, is named PHPFog (https://phpfog.com/). See Figure 12–1.This service allows you to run up to three "free" applications on their service. In fact, they have a one-button installer for running WordPress. After creating an account, create a new application (app) and click on the WordPress icon.

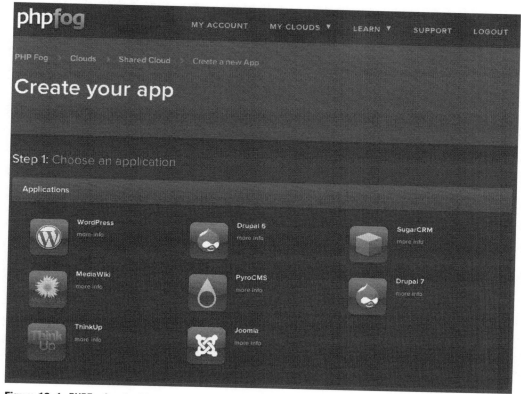

Figure 12–1. *PHPFogApp Dashboard*

After selecting a username and password for your database, as well as a domain name (it is fine to use the phpfogapp domain name), you will be redirected to a page that informs you that your application is being created.

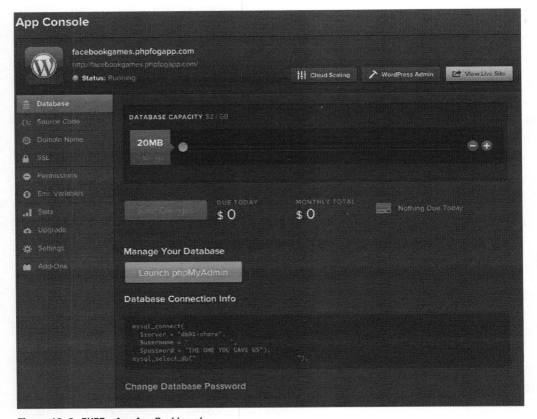

Figure 12–2. *PHPFogApp App Dashboard*

This page (Figure 12–2) will show you the general info for your application (I have blocked out the passwords and Git information here), but you will see that you can quickly have a WordPress installation up and running in the time it takes to click a few buttons. The nice thing about this is that it is very easy to scale this application. Simply drag the slider to add more database storage space if you need more storage. You can also upgrade your plan for the amount of RAM, CPU, and storage should you find you need more system resources. A silver account should be sufficient for most WordPress sites. See Figure 12–3.

Figure 12–3. *PHPFogApp Pricing Plans*

You can clone the project (it is a good way to have a local copy of what you have on the server), but it is not necessary when you are getting up and running.

Log on to your application (the WordPress Admin button on the dashboard) with the credentials you provided. Once logged in, you will see the WordPress dashboard, as shown in Figure 12–4.

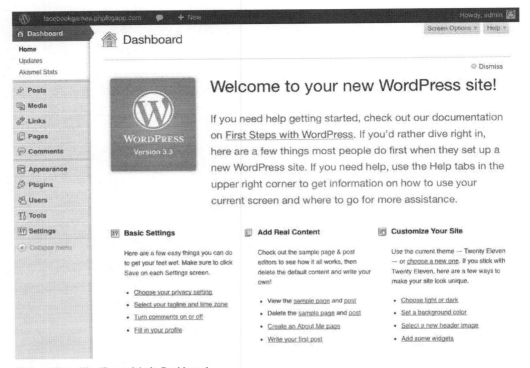

Figure 12–4. *WordPress Admin Dashboard*

WordPress Plugins

If you are new to WordPress, this page will provide you with some basics for working with WordPress. There are a few things beyond adding content, however, that you should do to configure your WordPress installation. First, a few plugins I always use can be installed by clicking on **Plugins ➤ Add New**. Just search for the plugins and click on "Install Now," as in Figure 12–5.

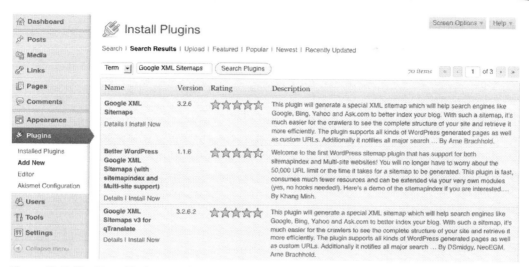

Figure 12–5. *WordPress Plugins*

- **Akismet**: Filters comments and track-backs for spam. You will need a key that you can sign up for at https://akismet.com/signup/ and the Pro account at $5 per month is well worth the money.

- **Google Analytics**: Knowing who is accessing your content, what they are looking at, and how they are using your content can go a long way in helping you tune your content to your users. You can also use the statistics to make sure your servers are responding in a timely manner to the load visitors are placing on them.

- **Google XML Sitemaps**: Generates an XML-Sitemap of your blog for search engines. This helps search engine spiders know about all of your content that you want to be crawled. This will help you have a better search rank in any engine that people are using to find your content.

- **WP Minify**: Combines and minifies JavaScript and CSS files on your site using the Minify engine. This greatly reduces the load time for these files, decreasing the time it takes to download those resourced from your server.

- **WP Super Cache**: A static caching plugin that generates HTML files that are served directly by your web server without processing PHP and MySQL results. Web servers are really great at serving static files, and this plugin will dramatically improve the performance of your application. In addition, if you are using a content delivery network (CDN) such as Amazon CloudFront, Cloudflare, or Akamai (among many others), there is integration with the plugin to send pull requests to propagate your content to all of the servers to ensure people living across the ocean from your servers will not see a lag in accessing your content.

Once you have set up these plugins, you will have a basic setup that will serve you well in general. But this is a book on Facebook, and there are a lot (A LOT) of plugins that help integrate WordPress with Facebook.

Social Plugins

There are literally thousands of WordPress plugins that integrate with Facebook. With this many, selecting ones that actually help (and not get in the way) of your workflow can be a bit overwhelming. These are some of the plugins that I have found work well with Facebook and are not too much of a pain.

- Facebook Like Button (http://wordpress.org/extend/plugins/facebook-like-button/): Adds a "Like" button to your posts. This plugin is highly configurable and allows you to add "Likes" with WordPress' shortcode commands in the editor.

- Facebook Comments (http://wordpress.org/extend/plugins/facebook-comments-for-wordpress/): Integrates Facebook's commenting system into your blog. Anywhere that a user can leave a comment is passed through Facebook. A great option for controlling spam on your site.

- Facebook Tab Manager (http://wordpress.org/extend/plugins/facebook-tab-manager/): Allows you to create content and tabs for Facebook Pages without programming. This is a great plugin for managing content in WordPress that is available only to your Facebook fans.

Facebook Pages

Facebook pages used to be called "Fan Pages," but were shortened to just Pages. Facebook Pages get high search engine positions because of how they are indexed (and the metadata provided on the Page). Unlike personal accounts that limit you to 5,000 friends, a Page can have an unlimited number of "fans." You can set up your Page with information, links to resources, a message forum, and pretty much anything else you want. A Facebook Page provides you with a convenient engaging way to interact with your "fans."

Creating Pages is simple, but a major consideration you need to make is in the name. Take care of the name of your Page, as once you have created a Page, and have more than 100 fans, you cannot change the name. The name is part of the URL and because of the search engine optimizations (SEO) that Facebook employs to drive traffic to your page, their policy is not to allow you to change the name. Unlike with other parts of Facebook, if you contact them directly, you will not be able to change the name.

To create a page, simply point your browser to the Facebook Pages page (`https://www.facebook.com/pages`) and click on the "Create a Page" button. You will be taken to a screen that asks you to categorize your page. See Figure 12–6.

Create a Page
Connect with your fans on Facebook.

Local Business or Place

Company, Organization or Institution

Brand or Product

Artist, Band or Public Figure

Entertainment

Cause or Community

Figure 12–6. *Facebook Pages*

This can be a little confusing. I wanted to create a Page for a game, so I clicked on Entertainment at first, but the options do not include "Game." This category is actually under Brand or Product. Click on Brand or Product and select "Game" from the drop-down menu. Give it a name (the name of your game), accept the Terms and Conditions, and click the Get Started button. See Figure 12–7.

Create a Page

Connect with your fans on Facebook.

Local Business or Place

Company, Organization or Institution

Brand or Product

Join your supporters on Facebook.

| Games / Toys ▼ |

| Alien Turtle Invasion |

☑ I agree to Facebook Pages Terms

[Get Started]

Artist, Band or Public Figure

Entertainment

Cause or Community

Figure 12–7. *Facebook Page Registration*

You will be directed to a wizard that will walk you through setting up your Page. The first step is to add an image for your Page. This image will be on the left-hand side of the Page and can be up to 180 pixels wide by 540 pixels high. There is a lot of creativity that goes into these images, with companies displaying hours, special offers, and other information for their fans. For my purposes here, I whipped up a quick text-based Page image and uploaded it to Facebook (Figure 12–8). For the time being, this will be a placeholder (you can change it later).

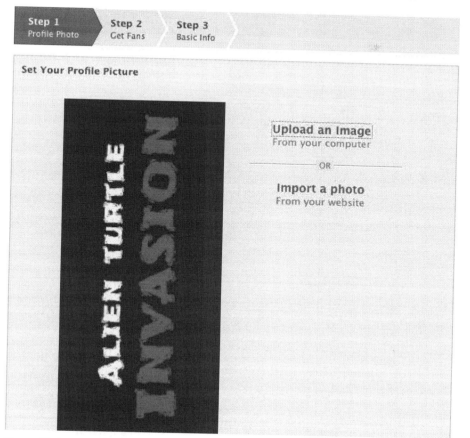

Figure 12–8. *Facebook Page Logo*

After your image has been uploaded, click on the Continue button to Step 2: Get Fans. If you are ready to roll, you can go ahead and invite your friends, but if you are in the initial stages of getting the Page up and running, you may want to uncheck the boxes next to "Share this page on my wall" and "Like this page" shown in Figure 12–9 (you can do this later).

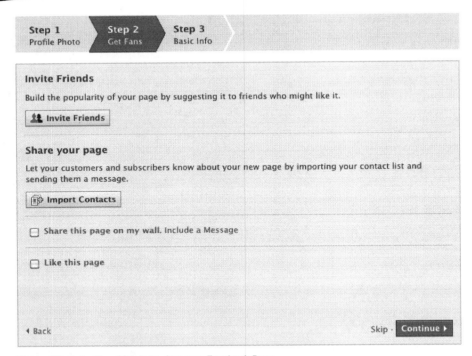

Figure 12–9. *Inviting friends to view your Facebook Page*

The last step is to add some basic information about your Page. If you have a website (like the one you set up earlier in the chapter), you can enter that on this screen as well as a short (255 characters) description of your Page (Figure 12–10).

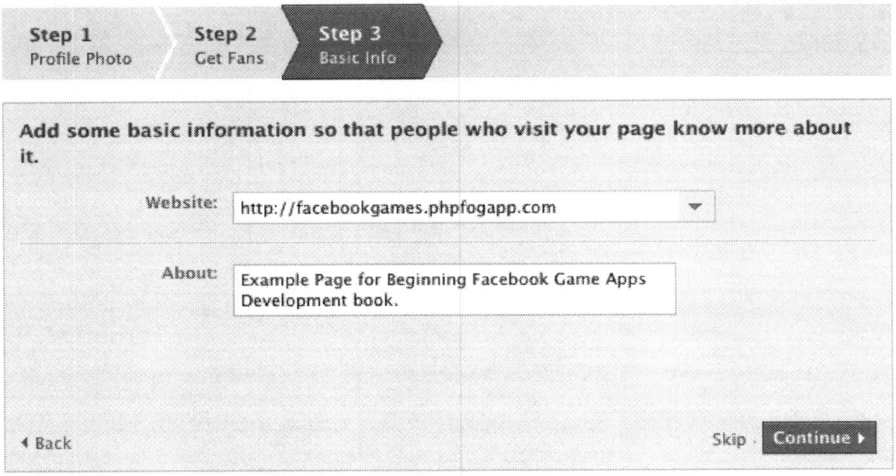

Figure 12–10. *Basic Information about your Facebook Page*

Click "Continue" and you will be redirected to your newly created Page (Figure 12–11).

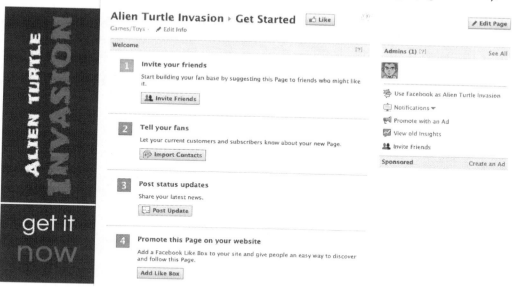

Figure 12–11. *Your Facebook Page*

I like to change the Page visibility while I am developing the content on the Page. Simply click on the "Edit Page" button and tick the "Unpublish page" (only admins can see this Page) option (Figure 12–12) and Save Changes.

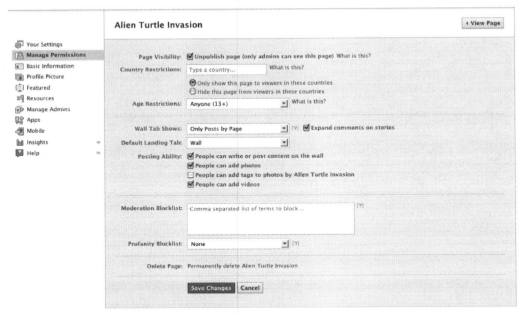

Figure 12–12. *Managing permissions*

Explore the rest of the tabs filling out any pertinent information for your Page.,

Customizing Your Page

After you have an initial page set up, you can start customizing the content. There are some major sections that you can edit, as well as sections that are on every Facebook Page.

Figure 12–13. *Facebook Page components*

I will go through each of the sections in more detail, but Figure 12–13 and the following show the basic layout of every Facebook Page.

1. Profile Picture: This is the image that represents your Page. If you are using this as a promotional device, you can change this easily in the Page admin panel.

2. Page Links: These are the links available to the users of the Page.

3. About: A very brief (255 characters) description of what your Page is about.

4. "Likes": Showcases how many likes you have on a Page and allows you to "Share" the Page with friends.

5. Page Title and Category: The title is editable until you reach 100 users, after that it is permanent. The category, however, can be edited at any time.

6. Page Body: Where new posts appear and where you can interact with "Fans."

7. Administrative Links: Only administrators will see this section and it provides links to options to control how the Page displays.

8. Sponsored Links: Facebook will place ads on your Page. You can also create advertisements to drive users to your Page from this link.

Profile Picture

The profile image is one of the most important pieces of your Page as it draws the eye of your visitors. With the Page I created earlier, you noticed that the image fit nicely on the Page. However, Facebook also generates thumbnails of the image at 50 by 50 pixels. By default, Facebook takes the center point of your image to generate its thumbnail. By default, the image I used for the page is resized as a thumbnail as shown in Figure 12–14.

Figure 12–14. *Default Facebook Page icon*

Not a compelling thumbnail image to grab the attention of potential users. You can move the thumbnail by clicking on the "Edit Thumbnail" at the bottom of the Profile Picture Page. You can either scale to fit the long image (this is actually better if you have a square image), or drag the image to get the thumbnail you want. See Figure 12–15.

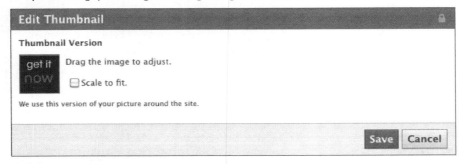

Figure 12–15. *Editing your Facebook Page icon*

Page Links

These links are on every Page and provide users with a consistent navigation scheme to different elements on the Pages. There is some editing you can do if you add new "tabs" to the Page, but for the most part this is a relatively static section of the Page.

About

As shown in Figure 12–16, this is a short sentence or two about your site. It is a good idea to have a link to your site here also. You can edit this either by clicking on the Edit link next to the About section, or in the Admin Panel under Basic Information. You can add a link to your website here and Facebook will automatically link it for you.

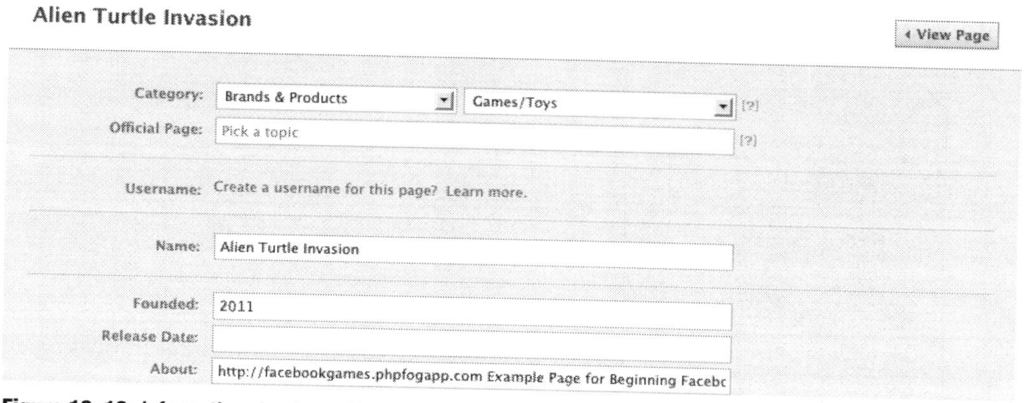

Figure 12–16. *Information about your Page*

"Like"

There are additional options for administrators, and beyond displaying the people who have "Liked" your Page and have participated by talking about it, there are tools to help you promote your Page. One of the more overlooked features is the ability to add "Favorites" to a Page. Essentially this allows you to promote other Pages you administer, or add other people's Pages (and, we hope, vice versa).

Simply click on the "Add to My Page's Favorites" and select the Page to which you want to add the Page, as in Figure 12–17.

Figure 12–17. *Adding a Page to the Favorites section*

This will add a link to the Page you have selected in the section.

If there are Pages you think should get included on your Page, you can navigate to their Page and click on the "Add to My Page's Favorites." To add Apress' site (the publisher of this book) to the game's Page, I simply go to their Page (https://www.facebook.com/pages/Apress/104141976287772), click on the "Add to My Page's Favorites," and select "Alien Turtle Invasion." You will then see a thumbnail with a link to the page in the Like section. See Figure 12–18.

0
like this

Likes

    Facebook API
         Developers Guide

    Apress

Add to My Page's Favorites

Remove from My Page's
Favorites

Get Updates via RSS

Share

Figure 12–18. *Favorites view on Facebook Page*

Title and Category

As mentioned previously, you can edit this title until you have 100 fans, but the category can be edited at any time. Generally if you need to change the title, you are encouraged to create a new Page from scratch. However, if you are really in a bind, one technique is to delete fans until you have 99 and change the title. Think long and hard about doing this as your fans probably won't like being deleted and may take a negative position toward your Page, content, and so on. That said, I cannot emphasize enough the importance of choosing a good name for your Facebook Page.

Page Body

You can add just about any type of content in the body of the Page. This is much like the post section on your user profile. When you post, it is publicly available, so make sure your spelling and punctuation are correct. If you submit a webpage or video that has thumbnails, you will see a preview that will allow you to select an appropriate image to display.

Administrative Links

These tools allow you to perform some common administrative efforts. You can "become" the page you administer on Facebook and post through it (useful for organizations with multiple administrators). From here you can also manage your notifications, promote your Page with an advertisement, view your Page's "insights" (analytics), and have the ability to "invite" your friends to look at the Page.

Promoting Your Page

Once you have your Page on Facebook set up, you can add a "Like" box to help drive traffic. Using the Social Plugins, you can generate a Like box that shows the current user's friends who have also liked your content on your website. If you are using WordPress for your website, you can use any number of plugins that will handle creating this box for you. If you have a custom HTML application (or want to add a "Like" button to a Page that your canvas game is running on), you can generate the code needed by going to the "Like Box" plugin generator that Facebook provides at (https://developers.facebook.com/docs/reference/plugins/like-box/). Simply paste in the Page you want to add a Like button for and click on the "Get Code" button to view the code to place on your Page (Figure 12–19). Be sure to select the proper application to use with your social plugin.

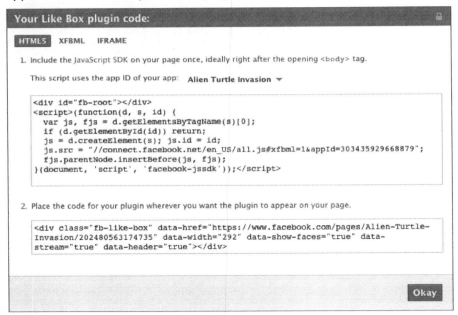

Figure 12–19. *"Like" box code*

The code (Figure 12–20) uses the Facebook JavaScript API to embed a widget on your Page displaying the friends of the user on your site.

Figure 12–20. *Embedded 'Like' button*

Advertising

Facebook has cleverly set itself up to allow individuals and companies to get their content in front of people through advertising. Getting new players to your game is important, and the way Facebook works is through "personal" endorsements (e.g., Joe Schmoe likes this). In order to get more people looking at your content, some carefully crafted ads for your content, as well as the social plugins and website content mentioned earlier in this chapter, go a long way in getting your game in front of more people. This section walks you through a cycle that should help you optimize the investment you make in advertising to help you get more people (and their friends) playing your game. There is a basic cycle you can use to promote your Page or Application that should work well for startups. The idea is to develop content, plug your application, create advertisements to push engagement, and then engage with your users. You will need to hit this cycle at least twice to optimize your Facebook application "adds," and the idea here is to gauge how much your costs are per "add" to optimize your advertising dollars.

Content

The first step in your Facebook campaign is getting some content set up. We hope that you have set this up with the information from earlier in the chapter, so you should have a good base from which to build. Having a Page allows you access to a lot of potential traffic.

Plug

After your content is in place, and you have all of the social plugins to promote your site, it is time to push out your content to your friends. This should get the ball rolling and get your Page a few "Likes". However, Facebook is set up in a manner that in order to really leverage the power of the platform, you will need to spend some money on advertising.

Targeting Ads

Once you have your initial content and users, you can greatly increase the people that you can access through advertising. Facebook provides some powerful tools that allow you to get a good idea of the estimated reach of any given advertising campaign. In the first pass, you want to keep the estimated reach relatively small by targeting those who are likely to click on your game. What you want are high-click-throughs to drive "Likes" to start a conversation (or other interactions) with the users. This will greatly expand the number of fans you can target on the second round of advertising.

Advertising Tips

Effective advertising targeting is only part of the puzzle. You also need to have effective ads. Always try to use a combination of simple bright images with very little text. This allows the eye to be drawn to the ad, and if cleverly worded, will intrigue the user to click on the ad. Images that convert well in general are headshots of some type and colorful logos (reds and yellows). You also want to change your art and copy very often. If your advertisements are not doing as well as you hope, change them and check back the next day. If they still are not performing well, pause or delete the Facebook Ad as the campaign is not targeted properly, or ineffective. There is no use in "wasting" money on ineffective ad campaigns.

One of the big things to keep in mind is having a spending level strategy. If you are just getting started, a very cheap campaign may be at the $20 to $50 per day level for a two-week campaign. As you grow more ambitious, you may want to raise the level to spending several hundred dollars a day.

A great way to find stock photography for your ads (if you are creating them yourself) is through a search engine such as compfight (`http://www.compfight.com`), iStockPhoto (`http://www.istockphoto.com/`), or stock.xchng (`http://www.sxc.hu/`). You can find royalty-free image assets that you can purchase for your ad campaigns at pretty reasonable prices.

Interaction

One of the most important things you can do when developing relationships with your "fans" is interact with them. If someone leaves a post on your Page's wall, or comments on a Page of your website, interact with him. Answer a question or start a discussion, anything that helps foster a relationship with the "fan." The more interactions you have with individuals, the more likely their interactions are to show up on their wall feed, showing your content to their users as an "endorsement" of your game, Page, and so on.

Cycle II

Once you have engaged users on your site, you should have a good base of users. Now it is time to repeat the cycle again, but this time focus on media. This could be an influential blog, a company you would like to work with (like Zynga), or anyone with a large trusted reach. A trick in this cycle is when targeting these individuals at companies, to point them at a target that requires them to click "Like" on your Page to get an "endorsement" of your content. If you are using social widgets from Facebook that can post to a user's wall, just be sure to be respectful. You do not want to be sending things to your users' walls that are unexpected; no one likes spam, and this can lose you "fans" very quickly if you are posting unexpected things to walls.

Cycle III

The first two cycles are meant to grow your base users and get some media exposure. It is hoped that at this point you are in a position where your users are generating content organically, and now you can do some things that will boost engagement. One inexpensive thing you can do is run a poll where your fans can vote on something that resonates with the community you are building. You could create a nomination system to feature a player of your game. Contests are also very popular, but you want to make sure you have a lot of fans before you engage in a contest, as they can be quite expensive. Lastly, you can target friends-of-fans for ads to expand your base.

At this point, you should also know what your revenue per fan is. If you have a game that generates revenue through in-game purchases using Facebook Credits, or ad revenue, you can calculate the revenue (and cost) of each user. As an example, if you have 50 users and each user spends an average of $5 (some may be a lot more, many less) on Facebook credits, each user is worth $5 to you. If you enter a campaign that costs you $2.50 to gain a new user, your revenue per user is $2.50. You will want to be tracking this to make sure you are spending your money wisely so you raise enough revenue to cover the costs of your servers, future development, and future advertising campaigns.

Driving Likes

One of the ways you can drive up your "Likes" (and hence your ranking on people's timeline) in the advertising cycles is with a "Tease and Reveal" where the user has to "Like" the Page in order to see some content. This section walks you through setting up a WordPress blog using the Facebook Tab Manager plugin for WordPress. You will need to install the Facebook Tab Manager plugin. (See the WordPress section earlier in this chapter.)

Create a WordPress Category

In this first step, log on to your WordPress installation and click on **Posts ➤ Categories** (Figure 12–21). You can name this anything you want, but I would suggest that you not use something like "facebook," or any other identifiers that you may use in your regular use of WordPress. I am using "facebook-exclusive" to denote that this is for this particular use. It actually does not matter what you call this, just as long as it makes sense to you. You do not need a slug, or description, and the default parent (none) is fine for our purposes.

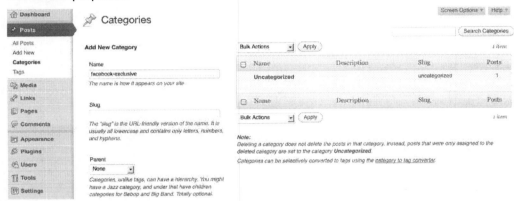

Figure 12–21. *Creating a Facebook Category*

Facebook Tabs

To add a tab for your Page to display some content, simply click on the Facebook Tabs menu on the left-hand side of the WordPress administrative interface (Figure 12–22). Click the "Add New."

Figure 12–22. *Facebook Tabs*

The screen should be quite familiar if you have used Facebook before. Simply add a title and some content (can be text, images, etc.). When you are ready, click on the Publish button. You will be redirected to the same Page, but there will be additional information at the bottom of the Page.

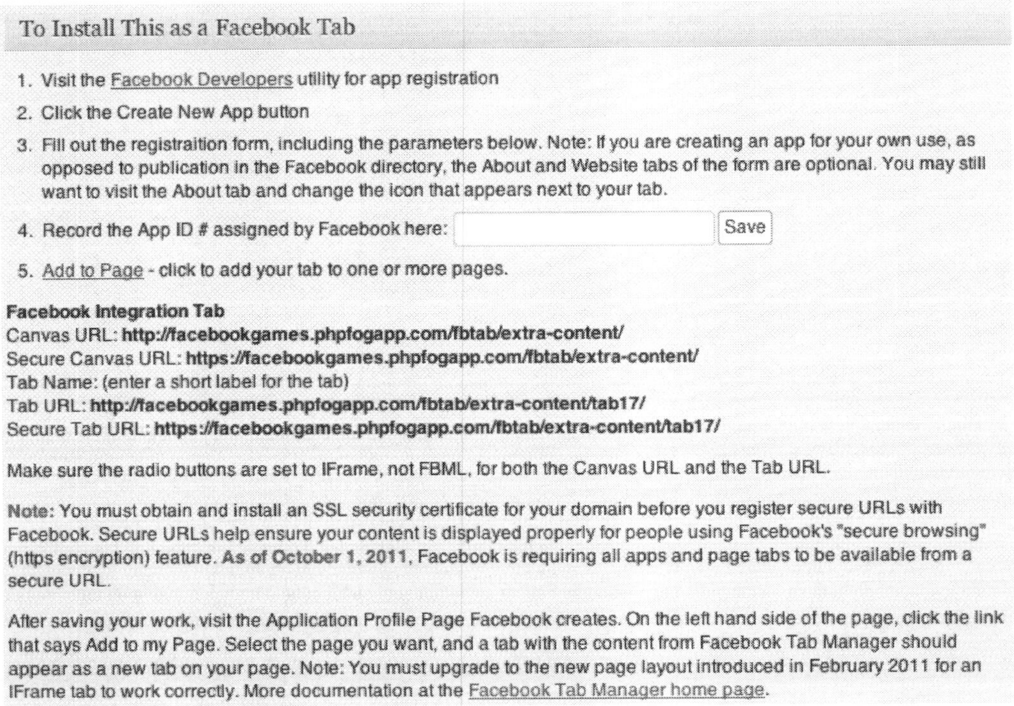

To Install This as a Facebook Tab

1. Visit the Facebook Developers utility for app registration

2. Click the Create New App button

3. Fill out the registraition form, including the parameters below. Note: If you are creating an app for your own use, as opposed to publication in the Facebook directory, the About and Website tabs of the form are optional. You may still want to visit the About tab and change the icon that appears next to your tab.

4. Record the App ID # assigned by Facebook here: [＿＿＿＿＿＿＿] [Save]

5. Add to Page - click to add your tab to one or more pages.

Facebook Integration Tab
Canvas URL: **http://facebookgames.phpfogapp.com/fbtab/extra-content/**
Secure Canvas URL: **https://facebookgames.phpfogapp.com/fbtab/extra-content/**
Tab Name: (enter a short label for the tab)
Tab URL: **http://facebookgames.phpfogapp.com/fbtab/extra-content/tab17/**
Secure Tab URL: **https://facebookgames.phpfogapp.com/fbtab/extra-content/tab17/**

Make sure the radio buttons are set to IFrame, not FBML, for both the Canvas URL and the Tab URL.

Note: You must obtain and install an SSL security certificate for your domain before you register secure URLs with Facebook. Secure URLs help ensure your content is displayed properly for people using Facebook's "secure browsing" (https encryption) feature. As of October 1, 2011, Facebook is requiring all apps and page tabs to be available from a secure URL.

After saving your work, visit the Application Profile Page Facebook creates. On the left hand side of the page, click the link that says Add to my Page. Select the page you want, and a tab with the content from Facebook Tab Manager should appear as a new tab on your page. Note: You must upgrade to the new page layout introduced in February 2011 for an IFrame tab to work correctly. More documentation at the Facebook Tab Manager home page.

Figure 12–23. *Facebook Tab App registration*

There is a lot of information here (Figure 12–23), but essentially you need to create a new application for this tab (or use an existing one) and enter the App ID in the box. Then, on the Facebook Application interface, enter the links for the Tab URL under Page Tab (Figure 12–24).

Select how your app integrates with Facebook

✓ **Page Tab**		✕
Page Tab Name: [?]	Games Page	
Page Tab URL: [?]	http://facebookgames.phpfogapp.com/fbtab/exclusive-content/	
Secure Page Tab URL: [?]	https://facebookgames.phpfogapp.com/fbtab/exclusive-content/	
Page Tab Edit URL: [?]		
✓ **Website**	I want to allow people to log in to my website using Facebook.	
✓ **App on Facebook**	I want to build an app on Facebook.com.	
✓ **Mobile Web**	I have a mobile web app.	
✓ **Native iOS App**	I have a native iOS app.	
✓ **Native Android App**	I have a native Android app.	

Figure 12–24. *Facebook Tabs*

Once you have the Page Tab set up on Facebook, you need to go back and click on the "Add to Page" link (number 5 in the instructions). This will redirect you to Facebook and prompt you for the Page to which you are adding the tab (Figure 12–25). In my case, I use the Page I created earlier in this chapter.

Figure 12–25. *Add a Facebook Page Tab*

Now, if you navigate to the Page, you will see the Games Page link that you defined in the application in the Page Links section of your Page.

Figure 12–26. *Facebook Page Tab*

This technique is useful to manage different Page content (Figure 12–26). However, one of the other useful things the Facebook Tab Manager provides is to enable you to have a "Like Reveal" where a user needs to click on the "Like" button in order to view the content. This is managed in the Reveal Tab Setup (**Facebook Tabs ➤ Reveal Tab Setup**). Simply make a selection of what a new visitor sees (one who has not "Liked" the Page) and what Page fans will see (Figure 12–27).

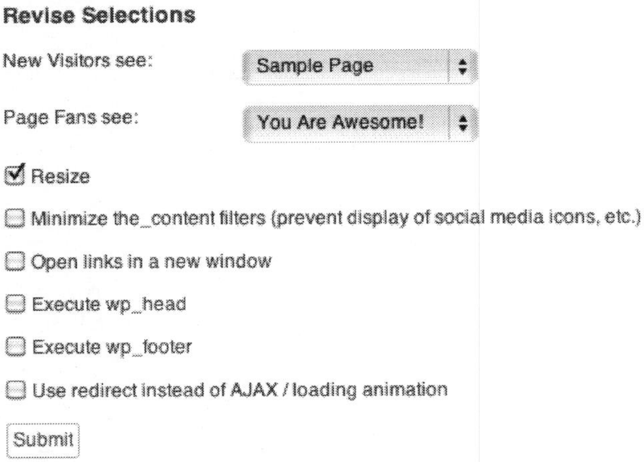

Revise Selections

New Visitors see: Sample Page ⬍

Page Fans see: You Are Awesome! ⬍

☑ Resize

☐ Minimize the_content filters (prevent display of social media icons, etc.)

☐ Open links in a new window

☐ Execute wp_head

☐ Execute wp_footer

☐ Use redirect instead of AJAX / loading animation

[Submit]

Figure 12–27. *Facebook Reveal Page*

I selected the Sample Page from the drop-down, and created a new Page that praises the fan for being awesome. You will then be presented with some links to update your Tab URLs, and a demo of what your user sees if she is a fan (Figure 12–28).

 Reveal Tab Setup

Tab URL: http://facebookgames.phpfogapp.com/fbtab/?fbreveal=10-22&resize=1

Secure Tab URL: https://facebookgames.phpfogapp.com/fbtab/?fbreveal=10-22&resize=1

Preview Fan Version: demo if page liked

Visitors see: New Post
Fans see: You Are Awesome!

Enter this (and https version) into the Facebook Developer app as the source for your page tab.

Figure 12–28. *Reveal Tab Setup*

You can now create clever content that helps users engage and want to "Like" your Page in visual ways and drive up your Page ranks in not only Facebook but other search engines including Google, Yahoo!, and Bing.

Notice that the CSS for the plugin looks quite minimal in your previews. This is because it is optimized to look good when it displays on your Facebook Page. See Figure 12–29.

Figure 12–29. *Rendered Facebook Page*

Launch Checklist

Once you have set up your web presence, take the time to walk through every page on your various sites and ensure that everything is correct. The following checklist should help you work through your content, ensuring there are no typos and there is a consistent look and feel across your different pages.

Content and Style

- Check all punctuation, especially apostrophes, quotes, hyphens, and dashes.
- Check all spelling and grammar.
- Check for capitalization consistency.
- Check writing tense.
- Check spelling variations.

- Check treatment of bulleted lists (punctuation at the end).
- Check for hard-coded links pointed at a staging domain.
- Ensure there is no test or filler content on the site.

Functional Testing

- Check the site on common browser variations (e.g., Internet Explorer, Firefox, and Chrome).
- Check the site with common screen resolutions (e.g., 1024 x 768, 1280 x 960, 1152 x 720).
- Test all forms (comments, contact) including anti-spam (e.g., Akismet) and email links.
- Check that links to external sites work.

Finishing Touches

- Set up monitoring alerts (http://aremysitesup.com/ provides a free service to monitor your sites).
- Create a backup schedule (save/export your WordPress data on a regular basis).

Ongoing

- Monitor and respond to feedback.
- Monitor your analytics for problems and popular content; adjust as necessary.
- Update your content.

Summary

This chapter covered how to set up a website for your application launch using WordPress. Getting up and running with the blogging platform is generally a breeze and there are many, many, many different ways you can set up a site. I also covered creating a Facebook Page, as well as an approach to advertising that aims to spread the reach of your voice. The advertising approach can be done in cycles and, it is hoped, gain you new revenue along the way. I also showed how to use the WordPress platform to interact with the Facebook platform to help drive users to "Like" your content. Remember, it is vitally important as you are starting out to interact with your fans and users. Engaging users will help you reach a greater number of them, and provide an engaging experience that will encourage users to revisit your Page.

To this point in the book, I have built the engine to run the game as needed. If you begin to do any type of real game development, designing your own game engine for every game can get quite repetitive and boring. In the next chapter, I cover some of the more popular options for HTML5 game engines that take much of the burden off you as the developer to manage the different types of interactions between components in your game, allowing you to focus on building a great gaming experience.

Chapter 13

HTML5 Game Engines

Game development for HTML5 has been progressing rapidly over the last several years. Browsers have come a long way in implementing the HTML 5 canvas specification, as well as optimizing the execution of JavaScript. As browsers have become better with JavaScript, and some really creative developers have put together compelling HTML5 games, frameworks to automate many of the repetitive tasks associated with game development have come onto the scene. These engines take care of loading assets, playing sounds, managing levels, offline storage—virtually all of the moving parts— allowing you to develop modular code and assets that you can (we hope) reuse on different games.

This chapter introduces several of the more popular game engines and their strengths and weaknesses, as well as how you may use these different engines with the Facebook Platform, and some simple examples of the engines' uses. These engines can be broken down to open source and paid products, each approach having its own tradeoffs.

Development

As you begin to develop your games, you will find that there are many different pieces that you will need for different components of your game. You may want to incorporate physics to simulate an explosion, or a bounce when an object collides with another object; you may need better methods of dealing with the edge cases for the browser's sound (Internet Explorer is still a strange beast compared to other browsers); you may need to provide better artificial intelligence for the enemies in your game, or other players. You may even want to provide different perspectives for your game. This is where a decent game engine will save you a lot of time, effort, and headache.

Game engines in general help you manage all of the moving parts associated with game development. Most of the engines for building HTML5 games provide a solution for building reusable software and asset (graphic and audio) components. Many also attempt to abstract the complexities of implementation between using the HTML5 canvas element, and the older HTML5 div elements. This allows you, as the developer of a game, to be able to change your game delivery from canvas to a div with a simple configuration option, hiding the complexities of the implementation details of each behind a self-contained engine that is developed independently of your game system. This should mean fewer bugs for you, allowing you more time to spend on developing a compelling game that people want to play.

There are a lot of different engines available for HTML game development, each with particular strengths. Depending on the type of game you are developing, and your personal coding style, you may choose a different engine to implement. The list of available engines keeps growing as more and more browsers become more capable of handling the needs of game developers. As a result, you can get a bit overwhelmed if you are looking at a long list of engines with various small differences. The rest of this chapter is devoted to investigating some of the more popular JavaScript engines for game development.

Open Source

Open source JavaScript engines provide a vast assortment of features for developers to collaborate on code to make their jobs easier. These engines come in a variety of flavors and completeness, as well as approaches to game development. Although an exhaustive list of open source game engines would be quite long, I discuss many of the engines that have gained some popularity in the HTML5 game development community.

With open source game engine solutions, it is important to remember that there is minimal support. Essentially you are reliant upon the kindness of strangers when resolving issues. You may run into a question about the syntax, a particular bug, or general issues that may pop up; you may (or may not) get a timely answer. However, when the community is thriving, you can often get faster responses to your questions, or even get a fix to a particularly vexing bug in a matter of hours as compared to the more formal chain that a bug goes through when backed by a company. These tradeoffs are a big factor in making an informed decision on which HTML engine you want to use.

Canvas Advanced Animation Toolkit

The Canvas Advanced Animation Toolkit (CAAT for short), is "a JavaScript based, multi-instance, director-based, scene-graph manager" that allows you to target canvas as well as WebGL (for 3D gaming). The library is hosted on Github (https://github.com/hyperandroid/caat) and has a front-facing project page at (http://labs.hyperandroid.com/static/caat/). That is a lot of technical jargon, but essentially it is a JavaScript engine that allows you to have more than one instance of CAAT running on a page (multi-instance). The library routes events and time through a single point (director-based), and manages entities and their state (scene-graph manager).

What sets CAAT apart from other engines is how it handles complex path and animation sequencing. This library is quite complex, but the base components can be thought of much like a movie scene. A "director" coordinates "actors" in a "scene" who are following a script. You are the writer telling the director what should happen in the scene, who the actors are, and how they will interact with one another in a scene from your game.

In the case of the HTML5 components, you create a director with at least the dimensions of the canvas you want, create a scene for the director, and begin an animation loop (how many frames per second the scene should receive). A "scene" is responsible for knowing how to get out of a scene and maintain a timeline for the "actors" as the "director" dictates. An "actor" in the CAAT implementation can be an image, shape, text, and so on, that has a location on the canvas, has a life cycle, and can be placed in a scene. The workflow in creating basic output for CAAT is to create a director, create a scene, add at least one scene to the director, and then add an actor to the scene.

Pros and Cons

CAAT does a good job at not only managing scenes and actors, but it also has facilities for managing audio. The library has support for preloading images, sprite images, packaging textures, support for local storage (e.g., for playing a game offline), and for complex collision detections (e.g., circles), and allows you to change easily between canvas and CSS methods of animating screens. However, it does lack the ability to add tiles and maps and the documentation is a bit difficult to find (it is actually in the tutorial section). If you are working on a game that needs some really advanced animation controls, this is definitely a tool for you. However, this is not as well suited for a side scroller or RPG as are some of the other game engines discussed in this chapter. The documentation is a bit on the light side, but the quality of the demos, and the fact that changing among CSS, canvas, and WebGL versions of a given game is practically seamless, this project is one to watch.

Quick Example

In order to use this library, you need a few elements in place. At a bare minimum you need to have the actual CAAT library and a template for loading the elements. Unfortunately you have to do a little digging for the boilerplate to instantiate the CAAT if it is the first time you are working with the library. You can write your own, but much of this is boilerplate that you can incorporate into a file for reuse in your code. Listing 13–1 is an example boilerplate for using CAAT with the HTML5 canvas, based on the examples from the author's demos (saved as `template.js`).

Listing 13–1. *CAAT Setup Boilerplate (template.js)*

```
CAAT.modules.initialization= CAAT.modules.initialization || {};


CAAT.modules.initialization.init = function( width, height, canvasId, imageURL,↵
  onEndLoading )   {

  var canvasContainer = document.getElementById(canvasId);

  /**
```

```
       * create a director.
       */
  var director = new CAAT.Director().
    initialize(
      width || 800,
      height || 600,
      canvasContainer);

    /**
     * Load splash images.
     */
  new CAAT.ImagePreloader().loadImages(
    imageURL,
    function on_load( counter, images ) {

      if ( counter == images.length ) {

        director.emptyScenes();
        director.setImagesCache(images);

        onEndLoading(director);
        CAAT.loop(60);

      }
    }
  );
};
```

This code instantiates the CAAT in its own namespace and will create a new `Director`. There are some defaults for the director, so you can generate a new `Director` with, or without, passing a width and height. If you do not pass a width and height to the constructor, a new `Director` will be created with a width of 800 pixels and a height of 600 pixels. There is also an ImagePreloader that will load any images passed to it into the `DirectorCache` to be used later.

Now in an HTML page we can use some HTML boilerplate (Listing 13–2) to create an HTML document with a link to the CAAT library (the `caat-min.js` from `https://github.com/hyperandroid/CAAT/tree/master/build`).

Listing 13–2. *HTML Boilerplate for CAAT Example (index.html)*

```
<!DOCTYPE HTML>
<html>
  <head>
    <meta charset="utf-8">
    <meta name="viewport" content="width=device-width,initial-scale=1">
    <title>CAAT Example</title>
  </head>
  <body>
    <canvas id="canvas"></canvas>

    <script src="javascripts/caat-min.js"></script>
    <script src="javascripts/template.js"></script>
    <script src="javascripts/logo.js"></script>

  </body>
</html>
```

Next, create the file `javascripts/logo.js`. Now comes the fun part: doing something with the library! For this example, I walk through adding a logo image that is split in two different parts and then recomposed in the middle. This is based on code provided in the examples for the library, but somewhat simplified for clarity here. With an image file named logo.png in the images directory, you can easily create an effect of breaking it apart and putting it back together in a random fashion with CAAT. See Figures 13–1 and 13–2 and Listing 13–3.

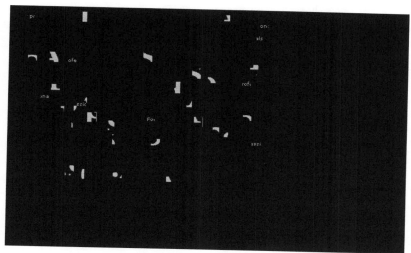

Figure 13–1. *Start of the CAAT animation*

Figure 13–2. *End of the CAAT animation*

Listing 13–3. *CAAT Example Code (logo.js)*

```
window.addEventListener(
  'load',
  function() {
    CAAT.modules.initialization.init(
      800, 500,
      'canvas',
      [
        {id: 'logo', url: 'images/logo.png'}
      ],
      scene1
    );
  },
  false);

function scene1(director) {
  var slide = director.createScene();
  slide.setFillStyle('#000');

  var rows = 4;
  var columns = 16;

  var logo_ci = new CAAT.SpriteImage().initialize(
    director.getImage('logo'), rows, columns
  );

  var i, j;
  var xoff  = (slide.width - logo_ci.width) / 2;
  var yoff  = (slide.height - logo_ci.height)/ 2;

  for( i = 0; i < rows; i++ ) {
    for( j=0; j < columns; j++ ) {
      var actor = new CAAT.Actor().
        setBackgroundImage( logo_ci.getRef(), true ).
        setSpriteIndex( j + i * columns ).
        setLocation(-100, -100);

      var bc = new CAAT.ContainerBehavior().
        setFrameTime(0, 23000).
        setCycle( true );

      var b1 = new CAAT.PathBehavior().
        setFrameTime( Math.random() * 2000, 5000+Math.random() * 2000 ).
        setValues(
          new CAAT.Path().
          setCubic(
            Math.random() < .5 ? slide.width + Math.random() * 50 : -50 -↵
Math.random() * slide.width,
            Math.random() < .5 ? slide.width + Math.random() * 50 : -50 -↵
Math.random() * slide.height,
            (Math.random() < .5 ?1 : -1) * Math.random() * slide.width,
            (Math.random() < .5 ?1 : -1) * Math.random() * slide.height,
            (Math.random() < .5 ?1 : -1) * Math.random() * slide.width,
            (Math.random() < .5 ?1 : -1) * Math.random() * slide.height,
            xoff + j * logo_ci.singleWidth,
            yoff + i * logo_ci.singleHeight
```

```
          )
        ).
          addListener({
          behaviorExpired : function(behavior, time, actor) {
            behavior.path.pathSegments[0].curve.coordlist[0].set(
              Math.random() < .5 ? slide.width+Math.random() * 50 : -20 -↵
Math.random() * slide.width,
                Math.random() < .5 ? slide.width+Math.random() * 50 : -20 -↵
Math.random() * slide.height
              )
          }
        });

      var b2 = new CAAT.PathBehavior().
        setFrameTime( 15000 + Math.random() * 2000, 5000 ).
        setValues(
          new CAAT.Path().
          setCubic(
            xoff + j * logo_ci.singleWidth,
            yoff + i * logo_ci.singleHeight,
            (Math.random() < .5 ? 1 : -1) * Math.random() * slide.width,
            (Math.random() < .5 ? 1 : -1) * Math.random() * slide.height,
            (Math.random() < .5 ? 1 : -1) * Math.random() * slide.width,
            (Math.random() < .5 ? 1 : -1) * Math.random() * slide.height,
            Math.random() < .5 ? slide.width+Math.random() * 50 : -20 -↵
Math.random() * slide.width,
              Math.random() < .5 ? slide.width+Math.random() * 50 : -20 -↵
Math.random() * slide.height
            )
        ).
          addListener({
          behaviorExpired : function(behavior, time, actor) {
            behavior.path.pathSegments[0].curve.coordlist[3].set(
              Math.random() < .5 ? slide.width+Math.random() * 50 : -20 -↵
Math.random() * slide.width,
                Math.random() < .5 ? slide.width+Math.random() * 50 : -20 -↵
Math.random() * slide.height
              )
          }
        });

    bc.addBehavior(b1);
    bc.addBehavior(b2);

    actor.addBehavior( bc );
    slide.addChild( actor );
  }
 }
}
```

We can walk through this a bit. First, logo.js calls the window.addEventListener method and sets up CAAT by calling the template file for some basic setup. I call the template initialization script and set a canvas size of 800 × 500 pixels, tell the function to attach to the canvas id on the page, pass an image file to the code to work with, and set a default function to call next (scene1).

The scene1() function tells the director to create a new scene named slide and sets the background color to black ("#000"). The logo is loaded as a sprite image and split into four rows and 16 columns, dynamically calculated by the size of the image. Each row and column is iterated through, and each part of the image is used to create a new Actor, with a position and name. A behavior for each actor is defined, as well as a time and a property that it should loop.

Two behaviors are then created that create random paths for the Actors (the pieces of the logo image). These use a cubic path (a Bezier curve with four control points), and a listener for the next instructions from the Director. The points for the curve are chosen randomly (but only once for the Scene) and cached by the Actor. The behaviors for the actor are added to the Scene, and each Actor is then added.

A quick note on the style here: one of the very convenient things in this library is its implementation of method chaining. Essentially this allows a developer to create an object and perform multiple operations on that object in the order they are listed; it is often referred to as a "sentence." For the behaviors above (without the parameters), you would see something like Listing 13–4.

Listing 13–4. *JavaScript Method Chaining*

```
var b1 = CAAT.PathBehavior().setFrameTime().setValues().addListener();
```

This makes coding a bit easier when you have complex objects such as you will often have in your game.

Cocos2d.js

Cocos2d.js is a web graphics engine based on the cocos2d engine, a game engine built for iOS development. This library is still in quite early development (0.2.0-beta at the time of the writing of this book), but does show quite a bit of promise. It can be downloaded from the project site (http://cocos2d-javascript.org/downloads). Alternatively, you can install the library with the nodeJS package manager npm. Unfortunately, the 0.1 version does not work in the more recent versions of npm, so until it is fully updated, Listing 13–5 shows a workaround to install the package successfully.

Listing 13–5. *Install cocos2d.js with npm*

```
npm remove -g cocos2d
git clone git://github.com/ryanwilliams/cocos2d-javascript.git
npm install -g cocos2d-javascript
```

One of the really nice features of this library is that it contains its own web server in the project, as well as a code generator to handle some of the boilerplate for you.

Although nodeJS is still gaining popularity, you could very easily integrate Facebook's JavaScript SDK if you want to stay in one environment (this is even supported on Heroku's cedar stack). If you choose to use a Facebook SDK such as the PHP or Ruby SDK, you still have a convenient way to get up and running with your game code.

Pros and Cons

Some of the projects that cocos2d relies on are changing rapidly and lead to some instabilities in the system. The developer is responsive to these issues as they pop up, but this does require you to run unstable code from time to time. It is still early in the project's development, and there are some kinks yet to be worked out. With those caveats in mind, the project, although lacking a sound manager, does have support for reading tile maps in both orthogonal (top down) and isometric (from above at an angle) perspectives. There is no built-in tool for editing maps, but you could easily add a tool such as Tiled Map Editor (an open source tile map editor) to create your tile maps to build worlds. Again, as with many Open Source projects, this project sees spurts of activity, and is community-supported through its forums (http://cocos2d-central.com/forum/19-cocos2d-jvscript-for-web-browsers-jvscript/). There is not a lot of traffic on the forum, but the developers do respond to issues that arise. This library is quite promising but may not suit your needs because of its rapid development cycles in the wild west of nodeJS, but if you are experimenting with new methods of developing games, this is definitely a library to check out.

Quick Example

Download the installer for your system from the cocos2d website (http://cocos2d-javascript.org/downloads) and install the packages on your system. This will include the installer code you need to run the nodeJS packages and compilers. To start a new project, simply type as in Listing 13–6:

Listing 13–6. *Creating a new cocos2d game*

```
cocos new gamename
```

This will create a skeleton project using the nodeJS framework.

> **NOTE:** Depending on your version of nodeJS (mine is v0.6.10), you may see an error thrown stating that the "require.paths is removed. Use node_modules folders, or the NODE_PATH environment variable instead."
>
> You can work around this issue by updating your NODE_PATH environmental variable to include the node_modules directory in your node installation. For my installation of node on OS X, I did the following.
>
> ```
> export NODE_PATH= /usr/local/lib/node_modules:$NODE_PATH
> ```
>
> There are issues such as this to work through in the library, and if you are not comfortable with major issues arising due to the rapidly changing node environment, this may not be the library for you.

Now we can look at the main code for the library in src/main.js, shown in Listing 13–7.

Listing 13–7. *Cocos2d JavaScript Template (main.js)*

```javascript
"use strict"  // Use strict JavaScript mode

var cocos  = require('cocos2d')    // Import the cocos2d module
, events = require('events')     // Import the events module
, geo    = require('geometry')   // Import the geometry module
, ccp    = geo.ccp              // Short hand to create points

var Test = cocos.nodes.Layer.extend(/** @lends Test# */{
    /**
     * @class Initial application layer
     * @extends cocos.nodes.Layer
     * @constructs
     */
  init: function () {
    // You must always call the super class version of init
    Test.superclass.init.call(this)

    // Get size of canvas
    var s = cocos.Director.get('sharedDirector.winSize')

    // Create label
    var label = cocos.nodes.Label.create({ string: 'Test', fontName: 'Arial',↵
 fontSize: 76 })

    // Add label to layer
    this.addChild({ child: label, z:1 })

    // Position the label in the centre of the view
    label.set('position', ccp(s.width / 2, s.height / 2))
  }
})

/**
 * Entry point for the application
 */
exports.main = function () {
  // Initialise application

  // Get director
  var director = cocos.Director.get('sharedDirector')

  // Attach director to our <div> element
  director.attachInView(document.getElementById('test_app'))

  // Wait for the director to finish preloading our assets
  events.addListener(director, 'ready', function (director) {
    // Create a scene
    var scene = cocos.nodes.Scene.create()

    // Add our layer to the scene
    scene.addChild({ child: Test.create() })

    // Run the scene
    director.replaceScene(scene)
  })
```

```
  // Preload our assets
  director.runPreloadScene()
}
```

When you are ready to test, you will need to start up a nodeJS web server to check your code in the browser. Fortunately, one is built in and you can start it up in your project directory with the code in Listing 13–8.

Listing 13–8. *Starting the Nodejs Web Server*

```
cocos server start
```

This will create a web server able to construct web views of your program. If you begin to make some progress with the library, you can also easily deploy the application to Heroku using their Cedar stack (e.g. `heroku create --cedar`).

Crafty

The CraftyJS engine works in a data-oriented paradigm using what is known as an entity–component. This is a method of object-oriented programming where each game object (e.g., character, enemy, coins, ball, etc.) is an entity and in order for the entity to do anything, it needs a component. This is a very intuitive way of approaching game development. The project has a growing number of tutorials and a growing community. As an intuitive way to develop software, this project has a lot of promise. As of the writing of this book, the library is at 0.4.4 status, and sports an impressive number of features.

As can most of these engines, CraftyJS can work with either the DOM or `canvas` element. It supports Tile maps (although you need to parse the XML output from an editor such as Tiled Map Editor yourself). Crafty supports a sound management system for different browsers, and supports adding multiple formats for browser compatibility.

CraftyJS works by building up scenes with entities and their components, which makes it quite easy to build up RPG and side scrolling games that make use of tile maps. The library also sports some quite advanced collision detection (convex polygons).

Pros and Cons

CraftyJS is quite feature rich, and there are a growing number of online tutorials and a growing community behind its use. There are also a growing number of useful plugins including a sprite map for using image-based fonts in your game. Building scenes (or levels) feels quite natural, and the library provides a lot of useful functionality in a reasonably easy-to-remember format (not an easy thing to do). I particularly liked the implementation of how components are added to an entity (as a string list), which makes it really easy to see immediately what a given entity has available to it.

CraftyJS is still in development and currently lacks a "real" physics engine that has friction or gravity. Work is progressing on this, but it is something to take into account when evaluating engines. If this is something you really need, you may need to keep looking at this point, but be sure to check the project as this feature may have been added by the time you are reading this.

Simple Example

In this example I create a simple isometric map automatically from a tile map of grass patterns using CraftyJS. First, download the basic boilerplate with the minified version from the CraftyJS website (http://craftyjs.com/) and place it in the javascripts directory. Next, download the "grass_and_water.png" file from Open Game Art (http://opengameart.org/content/grass-and-water-tiles) and save it in your images directory. Our boilerplate HTML, shown in Listing 13–9, should look familiar.

Listing 13–9. *CraftyJS HTML Boilerplate*

```
<!DOCTYPE HTML>
<html>
  <head>
    <meta charset="utf-8">
    <meta name="viewport" content="width=device-width,initial-scale=1">
    <title>Crafty Example</title>
  </head>
  <body>
    <script src="javascripts/crafty-min.js"></script>
    <script src="javascripts/isomap.js"></script>
  </body>
</html>
```

You may notice that there is no canvas element defined. This is actually taken care of by Crafty, and you can change easily between DOM and Canvas options for the entity when it is drawn.

In the javascripts/isomap.js file, add Listing 13–10 to generate a random isometric "map" from the first row of grass tiles in the grass_and_water.png file.

Listing 13–10. *CraftyJS isometric map (isomap.js)*

```
var width     = 800,
    height    = 600,
    spriteSize = 64;

Crafty.init(width, height);

Crafty.sprite(spriteSize, 'images/grass_and_water.png', {
    grass1: [0, 0, 1, 1],
    grass2: [1, 0, 1, 1],
    grass3: [2, 0, 1, 1],
    grass4: [3, 0, 1, 1]
});

iso = Crafty.isometric.size(spriteSize);

for (var y = 0; y < height / spriteSize * 3; y++) {
  for(var x = 0; x < width / spriteSize - 1; x++) {
    var which = Crafty.randRange(1, 4);
    var randomtile = 'grass' + which;
```

```
        var tile = Crafty.e('2D, Canvas, ' + randomtile);

      iso.place(x, y, 0, tile);
    }
}
```

This will randomly generate a map that looks like something along the lines of Figure 13–3.

Figure 13–3. *Randomly generated isometric map in Crafty*

Your image will most likely look slightly different, as a random image is chosen. If you look more closely at the code, you initialized Crafty, created a sprite with a width of 64 pixels that is in the images directory, and defined four areas and gave them a name. You told Crafty that this was an isometric map, and each tile was 64 pixels square.

The next part is a little clever piece. Because the tiles need to be placed on a Cartesian plane, and I want to pass x- and y-coordinates when placing the tile, I loop over each column (y) although the current column is less than the height (400) divided by the spriteSize (64) multiplied by 3 (400 / 64 * 3 = 18.75). I employ a similar technique for each row, but this time constraining the width of the tiles only to fill up the row. What this does is effectively draw the scene onto the full size of the canvas, but not overlapping the sides.

Next, the program chooses a random number between one and four, and then appends that number to the string "grass" to create a reference for the sprite. I created a new Entity named tile, and told it to be 2D, use the canvas element, and use the randomTile. Finally, the tile is placed at the x-, y-, and z-coordinates (there is no depth, so the z-index is 0).

LimeJS

LimeJS (http://www.limejs.com/) is a framework for building games that uses Python scripts to help manage not only the source files, but also generate optimized JavaScript with Google's Closure library. To use this library, you need to install Python and Java. LimeJS is also unique in its implementation of the engine on top of the Closure engine, providing a convenient method of loading your source files. This allows you to organize your source code in files that make sense, and let the Closure compiler optimize their integration into a deployable version of the code.

LimeJS uses a director/actor/scene ontology for developing games. The library's default templates append directly inside the body element, allowing developers some flexibility to resize content dynamically for "full-screen" views. LimeJS has shape primitives such as Circle, RoundedRect, and Polygon that allow you to simply pass as many co-ordinate points as required (a minimum of three).

Pros and Cons

LimeJS is a quite robust engine that leverages the power of Google's Closure libraries to add a lot of features. This does come at the cost of working within the idioms of Google's approach to software development. There is a bit of a learning curve not only from the library itself, but also the structures imposed by Closure. If you are already comfortable using Closure, or want a really good excuse to learn, this may just be the game engine for you. If, however, you object to a third-party tool changing your code (although this is good for code obfuscation), you may want to go in another direction. With Facebook full of game clones, having a development set of code that you work on and then deploying a harder to read version for game play will help you protect your game a bit from both cheaters and copycats.

Simple Example

The workflow with LimeJS is unique. Assuming you have both Java and Python installed on your computer, download LimeJS from their site (http://www.limejs.com/). To create a new project, simply enter the directory with LimeJS in the terminal and type Listing 13–11 to get the latest packages needed for the library; then create a new project:

Listing 13–11. *LimeJS Project Creation*

```
bin/lime.py init
bin/lime.py create gametime
```

This creates a new LimeJS project in the directory gametime with two files, gametime.html and gametime.js. The gametime.html file contains HTML boilerplate that should look quite familiar by now, as in Listing 13–12.

Listing 13–12. *LimeJS HTML Boilerplate*

```
<!DOCTYPE HTML>

<html>
<head>
        <title>gametime</title>
        <script type="text/javascript" src="../closure/closure/goog/base.js"></script>
        <script type="text/javascript" src="gametime.js"></script>
</head>

<body onload="gametime.start()"></body>

</html>
```

The gametime.js file contains boilerplate not only for adding modules to the Closure engine, but also for creating a new director, scene, and target. The boilerplate provides a generic circle with text on it that is draggable. The file ends with code required for the Closure library (Listing 13–13), and should not need to be edited.

Listing 13–13. *LimeJS JavaScript with Google Closure Libraries*

```
//set main namespace
goog.provide('gametime');

//get requirements
goog.require('lime.Director');
goog.require('lime.Scene');
goog.require('lime.Layer');
goog.require('lime.Circle');
goog.require('lime.Label');
goog.require('lime.animation.Spawn');
goog.require('lime.animation.FadeTo');
goog.require('lime.animation.ScaleTo');
goog.require('lime.animation.MoveTo');


// entrypoint
gametime.start = function(){

  var director = new lime.Director(document.body,1024,768),
  scene = new lime.Scene(),

  target = new lime.Layer().setPosition(512,384),
  circle = new lime.Circle().setSize(150,150).setFill(255,150,0),
  lbl = new lime.Label().setSize(160,50).setFontSize(30).setText('TOUCH ME!'),
  title = new lime.Label().setSize(800,70).setFontSize(60).setText('Now move⮐
me around!')
    .setOpacity(0).setPosition(512,80).setFontColor('#999').setFill(200,100,0,.1);

  //add circle and label to target object
  target.appendChild(circle);
  target.appendChild(lbl);

  //add target and title to the scene
  scene.appendChild(target);
  scene.appendChild(title);
```

```
director.makeMobileWebAppCapable();

//add some interaction
goog.events.listen(target,['mousedown','touchstart'],function(e){

  //animate
  target.runAction(new lime.animation.Spawn(
    new lime.animation.FadeTo(.5).setDuration(.2),
    new lime.animation.ScaleTo(1.5).setDuration(.8)
  ));

  title.runAction(new lime.animation.FadeTo(1));

  //let target follow the mouse/finger
  e.startDrag();

  //listen for end event
  e.swallow(['mouseup','touchend'],function(){
    target.runAction(new lime.animation.Spawn(
      new lime.animation.FadeTo(1),
      new lime.animation.ScaleTo(1),
      new lime.animation.MoveTo(512,384)
    ));

    title.runAction(new lime.animation.FadeTo(0));
  });

});

// set current scene active
director.replaceScene(scene);

}

//this is required for outside access after code is compiled in ADVANCED_COMPILATIONS↵
 mode
goog.exportSymbol('gametime.start', gametime.start);
```

Once your code is ready to deploy, you will need to run the build task included in the Python script (Listing 13–14).

Listing 13–14. *Compiling LimeJS Code*

```
bin/lime.py build gametime -o gametime/compiled/gametime.js
```

This will run your script through the Closure Compiler and build a single JavaScript file for you to deploy. By default, Closure will build a rather large JavaScript file as it includes all the needed libraries in a single file. This default example file is around 216 kB, which is a bit on the heavy side when compared to other game libraries mentioned in this chapter. You can significantly reduce the size of this file by using the "Advanced Options" in the Closure Compiler. There is a switch in the Python script to tell the Closure Compiler to use the Advanced Options, shown in Listing 13–15.

Listing 13–15. *Advanced Compilation of LimeJS Code*

```
bin/lime.py build gametime -o gametime/compiled/gt.js -a
```

By passing the "-a" flag, the Closure Compiler actually evaluates your code and renames variables and functions, removes unused code, and performs function inlining, which rewrites functions when safe. With these techniques, the 216 kB file is reduced to a much more respectable 56 kB. The one major downside of this compression is if you need to debug your production code when your development code is working. Because your variables and function names are rewritten (e.g., `function a(b,c){…}`) it can be a little difficult to find the particular line that is causing the issue. The Closure Compiler library is quite well documented, and there are tools available to make this debugging easier. If you do start to notice issues with your code after compiling a minified version, be sure to hit Google's Closure Compiler website for the latest information about the library (`http://code.google.com/closure/compiler/`).

To use the compiled JavaScript library on a production page, simply create a new HTML file in the project directory (e.g., index.html) with a link to the compiled source. See Listing 13–16.

Listing 13–16. *LimeJS HTML page with Minified Game Code*

```
<!DOCTYPE HTML>

<html>
  <head>
    <title>gametime</title>
    <script type="text/javascript" src="compiled/gt.js"></script>
  </head>

  <body onload="gametime.start()"></body>

</html>
```

Generally the rewriting of your code does not adversely affect the quality of your code. But however good the Google engineers working on the Closure Compiler are, there are new edge cases introduced all the time as browsers continue to implement more features. Because the code that is running is not the code you wrote, debugging can be a bit of an issue. However, you can generate a map of the functions in the code for debugging by generating a map that you can use with the Closure Inspector (Firebug Extension) to help sort out what is going on. To build the source map, pass the map flag (-m) to the build script and tell it where to save the source map (Listing 13–17).

Listing 13–17. *LimeJS HTML Page with Minified Game Code*

```
bin/lime.py build gametime -o gametime/compiled/gt.js -a -m gametime/compiled/map
```

This will generate a file in gametime/compiled/map that maps the original variable and function names to their compressed versions that the Firefox addon can read and make debugging much simpler. See the example in Listing 13–18.

Listing 13–18. *Example Closure Compiler Source Map*

```
{
"version":3,
"file":"",
"lineCount":2909,
"mappings":"AAAA,wCCAA;QAAS,GAAc,CAAC,CAAD,CAAsB;AAAG,QAAO,SAAQ,EAAG;AAAC,UAAO,KAAA, ↵
CAAK,CAAL,...",
```

```
"sources":["../../closure/closure/goog/base.js","class com.google.javascript↵
.jscomp.FunctionRewriter$GetterReducer:helper",...]
"names":["goog.global","goog.nullFunction","goog.typeOf","value","s","Array",...]
}
```

melonJS

The melonJS library is a 2D sprite-based engine that uses the object–entity paradigm for game generation. Once more, it supports the Tiled map specification out of the box, allowing you to use a third-party tool such as Tiled (http://www.mapeditor.org/). In fact, if you do use Tiled, you can actually define elements and properties in the GUI editor and use them in your game. The library has some nice support for parallax scrolling, audio channels, tweens, and a customizable loader for the game. I cover the melonJS engine in quite a bit of detail in the next chapter, so I forgo an example here.

Pros and Cons

The integration with the Tiled editor is really fantastic, and provides an excellent way to create levels for your game. By building up the scene visually, you have a good handle on what the scene will look like before you render it on the screen (or attempt to pick a section of a sprite programmatically based on its position on the sheet). This is a good engine if you want to build a game that requires good level editing in both isometric and orthogonal display. Currently this is the strength of the library, and if you are not building a sprite-based game, you may find that one of the other engines suits your needs better.

Play My Code

I wanted to mention Play My Code (http://www.playmycode.com), which is a slightly different approach and a good way to learn techniques of game development. Play My Code (Figure 13–4) is a hosted web service that provides a browser-based editor that allows developers to write games in a language named Quby (with a Ruby-like syntax) to build a game directly in the browser. You can then embed the game that you have developed within an iframe, with your code remaining on the Play My Code website. The site allows you (or better stated, requires you) to share your game with others. This is really great to see how someone approached designing a game, fork their code to yours, and add improvements. This may not be the final destination for your Facebook game, but it will provide you with an environment in which to experiment, explore ways in which to implement different mechanics, or quickly prototype an idea.

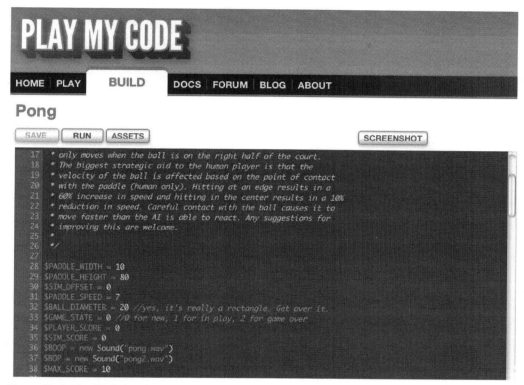

Figure 13–4. *Play My Code editor*

PixieEngine

PixieEngine (http://pixieengine.com/) is another browser-based game creation tool. PixieEngine (Figure 13–5) allows you to create a single game with its interface, and provide a Premium account if you would like to make more. PixieEngine has a nice interface for building sprites, and can help you get practice building these game assets. Beyond that, you edit the files using the CoffeeScript language (a language that preprocesses down to JavaScript) all through a web interface. This is quite a bit more sophisticated than Play My Code, but there are some nice tutorials on the site. If you are comfortable with CoffeeScript, this may be a very attractive solution as you can export your projects to zip files for deployment on your own server (you can also publish directly to the Chrome Web Store).

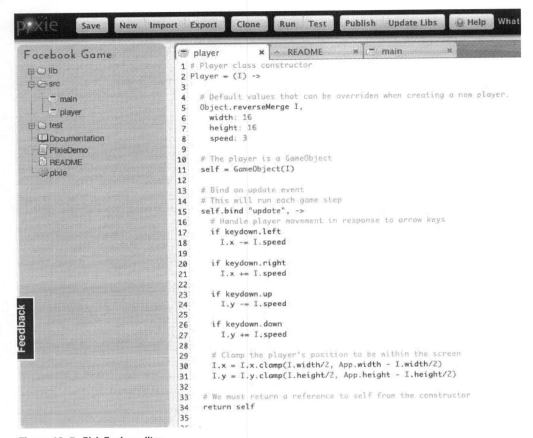

Figure 13–5. *PixieEngine editor*

Paid Game Engines

There are a few paid solutions for developing HTML games, and they do an excellent job on a few different fronts. Where this software excels is in providing a stable platform that has additional tools to ease development. Unlike many open source projects, there is (presumably) a developer who is making his or her livelihood from the sale of the software, and providing a feature-rich environment that is easy to work with ensures that the business will grow. Should you run into an issue, you will be able to get support to help resolve it. If you are interested in using a professional tool to help build a professional product, without the uncertainties associated with nascent open source engines, you may want to pay a company for its software.

ImpactJS

ImpactJS (http://impactjs.com/) has been well received by game developers for its robust feature set. The engine has built-in support for device targeting (e.g., provides a different canvas size for an iPhone 4, which has more pixels than other mobile devices). Perhaps the most compelling piece of the software is the built-in visual editor for building tile maps named Weltmeister.

Beyond the tools, ImpactJS has an excellent (and growing) list of tools that work well with the library. One of these third-party tools is the appMobi XDK which runs through Chrome and allows you to build native iOS applications without running XCode or even OS X. The editors for working with ImpactJS are integrated into appMobi, but provide hardware accelerators for mobile devices. If you are interested in Impact, you may want to take a look at appMobi first as they cost the same, but it comes with a five-game license for ImpactJS and the level editor. If you are interested in native mobile, this may be a solution that helps you get there quickly.

Another of the integration points is TapJS (http://tapjs.com/), a platform for your game that provides simple ways to save your high score, add badges, and manage community features. It also has Facebook integration baked into the administrative interface. Simply include jQuery and the TapJS API, and you are ready to roll.

Pros and Cons

ImpactJS is designed for action-style games and has an easy-to-use level editor. There are built-in components for managing a player's (or enemy's) health, as well as nice acceleration and velocity parameters for all entities. There are controls for volume, loading screens, and controlling the next level. ImpactJS is a great engine for platformers and 2D shooters, but not as good when developing more puzzle-based games such as Chess or Words with Friends. Also, there is no trial license, and the $99 price tag can be a little much to see if the engine may be right for a lot of people getting started in games development. The developer has been addressing some of the critiques of the software, and the library continues to progress, which is a good sign for browser-based game developers. With a growing ecosystem for supporting the ever-evolving browser standards and technologies, paid applications such as this will (we hope) continue to lead the way and blaze new ground for browser-based games development.

Isogenic

The Isogenic Game Engine (http://www.isogenicengine.com/) sells itself as a web-based MMO game engine. The engine is particularly suited to generating isometric map-based games. This engine has support for "real-time" events, and so there is a bit of infrastructure that you will need to have running. Isogenic runs on nodeJS with a database named MongoDB to store its information. Again, you can run this code on Heroku, or any number of other hosts (you can try out a hosted MongoDB instance at http://mongolab.com), but Isogenic does provide some hosting solutions to help you get started.

Isogenic is an ideal engine for developing a game with real-time elements, and has Facebook integrated in the engine. This is a nodeJS solution, so to test some of the code, you will need to have your computer set up to run a node server locally. However, there is good documentation on their site (and with the software) to help get you up and running quickly.

Pros and Cons

Isogenic has some impressive tools building server-based MMO games. They include a lot of technology designed to scale on cloud services including Amazon's EC2 service. They are building a system capable of handling very large loads of traffic that a Facebook game may drive, but there is a tradeoff with using nascent technologies such as MongoDB and nodeJS so heavily. If you are not developing an MMO-style of game, you may find this engine does not fit your needs; but if you are working on developing an MMO and plan on having a lot of concurrent players, this is the best engine out there. With the different hosting packages, you have some options to get the service up and running with a minimal amount of effort on your part.

Summary

This chapter covered some of the popular open and closed source game engine solutions that are currently being developed. I covered some of the basics about how each engine approaches game development, and displayed something at which the engine excels. All of the engines have strengths and are designed to tackle a particular type of problem well. There are tradeoffs with all of these, and making an informed decision *before* you start coding will save you a lot of time (or at least you will know a little more about what you are getting yourself into).

In the next chapter, I discuss how to use a game engine (melonJS) to develop a game for Facebook, and how using a game engine helps make managing the pieces of your game easier.

Chapter 14

Facebook Fuzed

In the last chapter we took a look at several of the different game engine options available to build HTML5 games. Several of these engines even have Facebook integration already built in! In this final chapter, I take a closer look at one of these engines, work through developing a game with it, and then integrate it into the Facebook platform using the score API. Although all of the engines discussed in the previous chapter make good candidates, I thought it was important to show how using tilesets in games with a good editor can make prototyping and polishing a game a cinch.

After looking at all of the different options available for developing an HTML5 game using an open source project, I wanted to actually walk through implementing a simple game. The question became which one? All of the engines have somewhat similar features, but some are better suited for certain types of games. I wanted to create a game that used tiles and sprites to build up a side-scroller game. This is actually something that ImpactJS does quite well with its level editor, and the closest open source game engine that has a level editor is melonJS.

If you recall in the previous chapter, melonJS uses the Tiled Map Editor (Tiled for short) for level editing, and allows you to manipulate the maps both programmatically and with keywords in Tiled. Using a graphical tool to build up maps makes designing levels less painful (the alternative is to keep track of the tiles yourself). You may find some limitations with melonJS and Tiled, but if the development mode suits you, you should definitely spring for the ImpactJS SDK as it has a really great level editor.

Game

This game will be a straightforward side-scroller (sometimes called platformer for the platforms the player jumps on). The object of the game will be to complete the level, collecting coins to gain points along the way. If you have ever played Super Mario Brothers, Contra, or Sonic the Hedgehog, you will be familiar with the basic gameplay. When designing levels, they should be relatively easy in the beginning, increasing in complexity as the player progresses through the game. We do not work through the creation of all the levels, but you will have the graphic assets and knowledge basics to take this game to the next level (literally).

You also need to come up with a story that goes along with the game. Who is the player? Why is she trying to get to the other side? Why are some of the entities bad? Determining the story behind the game will help you keep the overall design of the levels, character interactions, and goals of the game at the forefront of your game decisions, making for more compelling gameplay.

Tiled Map Editor

Tiled is a general-purpose tile map editor that uses an XML-based map format with support for both orthogonal and isometric maps. There are versions for Windows, OS X, and Linux flavors, and it can be used with a variety of open source game engines. There are some really great features in the latest release, including support for polygon objects, support for tile rotation, and an "auto-mapping" feature that allows you to create rules to speed up creating maps and reducing errors in the map. Basically, this auto-mapping feature allows you to make sure you do not accidentally overwrite the wrong tile, an issue you will need to deal with as you design more complex levels. All of these generate game maps using the TMX (Tile Map XML) format to describe a tile-based map.

You can download an installer for your platform from the project's website (http://www.mapeditor.org/). Once installed, you will need to change the output format for the TMX files from Base64 compressed to Base64 uncompressed as melonJS only supports uncompressed tilemaps. In your version's preferences, select the Base64 (uncompressed) in the Saving and Loading section as shown in Figure 14.1.

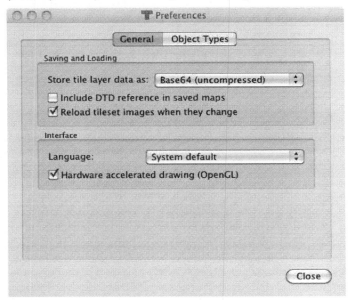

Figure 14-1. *Setting Tiled's output to Base64 (uncompressed)*

The game we develop has a canvas size of 640 × 480, a standard 4:3 aspect ratio for games. With the default size of the Facebook canvas (the space they use to display your application, not the HTML canvas element) set at 760 pixels by default, this size game fits into that space well. There is a bit of math required to determine the size of the tiles for creating a new map. Depending on the size of the tiles you are using, you need to calculate how many tiles will fit in a given view of the map. If you have tiles that are 32 × 32 pixels large, you are working a 20 × 15 area for your tiles. If you want more than one "scene" on a map, you can adjust the number of rows in the grid. If you want two screens as shown in Figure 14–2, you would define a map that is 40 × 15. If your tiles are 16 × 16, your tile map sizes need to be adjusted appropriately (e.g., 40 × 30).

Figure 14–2. *A two panel scene*

The great tutorial that is on the melonJS site uses a modified version of the tiles the SpicyPixel.net made available under the Common Public License (http://www.spicypixel.net/2008/01/10/gfxlib-fuzed-a-free-developer-graphic-library/). We actually use the original files (which include additional level tiles) and get a bit more in depth.

Download the GfxLib-Fuzed library from the SpicyPixel.net site and place it in a new project directory (e.g., fuzed). Create a new map in Tiled (**File ➤ New**) that is orthogonal with a map size of 80 × 30 tiles, with a tile size of 16 × 16. See Figure 14–3.

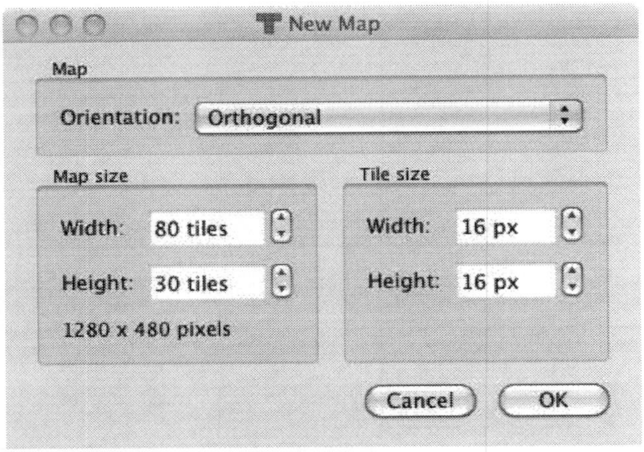

Figure 14–3.*Creating a new orthogonal map*

Save the file in the "data" directory in your project as area01.tmx. Now we can start adding some of the tiles to create a map. Click on **Map ➤ New Tileset** and navigate. Click on the file browser next to the Image field and navigate to gfx-fuzed/Backgrounds/lev01_checkers/area01_tileset/area01_level_tiles.png and click Open. Be sure that the "Use transparent color" checkbox is selected and the color is the hot-pink color that is the background on the image. Also, be sure that the tile sizes are correct (16 px for both the height and width). See Figure 14–4.

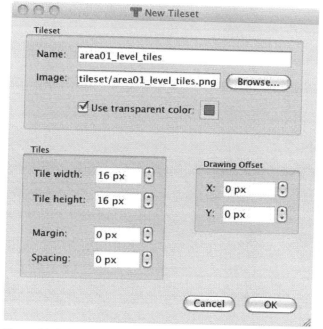

Figure 14–4. *Importing a tileset*

After you click OK, you will see the tiles you just imported on the bottom right in the Tilesets tab (Figure 14–5).

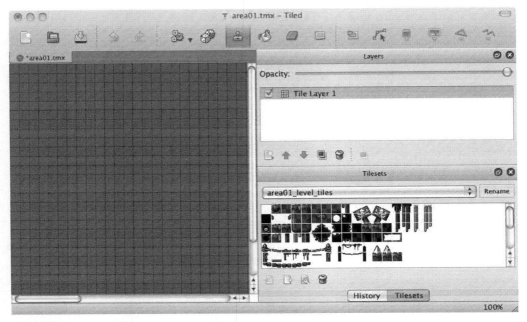

Figure 14–5. *Imported tile set*

I always try to name the layers logically, so go ahead and rename "Tile Layer 1" as "background." There is not really a naming convention for this, but I do try to pick a name that is logical to remind me what the purpose of that layer is. You may want to place some of the tiles on top of each other. You can easily add another layer (e.g., foreground) to the mix to hold those elements that need to be on top of the background by adding a new Tile Layer (**Layer ➤ Add Tile Layer**).

Now is your chance to be artistic. Select a tile you want to use and simply click on the square you want it to display. If you hold down the left mouse button, you can "paint" tiles with the tile you have selected. If you find that you want to replace a tile, just select a tile and replace it in the editing area. Make something that looks nice with the tiles available. Mine ended up looking like Figure 14–6.

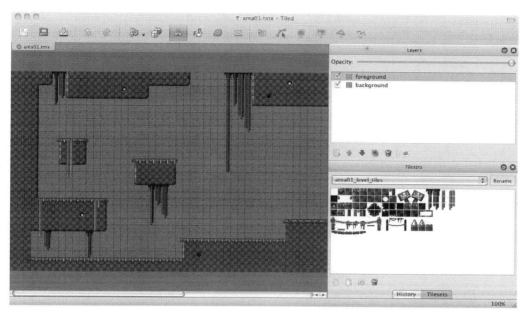

Figure 14–6. *First level tiles*

The last thing to do before starting to work with the code is to set a default background color. I thought this should have something like a sky-blue color (for now), so I decided to use #00c0ff. To add the background, select **Map ➤ Map Properties** and set a value for the "background_color" to "#00c0ff" as in Figure 14–7.

Figure 14–7. *Setting background_color property*

The melonJS library allows you to set keywords and values in the code or on individual elements in the Tiled editor. This gives you a lot of flexibility, but it is important to remember to be consistent. If you set some properties in the TMX file, and others in the

JavaScript, it can get confusing as to which file contains the information when debugging. I like having all of the properties for my game in the TMX file and keeping my game logic in JavaScript. You may run into a case where this is not possible and you need to put some of this into the JavaScript file. If you do run into this situation, just be sure to add a big comment on that value.

melonJS Framework

You now have a level that could be used in a variety of game engines, but we use the melonJS framework for this HTML5 game. The framework code comes in a raw format that you will need to compile to have a minified version for use in your game. Download the latest version of the code from the melonJS website (`http://www.melonjs.org/`). You can download the zip, or clone the github repository (`https://github.com/obiot/melonJS`). I chose to download the zip file, which is just a tagged version of the source code.

Now we need to compile the source. There is a script that compiles the source, but you need to create a `build` directory first (or edit the Makefile if you are comfortable), then run the make command in the melonJS source (you need to insert the correct path for your system in the following examples). See Listing 14–1.

Listing 14–1. *Building the melonJS Files*

```
cd /path/to/melonJS/files
mkdir build
make
```

This will concatenate all of the source files into a single file (e.g., `melonJS-0.9.2.js`) and build a compressed derivative of the code in the build directory. For our game, we use the minified version (e.g., `melonJS-0.9.2-min.js`). Copy this file into a `javascript` directory in your game project as in Listing 14–2.

Listing 14–2. *Moving Compiled Sources to Your Project*

```
cd path/to/your/game/
mkdir javascript
cd path/to/melon/source
cp build/melon-0.9.2-min.js path/to/your/game/javascript/
```

Creating the Game files

Now we need some HTML for our game. Create an `index.html` file in your game directory with the code shown in Listing 14–3.

Listing 14–3. *HTML for Your Game*

```
<!DOCTYPE HTML>
<html>
<head>
  <meta charset="utf-8">
  <meta name="viewport" content="width=device-width,initial-scale=1">
  <title>Fuzed for Facebook</title>
```

```
<style>
  body { background-color: #000 }
  #info { width: 640px; }
  #fps { float: right; }
  #framecounter { font-size: 10px; font-family: Courier, 'Courier New'; color:
#c0c0c0;}
  </style>
</head>
<body>
  <div id="info">
    <div id="fps">
      <span id="framecounter">(0/0 fps)</span>
    </div>
  </div>

  <div id="jsapp"></div>
  <script src="javascript/melonJS-0.9.2-min.js"></script>
</body>
</html>
```

The first section (info) is for development purposes and will provide you with feedback on the frames-per-second at which your game is performing. You can easily change this setting by changing the CSS for info and add "display: none;" to the CSS.

It is a good idea to keep your code separate, so we need to create a new file in the javascript directory to hold the code for our game. There are different conventions for naming the code that contains the game; developers with a lot of C experience name this file "main" and other schools name this file something more meaningful. With just a few files this is not that big a deal, but if you have a large project with a lot of different files, having a consistent naming convention for your code will save you a lot of headaches. For this example, though, I use the convention of "main" containing the game logic and create the file main.js in the javascript directory.

The file needs some code to set up. We need to tell the framework what to do when loading (e.g., create a canvas element, initialize audio components, load the maps), and what to do once all of the components have been loaded (start playing a game). See Listing 14-4.

Listing 14-4. *Building the melonJS Files (main.js)*

```
// game resources
var g_resources = [];

var jsApp = {

  onload: function() {

    // init the video
    if (!me.video.init('jsapp', 640, 480, false, 1.0)) {
      alert("Sorry but your browser does not support html 5 canvas.");
      return;
    }

    // initialize the "audio"
    me.audio.init("mp3,ogg");
```

```
        // set all resources to be loaded
        me.loader.onload = this.loaded.bind(this);

        // set all resources to be loaded
        me.loader.preload(g_resources);

        // load everything & display a loading screen
        me.state.change(me.state.LOADING);
    },

        // callback when everything is loaded

    loaded: function() {
        // set the "Play/Ingame" Screen Object
        me.state.set(me.state.PLAY, new PlayScreen());

        // start the game
        me.state.change(me.state.PLAY);
    }

};// jsApp

/* the in game stuff*/
var PlayScreen = me.ScreenObject.extend({

    onResetEvent: function() {
        // stuff to reset on state change
    },

    // action to perform when game is finished (state change)
    onDestroyEvent: function() {
    }

});

window.onReady(function() {
    jsApp.onload();
});
```

A quick note on style here; in JavaScript you can run into issues with your code in the Global namespace. The melonJS engine uses a best practice of placing its code into appropriate namespaces, in the case of this game, the "jsApp" namespace. Functions are defined using this style with a name colon and a function definition. You then have access to the code in dot notation (e.g., jsApp.onload()). This can feel a little funny at first, but once you get used to it, and realize all the problems it prevents you from having, this format is quite appealing.

We need to tell our main application about this new file to load it in the browser. Under the <script> tag that calls the melonJS library, add the code in Listing 14–5.

Listing 14–5. *Adding Game Code to index.html*

```
<script src="javascript/main.js"></script>
```

If you reload the main web page, you will now see a loading screen; because there is nothing to load yet, nor have we defined what to do next, you will just see the loading screen for melonJS (Figure 14–8).

Figure 14–8. *melonJS loading screen*

We need to load some resources and we use the g_resources container to define what and where our assets are located. First we need to define where the tile image is that we are using (area01_level_tiles.png), and where the TMX file is. See Listing 14–6.

Listing 14–6. *Adding Game Resources (main.js)*

```
var g_resources = [{
    name: "area01_level_tiles",
    type: "image",
    src: "data/gfxlib-↵
fuzed/Backgrounds/lev01_checkers/area01_tileset/area01_level_tiles.png"
}, {
    name: "area01",
    type: "tmx",
    src: "data/area01.tmx"
}];
```

Now we just need to code the PlayScreen object to load the level once the assets have been loaded by updating the onResetEvent method to load area01 from the game resources as in Listing 14–7.

Listing 14–7. *Loading the area01 map (main.js)*

```
var PlayScreen = me.ScreenObject.extend({

  onResetEvent: function() {
    // stuff to reset on state change
    me.levelDirector.loadLevel('area01');

},

  // action to perform when game is finished (state change)
  onDestroyEvent: function() {

}

});

window.onReady(function() {
  jsApp.onload();
});
```

When you save the main.js file and refresh the web page, you should now see your level loaded on the screen, as in Figure 14.9.

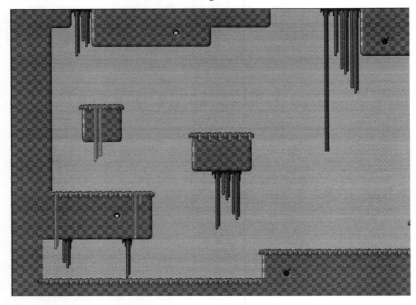

Figure 14–9. *Map for melonJS game loaded*

You map may look a bit different depending on how you designed your level in Tiled. Now that there is a map, we need to bring in the main player. There are a lot of sprites included in the gfx-fuzed library, but for our purposes here, we use "gripe.run_right.png". We first need to add the file to the game resources, and then define a new object to define how the object walks and interacts with the keyboard. It is a good idea to get in the habit of creating new files for any of the entities in your game that are their own object. This helps you focus on the actual object you are working on, and allows you to reuse the components in future projects more easily. For our purposes here, we add a new image to the g_resources container and then create a new file named player.js to define the PlayerEntity as shown in Listing 14–8.

Listing 14–8. *Adding the Player to the Entity Loader*

```
var g_resources = [{
  name: "area01_level_tiles",
  type: "image",
  src: "data/gfxlib-
fuzed/Backgrounds/lev01_checkers/area01_tileset/area01_level_tiles.png"
}, {
  name: "area01",
  type: "tmx",
  src: "data/area01.tmx"
}, {
  name: "gripe_run_right",
  type: "image",
  src: "data/gfxlib-fuzed/Sprites/gripe.run_right.png"
}
];
```

Now we need to build the Player entity in player.js (Listing 14–9), setting it in position, where the camera should focus, and how fast it should walk and jump.

Listing 14–9. *Building the Player Entity (player.js)*

```
// player entity
var PlayerEntity = me.ObjectEntity.extend({
  init: function(x, y, settings) {
    // call ObjectEntity constructor
    this.parent(x, y, settings);

    // set walking and jumping speed
    this.setVelocity(3, 15);

    // set display to follow player's position on x and y axis
    me.game.viewport.follow(this.pos, me.game.viewport.AXIS.BOTH);
  },

  // update player position
  update: function() {
    if(me.input.isKeyPressed('left')) {
      this.doWalk(true);
    } else if (me.input.isKeyPressed('right')) {
      this.doWalk(false);
    } else {
      this.vel.x = 0;
    }

    if (me.input.isKeyPressed('jump')) {
      this.doJump();
    }

    // check and update player movement
    this.updateMovement();
```

```
          // update animation if necessary
          if(this.vel.x !== 0 || this.vel.y !== 0) {
            // update object animation
            this.parent(this);
            return true;
          }

          return false;

      }
});
```

There is some magic going on here that allows you to use some predefined helper functions in the melonJS engine to help you write less code. The doWalk(), doJump(), and setVelocity() functions are defined in melonJS and give you some basic "walking" and "jumping" capabilities. You may find that they are not sufficient if you develop something a bit more complex, but there is some base code so you can develop your own code from the melonJS source (in src/entity/entity.js).

We need to load the new player.js file before our main.js file, and then define a callback in the main.js file to bind the keys to the player object when the application is loaded. We update the jsApp.loaded function to read as Listing 14–10.

Listing 14–10. *Adding Key Bindings to Move*

```
loaded: function() {
    // set the "Play/Ingame" Screen Object
    me.state.set(me.state.PLAY, new PlayScreen());

    // add the player to the entity pool
    me.entityPool.add('mainPlayer', PlayerEntity);

    // bind to the keyboard
    me.input.bindKey(me.input.KEY.LEFT, "left");
    me.input.bindKey(me.input.KEY.RIGHT, "right");
    me.input.bindKey(me.input.KEY.X, "jump", true);

    // start the game
    me.state.change(me.state.PLAY);
}
```

With PlayerEntity defined in player.js, and loaded before main.js in the index.html file, we have the code defined to handle the player object. However, we need to go back into Tiled and define a new object layer and entity in order to view the player in the game.

In Tiled, click on **Layer ➤ Add Object Layer** and rename it "Entities". Now add an object to the Object layer (type the letter "O" on the keyboard) and click somewhere on the map. This will put a gray box on the screen (Figure 14–10); right-click on it and set these properties:

- Name: mainPlayer (or the label you used when you added the PlayerEntity to the entityPool in the jsApp.loaded() method).

- image: gripe_run_right

- spritewidth: 32

Figure 14–10. *Adding the main player*

After you save the area01.tmx file, you may be tempted to look at the web page. You may see your sprites on the page, but then fall off the screen. Kind of a cool effect, but it does not make for compelling gameplay! We need to add another layer that defines a solid tile for the sprite to walk on, thus we need to create our own tile map to do this. For this case, you can create a 16 × 16 pixel square and make it red (you want to make sure it is obvious that this is not for display in the game) in your favorite image program. I put an "S" on my square (for solid) for good measure. Save the file in your project's data directory (e.g., project/data/metatiles.png).

In Tiled, create a new Tileset (**Map ➤ New Tileset…**) and navigate the image field to where you just saved the metatiles.png file. See Figure 14–11.

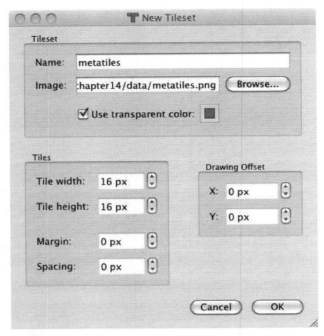

Figure 14–11. *Adding the metatiles tileset*

Once added, select the red tile, right-click, and select "Tile Properties…" to add a type property of solid to the tile (Figure 14–12).

Figure 14–12. *Adding a type to a tileset*

Add a new layer with the keyword "collision" (must be lowercase) for melonJS to recognize this as a collision layer. Be sure you have the collision layer selected and draw where the game should recognize something as solid. Mine looked like that shown in Figure 14–13.

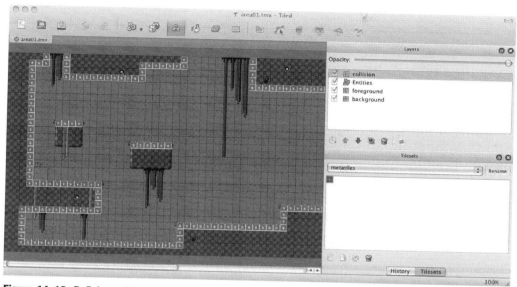

Figure 14–13. *Defining solid surfaces*

Now if you reload the page, you will see the sprite on the canvas and have the ability to move and jump the player entity. See Figure 14–14.

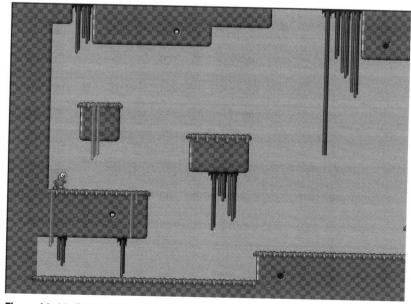

Figure 14–14. *Rendered scene*

NOTE: If you are getting strange error messages in alert messages (e.g., cannot load undefined), make sure you did not accidentally add an extra object in the Entities layer. If you did, right-click the object and select "Remove Object."

What about that pink box around the sprite, though? The background of the sprite is that pink color. Tiled has a setting to use a default transparency color for layers, but this is not currently an option for objects. The easiest way to get rid of this background is to edit the file itself. Most image editing tools have a "magic-wand" tool that will let you click on a pixel and it will select all pixels of that color. Open the gripe_run_right.png file, use the magic-wand tool, and select the pink background; then delete that color. You should be left with the original sprites without the pink background as in Figure 14–15.

Figure 14–15. *Gripe sprite without pink background*

Everything should look much better when you reload the page. See Figure 14–16.

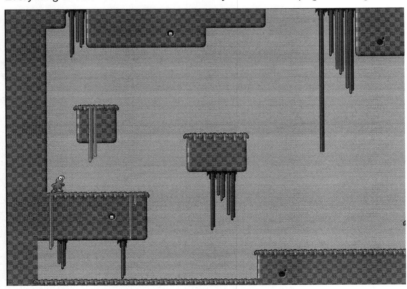

Figure 14–16. *Game with sprite background removed*

> **NOTE:** While you are developing your game, it may be useful to have a hitBox around your sprite to help you visually verify that any collisions that are expected to occur actually do. In the main.js file, edit the jsApp.loaded() method after the sprite has been loaded to include the following to place a bounding box around the sprite.
>
> ```
> // debugging
> me.debug.renderHitBox = true;
> ```
>
> This will place a box around any entities that can collide, allowing you visually to verify the collision box around an entity. However, be sure to comment this line out before pushing into a production environment!

If you look at the bounding box for the sprite, you may notice that there is a bit of whitespace on each side of the tile. We can update the bounding box in the player.js file to take in the correct dimensions of the sprite. This is done in the `PlayerEntity.init()` function by calling the `updateColRect` function, passing the *x*-offset, width, *y*-offset, and height for the hit box. For our purposes here, we want to shift the *x*-offset of the bounding box by 4 pixels, and give it a new width of 20 (16 pixel width + 4 pixel offset). We take the *y*-offset to –1 (to prevent the sprite from jumping around) and leave the height alone. See Listing 14–11.

Listing 14–11. *Initializing the Player*

```
init: function(x, y, settings) {
    // call ObjectEntity constructor
    this.parent(x, y, settings);

    // set walking and jumping speed
    this.setVelocity(3, 15);

    // update the hitbox
    this.updateColRect(4, 20, -1, 0);

    // set display to follow player's position on x and y axis
    me.game.viewport.follow(this.pos, me.game.viewport.AXIS.BOTH);
},
```

Now when the player is in the game, they can get a little bit closer to the collision tiles.

Background

Now that the game has some interaction, we can add the background that the gfx-fuzed library came with for this level. We add a parallax effect where the foreground moves faster than the background here. The images for this level are in the `data/gfxlib-fuzed/Backgrounds/lev01_checkers/area01_parallax/` directory. See Listing 14–12.

We first need to add these images (`area01_bkg0.png` and `area01_bkg1.png`) to the `g_resources` in main.js.

Listing 14–12. *Adding the Backgrounds to the Game Resources*

```
var g_resources = [{
  name: "area01_level_tiles",
  type: "image",
  src: "data/gfxlib-
fuzed/Backgrounds/lev01_checkers/area01_tileset/area01_level_tiles.png"
}, {
  name: "area01",
  type: "tmx",
  src: "data/area01.tmx"
}, {
  name: "gripe_run_right",
  type: "image",
  src: "data/gfxlib-fuzed/Sprites/gripe.run_right.png"
}, {
  name: "area01_bkg0",
  type: "image",
  src: "data/gfxlib-fuzed/Backgrounds/lev01_checkers/area01_parallax/area01_bkg0.png"
}, {
  name: "area01_bkg1",
  type: "image",
  src: "data/gfxlib-fuzed/Backgrounds/lev01_checkers/area01_parallax/area01_bkg1.png"
}
];
```

To use these, go back into Tiled and create two new tile layers (**Tile ➤ New Tile Layer**) that are prefixed with the keyword "parallax." This keyword tells melonJS to handle these images as parallax layers, and to use the resource pointer defined in the main.js file. These tile layers need to be behind all the other layers, so push them down the layer stack by clicking on the down arrow in the layer view (Figure 14–17).

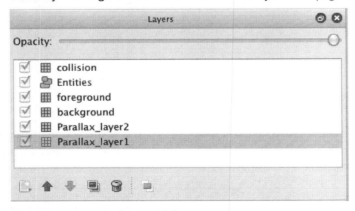

Figure 14–17. *Parallax layers added*

Now assign properties to the parallax layers of imagesrc to the appropriate symbol defined in main.js as in Figure 14–18. On my layer, Parallax_layer1 has an imagesrc of area01_bkg0 and Parallax_layer2 uses area01_bkg1.

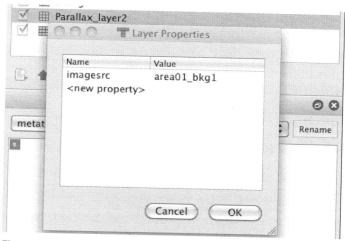

Figure 14–18. *Defining parallax layers in Tiled*

Reload the page and you should see the parallax effect with the stars in the background, and a hideous pink background (Figure 14–19). We can fix that the same way we did previously by opening up the area01_bkg1.png file and removing the pink background.

Figure 14–19. *Parallax with solid pink background*

After removing the pink background from the image using a transparent color, your game will look much nicer (Figure 14–20).

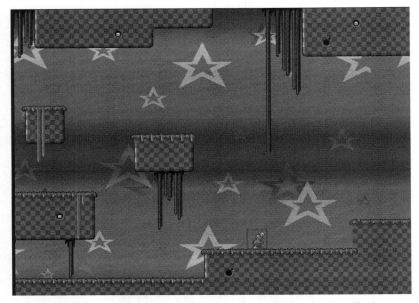

Figure 14–20. *Game with correct parallax background and debugging bounding box around player*

When you move your sprite around on the screen, you should see the two different fields moving, giving the game extra dimension and depth.

Game Components

Running around is fun, but we need to add some more components that provide more game-playing elements. Ever since Super Mario, people have been collecting coins, and there are some nice enemy and coin images in the gfx-fuzed library. We add in the spinning_coin_gold.png and the wheelie_right.png in the Sprites directory. As before, we need to get rid of the annoying pink background. After you save the file, add them to the g_resources to load as in Listing 14–13.

Listing 14–13. *Adding an Enemy to the Game Resources*

```
var g_resources = [{
  name: "area01_level_tiles",
  type: "image",
  src: "data/gfxlib-
fuzed/Backgrounds/lev01_checkers/area01_tileset/area01_level_tiles.png"
}, {
  name: "area01",
  type: "tmx",
  src: "data/area01.tmx"
}, {
  name: "gripe_run_right",
  type: "image",
  src: "data/gfxlib-fuzed/Sprites/gripe.run_right.png"
}, {
```

```
      name: "area01_bkg0",
      type: "image",
      src: "data/gfxlib-fuzed/Backgrounds/lev01_checkers/area01_parallax/area01_bkg0.png"
    }, {
      name: "area01_bkg1",
      type: "image",
      src: "data/gfxlib-fuzed/Backgrounds/lev01_checkers/area01_parallax/area01_bkg1.png"
    }, {
      name: "spinning_coin_gold",
      type: "image",
      src: "data/gfxlib-fuzed/Sprites/spinning_coin_gold.png"
    }, {
      name: "wheelie_right",
      type: "image",
      src: "data/gfxlib-fuzed/Sprites/wheelie_right.png"
    }
];
```

You could define the Coin in Tiled, but we want to add some additional components and actions to the coin (e.g., score and sound). For this, create a new file (coin.js) and extend the CollectableEntity in melonJS, as in Listing 14–14.

Listing 14–14. *Coin entity*

```
var CoinEntity = me.CollectableEntity.extend({

  init: function(x, y, settings) {
    settings.image = 'spinning_coin_gold';
    settings.spritewidth = 16;

    this.parent(x, y, settings);
  },

  // called by the engine when an object is destroyed
  onDestroyEvent: function() {
    // do something when collected
  }
});
```

For the enemies, we create a new file, but this is a little more complex as we want to give them a little bit of AI to move back and forth, as well as be able to collide when the player runs into the enemy; see Listing 14–15.

Listing 14–15. *Adding an Enemy*

```
var EnemyEntity = me.ObjectEntity.extend({
  init: function(x, y, settings) {
    // define this here instead of tiled
    settings.image = 'wheelie_right';
    settings.spritewidth = 32;

    // call the parent constructor
    this.parent(x, y, settings);

    this.startX = x;
    this.endX = x + settings.width - settings.spritewidth;
    // size of sprite
```

```
            // make him start from the right
            this.pos.x = x + settings.width - settings.spritewidth;
            this.walkLeft = true;

            // walking & jumping speed
            this.setVelocity(2, 6);

            // make it collidable
            this.collidable = true;
            // make it a enemy object
            this.type = me.game.ENEMY_OBJECT;

        },

        // call by the engine when colliding with another object
        // obj parameter corresponds to the other object (typically the player) touching ↵
    this one
        onCollision: function(res, obj) {

            // res.y >0 means touched by something on the bottom
            // which mean at top position for this one
            if (this.alive && (res.y > 0) && obj.falling) {
                this.flicker(45);
            }
        },

        // manage the enemy movement
        update: function() {
            // do nothing if not visible
            if (!this.visible)
                return false;

            if (this.alive) {
                if (this.walkLeft && this.pos.x <= this.startX) {
                    this.walkLeft = false;
                } else if (!this.walkLeft && this.pos.x >= this.endX) {
                    this.walkLeft = true;
                }
                this.doWalk(this.walkLeft);
            } else {
                this.vel.x = 0;
            }

            // check and update movement
            this.updateMovement();

            // update animation if necessary
            if (this.vel.x !== 0 || this.vel.y !== 0) {
                // update objet animation
                this.parent(this);
                return true;
            }
            return false;
        }
    });
```

You need to include these files in the index.html file before main.js called (Listing 14–16).

Listing 14–16. *Adding the JavaScript to the Main HTML Page (index.html)*

```
<script src="javascript/melonJS-0.9.2-min.js"></script>
<script src="javascript/player.js"></script>
<script src="javascript/coin.js"></script>
<script src="javascript/enemy.js"></script>
<script src="javascript/main.js"></script>
```

And now edit main.js to add the coin and enemy to the EntityPool in the `jsApp.loaded()` method (Listing 14–17).

Listing 14–17. *Loading the Enemies into the Game (main.js)*

```
loaded: function() {
    // set the "Play/Ingame" Screen Object
    me.state.set(me.state.PLAY, new PlayScreen());

    // add the player to the entity pool
    me.entityPool.add('mainPlayer', PlayerEntity);
    me.entityPool.add('CoinEntity', CoinEntity);
    me.entityPool.add('EnemyEntity', EnemyEntity);

    // bind to the keyboard
    me.input.bindKey(me.input.KEY.LEFT, 'left');
    me.input.bindKey(me.input.KEY.RIGHT, 'right');
    me.input.bindKey(me.input.KEY.X, 'jump', true);

    // debugging
    me.debug.renderHitBox = true;

    // start the game
    me.state.change(me.state.PLAY);
}
```

Jump back into Tiled and create a new Object layer (**Layer ➤ Add Object Layer**) and rename it EnemyEntities. Use the Insert Object tool (O on the keyboard) and draw an object where you would like an enemy or a coin. After drawing the box, right-click and give it a name of either `CoinEntity` or `EnemyEntity` in the Object Properties. Create a few coins and an enemy or two on the map and when you are done, you will have a screen that looks something like Figure 14–21 in Tiled:

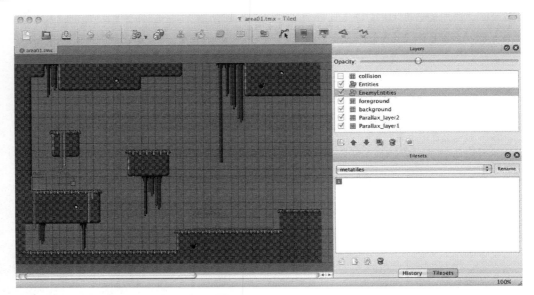

Figure 14–21. *Adding coins and enemies in Tiled*

When you reload the page, you should see some coins spinning and the "enemy" sprite moving back and forth. However, we have yet to define how the player will interact with these other entities. We need to update the player.js file to check if it has collided with something (a coin or an enemy). The section checking for collision evaluates if the collision is with an enemy, and where it is, to respond accordingly. If the sprite jumps on top of the enemy, the enemy flickers; all other collisions cause the sprite to flicker. See Listing 14–18.

Listing 14–18. *Adding Interactions with the Enemy (main.js)*

```
update: function() {
    if (me.input.isKeyPressed('left')) {
      this.doWalk(true);
    } else if (me.input.isKeyPressed('right')) {
      this.doWalk(false);
    } else {
      this.vel.x = 0;
    }

    if (me.input.isKeyPressed('jump')) {
      this.doJump();
    }

    // check and update player movement
    this.updateMovement();

    // check for a collision
    var res = me.game.collide(this);

    if (res) {
      // collide with an enemy
```

```
        if (res.obj.type == me.game.ENEMY_OBJECT) {
            // check if enemy was jumped on
            if ((res.y > 0) && ! this.jumping) {
                // bounce
                this.forceJump();
            } else {
                // flicker when touched
                this.flicker(45);
            }
        }
    }
}

    // update animation if necessary
    if (this.vel.x !== 0 || this.vel.y !== 0) {
        // update object animation
        this.parent(this);
        return true;
    }

    return false;

}
```

Adding Feedback

You definitely want to provide some feedback for your users as they play the game. We can use the 16 × 16_font.png (removing the pink background) in the Sprites directory to display information to the user. As we have done previously, we need to add the font to the game resources (see Listing 14–12), then create a new object to record the Score (in score.js). The code for the Score (Listing 14–18) will extend the HUD (heads up display) in melonJS and use the 16 × 16_font as its letters. This essentially treats the fonts as a sprite sheet and converts your letters to the image equivalent. See Listing 14–19.

Listing 14–19. *Creating the ScoreObject (score.js)*

```
var ScoreObject = me.HUD_Item.extend({
  init: function(x, y) {

    this.parent(x, y);
    // create a font
    this.font = new me.BitmapFont('16x16_font', 16);
  },

  update: function(value) {
    this.parent(value);

    if (this.value > me.gamestat.getItemValue('highscore')) {
      me.gamestat.setValue('highscore', this.value);
    }

    return true;
  },


  draw: function(context, x, y) {
```

```
        this.font.draw(context, this.value, this.pos.x + x, this.pos.y + y);
    }

});

var HighScoreObject = me.HUD_Item.extend({

    init: function(x, y, val) {
        this.parent(x, y, val);
        this.font = new me.BitmapFont('16x16_font', 16);
        this.font.set('left');
    },

    draw: function(context, x, y) {
        this.font.draw(context, 'HIGH SCORE', this.pos.x + x, this.pos.y + y);
        this.font.draw(context,
                        me.gamestat.getItemValue('highscore'),
                        this.pos.x + x,
                        this.pos.y + y + 16
                    );

    }
});
```

With an object keeping track of the score, we can update the PlayScreen object (in main.js) to use the object to display the score on the game; see Listing 14–20.

Listing 14–20. *Adding a Score to the Main View (main.js)*

```
var PlayScreen = me.ScreenObject.extend({

    onResetEvent: function() {
        // stuff to reset on state change
        me.levelDirector.loadLevel('area01');

        me.game.addHUD(0, 430, 640, 60);
        me.game.HUD.addItem("score", new ScoreObject(620, 10));

        me.game.sort();
    },

    // action to perform when game is finished (state change)
    onDestroyEvent: function() {
        me.game.disableHUD();
    }

});
```

This will add the score HUD at the bottom-right of the play screen. The score object has been assigned to "score" so it can be easily updated in other places in the code. To get a score from the onDestroyEvent method of the CoinEntity see Listing 14–21.

Listing 14–21. *Updating the Score (coin.js)*

```
onDestroyEvent: function() {
    // do something when collected
    me.game.HUD.updateItemValue('score', 250);
}
```

Now, when a coin is collected by the player, the score on the HUD will be updated by 250.

Adding Audio

We need some sounds for this game. For starters, we need some background tunes, a sound for collecting a coin, jumping, and stomping on an enemy. For the background music, head over to NoSoapRadio (http://www.nosoapradio.us/) and pick something appropriate from the Platform/Puzzle section (or any section really). I picked GameOn for this level and saved it in the data/audio directory. Convert the mp3 to an ogg in there too (same file name) using Audacity as we covered in Chapter 10 (see the Music section).

Next I headed over to OpenGameArt.org and did some searching for coin and jumping sounds. I found a great set of coin sounds by Luke.RUSTLTD (http://opengameart.org/content/10-8bit-coin-sounds) and a nice jumping sound effect over on SoundBible.com named Mario Jumping Sound (http://soundbible.com/1601-Mario-Jumping.html) and Bounce Sound (http://soundbible.com/1120-Bounce.html) both by Mike Koenig. I grabbed all the files making mp3s and ogg versions of each sound in Audacity, also cutting down long sounds (Mario_Jump and Bounce were each about two seconds long; I adjusted them down to about a second. My final audio directory contained the files in Listing 14–22.

Listing 14–22. *Files in the Audio Directory*

```
Bounce.mp3
Bounce.ogg
coin1.mp3
coin1.ogg
DST-GameOn.mp3
DST-GameOn.ogg
Mario_Jumping.mp3
Mario_Jumping.ogg
```

The melonJS framework has a decent audio manager, and instead of adding individual files, you add the path and a base file name to load the different versions of the sound (Listing 14–23).

Listing 14–23. *Adding Sounds to Game Resources (main.js)*

```
// game resources
var g_resources = [{
  name: "area01_level_tiles",
  type: "image",
  src: "data/gfxlib-
fuzed/Backgrounds/lev01_checkers/area01_tileset/area01_level_tiles.png"
}, {
  name: "area01",
  type: "tmx",
  src: "data/area01.tmx"
}, {
  name: "gripe_run_right",
  type: "image",
  src: "data/gfxlib-fuzed/Sprites/gripe.run_right.png"
```

```
}, {
  name: "area01_bkg0",
  type: "image",
  src: "data/gfxlib-fuzed/Backgrounds/lev01_checkers/area01_parallax/area01_bkg0.png"
}, {
  name: "area01_bkg1",
  type: "image",
  src: "data/gfxlib-fuzed/Backgrounds/lev01_checkers/area01_parallax/area01_bkg1.png"
}, {
  name: "spinning_coin_gold",
  type: "image",
  src: "data/gfxlib-fuzed/Sprites/spinning_coin_gold.png"
}, {
  name: "wheelie_right",
  type: "image",
  src: "data/gfxlib-fuzed/Sprites/wheelie_right.png"
}, {
  name: '16x16_font',
  type: 'image',
  src: 'data/gfxlib-fuzed/Sprites/16x16_font.png'
}, {
  name: 'DST-GameOn',
  type: 'audio',
  src: 'data/audio/',
  channel: 1
}, {
  name: 'Bounce',
  type: 'audio',
  src: 'data/audio/',
  channel: 1
}, {
  name: 'coin1',
  type: 'audio',
  src: 'data/audio/',
  channel: 1
}, {
  name: 'Mario_Jumping',
  type: 'audio',
  src: 'data/audio/',
  channel: 1
}
];
```

To play the background sound (DST-GameOn), we tell melonJS to play the track in the PlayScreen.onResetEvent, and stop the sound in the onDestroyEvent as in Listing 14–24.

Listing 14–24. *Adding a Track to the Game (main.js)*

```
var PlayScreen = me.ScreenObject.extend({

  onResetEvent: function() {
    // stuff to reset on state change
    me.levelDirector.loadLevel('area01');

    me.game.addHUD(0, 430, 640, 60);
    me.game.HUD.addItem("score", new ScoreObject(620, 10));
```

```
      me.game.sort();

      me.audio.playTrack('DST-GameOn');
    },

    // action to perform when game is finished (state change)
    onDestroyEvent: function() {
      me.game.disableHUD();

      // stop the music
      me.audio.stopTrack();
    }

});

window.onReady(function() {
  jsApp.onload();
});
```

To play the coin1 sound, we attach that to the `CoinEntity.onDestroyEvent()`. See Listing 14–25.

Listing 14–25. *Adding a Sound when the Coin Is Collected (coin.js)*

```
var CoinEntity = me.CollectableEntity.extend({

  init: function(x, y, settings) {
    settings.image = 'spinning_coin_gold';
    settings.spritewidth = 16;

    this.parent(x, y, settings);
  },

  // called by the engine when an object is destroyed
  onDestroyEvent: function() {
    // do something when collected
    me.audio.play('coin1');

    me.game.HUD.updateItemValue('score', 250);
  }
});
```

For the jump sound, we need to play the sound for the player jumps. Add the sound when the jump is completed in the player.js, as in Listing 14–26.

Listing 14–26. *Adding a Sound to the Player Jump (player.js)*

```
if (me.input.isKeyPressed('jump')) {
    if (this.doJump()) {
      me.audio.play('Mario_Jumping');
    }
}
```

And lastly, add the "stomp" sound (Bounce in our case) when a player jumps on the head of an enemy. Update the player.js logic when the player is on top of an enemy to play "Bounce" (see Listing 14–27). Later in the chapter, we add in code to end the game when the player runs into the enemy.

Listing 14–27. *Adding a Bounce to an Enemy (player.js)*

```
if (res) {
      // collide with an enemy
      if (res.obj.type == me.game.ENEMY_OBJECT) {
        // check if enemy was jumped on
        if ((res.y > 0) && ! this.jumping) {
          // bounce
          me.audio.play('Bounce');
          this.forceJump();
        } else {
          // flicker when touched
          this.flicker(45);
        }
      }
}
```

Adding a Level

We now have a sprite running on a map, coins to earn points, enemies, and sounds that work together as a unit. One level is fine, but you will want to add more levels to keep things interesting. There is an object in melonJS named me.LevelEntity that you can add in Tiled to denote the area for a player to get to in order to advance to the next level.

In Tiled, select the Entities layer, add a new Object (O on the keyboard), and set the property name to me.LevelEntity, with a duration property of 250, a fade of #000000, and to (which map you want to load next) of area02. You can create a new TMX file named area02.tmx in the data directory, and when the player reaches the me.LevelEntity, the next map will be loaded. See Figure 14–22.

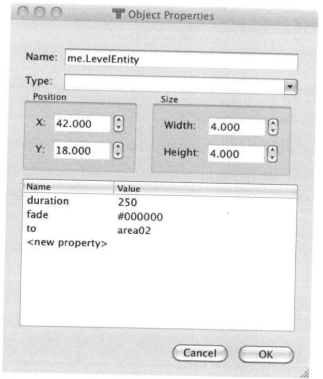

Figure 14–22. *Adding the next level*

You can play with these settings to get the desired fade-in/fade-out effect and colors. Use the different level tile sheets that are in the gfxlib-fuzed directory to come up with interesting maps to figure out. Remember, too, to play the different levels. Make sure that the beginning levels are relatively easy to give players a sense of accomplishment, and make sure that there are not things such as coins that are out of reach of your PlayerEntity.

Title Screen

The gfxlib-fuzed library comes with a title screen, and makes for a nice finishing touch to the game. As we have done numerous times in this chapter, we create a new file (title_screen.js) that we include in the index.html file. We add the title screen to the g_resources, then set the screen to use the 16x16_font to provide information about the game to the user.

The file we use is in data/gfxlib-fuzed/GUI/title_screen.jpg, so I define that in the g_resources in main.js as in Listing 14–28.

Listing 14–28. *Adding a Title Screen (main.js)*

```
{
  name: 'title_screen',
  type: 'image',
  src: 'data/gfxlib-fuzed/GUI/title_screen.jpg'
}
```

Next I add title_screen.js to the list of scripts that index.html loads (Listing 14–29).

Listing 14–29. *Adding the Title Screen to the HTML Page (index.html)*

```
<script src="javascript/melonJS-0.9.2-min.js"></script>
<script src="javascript/player.js"></script>
<script src="javascript/coin.js"></script>
<script src="javascript/enemy.js"></script>
<script src="javascript/score.js"></script>
<script src="javascript/title_screen.js"></script>
<script src="javascript/main.js"></script>
```

Now create the title_screen.js file with the code in Listing 14–30. Remember, the 16x16_font file does not have any lowercase characters, so all text needs to be uppercase in order to be viewed on the screen.

Listing 14–30. *Adding Text to the Title Screen (title_screen.js)*

```
var TitleScreen = me.ScreenObject.extend({

    init: function() {
      this.parent(true);

          // title screen image
          this.title = null;

          this.font = null;
          this.scrollerfont = null;
          this.scrollertween = null;

          this.scroller = 'AN EXAMPLE FACEBOOK GAME USING THE MELONJS GAME ENGINE        ';
          this.scrollerpos = 600;
    },

    onResetEvent: function() {
      if (this.title == null) {
        this.title = me.loader.getImage('title_screen');

        // font to use
        this.font = new me.BitmapFont('16x16_font', 16);
        this.font.set('left');

        // set the scroller
        this.scrollerfont = new me.BitmapFont('16x16_font', 16);
        this.scrollerfont.set('left');
      }
```

Now we just need to change the code jsApp.loaded() method to register a new game state for the Menu, and use it as the default state (where it had been play) as in Listing 14–31.

Listing 14–31. *Adding the Title Screen to the Game Loader (main.js)*

```
loaded: function() {
    me.state.set(me.state.MENU, new TitleScreen());

    // set the "Play/Ingame" Screen Object
    me.state.set(me.state.PLAY, new PlayScreen());

    // add the player to the entity pool
    me.entityPool.add('mainPlayer', PlayerEntity);
    me.entityPool.add('CoinEntity', CoinEntity);
    me.entityPool.add('EnemyEntity', EnemyEntity);


    // bind to the keyboard
    me.input.bindKey(me.input.KEY.LEFT, 'left');
    me.input.bindKey(me.input.KEY.RIGHT, 'right');
    me.input.bindKey(me.input.KEY.X, 'jump', true);

    // debugging
    //me.debug.renderHitBox = true;

    // start the game
    me.state.change(me.state.MENU);
}
```

Now, when you reload the web page, you should see the title screen with a scroller across the bottom of the game.

Figure 14–23. *Fuzed for Facebook Title Screen*

Have some fun adding and tweaking levels. Remember the gfxlib-fuzed library comes with several good tilesets for different levels. Adding in sounds from sources on the Internet (or creating your own) is easy, as is building in form functionality for the game. For instance, there are gems, silver coins, mines, explosions, and a few different enemies in the Sprites directory, and several different screens to use in a credits and menu system.

NOTE: If you really like Tiled for editing, you may also like the iPad/iPod app iTileMaps (`http://www.klemix.com/page/iTileMaps.aspx`). This app allows you to edit/create TMX maps on your mobile device, and has iCloud and Dropbox integration so you can work on your maps even when you are not at your desk. The main limitation right now for use with melonJS is that iTileMaps only uses base64 compressed TMX. You can change this setting in Tiled (you will need to resave after you change it to uncompressed), but it is an extra step to be aware of if you use iTileMaps.

Facebook Score API

The game we just developed could be deployed in a lot of places right now because it is just HTML code. You could make it playable from a website and code a high-score system into the game that uses your browser's LocalStorage API to record a user's high score. This would be relatively straightforward, but you really are limited to seeing your own high scores. You could write your own database system for recording high scores as we did in Chapter 12. There are some limitations with a solution like this, especially if you need to develop an authentication/authorization system (there are a lot of talented site crackers out there). This is actually a big plus for a framework such as the Facebook platform, to manage some of these concerns so you do not need to think (as much) about them.

Facebook provides a great API for registering high scores for applications that are categorized as games. With the "publish_actions" permission in your application, you can create and update scores for your players, then display both the user's high score and the high score of that user's friends (but not an overall high score). This encourages groups of friends to play together, while respecting their privacy.

So how do we integrate the game we have just created into the Facebook framework? The process is much like what I outlined in Chapter 10 when we moved from using a dummy image to integrating with a user's images. However, because the game is contained in itself, the graph calls can be simplified quite a bit. We also need to update the game somewhat to send the score to the API when the game is in an "over" state.

First, set up a new application in the Facebook Developer application and add the Cloud Services hosting. Clone the Git repo from Heroku (log on to heroku.com to see your applications); then we can start merging the game files into the PHP template Heroku adds. Also be sure to change the category to "Game."

Next we need to copy the `javascript` and `data` directories from our game into the Heroku application. After you have all of the components in place, add them to your Git repository (`git add data javascript`) and then commit them (`git commit -am "Added JavaScript and data from html game"`). Now we can update the `index.php` file to pull the game together. Either move the `index.php` file (e.g., `mv index.php index.php.bak`) or delete the contents and replace them with those shown in Listing 14–32..

Listing 14–32. *Application Template for Fuzed (index.php)*

```php
<?php

// Provides access to app specific values such as your app id and app secret.
// Defined in 'AppInfo.php'
require_once('AppInfo.php');

// Enforce https on production
if (substr(AppInfo::getUrl(), 0, 8) != 'https://' && $_SERVER['REMOTE_ADDR'] !=↵
  '127.0.0.1') {
  header('Location: https://'. $_SERVER['HTTP_HOST'] . $_SERVER['REQUEST_URI']);
  exit();
}

// This provides access to helper functions defined in 'utils.php'
require_once('utils.php');

// include the Facebook SDK
require_once('sdk/src/facebook.php');

$facebook = new Facebook(array(
  'appId'  => AppInfo::appID(),
  'secret' => AppInfo::appSecret(),
));

$user_id = $facebook->getUser();
if ($user_id) {
  try {
    // Fetch the viewer's basic information
    $basic = $facebook->api('/me');
  } catch (FacebookApiException $e) {
    // If the call fails we check if we still have a user. The user will be
    // cleared if the error is because of an invalid accesstoken
    if (!$facebook->getUser()) {
      header('Location: '. AppInfo::getUrl($_SERVER['REQUEST_URI']));
      exit();
    }
  }

  //$app_token = $facebook->getAccessToken();

}

// Fetch the basic info of the app that they are using
$app_info = $facebook->api('/'. AppInfo::appID());

$app_name = idx($app_info, 'name', '');

?>
```

```
<!DOCTYPE html>
<html xmlns:fb="http://ogp.me/ns/fb#" lang="en">
  <head>
    <meta charset="utf-8" />
    <meta name="viewport" content="width=device-width, initial-scale=1.0,↵
maximum-scale=2.0, user-scalable=yes" />

    <title><?php echo he($app_name); ?></title>
    <link rel="stylesheet" href="stylesheets/screen.css" media="Screen"↵
type="text/css" />
    <link rel="stylesheet" href="stylesheets/mobile.css" media="handheld, only screen↵
and (max-width: 480px), only screen and (max-device-width: 480px)" type="text/css" />

    <!--[if IEMobile]>
    <link rel="stylesheet" href="mobile.css" media="screen" type="text/css"  />
    <![endif]-->

    <meta property="og:title" content="<?php echo he($app_name); ?>" />
    <meta property="og:type" content="game" />
    <meta property="og:url" content="<?php echo AppInfo::getUrl(); ?>" />
    <meta property="og:image" content="<?php echo AppInfo::getUrl('/images/logo.png');↵
?>" />
    <meta property="og:site_name" content="<?php echo he($app_name); ?>" />
    <meta property="og:description" content="Fuzed for Facebook is a sidesroller game↵
developed as a demo application for the Beginning Facebook Games Apps Development." />
    <meta property="fb:app_id" content="<?php echo AppInfo::appID(); ?>" />
    <meta property="fb:admins" content="[Your Facebook user id]" />

    <style>
      #info { width: 640px; }
      #fps { float: right; }
      #framecounter { font-size: 10px; font-family: Courier, 'Courier New';↵
color: #c0c0c0;}
      #game {
        border-left: 1px solid #B3B3B3;
        border-right: 1px solid #B3B3B3;
        border-bottom: 1px solid #B3B3B3;
        padding-bottom: 15px;
        padding-left: 35px;
      }
    </style>

    <script type="text/javascript" src="/javascript/jquery-1.7.1.min.js"></script>

    <script type="text/javascript">
      function logResponse(response) {
        if (console && console.log) {
          console.log('The response was', response);
        }
      }

      $(function(){
        // Set up so we handle click on the buttons
        $('#postToWall').click(function() {
          FB.ui(
            {
              method : 'feed',
```

```
            link    : $(this).attr('data-url')
          },
          function (response) {
            // If response is null the user canceled the dialog
            if (response != null) {
              logResponse(response);
            }
          }
        );
      });

      $('#sendToFriends').click(function() {
        FB.ui(
          {
            method : 'send',
            link    : $(this).attr('data-url')
          },
          function (response) {
            // If response is null the user canceled the dialog
            if (response != null) {
              logResponse(response);
            }
          }
        );
      });

      $('#sendRequest').click(function() {
        FB.ui(
          {
            method  : 'apprequests',
            message : $(this).attr('data-message')
          },
          function (response) {
            // If response is null the user canceled the dialog
            if (response != null) {
              logResponse(response);
            }
          }
        );
      });
    });
  </script>

  <!--[if IE]>
    <script type="text/javascript">
      var tags = ['header', 'section'];
      while(tags.length)
        document.createElement(tags.pop());
    </script>
  <![endif]-->
</head>
<body>
  <div id="fb-root"></div>
  <script type="text/javascript">
    window.fbAsyncInit = function() {
      FB.init({
        appId        : '<?php echo AppInfo::appID(); ?>', // App ID
```

```
          channelUrl : '//<?php echo $_SERVER["HTTP_HOST"]; ?>/channel.html',↵
// Channel File
          status     : true, // check login status
          cookie     : true, // enable cookies to allow the server to access the session
          xfbml      : true // parse XFBML
      });

      // Listen to the auth.login which will be called when the user logs in
      // using the Login button
      FB.Event.subscribe('auth.login', function(response) {
          // We want to reload the page now so PHP can read the cookie that the
          // Javascript SDK sat. But we don't want to use
          // window.location.reload() because if this is in a canvas there was a
          // post made to this page and a reload will trigger a message to the
          // user asking if they want to send data again.
          window.location = window.location;
      });

      FB.Canvas.setAutoGrow();
    };

    // Load the SDK Asynchronously
    (function(d, s, id) {
      var js, fjs = d.getElementsByTagName(s)[0];
      if (d.getElementById(id)) return;
      js = d.createElement(s); js.id = id;
      js.src = "//connect.facebook.net/en_US/all.js";
      fjs.parentNode.insertBefore(js, fjs);
    }(document, 'script', 'facebook-jssdk'));
  </script>

  <header class="clearfix">
    <?php if (isset($basic)): ?>
    <p id="picture" style="background-image: url(https://graph.facebook.com/↵
<?php echo he($user_id); ?>/picture?type=normal)"></p>

    <div>
      <h1>Welcome, <strong><?php echo he(idx($basic, 'name')); ?></strong></h1>
      <p class="tagline">
        You are playing
        <a href="<?php echo he(idx($app_info, 'link'));?>" target="_top">↵
<?php echo he($app_name); ?></a>
      </p>

      <div id="share-app">
        <p>Share your app:</p>
        <ul>
          <li>
            <a href="#" class="facebook-button" id="postToWall" data-url="↵
<?php echo AppInfo::getUrl(); ?>">
              <span class="plus">Post to Wall</span>
            </a>
          </li>
          <li>
            <a href="#" class="facebook-button speech-bubble" id="sendToFriends"↵
  data-url="<?php echo AppInfo::getUrl(); ?>">
              <span class="speech-bubble">Send Message</span>
```

```
                    </a>
                  </li>
                  <li>
                    <a href="#" class="facebook-button apprequests" id="sendRequest"↵
    data-message="Test this awesome app">
                      <span class="apprequests">Send Requests</span>
                    </a>
                  </li>
                </ul>
              </div>
            </div>
            <?php else: ?>
            <div>
              <h1>Welcome to Fuzed</h1>
              <p>Log on to Facebook to play the game.</p>
              <div class="fb-login-button" data-scope="user_likes,user_photos,↵
    publish_actions"></div>
            </div>
            <?php endif; ?>
          </header>

          <?php if($user_id): ?>

          <section id="game" class="clearfix">
            <div id="info">
              <div id="fps">
                <span id="framecounter">(0/0 fps)</span>
              </div>
            </div>

            <div id="jsapp"></div>
          </section>

          <script src="javascript/melonJS-0.9.2-min.js"></script>
          <script src="javascript/player.js"></script>
          <script src="javascript/coin.js"></script>
          <script src="javascript/enemy.js"></script>
          <script src="javascript/score.js"></script>
          <script src="javascript/title_screen.js"></script>
          <script src="javascript/main.js"></script>

          <script>
            var user_id = '<?php echo $user_id; ?>';
          </script>

          <?php endif; ?>

      </body>
</html>
```

Remember that we need to tell Facebook that this is a game (and not a website); we
need to add the og:type metadatato the call. Note that in the line with the Facebook
login button (fb-login-button), we need to add the publish_actions permission to the
data-scope request. This is the permission that will allow us to send scores to the
Facebook Score API.

In order to actually post a score, we need to get the game to have an end state, and then pass the score to the Facebook API. First, let us implement a game-over screen. We need to create a new file in the `javascript` directory (`game_over.js`) and add Listing 14–33 to define the GameOverScreen.

Listing 14–33. *Defining the Game-Over Screen (game_over.js)*

```
/*
 * Game over screen
 */
GameOverScreen = me.ScreenObject.extend({
  init: function() {
    this.parent(true);

    this.font = null;
    this.background = null;
    this.saveScore = false;
  },

  onResetEvent: function(levelId) {
    if (this.background === null) {
      this.background = me.loader.getImage('game_over');

      // font to use
      this.font = new me.BitmapFont('16x16_font', 16);
      this.font.set('left');
    }

    // enable keyboard
    me.input.bindKey(me.input.KEY.ENTER, 'enter', true);
  },

  update: function() {
    if (!this.saveScore) {
      try {
        // post to Facebook
        logResponse('post to facebook');
      } catch (error) {}

      this.saveScore = true;


      if (me.input.isKeyPressed('enter')) {
        me.state.change(me.state.PLAY);
      }
    }
    return true;
  },

  draw: function(context) {
    context.drawImage(this.background, 0, 0);

    this.font.draw(context, 'GAME OVER!', 260, 240);
    this.font.draw(context, 'PRESS ENTER TO PLAY AGAIN', 140, 292);

  },
```

```
  onDestroyEvent: function() {
    me.game.disableHUD();

    me.input.unbindKey(me.input.KEY.ENTER);
  }

});
```

The effect (after loading the data/gfxlib-fuzed/GUI/generic_menus.jpg as game_over in
the g_resources), will look like that shown in Figure 14–24.

Figure 14–24. *Fuzed for Facebook Title Screen*

What we need to do is pick a logical point to cause the game to end, and register that
with the loader. For demonstration purposes, we just end the game when the player is
hit by an enemy, but you can plan a more elaborate system. To accomplish this, I first
added the resource in the main.js file and registered the state as we did earlier with the
MENU and PLAY states in the jsApp.loaded() method. See Listing 14–34.

Listing 14–34. *Adding the Game Over screen to the Game Loader (main.js)*

```
loaded: function() {
    me.state.set(me.state.MENU, new TitleScreen());

    // set the 'Play/Ingame' Screen Object
    me.state.set(me.state.PLAY, new PlayScreen());

    // game over
    me.state.set(me.state.GAMEOVER, new GameOverScreen());

    // add the player to the entity pool
    me.entityPool.add('mainPlayer', PlayerEntity);
```

```
    me.entityPool.add('CoinEntity', CoinEntity);
    me.entityPool.add('EnemyEntity', EnemyEntity);


    // bind to the keyboard
    me.input.bindKey(me.input.KEY.LEFT, 'left');
    me.input.bindKey(me.input.KEY.RIGHT, 'right');
    me.input.bindKey(me.input.KEY.X, 'jump', true);

    // debugging
    //me.debug.renderHitBox = true;

    // start the game
    me.state.change(me.state.MENU);
},
```

We also need to change the logic in the player.js file so when the player collides with an enemy, the game state will change to GAMEOVER. Where we earlier defined the player to flicker, we can comment out that line and change the game state, as in Listing 14–35.

Listing 14–35. *Logic to End the Game (player.js)*

```
if (res) {
      // collide with an enemy
      if (res.obj.type === me.game.ENEMY_OBJECT) {
        // check if enemy was jumped on
        if ((res.y > 0) && ! this.jumping) {
          // bounce
          me.audio.play('Bounce');
          this.forceJump();
        } else {
          me.state.change(me.state.GAMEOVER);
          // flicker when touched
          //this.flicker(45);
        }
      }
}
```

Great! Now when the player hits the enemy, the game will be over, but we still need to register the score. To add a little more flexibility, we use the LocalStorage API to help keep track of the player's high score, posting new high scores as they occur to Facebook. Essentially we will be keeping a cached copy of the high score on the local system to decrease the bandwidth for the API calls.

We need to write two new methods in main.js to read and write the scores, as well as set up a new game statistic. The jsApp object needs two new methods, writeHighScore and readHighScore, as shown in Listing 14–36.

Listing 14–36. *Saving a High Score Locally (main.js)*

```
// write High score
  writeHighScore: function(val) {
    if (me.sys.localStorage) {
      try {
        localValue = this.readHighScore();
        if (val > localValue) {
```

```
          localStorage.setItem('fuzed_highscore', val);
        }
      } catch (e) {
        // no save
      }
    }
  },

  // read score from local storage
  readHighScore: function() {
    if (me.sys.localStorage) {
      try {
        return localStorage.getItem('fuzed_highscore') || 0;
      } catch (e) {}
    }

    return false;
  }
```

Register the fuzed_highscore game statistic in the loaded method, as in Listing 14–37.

Listing 14–37. *Add a Highscore Game Statistic (main.js)*

```
me.gamestat.add('highscore', this.readHighScore());
```

And using Listing 14–38, add a new highScore object in scores.js to display the high score:

Listing 14–38. *Defining the ScoreObject (scores.js)*

```
var ScoreObject = me.HUD_Item.extend({
  init: function(x, y) {

    this.parent(x, y);
    // create a font
    this.font = new me.BitmapFont('16x16_font', 16);
  },

  update: function(value) {
    this.parent(value);

    if (this.value > me.gamestat.getItemValue('highscore')) {
      me.gamestat.setValue('highscore', this.value);
    }

    return true;
  },


  draw: function(context, x, y) {
    this.font.draw(context, this.value, this.pos.x + x, this.pos.y + y);
  }

});

var HighScoreObject = me.HUD_Item.extend({

  init: function(x, y, val) {
    this.parent(x, y, val);
```

```
      this.font = new me.BitmapFont('16x16_font', 16);
      this.font.set('left');
    },

  draw: function(context, x, y) {
      this.font.draw(context, 'HIGH SCORE', this.pos.x + x, this.pos.y + y);
      this.font.draw(context,
                     me.gamestat.getItemValue('highscore'),
                     this.pos.x + x,
                     this.pos.y + y + 16
                    );

  }
});
```

And finally, using Listing 14–39, update the `PlayerScreen` in `main.js` to display the high score in the lower-left corner of the screen, as shown in Figure 14–25.

Listing 14–39. *Adding the Highscore to the Player Screen (main.js)*

```
var PlayScreen = me.ScreenObject.extend({

  onResetEvent: function() {
      // stuff to reset on state change
      me.levelDirector.loadLevel('area01');

      me.game.addHUD(0, 430, 640, 60);
      me.game.HUD.addItem('score', new ScoreObject(620, 10));

      me.game.HUD.addItem('highscore', new HighScoreObject(10, 10, me.gamestat↵
.getItemValue('highscore')));

      me.game.sort();

      me.audio.playTrack('DST-GameOn');
  },

  // action to perform when game is finished (state change)
  onDestroyEvent: function() {
      jsApp.writeHighScore(me.gamestat.getItemValue('highscore'));


      me.game.disableHUD();

      console.log(me.gamestat.getItemValue('highscore'));

      // stop the music
      me.audio.stopTrack();
  }

});
```

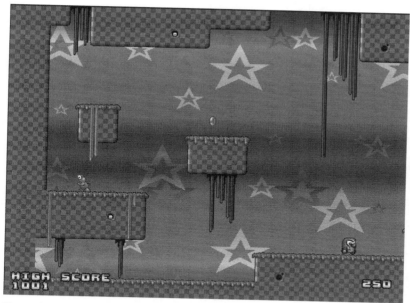

Figure 14–25. *High score added to the HUD*

Now we just need to send an AJAX post of the score to Facebook. We use the same technique as we did in Chapter 12 to post an Achievement to Facebook, using jQuery to post the high score at the end of the game; see Listing 14–40.

Listing 14–40. *Adding AJAX Call to score.php (game_over.js)*

```
update: function() {
    if (!this.saveScore) {
      try {
        // post to Facebook
        dataString = {
          score: me.gamestat.getItemValue('highscore'),
          user_id: user_id
        };

        $.ajax({
          type: 'POST',
          data: dataString,
          url: 'score.php'
        });
      } catch (error) {}

    this.saveScore = true;

  }

  if (me.input.isKeyPressed('enter')) {
    me.state.change(me.state.PLAY);
  }
```

```
   return true;
  },
```

To post the score to Facebook, we create a new file (score.php) and use the code in Listing 14–41 to send the score to Facebook's servers.

Listing 14–41. *Posting a Score to Facebook Score API (score.php)*

```php
<?php

require_once('AppInfo.php');
require_once('sdk/src/facebook.php');

if (!isset($_POST['score'])) {
  header('HTTP/1.1 403 Forbidden');
  die;
}

$score = $_POST['score'];
$user = $_POST['user_id'];

$facebook = new Facebook(array(
  'appId'  => AppInfo::appID(),
  'secret' => AppInfo::appSecret(),
));

$access_token = AppInfo::appID() . '|' . AppInfo::appSecret();

$payload = array('score' => $score, 'access_token' => $access_token);

$response = $facebook->api('/' . $user . '/scores', 'POST', $payload);

print_r($response);
```

You can also grab scores for the application to use them in a display with Listing 14–42.

Listing 14–42. *Retrieving User's Scores from Facebook API*

```php
$scores = idx($facebook->api(AppInfo::appID() . '/scores'), 'data', array());
```

The $scores variable will contain an array of the scores for the current user and their friends who have authorized the application. You can use this information to create a leaderboard that shows an individual's ranking among their friends. Since this is just an array of scores and user ids, you are free to style this as you wish to have a leaderboard for your game that fits the overall look, and feel, of your application.

Summary

This chapter took a lot of the different concepts that were covered in previous chapters and used them with a great open source game engine, melonJS. This engine does a fantastic job in managing different elements of your game, from sound, to images, and state. Not only does it manage these assets and the game state, but it also integrates nicely with the Tiled Map Editor, allowing you to reuse your maps on other platforms that use the TMX format (such as cocos2d). Integrating the game with the Facebook graph is quite straightforward, and takes care of some of the gameplay concerns for you, including achievements, scores, and authentication.

These are some of the basics of using a game engine to create a game using different components. It is now up to you to use your creativity and knowledge to build great games that people want to play on Facebook. One of the really great things about developing HTML5 games is the community. There are supportive forums for all of the major game engines, and the #bbg (browser-based games) irc channel on freenode has some great conversations and the people that hang out are quite friendly (including the authors of some of the game engines discussed in this book).

There are a lot of companies building game development software and getting them into the hands of people who will enjoy them. There is a lot of promise in the realm of HTML game development to build exciting content in new and engaging ways. We hope this book has given you some tools to explore this world with more confidence, and an eagerness to learn more about the world of game development.

Index

■A

Adobe Fireworks, 83
Adobe Illustrator, 84
Adobe Photoshop, 84
Alien Turtle Invasion game
  boilerplate code, 113
    basic HTML code, 111–113
    Game CSS, 113
    game directory, setup, 111
    HTML and CSS code, 111, 112
    projects directory, creation, 111
  competition, 110
  engine coding
    background drawing and redraw, 115
    build and hone, 114
    canvas element, 114
    checkhits, 125–126
    drawing, spaceship, 116
    fire projectiles, spaceship, 120
    fireLaser() function, 119
    full game code, 129–136
    game loop function, 114, 115, 118, 121
    game state setting, 120
    hit detection, 122, 123
    invaders and spaceship shooting, 126
    invaders drawing, 120
    invasion, 122
    keyboard events, 117
    lasers drawing, 118, 119
    position and checking, collisions, 123–124
    position, spaceship, 117
    requestAnimationFrame()function, 118
    spaceship firing, random intervals, 124–125
    spaceship object, 116
    stand-in shape, spaceship, 116
    updateInvaders() and drawInvaders()function, 121
    updateSpaceship() function, 123
    updating, invader position, 121
    updating, game state, 126–129
  objectives and rules, 109
  sound
    audio loading, 141
    explosions and missile firing, 140
    playing, 142
    "whoosh" effect, 141
  targeted audience, 110
  textures
    draw functions, 138–139
    game, 140
    game loading resources, 138
    inkscape export, starship.svg, 137
    loading image resources, 138
    projectile1.svg, 137
    public domain download, 136
    starship.svg, 137
    torpedo.svg, 137
    ufo.svg, 137
Apache 2.0, 106
Application idea, design process
  artistic direction, 73
  audience research, 71
  brainstorming, 70–71
  coding, 77

competitor identification, 72
concept, 69
deployment, 77–78
feature cull, 75–76
launching, 78
planning, 76–77
project review and checklist, 74–75
user testing, 78
Application Programming Interface
(API), 9, 171
AJAX, 401
browser's LocalStorage, 390
game statistic, 399
GAMEOVER, 398
game-over screen, 396
Heroku application, 391
index.php file, 391–395
MENU and PLAY, 397–398
playerScreen, 400–401
publish_actions permission, 390,
395
retrieving user's scores, 402
score.php, 402
ScoreObject, 399
writeHighScore and readHighScore,
398

B

Beginner hardware, 101

C

Cakewalk, 100
Canvas Advanced Animation Toolkit
(CAAT)
animation, 337
boilerplate, 335–336
HTML5 components, 335
JavaScript method chaining, 340
library, 334
logo, 338–339
pros and cons, 335
scene1() function, 340
Cocos2d.js web
installation, 340

JavaScript template, 342–343
new gamename, 341
Nodejs Web Server, 343
pros and cons, 341
Content delivery network (CDN), 267
Content management system (CMS),
301
CraftyJS engine
HTML boilerplate, 345
isometric map, 344–345
pros and cons, 343
working principle, 343
Creative Commons 0 (CC0), 105
Creative Commons—BY—Share Alike
(CC-BY-SA), 105
Creative Commons—BY(CC-BY), 105
Cubase, 99

D

Data definition language (DDL), 275
2D context canvas
arcTo method, 53
beginPath method, 53
bezierCurveTo method, 53
Cartesian co-ordinate system, 50–51
character encoding, 52
clearRect method, 53
clip method, 53
closePath method, 53
270 × 270 co-ordinates, 52
debugging tools, 66–67
DOM elements, 52
drawImage method, 53
fill method, 53
fillRect method, 54
fillText method, 54
keyboard control
binding keyboard events, 66
coding, 64–65
WASD and arrow control system,
63
window.addEventListener, 65
lineTo method, 54
moveTo method, 54
quadraticCurveTo method, 54

rect method, 54
rectangle, 51
rendered canvas rectangle, 53
restore and rotate method, 54
save and scale method, 54
setTransform method, 54
simple motion
    coding, 61–62
    "moving" scene, 60
    object in motion, 63
    static shapes and change, 60
    window.setInterval, 62
    x- and y-co-ordinates sets, 63
smart mobile devices, 67
strokeRect and Text method, 54
transform and translate method, 54
translation and rotation, 58–60
transparency, 56–58
triangles and lines, 55–56
Do/while loop, 36–37
Dual/Multi License, 106

E

Essential game components
Apache 2.0, 106
audio, 97–98
browse menu, 104
CC0, 105
CC-BY, 105
CC-BY-SA, 105
colors, 95
context, 104
copyright exclusive rights, 104
depth, 94, 95
design process
    Bezier tool, Inkscape, 89
    new layer, Inkscape, 87–88
    refine, 86
    sketch, 85–86
drop shadows, 97
dual/multi license, 106
focus and blur, 96
GPL, 105
graphics type
    Adobe Fireworks, 82

JPEG format, 82
Portable Network, 82
raster and raster based circle, 81, 82
vector-based circle, Inkscape, 82
vector graphics, 81, 82
lighting
ellipse shape, 92
Fireworks, 91
radial gradient, 93–94
shadow location, 91
WebGL, 90
MIT, 106
movement, 96
OpenGameArt.org search page, 105
sounds
Ableton's Live sound editor, 100
audacity, 99
audio preparation, 103
audition, 99
Cubase, 99
entry level hardware, 101
GarageBand, 98
Logic Studio, 99
mid-range hardware, 101
professional hardware, 101
protools, 100
recording, 101–102
royalty-free sounds, 102–103
Sonar, 100
sound studio, 99
tools, graphics
acorn, 83
Adobe Fireworks, 83
Adobe Illustrator, 84
GIMP, 83
Inkscape, 83
Paint.net, 84
scanner, 84

F

Facebook
game genres
    action, 12
    adventure, 13

casinos, 13
FPS, 13
horror, 13
puzzle, 13
RPGs, 13
simulation, 13
sport, 13
strategy, 13
game terminology
    Armagetron Advanced courtesy, 8
    chase, 5
    Dwarf Fortress World Creation, 5
    Extreme Tux Racer courtesy, 6
    first person, 6
    isometric, 4
    side scroller, 5
    side-scrolling, 5
    third person view, 7
    top-down, 4
    Urban Terror courtesy, 7
gaming browser, 1
general terms
    AAA game, 8
    algorithm, 8
    API code, 9
    artificial intelligence, 9
    assets, 9
    Avatar, 9
    collison detection, 9
    framework, 9
    map, 9
    multiplayer, 9
    raster-based fish, 10
    raster graphics, 9
    realtime, 10
    render, 10
    single player game, 10
    sprite, 10
    turn-based game, 11
    vector graphics, 11, 12
HTML5 canvas element, 2
social games and interaction, 1
Facebook achievement system
    description, 213
    dummy objects, 214
    open graph

earn action, 212
metadata, 211
preview, 214
timeline story, 215
user timeline, 210
Facebook components
    assigning achievements, 287–288
    authorization dialog customization
        Auth Dialog form, 288–289
        privacy policy, 290
        puzzle icon, 289
        terms of service and privacy
          policy, 292
        terms of service agreement,
          291–292
    deployment concerns
        ant-build-script repository, 294
        ANT script, 294–297
        bash/Windows batch file, 294
        Git-Heroku Deployment
          Workflow, 298
        HTML5 Boilerplate, 294
        JavaScript and CSS code, 297
        magnification libraries, 293
        whitespace removal, 293
Heroku
    ALTER TABLE statement, 275
    command-line interface, 273
    comment out dangerous parts,
      277–278
    CREATE TABLE statement, 276
    database connection URL, 274
    db_manager.php, 274–275
    DDL, 275–276
    environmental variables, 273
    Git repository, 277
    MySQL, 275
    PostgreSQL, 273
    puzzle_tracker table, 276
    setup.php, 276, 277
    timestamp, 276
    uid field, 276
levels, adding
    CDN, 267
    data-level attribute, 267
    DOM element, 266

Google Font directory, 269
grid size, 266
HTML5 specification, 266
index.php file, 266
instantiation parameter, 265
'level' container, 267
#splash container, 267
Splash screen. *(see* Splash
    screen)
stylesheets/base.css, 269
puzzle information
    AJAX code, 278
    completion_time field, 282
    date formatter, 282
    Hall of Fame, 283
    highscore.php, 280
    inserts protection, 280–282
    javascripts/puzzle.js file, 278
    $my_id variable, 279
    player_id field, 283
    puzzle.js AJAX call, 279
    score object, 278
    score.uid Value, 279
    server-side code, 278
    setTimeout() function, 279
    time format, 282
timer, 271–273
tracking achievements
    database table, 284
    displaying achievements,
        285–286
    Facebook Achievement
        Registration Response, 287
    Facebook Graph API, 287
    Facebook Object Debugger, 286
    id URL parameter, 286
    Open Graph debugging tool, 286
    Open Graph protocol, 283
    setting up achievements, 283
Facebook developer tools
    applications, 201
    credits
        application credits configuration,
            221
        Callback processing template,
            219– 220

callback status values, 223
company registration, 218
configuration, 217
credits as currency, 216
JSON object, 221
purchase credits, 222
troubleshooting, 223
insights
    application, 226
    excel data, 228
    export data, 228
    facebook insights, 227
open graph protocol
    activities, 204
    businesses, 204
    custom metadata, 205
    Google Rich Snippet Testing
        Tool, 203
    groups, 204
    HTML metadata elements, 201
    metadata, 202
    organizations, 204
    people, 204
    products and entertainment, 205
    RDFa, 202
    Rich Snippets Testing Tool, 203
    song metadata, 203
    Timeline, 201
    websites, 205
open graph stories
    achievement system. *(see*
        Facebook achievement system)
    aggregations, 209–210
    configuration, 208
    dashboard, facebook application,
        206
    Facebook Developer Application,
        206
    start, facebook, 207
    World of Warcraft, 210
roles, 224–226
Facebook fuzed, 355
    API
        AJAX, 401
        browser's LocalStorage, 390
        game statistic, 399

GAMEOVER, 398
game-over screen, 396–397
Heroku application, 391
index.php file, 391–395
MENU and PLAY, 397–398
PlayerScreen, 400–401
publish_actions permission, 390, 395
retrieving user's scores, 402
ScoreObject, 399
score.php, 402
title screen, 397
writeHighScore and readHighScore, 398
game, 355
melonJS Framework. (see melonJS Framework)
tiled map editor
auto-mapping, 356
background_color, 361
Base64 compressed, 356
GfxLib-Fuzed library, 357
melonJS library, 361
melonJS site, 357
orthogonal map, 358
panel scene, 357
tile layer, 360
tilesets tab, 359
TMX format, 356
use transparent color, 358
XML-based map format, 356
Facebook game
audience identification, 232
competition, 232–233
game code
background music, 248
canvas, puzzle.js, 237
click events and tile drawing, 243
click location container, 242
complete game code, 244–246
display play/pause controls, 248
distance calculation, 242
DOM element, 237
drawImage()method, 238
eventHandler()function, 248
eventListener()method, 238

Flickr, 235
Full drawImage Method, resizing, 238
gnuckx image, 235, 236
7×7 grid image, 246
image processing and loading, 237, 238
MP3 play game, 247
Ogg Vorbis format, 247
pause/play background music, 248
playMusic function, 248
rendered image, 239
resizing, drawImage Method, 238
Rialto song, 247
setBoard() function, 240
tile positions calculation, 241
tile size calculation, 239
tiles and check, 242–243
HTML Container Boilerplate, 234
image puzzle
checkSolved() function, 261
corrected image puzzle, 262
drawTiles() function, 260
game application, PHP block, 251– 252
HTML code, 253–256
image slider puzzle, 262
main content, 252
Math.floor() function, 258
onclick = function(), 260
PHP image array data, 249–251
picking, random image, 251
playMusic(musicPath, filename) function, 261
pulling your photos, 249
random image, 257
random image function, 249
script tag, 252
setBoard() function, 260
tileHeight and tileWidth variables, 258, 259
tileSize variable, 258
Your Git Repository creation, 257
rules, 231

Facebook Pages
  advertising, 321
    content, 321
    cycle II, 323
    cycle III, 323
    plug, 321
    tips, 322
  basic information, 312
  content and style, 329–330
  creation, 309
  customization
    administrative links, 319
    favorite section, 317–319
    page body, 319
    page components and
      information, 314–317
    page links, 317
    profile picture, 316
    title and category, 319
  driving likes, 323
    facebook tabs, 324–329
    WordPress category, 324
  functional testing, 330
  interaction, 322
  inviting friends, 311–312
  Logo, 310–311
  name setting, 309
  permission management, 313
  promotion, 320–321
  registration, 309–310
  search engine optimizations, 308
Facebook platform
  API, 172
  API graph
    abridged request, 189
    API events request, 190
    API URL structure, 190
    authentication, 188
    documentation, 191–192
    event response, 191
    facebook graph request, 189
    geospatial place search, 196
    graph for coffee shops, 193–195
    graph theory, 187
    JSON format, 187
    request, 188
    search, 193
    search response, 193–194
    type search, 193
    unauthentication, 188
    URLs, 188, 189
  App Display Name, 176
  App Domain, 176
  App Namespace, 176
  App on Facebook, 177
  application ID and secret, 175
  application request architecture, 173
  application, new, 175
  category, 176
  cloud services, 176
  contact email, 176
  FBML, 172
  first application
    Git, 178–179
    Heroku, 181–183
    ruby, 179
    windows, 179–180
  Mobile Web integration, 177
  Native Android App, 177
  Native iOS App integration, 177
  new application form, 174
  Page Tab, 178
  policies, 174
  query Language
    FQL query, 196
    friends from facebook, 197
    friends_using_app method, 197
    Graph API Explorer, 197
    response to FQL query, 196
    selecting elements, 196
REST functions, 172
SDKs
  cloud services, 199
  development cycle, 198
  Env Variables, Apache, 199
  external web APIs, 198
  Graph API response, 199
  GUI, 199
  Heroku, 199
  Koala, 198
  MAMP server, 198
software development kits, 178

Website integration, 177
Facebook Query Language (FQL), 196
Farmville, 146
Feature cull, 75–76
Firebug
    Addons directory, 18
    Aurora Scratchpad, 19
    button, Firefox, 18
    console evaluating, 19
    Firefox user, 18
First-Person Shooter (FPS), 13
For Loop, 36

▓G

Game tracking
    bitwise operations, 154
    checking and drawing, 154–155
    clickHandler() function, 153
    data array, 152
    drawBoard() function, 153
    grid x-axis pixel co-ordinates, 153
    X and Oboards and game state, 153
    X marks, game board, 156
Gameplay mechanics
    artificial intelligence
        Answers and Draw Guess board,
            159–160
        calculateRatio() function, 158
        tic-tac-toe, 157–158
        X marks board, tic-tac-toce, 161
    Farmville, 146
    Neopets, 146
    scoreboard, 162–163
    sound, 163–170
    tic-tac-toe
        "Boilerplate" section, 147
        CSS using Google Font, 148
        em scales, 148
        game board, grid lines, 152
        Google Fond API, Boilerplate
          code rendered, 149
        "hot metal" typesetting, 148
        HTML Boilerplate, 147
        JavaScript, 150–151
        rules, 150

tracking. *(see* Game tracking)
Web Page adding, 151
GIMP, 83
Git-Heroku Deployment Workflow, 298
Gnu General Public License (GPL), 105
Google Font directory, 269
Graphical user interface (GUI), 199

▓H

Heroku
    application, 391
    cloning application, 186
    command-line client application, 181
    command-line tool, 182
    confirmation, 184
    developer app, 183
    Facebook
        basic application, 185
        cloud services, 183
        login, 184
        setup, 184
    Gem (OS X) installation, 181
    gem output, 182
    installation, 181
    rename application screen, 186
    SSH kgeneration, 187
HTML5 Boilerplate, 294
HTML5 game engines
    canvas. *(see* Canvas Advanced
      Animation Toolkit)
    Cocos2d.js. *(see* Cocos2d.js web)
    CraftyJS. *(see* CraftyJS engine)
    development, 333–334
    LimeJS. *(see* LimeJS)
    melonJS, 350
    paid games. *(see* Paid game
      engines)
    PixieEngine, 351–352
    Play My Code, 350–351

▓I

ImpactJS, 353
Inkscape, 83

Integrated development environments (IDE), 111
Isogenic game engine, 353

J, K

JavaScript
ActionScript, 16
boolean, 22
break loop statement, 37
browser engines and platforms, 17, 46
comments, 21–22
continue loop statement, 37–38
data structure
array, 32
array iteration, 33–34
array length, 33
array literals, 33
data types, 22
Do/while loop, 36–37
document object model, 42
duck-typed language, 16
ECMAScript, 16
Facebook application, 17
flow control
if..else, 34
Switch, 35
Typeof, 35
For Loop, 36
functions
constant variable, 41
function and function call, 39
global keyword, 39
global scope clarity, 40
global scope confusion, 40
global variables, 41, 42
scope and confusion, 39–41
jQuery, 16
NaN, 23
null data, 23
number game
checkGuess function, 44
Facebook, 43
high–low complete game, 45
high–low game, 46

high–low game components, 43
high-low global variables, 43
HTML Wrapper, 44
jQuery Loader, 44
randomNumber function, 44
numeric data, 22
operators
arithmetic, 27
assignment, 25
Chrome Developer Tools, 29
comparison, 26
if/else code, 30
logical, 28
New, 31
string, 28–29
string shorthand operator, 29
ternary, 30–31
This, 31
typeof, 31, 32
prototype-based language, 15
strings data, 22
style programming, 15
testing
Chrome, 19–20
debugging, 20–21
Firebug. (see Firebug)
undefined data, 23
variables, 23–25
W3C, 16
While Loops, 36
JavaScript frameworks, 267
jQuery, 267

L

LimeJS
Closure Compiler Source Map, 349
compiling, 348
Google Closure Libraries, 347–348
HTML Boilerplate, 346
library, 346
minified game code, 349–350
project creation, 346
pros and cons, 346

■M, N, O

melonJS framework
  adding audio
    Audacity, 383
    Bounce, 385–386
    CoinEntity, 385
    directory, 383
    game resources sounds,
      383–384
    NoSoapRadio, 383
    onDestroyEvent, 384
    OpenGameArt.org, 383
    player jumps, 385
  area01 map, 366
  building, 362
  compiled sources, 362
  entity loader, 367
  game components
    coin entity, 377
    enemy, 377–378
    enemyEntities, 379–380
    enemy sprite, 380–381
    entityPool, 379
    game resources enemy, 376
    JavaScript, 378–379
  game files, 362
    HTML, 362
    main.js, 363–364
  game loaded, 366
  game resources, 365
  game resources backgrounds, 374
  gfxlib-fuzed directory, 387
  key bindings, 368
  LevelEntity, 386–387
  loading screen, 365
  mainPlayer, 368–369
  metatiles tileset, 369
  parallax layers
    debugging bounding box,
      375–376
    resource pointer, 374
    solid pink background, 375
    tiled, 374–375
  pink background, 372
  player entity, 367–368
  PlayScreen object, 382

  rendered scene, 371
  score HUD, 382
  ScoreObject, 381–382
  solid surfaces, 370–371
  sprite background, 372
  tile properties, 370
  title screen, 387
    adding and tweaking levels, 390
    Game Loader, 389
    gfxlib-fuzed library, 387
    index.html loads, 388
    iTileMaps, 390
    main.js, 387
    title_screen.js, 388
    web page reload, 389
  updateColRect function, 373
melonJS library, 350
MIT, 106

■P, Q

Paid game engines, 352
  ImpactJS, 353
  Isogenic, 354
Paint.net, 84
PixieEngine, 351–352
Play My Code, 350–351
Play-by-email (PBeM) game, 145
PostgreSQL, 273

■R

Relational database management
  system (RDBMS), 273
Role-Playing Games (RPGs), 13
Rresource description framework
  (RDFa), 202

■S

Splash screen
  code, 266
  CSS, 268–270
  initial screen, 266
  styled screen, 269, 271

■T, U, V

Tic-tac-toe

"Boilerplate" section, 147

CSS using Google Font, 148

em scales, 148

game board, grid lines, 152

Gogole Font API, Boilerplate code
rendered, 149

"hot metal" typesetting, 148

HTML Boilerplate, 147

JavaScript, 150–151

rules, 150

Scoreboard, 162–163

sound, 163–170

track. (*see* Game tracking)

Web Page adding, 151

■W, X, Y, Z

WordPress

Admin dashboard, 305–306

Heroku service, 302

MySQL database, 302

PHPFogApp

dashboard, 302–304

pricing plan, 304–305

plugins

Akismet, 307

Google Analytics, 307

Google XML Sitemaps, 307

installation, 306–307

social plugins, 308

WP Minify, 307

WP Super Cache, 308

shared hosting solution, 302

web host, 302

World of Warcraft, 146

World Wide Web Consortium (W3C), 16